Social History of the
United States

Titles in ABC-CLIO's
Social History of the United States

Social History of the United States
The 1920s

Linda S. Watts
Alice L. George
Scott Beekman

Series Editors
Daniel J. Walkowitz and Daniel E. Bender

A B C • C L I O

Santa Barbara, California   Denver, Colorado   Oxford, England

Library of Congress Cataloging-in-Publication Data

Watts, Linda S., 1960-
    Social history of the United States : the 1920s / Linda S. Watts, Alice L. George, and Scott Beekman.
        p. cm. — (Social history of the United States)
    Includes bibliographical references and index.
    ISBN 978-1-85109-972-6 (hard copy : alk. paper) — ISBN 978-1-59884-127-5 (set)
    EISBN 978-1-85109-973-3 (ebook)
    1. United States—Social conditions—1918–1932.   2. United States—Social life and customs—1918–1945.   3. Nineteen twenties.   I. George, Alice L., 1952–
II. Beekman, Scott.   III. Title.
    HN57.W355   2009
    306.0973'09042—dc22   2008017168

12 11 10 09   1 2 3 4 5

Senior Production Editor: Vicki Moran
Production Manager: Don Schmidt
Media Editor: Julie Dunbar
Media Resources Manager: Caroline Price
File Management Coordinator: Paula Gerard

This book is also available on the World Wide Web as an eBook.
Visit www.abc-clio.com for details.

ABC-CLIO, Inc.
130 Cremona Drive, P.O. Box 1911
Santa Barbara, California 93116–1911

This book is printed on acid-free paper ∞
Manufactured in the United States of America

Contents

Series Introduction

Ordinary people make history. They do so in ways that are different from the ways presidents, generals, business moguls, or celebrities make history; nevertheless, the history of ordinary people is just as profound, just as enduring. Immigration in the early decades of the 20th century was more than numbers and government policy; it was a collective experience of millions of men, women, and children whose political beliefs, vernacular cultural expression, discontent, and dreams transformed the United States. Likewise, during the Great Depression of the 1930s, President Franklin Delano Roosevelt advanced a broad spectrum of new social policies, but as historians have argued, ordinary Americans "made" the New Deal at the workplace, at the ballot box, on the picket lines, and on the city streets. They engaged in new types of consumer behavior, shifted political allegiances, and joined new, more aggressive trade unions. World War II and the Cold War were more than diplomatic maneuvering and military strategy; social upheavals changed the employment patterns, family relations, and daily life of ordinary people. More recently, the rise of the Christian Right in the last few decades is the expression of changing demographics and emerging social movements, not merely the efforts of a few distinct leaders.

These examples, which are drawn directly from the volumes in this series, highlight some of the essential themes of social history. Social history shifts the historical focus away from the famous and the political or economic elite to issues of everyday life. It explores the experiences ordinary Americans—native-born and immigrant, poor and rich, employed and unemployed, men and women, white and black—at home, at work, and at play. In the process, it focuses new attention on the significance of social movements, the behavior and meanings of consumerism, and the changing expression of popular culture.

In many ways, social history is not new. American historians early in the 20th century appreciated the importance of labor, immigration, religion, and urbanization in the study of society. However, early studies shared with political history the emphasis on leaders and major institutions and described a history that was mostly white and male—in other words, a history of those who held power. Several cultural shifts combined to transform how social history was understood and written in the last half of the 20th century: the democratization of higher education after World War II with the GI Bill and the expansion of public and land grant universities; the entry of women, children of immigrants, and racial minorities into the universities and the ranks of historians; and the social movements of the 1960s. Historians created new subjects for social history, casting it as "from the bottom." They realized that much was missing from familiar narratives that stressed the significance of "great men"—presidents, industrialists, and other usually white, usually male notables. Instead, women, working people, and ethnic and racial minorities have become integral parts of the American story along with work, leisure, and social movements.

The result has not simply been additive: ordinary people made history. The story of historical change is located in their lives and their struggles with and against others in power. Historians began to transform the central narrative of American history. They realized that—in the words of a popular 1930s folk cantata, "Ballad for Americans"—the "'etceteras' and the 'and so forths' that do the work" have a role in shaping their own lives, in transforming politics, and in recreating economics. Older themes of study, from industrialization to imperial expansion, from party politics to urbanization, were revisited through the inclusion of new actors, agents, and voices. These took their place alongside such new topics as social movements, popular culture, consumption, and community. But social history remains socially engaged scholarship; contemporary social issues continue to shape social historians' research and thinking. Historians in the 1970s and 1980s who focused on the experiences of working people, for instance, were challenged by the reality of deindustrialization. Likewise, historians in the 1990s who focused on popular culture and consumer behavior were influenced by the explosion of consumerism and new forms of cultural expression. Today's historians explore the antecedents to contemporary globalization as well as the roots of conservatism.

The transformation of the questions and agendas of each new era has made it apparent to historians that the boundaries of historical inquiry are not discrete. Social history, therefore, engages with other kinds of history. Social history reinterprets older narratives of politics and political economy and overlaps both areas. Social historians argue that politics is not restricted to ballot boxes or legislatures; politics is broad popular engagement with ideas about material wealth, social justice, moral values, and civil and human rights. Social historians, naturally, remain interested in changing political affiliations. They have, for example, examined the changing political allegiances of African Americans during the 1930s and the civil rights movement of the 1960s. So too have they examined the relationship of socialist and communist parties to working-class and immigrant communities. At the same time, social historians measure change by looking at such issues as family structure, popular culture, and consumer behavior.

For the social historian, the economy extends far beyond statistical data about production, gross domestic product, or employment. Rather, the economy is a lived experience. Wealthy or poor, Americans have negotiated the changing reality of economic life. Social historians ask questions about how different groups of Americans experienced and resisted major economic transformations and how they have grappled with economic uncertainty. The Great Depression of the 1930s, for example, left both urban workers and rural farmers perilously close to starvation. During the 1970s and 1980s, factories in the Rust Belt of the Midwest and Northeast shuttered or moved, and many Americans began laboring in new parts of the country and working new kinds of jobs, especially in the service sector. Americans have also grappled with the unequal distribution of wealth; some people advanced new ideas and engaged with emerging ideologies that challenged economic injustice, but others jealously guarded their privilege.

As social history has broadened its purview, it has transformed our sense of how historical change occurs. Social history changes our conception of chronology; change does not correspond to presidential election cycles. Social history also changes how we understand sources of power; power is constituted in and challenged by diverse peoples with different resources. Social historians, then, look at the long history of the 20th century in the United States and examine how the terrain has shifted under our feet, sometimes slowly and sometimes dramatically and abruptly. Social historians measure change in complex ways, including but also transcending demographic and geographic expansion and political transformation. How, for example, did the institution of the family change in the face of successive waves of immigration that often left spouses and children separated by national borders and oceans? Or during years of war with rising rates of women's wage and salary employment? Or following moralist reaction that celebrated imagined traditional values, and social movements that focused on issues of sexuality, birth control, homosexuality, and liberation? Historical change can also be measured by engagement with popular culture as Americans shifted their attention from vaudeville and pulp novels to radio, silent films, talkies, television, and finally the Internet and video games. The volumes in this series, divided by decades, trace all these changes.

To make sense of this complex and broadened field of inquiry, social historians often talk about how the categories by which we understand the past have been "invented," "contested," and "constructed." The nation has generally been divided along lines of race, class, gender, sexuality, and ethnicity. However, historians have also realized that analysts—whether in public or professional discourse—define these "categories of analysis" in different ways at different moments. Waves of immigration have reconfigured understandings of race and ethnicity, and more recent social movements have challenged the meanings of gender. Similarly, to be working class at the dawn of the age of industry in the 1900s meant something very different from being working class in the post-industrial landscape of the 1990s. How women or African Americans—to cite only two groups—understand their own identity can mean something different than how white men categorize them. Social historians, therefore, trace how Americans have always been divided about the direction of their lives and their nation, how they have consistently challenged and rethought social and cultural values and sought to renegotiate relationships of power, whether in the family, the workplace, the university, or the military. Actors do this armed with differing forms of power to authorize their view.

To examine these contestations, social historians have explored the way Americans articulated and defended numerous identities—as immigrants, citizens, workers, Christians, or feminists, for example. A post–World War II male chemical worker may have thought of himself as a worker and trade unionist at the factory, a veteran and a Democrat in his civic community, a husband and father at home, and as a white, middle-class homeowner. A female civil rights worker in the South in the 1960s may have seen herself as an African American when in the midst of a protest march or when refused service in a restaurant, as working class during a day job as a domestic worker or nurse, and as a woman when struggling to claim a leadership role in an activist organization.

Social historians have revisited older sources and mined rich new veins of information on the daily lives of ordinary people. Social historians engage with a host of materials—from government documents to census reports, from literature to oral histories, and from autobiographies to immigrant and foreign-language newspapers—to illuminate the lives, ideas, and activities of those who have been hidden from history. Social historians have also brought a broad "toolbox" of new methodologies to shed light on these sources. These methodologies are well represented in this series and illustrate the innovations of history from the bottom up. These volumes offer many tables and charts, which demonstrate the ways historians have made creative use of statistical analysis. Furthermore, the volumes are rich in illustrations as examples of the new ways that social historians "read" such images as cartoons or photographs.

The volumes in this series reflect the new subject matter, debates, and methodologies that have composed the writing of the United States' 20th-century social history. The volumes have unique features that make them particularly valuable for students and teachers; they are hybrids that combine the narrative advantages of the monograph with the specific focus of the encyclopedia. Each volume has been authored or co-authored by established social historians. Where the work has been collaborative, the authors have shared the writing and worked to sustain a narrative voice and conceptual flow in the volume. Authors have written the social history for the decade of their expertise and most have also taught its history. Each volume begins with a volume introduction by the author or authors that lays out the major themes of the decade and the big picture—how the social changes of the era transformed the lives of Americans. The author then synthesizes the best and most path-breaking new works in social history. In the case of the last three volumes, which cover the post-1970 era, scholarship remains in its relative infancy. In particular, these three volumes are major original efforts to both define the field and draw upon the considerable body of original research that has already been completed.

The ten volumes in the series divide the century by its decades. This is an avowedly neutral principle of organization that does not privilege economic, political, or cultural transformations; this allows readers to develop their own sense of a moment and their own sense of change. While it remains to be seen how the most recent decades will be taught and studied, in cases such as the 1920s, the 1930s, and the 1960s, this decadal organization replicates how historians frequently study and teach history. The Progressive Era (ca. 1890–1920) and postwar America (ca. 1945–1960) have less often been divided by decades. This highlights the neutrality of this division. In truth, all divisions are imposed: we speak of long decades or short centuries, and so forth. When historians teach the 1960s, they often reach back into the 1950s and ahead into the 1970s. The authors and editors of these volumes recognize that social processes, movements, ideas, and leaders do not rise and fall with the turn of the calendar; therefore, they have worked to knit the volumes together as a unit.

Readers can examine these texts individually or collectively. The texts can be used to provide information on significant events or individuals. They can provide an overview of a pivotal decade. At the same time, these texts are designed to allow readers to follow changing themes over time and to develop their own sense of chronology. The authors regularly spoke with one another and with the series editors to establish the major themes and subthemes in the social history of the century and to sustain story lines across the volumes. Each volume divides the material into six or seven chapters that discuss major themes such as labor or work; urban, suburban, and rural life; private life; politics; economy; culture; and social movements. Each chapter begins with an overview essay and then explores four to six major topics. The discrete essays at the heart of each volume give readers focus on a social movement, a social idea, a case study, a social institution, and so forth. Unlike traditional encyclopedias, however, the narrative coherence of the single-authored text permits authors to break the decade bubble with discussions on the background or effects of a social event.

There are several other features that distinguish this series.

- Many chapters include capsules on major debates in the social history of the era. Even as social historians strive to build on the best scholarship available, social history remains incomplete and contested; readers can benefit from studying this tension.

- The arguments in these volumes are supported by many tables and graphics. Social history has mobilized demographic evidence and—like its sister field, cultural history—has increasingly turned to visual evidence, both for the social history of media and culture and as evidence of social conditions. These materials are not presented simply as illustrations but as social evidence to be studied.

- Timelines at the head of every chapter highlight for readers all the major events and moments in the social history that follows.

- A series of biographical sketches at the end of every chapter highlights the lives of major figures more often overlooked in histories of the era. Readers can find ample biographical material on more prominent figures in other sources; here the authors have targeted lesser known but no less interesting and important subjects.

- Bibliographies include references to electronic sources and guide readers to material for further study.

- Three indices—one for each volume, one for the entire series, and one for all the people and events in the series—are provided in each volume. Readers can easily follow any of the major themes across the volumes.

Finally, we end with thanks for the supportive assistance of Ron Boehm and Kristin Gibson at ABC-CLIO, and especially to Dr. Alex Mikaberidze and Dr. Kim Kennedy White, who helped edit the manuscripts for the press. But of course, these volumes are the product of the extraordinary group of historians to whom we are particularly indebted:

The 1900s: Brian Greenberg and Linda S. Watts
The 1910s: Gordon Reavley
The 1920s: Linda S. Watts, Alice L. George, and Scott Beekman
The 1930s: Cecelia Bucki
The 1940s: Mark Ciabattari
The 1950s: John C. Stoner and Alice L. George
The 1960s: Troy D. Paino
The 1970s: Laurie Mercier
The 1980s: Peter C. Holloran and Andrew Hunt
The 1990s: Nancy Cohen

Daniel J. Walkowitz, Series Editor
Daniel E. Bender, Series Associate Editor

Volume Introduction

DID THE 1920s ROAR?

The 1920s in America spanned the period from the end of World War I to the stock market crash of 1929. On first glance, then, the 1920s might be regarded as the interlude between the Progressive era and the Depression. Once World War I concluded, Americans turned their attention to the home front and to establishing a peacetime economy. After a relatively brief depression in 1920–1921, the United States experienced a time of postwar prosperity. Food was plentiful and cheap, due in large part to the productivity of America's farmers. Mass production and technological innovations changed the ways Americans worked, played, and spent their earnings (and occasionally spent more than their earnings). The era's abundance expressed itself through materialism, as consumer goods became mass marketed. The period marked a time during which Americans, especially the nation's young people, questioned traditional values and morality. War had disillusioned some and robbed many other Americans of their sense of youthful innocence. Americans looked for new manners and customs that better reflected their outlook than did those of their parents' generation. Modernity came to represent change and movement away from conventional practice—in economic, cultural, and social terms.

The decade of the 1920s also represented a key stage in the development of a national culture, yet there was no consensus about what that culture should ideally be. In many respects, the urban and rural residents of the United States belonged to two distinct cultures. Often these outlooks clashed, as in the conflicts over immigration policy, Prohibition, fundamentalism, and the Red Scare. In most cases, these issues involved disputes between traditional values and practices associated with an agrarian way of life on one hand and the modern temper of America's diverse and rapidly growing cities on the other.

The 1920s were a time in which differences of race, class, ethnicity, region, and religion divided Americans. Still, there were technological developments that helped to bridge the gaps among the United States' consumers, particularly between members of the middle and upper classes. As the cost involved in the production of Ford automobiles dropped, for example, more Americans were able to become car owners. Trends in buying on credit, and especially install-ment loans, made it possible for Americans to possess status items before they had the full cost of those purchases in hand. The mass media also helped close the distance between the social classes because families of different economic stations might listen to the same radio programming or attend the same motion pictures. A national culture was developing, and while it could not erase cul-tural distances and differences, it began to narrow the gulf between haves and have-nots in terms of such activities as leisure and mass communication.

CHARACTERIZING AN ERA

Haves and Have-Nots in the 1920s

The popular image of the 1920s involves raised hemlines, bathtub gin, and over-whelming prosperity. This portrait finds expression in Fitzgerald's *The Great Gatsby* (1925), the quintessential novel of the era. Fitzgerald's images of affluent partygoers, coupled with John Held Jr.'s illustrations of carefree youth driving about in "tin lizzies," helped define the decade in the popular imagination—then and now. Their iconic depictions of carefree, pleasure-seeking Americans suggested a world without worries, without wants.

While Fitzgerald's and Held's depictions were apt in capturing something of the flavor of an era, they are far from sufficient for understanding this time in American social history. As chronicler of the age J. C. Furnas notes, "To say 'the Roaring Twenties' tempts those born too late for direct experience of that renowned decade into a swirl of clichés: a girl with bobbed hair, a fuzzy per-manent and a Cupid's bow mouth dancing the Charleston on a table; raccoon coats and hip flasks; Wall Street spinning like a toddle top; mounted police rid-ing down demonstrators; Hoover's high colors, Coolidge in a ten-gallon hat; two cars in every garage, one a Stutz, the other a Packard; a shining castle built upon the sand. . . . That is the nostalgia-monger's montage. It's all pertinent, only the scope is too narrow for the diverse realities. Yes, the 1920s were like that, only

Table 1. U.S. Unemployment Rates and Percentages, 1921–1929 (annual averages for persons 14 and older)

Year	Unemployment Rate	% of Civilian Labor Force
1921	4,918,000	11.7
1922	2,859,000	6.7
1923	1,049,000	2.4
1924	2,190,000	5.0
1925	1,453,000	3.2
1926	801,000	1.8
1927	1,519,000	3.3
1928	1,982,000	4.2
1929	1,550,000	3.2

Source: Bureau of the Census 1976, 126, as presented in Ross 1995, 101; Stricker 1983, 19.

they were so much more. . . ." (Furnas 1974, 367). In reality, the 1920s offered a much more complex story than raccoon coats and roadsters alone could ever convey. To discover this other story, it becomes necessary to look beyond an iconic image of 1920s America.

Postwar Prosperity

Taken as a whole, America did prosper during the 1920s. Once the economy underwent the usual adjustments from war to a peacetime society, financial growth was brisk. On average, although workweeks were shortened since the previous decade, 1920s wages/salaries still rose. Gross wages in the United States rose 26 percent from 1919 to 1929. Real wages lagged behind, growing only 8 percent during the period from 1923 to 1929. Average annual per capita salaries grew from $1,236 in 1920 to $1,368 in 1930. Nationally, savings went from $19.7 billion to $28.4 billion. Death rates continued to decline. Life insurance policy values increased from $9.4 billion to $15.9 billion. From 1921 to 1929, the nation's gross national product went from $74 billion to $104.4 billion. Manufacturing output during the years between 1920 and 1929 grew in excess of 60 percent. The value of new construction went from $12 billion in 1919 to $17 billion in 1928. All of these figures function as indicators of a society's general prosperity. Still, statistics that aggregate American experience may obscure real and stark differences in condition among the living conditions of the nation's people (Broer and Walther 1990, 27; Drowne and Huber 2004, 294, 5; Grant and Katz 1998, 222).

While it is true that the 1920s represented a time of abundance for some Americans, this affluence did not extend to all the nation's residents. According to

Did 1920s' Prosperity "Trickle Down"?

Although many economic indicators improved during the 1920s, not all Americans benefited equally from that growth. In this sense, historical statistics can distort the real disparities between the rich and poor during this decade. As early as 1929 cultural observer Stuart Chase contended that the decade's affluence was concentrated in a small portion of the country's people. He claimed that "America's prosperity is only 24 per cent of the people, and this percentage owns all the wealth of this country. . . . In the time this excess has been accumulating, public charities have increased their expenditures 132 per cent" (Chase 1929, 24).

People who had already inherited or amassed wealth as the 1920s opened continued to grow that wealth during the decade. They were able to conduct the lives of opulence commonly associated in the popular imagination with 1920s America, at least until the stock market crashed in 1929.

Those who worked or invested in major areas of the era's economic boom, such as construction, printing, hosiery/knitwear, automobile manufacture, and some branches of the leisure and entertainment industries, derived the most new economic advantages. Furthermore, individuals who involved themselves in lucrative but illegitimate enterprises, such as bootlegging, gambling, narcotics, prostitution, and other forms of organized crime, often managed impressive incomes from their ventures of the 1920s.

People who worked or invested in declining businesses and industries of the period, such as railroad, horse-drawn carriage, and streetcar operations, suffered. With the growth in automobile ownership and motorized private transportation during the 1920s, public transportation was not used as extensively, and so these operations, among others, experienced significant economic setbacks.

Other populations hit hard in the economy of the 1920s included coal miners, leather workers, and textile workers. America's farmers occupied what was perhaps the most difficult place within the decade's economy. Early in the 1920s, agriculture experienced a depression. The agricultural price index crashed during the period from 1920 to 1921, resulting in a combined 40 percent drop (Emmet and Jeuck 1950, 205). Compounding these economic challenges for rural Americans were natural disasters such as floods and droughts that not only threatened crop yield but also endangered personal safety. As one historian summarized the decade of the 1920s in the United States, "This was a period of winners and losers in the United States, with the business community entering a 'golden age' and the small farmer and certain segments of the labor market beginning a long cycle of decline" (Goldberg 2003, xii).

Although they cannot readily be identified solely by industry or profession, several other groups in the United States typically did not achieve financial independence during this decade. Americans who shared least in the era's purported prosperity were the unemployed, new immigrants, people of color, homemakers, and others who performed unpaid labor.

Social History of the United States: The 1920s

Did 1920s' Prosperity "Trickle Down"?, Continued

Furthermore, contrary to the term's suggestion, "1920s prosperity" did not extend throughout the entire decade. The period of abundance typically denoted by the term "Jazz Age" (1920–1927) was shorter in duration. Near the decade's end, a major stock market crash had an adverse impact on the economic condition of most Americans.

Therefore, it is fair to say that the popular imagery of the 1920s hints at levels of affluence few Americans recognized, and even fewer experienced, during that era. In fact, the average U.S. worker's salary rose only slightly during the 1920s, from $1,236 in 1920 to $1,368 in 1930. Historians such as Frank Stricker have helped clarify this gap between 1920s reality and perception. His research, along with that of other recent scholars, reveals that while living standards rose during this decade, most Americans remained concerned with achieving economic security.

---

historian Myra Weatherly, "Census data for the 1920s gathered by the Bureau of the Census classified between one-third and two-fifths of the American population as poor" (Weatherly 2006, 14).

MEASURED PROGRESS

The 1920 Census

Historian Hyman Alterman has called the United States decennial census "the 'diary' of America" (Alterman 1969, 305). For one thing, the census tracks growth in the total population in the United States. The census provides more information, however, than a mere headcount. It regularly records significant events, trends, and changes for the nation's people.

The United States Constitution calls for a census to be taken every ten years. It is on the basis of these findings that the nation determines levels of representation in Congress and taxation practices. The Census Bureau collects information about the nation's changing population. Each time the census is conducted, a detailed questionnaire determines what type of information will be collected. The ideal census is an inclusive one, capturing a full and accurate data set for the entire residential population of the United States.

While the list of questions included changes somewhat from one census to the next, typical information collected includes name, gender, race, age, marital status, and place of birth. The 14th census, conducted in 1920 at a cost of

$2,511,700, offers not only a great deal of data but also a sketch of the time and its concerns (Gauthier 2002, 1). For example, although the format of the 1920 census resembled that of the 1910 census, it did not ask some of the questions previous ones had asked. Questions about number of children born, length of marriage, Union or Confederate service history, or unemployment were dropped. Instead, the 1920 census added four new questions. These newly introduced questions included one about year of naturalization and three about the respondent's native language. Those shifts suggest that the designers of the census survey instrument were more interested in the societal challenges surrounding turn-of-the-century immigration rates than in the Civil War status of those interviewed.

The Changing American Family

On January 13, 1921, the findings of the 1920 census became available as a report. The nation's population had grown from 76,094,000 in 1900 to 106,021,537 in 1920 (Time-Life 1998, 35). During the decade of the 1920s, the United States population would continue to rise, reaching 123,202,624 in 1930 (Drowne and Huber 2004, 294). There was more to notice about the census findings, however, than an increase in the nation's total population. Data gathered in the 1920 census and related studies also revealed a great deal about American family life.

For instance, life expectancy in America at this time was 54.6 years of age for men and 53.6 years of age for women (Drowne and Huber 2004, 294). Of those Americans age 15 or older, over 60 percent were married and less than 1 percent were divorced (Gregory 1995, 170). Census-takers determined that the average household size in 1920 was 4.3 people, smaller than the previous census averages of 4.5 in 1910 and 4.8 in 1900 (U.S. Department of Commerce/Bureau of the Census 1960, 41). Infant mortality remained a concern, as evidenced by

Table 2. Marital Status of Persons Age 15 or Older in the United States, 1920–1940

Marital Status	1920	1930	1940
Single	12,967,565	14,953,712	16,376,595
Married	21,849,266	26,327,109	30,191,087
Widowed	1,758,308	2,025,036	2,143,552
Divorced	285,284	489,478	624,398
Unknown	110,240	85,686	—
Total	36,970,663	43,881,021	49,335,632

Source: Bureau of the Census, Statistical Abstract of the United States 1947, 42, as presented in Gregory 1995, 170.

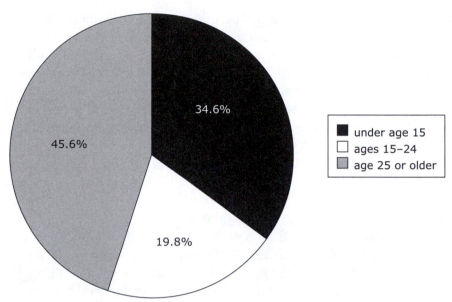

Figure I.1 *1920 U.S. Census Findings on Age in America. Compare these figures,*
particularly in terms of the percentage of Americans age 25 or older, with figures for
1880: 38.2% under age 15, 20.6% ages 15–24, and 41.2% age 25 or older. Source:
U.S. Department of Commerce/Bureau of Statistics 1989, 15.

such measures as the Sheppard-Towner Maternity and Infancy Protection Act of
1921. This law sought to promote public health, particularly for infants and their
mothers. The U.S. infant death rate dropped 17 percent during the 1920s (Haines
2005, online).

Youth Culture Flourishes . . . and Rebels

The 1920 census also established that an important shift in age distribution in
the nation's population had taken place. Chiefly, it revealed how young the
nation's population had become. Due to increased birth rates and decreased
infant and child mortality rates, in 1920, 34.6 percent of America's residents were
under the age of 15; 19.8 percent were ages 15 to 24. Taken together, then, 54.4
percent of the population was 24 or younger, 72.1 percent of the nation was
age 34 or younger, and 27.9 percent was age 35 or older. This age distribution
marked a contrast to the comparable population statistics for 1900, at which
time 33.4 percent of Americans were under age 35 and 66.6 percent were 35 or
older (U.S. Department of Commerce/Bureau of Statistics 1989, 15).

In many ways, the 1920s represented a time of opportunity and optimism
for America's youth. The nation had realized a reduction in the use of child labor, although undocumented forms of child labor persisted among families of

sharecroppers and migrant workers. The United States experienced the highest ever rates of school attendance, including at institutions of higher education. A playground movement aimed to provide America's youth with healthful and safe places to enjoy recreation. There were also voluntary associations dedicated to developing boys and girls as the leaders of tomorrow. During the 1920s many organizations sought to exert positive influences on American young people, including the farm and 4-H clubs, Girl Scouts, Boy Scouts, YMCA, and YWCA. By 1927 over 25 percent of the nation's boys were members of the Boy Scouts of America (Leinwand 2001, 1927).

It would be misleading, then, to suggest that all youth rejected the mores of their parents. Still, with a national median age of 25, it is no wonder that many historians consider that the generation gap had its origins in the 1920s. This decade's youth felt a distance from Victorian notions of conduct and morality. For many this youth rebellion helped define the era. As historian Paula S. Fass writes, "The image that teases the historical imagination is of a rebellious youth, iconoclastic, irreverent, frivolous, lost to social responsibility, and even more lost to traditional values and beliefs" (Fass 1977, 6). This attitude of rebellion shaped a whole range of behaviors by America's young people during the 1920s.

Postwar youth were not just critical of the older generation's habits and attitudes but also of their legacy to the next generation. Writing in 1920, cultural observer John F. Carter asserted, "The older generation had certainly pretty well ruined this world before passing it on to us." He goes on to explain how "they give us this thing, knocked to pieces, leaky, red-hot, threatening to blow up; and then they are surprised that we don't accept it with the same attitude of pretty, decorous enthusiasm with which they received it, way back in the 'eighties'" (Carter 1920, 301). America's young people questioned the actions, values, and priorities of previous generations, and they struck out to create a different way of life than their parents had known.

WHO LIVED WHERE?

American Regions and Population Shifts

Author Gertrude Stein has been quoted as saying, "In the United States there are more places where nobody is than where somebody is. That is what makes America what it is" (Norris 1994, 105). For many years, that had been the story told by the national census. The American West stood as the frontier, an area perceived as open and unoccupied. The story of westward expansion was typically narrated as the closing of the American frontier. With time, however, the story to be told on the basis of census data had less to do with unoccupied space ("where nobody is") and more to do with how and where people congregated ("where somebody is").

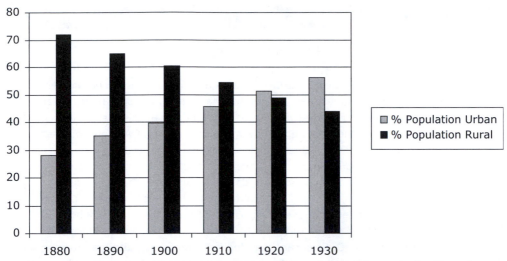

Figure I.2 *Comparative Bar Graph, Urban and Rural Populations in the United States, 1880–1930.* Source: *Bureau of the Census, 1939,* Urban Population in the United States from the First Census (1790) to the Fifteenth Census (1930). *Washington, D.C.: Bureau of the Census, as presented in Emmet and Jeuck 1950, 194.*

More Urban than Not

Of all the census findings during 1920, the most remarked change, both at the time and since, had to do with where Americans lived. The 1920 census was the first such survey to demonstrate that a majority of Americans resided in urban rather than rural areas. Furthermore, fewer than 30 percent of the nation's population were supporting themselves through farming. Within the classifications used for the 1920 census, an urban place of residence included any location with more than 2,500 residents. Therefore, not everyone categorized as urban in the census lived in a large city. Still, this census was the first one in the nation's history to find that a majority of Americans no longer resided in rural areas. In addition, over 50 percent of America's urban dwellers did inhabit cities of 100,000 or more residents.

More Mobile than Ever

A related finding within the census report also had to do with population movements. One of the most telling aspects of the 1920 census

Table 3. Net Loss in Farm Population as a Result of Migration into Cities, United States, 1910–1927

Year(s)	Loss*
1910–1920	463,000
1920–1925	2,000,000
1925	441,000
1926	649,000
1927	193,000

*Losses are estimated.

Source: United States Department of Agriculture data, as presented in Wolman 1929, 72.

The Harlem Renaissance

During the early 1920s, New York City became a mecca for displaced and disenfranchised people. Harlem, an area within Manhattan, became home to an extraordinary artistic and expressive movement now known as the Harlem Renaissance. Also known as the New Negro Movement, this group of African American artists, writers, and intellectuals promoted racial pride and social consciousness. Out of this movement came sports clubs, musicals, music recordings including the so-called race records, books, periodicals, dances, sculptures, and paintings. Two particularly important magazines linked to the Harlem Renaissance were *Opportunity* and *Crisis.* Both lent expression and credibility to voices for racial equality and acceptance. Among the writers affiliated with the Harlem Renaissance were Countee Cullen, W. E. B. DuBois, Langston Hughes, Alain Locke, and Jean Toomer. Alain Locke's 1925 anthology, *The New Negro,* helped convey the range and richness of the movement's work, disseminating its message of the Harlem Renaissance to a readership beyond New York.

was its set of findings regarding Americans' place of residence. As did census reports before it, the 1920 census documented rates of immigration. The 1920 census reported 13 percent were first-generation immigrants, most of whom resided in the nation's major cities. Other population shifts had to do with movements within the United States. For instance, during this period, growth in the population of the Western states continued. In addition, a significant number of African Americans participated in a movement known as the Great Migration. These individuals left the rural South to travel to Northern cities where they sought better jobs and better schools as well as a reprieve from racial violence such as lynching and other forms of racism.

The era's shift toward automobile travel brought Americans into greater contact with one another. It also produced several benefits to America's farming families. Farms no longer needed to be situated close to rail lines to distribute their crops. In addition, farmers no longer experienced the isolation of remote regions because travel by automobile was increasingly common during the 1920s. Developments such as telephone service, rural free delivery, and mail-order buying all helped bridge the distance between rural residents and their urban counterparts. The gap between country and city, farm and factory narrowed.

In terms of the nation's historical imagination, then, a sharp divide continues to separate popular perceptions of the 1920s from the actual living conditions experienced by ordinary Americans at that time. While it is true that bobbed hair, raccoon coats, and bugle beads helped form the backdrop for this decade, the 1920s involved more profound and enduring changes than those typically associated with style and fashion. Behind the flapper era's exuberant application of rouge stood starker conflicts and more complex realities.

REFERENCES AND FURTHER READINGS

Allen, Frederick Lewis. 1931. *Only Yesterday*. New York: Bantam.

Alterman, Hyman. 1969. *Counting People: The Census in History*. New York: Harcourt, Brace and World.

Broer, Lawrence R., and John D. Walther, eds. 1990. *Dancing Fools and Weary Blues: The Great Escape of the Twenties*. Bowling Green, OH: Bowling Green State University Popular Press.

Carter, John F., 1920. "These Wild Young People, by One of Them." *Atlantic Monthly* 126 (September): 301–304.

Chase, Stuart. 1929. *Prosperity: Fact or Myth*. New York: C. Boni.

Drowne, Kathleen, and Patrick Huber, 2004. *The 1920s*. Westport, CT: Greenwood Press.

Editors of Time-Life Books. 1998. *Our American Century,* 1998. Alexandria, VA: Time-Life Books.

Emmet, Boris, and John E. Jeuck. 1950. *Catalogues and Counters: A History of Sears, Roebuck and Company*. Chicago: University of Chicago Press.

Fass, Paula S. 1977. *The Damned and the Beautiful: American Youth in the 1920s*. New York: Oxford University Press.

Furnas, J. C., 1974. *Great Times: An Informal Social History of the United States, 1914–1929*. New York: Putnam.

Gauthier, Jason G. 2002. *Measuring America: The Decennial Censuses from 1790 to 2000*. Washington, DC: U.S. Census Bureau.

Goldberg, Ronald Allen. 2003. *America in the Twenties*. Syracuse, NY: Syracuse University Press.

Grant, Robert B., and Joseph Katz. 1998. *The Great Trials of the Twenties: The Watershed Decades in America's Courtrooms*. Rockville Center, NY: Sarpedon.

Gregory, Ross. 1995. *Modern America, 1914–1945*. New York: Facts on File.

Haines, Michael. 2005. "Fertility and Mortality in the United States." *EH.Net Encyclopedia*. Edited by Robert Whaples. http://eh.net/encyclopedia/article/haines.demography (accessed September 11, 2006).

Leinwand, Gerald. 2001. *1927: High Tide of the Twenties*. New York: Four Walls Eight Windows.

Norris, Scott, ed. 1994. *Discovered Country: Tourism and Survival in the American West*. Albuquerque: Stone Ladder Press.

U.S. Department of Commerce/Bureau of the Census. 1960. *Historical Statistics of the United States: Colonial Times to 1957*. Washington, DC: GPO.

Weatherly, Myra. 2006. *Living in 1920s America*. Farmington Hills, MI: Greenhaven Press/Thomas Gale.

Issues of the 20th Century

Work and the Workplace

Modernity and Mass Production

OVERVIEW

Mass production's mechanization and regimentation reshaped American life in the 1920s. This was a time of surprising growth and newfound prosperity, exciting innovations, and devastating collapses. The economy stumbled in 1921 and then regained its footing in a period of sustained prosperity before taking a disastrous dive into the Great Depression in late 1929. During the decade's middle years, industrialization's prospects seemed almost limitless. As cars rolled off assembly lines in Detroit and clattered down the streets of the United States, a vigorous economy embellished American lives and revolutionized manufacturing. Mass production quickened the pulse of American business, and in the 1920s' feverish economic boom, many Americans envisioned the prospect of even more.

The boom clearly did not affect all demographic groups equally. More than half of all Americans earned just enough to support themselves, but the boisterous prosperity of the 1920s spawned the decade's image. Indeed, a reduction in average working hours joined with rising per capita income to generate striking improvements in the standard of living. Technological advances transformed American life at a rapid pace. A person 30 years old in 1920 had witnessed the proliferation of electricity, telephones, and automobiles, all of which had profoundly affected the way the United States did business and the way Americans lived. The capacity of cheap electricity alone accelerated production of consumer goods that would change newly electrified American households.

Big Business and its leaders played a prominent role in the nation's culture during this era when movie stars had only begun to twinkle on the American horizon. As new business practices created mechanical wonders, business tycoons served as role models. The success of men like automobile manufacturer Henry Ford and financier Andrew Mellon helped to shape an American dream that promised wealth for the multitudes. Many Americans flourished as the swiftly evolving economy created new white-collar job opportunities, which opened the door to a broader middle class. As more educated men moved into the offices of American workplaces, many enjoyed higher wages. Complicated operations required a white-collar bureaucracy at the same time that increased mechanization allowed factories to increase their capacities without adding to the blue-collar work force. The successes of mass production gave birth to new problems. For many, the nature of work was changing. Both mass production and bureaucracy generated jobs governed by a routine that did not supply the satisfaction many workers sought. For an office worker, replicating the same activities day after day could be stifling. And assembly lines lessened both the status and the monetary value assigned to many skilled laborers' jobs. Instead of using their skills, they sometimes found themselves performing one simple procedure over and over again throughout the day. These workers had few options because Big Business's ascendance had coincided with a decline in the power of organized labor. As a result, many workers felt like insignificant cogs in the great machine of mass production.

For those with enough money, entrepreneurships still offered opportunities, even for members of immigrant and minority groups. Small specialized stores continued to dominate the retail market as the range of consumer products expanded. Neighborhood operations with a loyal clientele prospered although chain stores also experienced rapid growth from 29,000 in 1918 to 160,000 in 1929 (Leuchtenburg 1993, 191). Construction enjoyed a period of increased activity. After a virtual halt during World War I, this industry contributed to the blossoming of the suburban communities that were to house the expanding middle class. Some towns grew by as much as 1,000 percent (Leuchtenburg 1993, 183). In American cities, towering skyscrapers, some reaching as high as sixty stories, changed the landscape dramatically.

While the industrial and retail economies thrived, American farmers suffered. By 1921, prices for U.S. crops had plummeted as worldwide demand dropped following Europe's recovery from the ravages of World War I. And over the course of the decade, nature unleashed multiple assaults on agriculture in the form of droughts, floods, and insect infestations. Despite these setbacks, farmers' worlds faced a possible transformation as the use of machines, such as tractors and trucks, offered the possibility of accomplishing more work with fewer people. In addition, newly developed hybrid seeds and chemical fertilizers enabled larger operations to increase their yield per acre. As a result, prosperous farmers were able to make better use of land, devoting fewer acres to feed for horses and mules, thus expanding the amount of acreage for cash crops. However, most small farmers could not afford to buy new technology; consequently, they had difficulty competing with expanding agribusinesses.

Women represented roughly one-fifth of the work force throughout a decade that offered them new opportunities without large economic rewards. Business offices, alive with the sounds of typewriters, telephones, and adding machines, provided a variety of options for women who wanted to find work outside the factory. These new "pink collar" jobs cast women in supporting roles within the offices that governed American businesses. They performed necessary work, but their jobs rarely offered any hope of promotion to important decision-making jobs. Many women found work behind a desk while the retail economy welcomed more and more women into stores as clerks.

African Americans joined the urban economy in increasing numbers at this time. By moving away from the South, African Americans could escape the stigma of legalized segregation and the frustrating life of tenant farming and sharecropping. In some companies, African American men found unskilled jobs alongside white workers; however, most employers assigned them to the factories' worst jobs. Because African American men seldom held well-paying jobs, most African American women had to work to increase family incomes. During this prosperous decade, they generally found themselves confined to domestic labor on the bottom rung of the economic ladder to success.

As the decade progressed, the tentacles of economic distress gradually began to place a stranglehold on the lives of the most vulnerable workers. After the stock market crash in late 1929, the crisis became a threat to workers at all levels. The Great Depression would destroy many American businesses and move millions of workers into the ranks of the unemployed. A glittering mirage of economic potential tantalized many Americans during the 1920s, but that dream collapsed under the weight of uncertainty and decline at the decade's end.

TIMELINE

1920   Arkansas River floods, claiming 1,500 casualties and causing millions of dollars in property damage. Disaster adds to nature's toll on farmers.

Latest figures show that the United States has more than 265,000 miles of railroad track.

Organized labor reaches high point of 5 million members, including 400,000 women.

Product surpluses lead to recession in mid-year that cripples economy through the following year.

1921   The Farm bloc has its first meeting, begins pushing legislation to protect farmers.

1922   U.S. economy begins to rebound.

A mechanical switchboard begins work in New York's telephone system.

Approximately 60,000 New England textile workers strike in February, setting off a series of walkouts.

About 600,000 coal miners walk off the job April 1.

Roughly 400,000 workers join July 1 railroad strike after the threat of a wage cut.

Jamaican Marcus Garvey, who attempts to demonstrate the potential for business success to African Americans, suffers a setback when his Black Star Line of ships fails; he is indicted.

Capper–Volstead Act exempts farm cooperatives from antitrust laws.

1923   Judge orders U.S. Steel to discontinue the twelve-hour workday.

Approximately 13.3 million automobiles are registered.

1924   DuPont manufactures Cellophane for first time in the United States.

1925   Manufacturers produce five million enameled bathroom fixtures to embellish American homes.

Henry Ford initiates the five-day workweek.

Ford rolls completed car off assembly line every 10 seconds in one October day.

General Motors unveils K Model Chevrolet with color finish.

A. Philip Randolph founds the Brotherhood of Sleeping Car Porters.

Survey of low- to mid-level office workers shows that 86 percent have some high school education, and 64 percent have some commercial training.

1926   A disastrous tornado ends Florida land boom.

1927   Congress approves the McNary–Haugen Farm Relief Bill; Calvin Coolidge vetoes it.

Ford Motor Company produces its 15 millionth car. Henry Ford drives the car off assembly line.

International Harvester becomes the first company to offer two-week annual vacation.

The Mississippi, Ohio, and Missouri rivers overflow, causing widespread devastation. Farmers are especially hard hit.

1928   Congress again passes McNary–Haugen Farm Relief Bill; Coolidge again vetoes it.

Ford announces plans for Model A; 500,000 buyers make down payments based on reputation alone.

Film director King Vidor's *The Crowd* portrays a young man's attempts to succeed while lost in the bureaucracy of a large company.

The *New York Times* mounts the first electric sign on Times Square.

1929   Twenty-seven million automobiles are registered in the United States.

Automobile manufacturers produce 4.8 million vehicles and employ more than 7 percent of all factory workers.

Per capita income reaches $681, up more than 40 percent over 1900 figure.

The average worker is on the job 44.2 hours per week.

Sixteen holding companies control more than 90 percent of the nation's electrical power.

Union membership is down almost 1 million since 1920.

Farmers hold only 9 percent of nation's wealth, a plunge from 16 percent a decade earlier.

October 24 stock market crash signals the end to widespread prosperity and the start of the Great Depression.

CHANGES IN INDUSTRIAL PRODUCTION

Powered by the techniques of mass production, a startling revolution surged through the U.S. economy during the 1920s. Less than ten years after Henry Ford had introduced the assembly line, the United States distinguished itself as a worldwide leader in manufacturing. Factories buzzed with activity facilitated by

Workers in a Goodyear Tire factory in Akron, Ohio, labor to satisfy a growing demand for tires sparked by growth of the auto industry. (Library of Congress)

a large pool of unskilled workers from the ranks of European immigrants and African American migrants. Automobile manufacturing and the related industries of steel, rubber, glass, and gasoline led the business bonanza. With electricity making more rapid production possible, manufacturers focused on efficiency, increased output, and greater profits. Cutting-edge companies set aside manpower for research that would develop new products and procedures. Not surprisingly, this dedication to science bolstered the chemical industry, but experimentation also played a key role in production of widely used products such as automobiles and household appliances. By the mid-1920s, more sophisticated consumers placed higher demands on manufacturers. Ford's unassuming Model-Ts could no longer satisfy public demand. Therefore, manufacturers turned their attention to factory enhancements that could generate sales.

Combining these management strategies with ingenious marketing techniques enabled industries to increase production by 64 percent without adding to the total number of factory workers (Dumenil 1995, 58). This was good news for manufacturers but not necessarily for workers. Management decisions to replace skilled laborers with machines threatened jobs and lowered wages. For example, a single warp-tying device in a textile plant could eliminate the jobs of ten to fifteen workers and devalue the remaining laborers. The United States could take pride in a skyrocketing 264 percent increase in industrial production over the first three decades of the 20th century; however, the work force often suffered financially as employers profited (Leuchtenburg 1993, 180).

In the economy at large, growth led to many business mergers, which concentrated the control of American industry and commerce in fewer hands. Between 1919 and 1930, approximately 8,000 companies were swallowed up by other companies in mergers (Dumenil 1995, 39). Generally, these consolidations worked to broaden a business's geographic reach rather than to wipe out its competitors. The spread of businesses from state to state and the emerging growth of chain stores enhanced the sense of a national economy and diminished the links that tied owners to their employees and to their customers. Because the prosperous years of the 1920s coincided with a decline in the power of organized labor, this truly was an era in which the captains of industry reigned su-

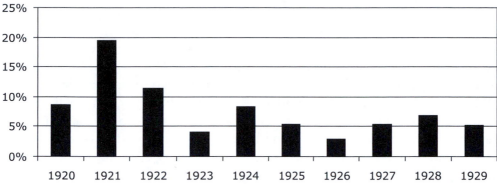

Figure 1.1 *Non-farm Civilian Work Force: 1920 to 1930 (percent unemployed).*
Source: *United States Bureau of the Census.*

preme in the workplace and, to a surprising extent, in popular culture. *The Man Nobody Knows,* a 1925 best seller by Bruce Barton, portrayed Jesus Christ as a successful executive. Jesus, according to Barton, had "picked up twelve men from the bottom ranks of business and forged them into an organization that conquered the world" (Leuchtenburg 1993, 188). Barton also called the parables "the most powerful advertisements of all time." Mass production had become the lens through which many Americans saw their world.

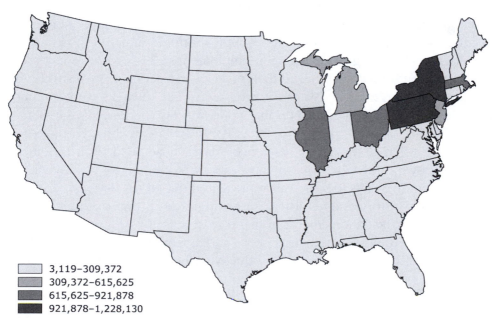

3,119–309,372	
309,372–615,625	
615,625–921,878	
921,878–1,228,130	

Map 1.1 *Average Number of Wage Earners in Manufacturing in 1920*

Economy Erratic Early in Decade

For American business, the new decade began on a positive note. Throughout 1920 and the early months of 1921, the United States experienced the remnants of a postwar boom. Consumer demand, which had been stifled by wartime scarcity and rationing, blossomed anew. The availability of easy credit and continued demand for American products in war-ravaged European nations bolstered the economy. And few strikes stood as obstacles to business. In 1920 Henry Ford rolled a car off the assembly line every 60 seconds. The idea behind the assembly line—breaking down a complicated operation into a chain of simple actions with each being performed by a different worker—had tightened the efficiency of industrial production while broadening the perception of what industry could accomplish. Businessmen increasingly invested with the goal of coming one step closer to the mesmerizing goal of full mechanization.

By mid-1921, however, a deep recession had taken hold, generating unemployment and wages cuts. Wartime production had primed the pump of industrial growth, so the decline in demand for military matériel led to overproduction. In addition, the returning flood of veterans into the workforce raised the total number of people competing for civilian jobs. And a 1920 jump in oil prices contributed to the crisis in a culture increasingly dependent on petroleum products. Wholesale prices plummeted at a rate not seen since the American Revolution. At the same time, production of minerals dropped sharply. In the first 10 months of 1920 and the comparable period in 1921, mail-order businesses Sears-Roebuck and Montgomery Ward experienced a huge sales drop from $301 million to $206 million (Persons 1922, 14). The jobless rate in manufacturing peaked at just over 20 percent. When companies implemented layoffs, they sometimes targeted workers with a shorter tenure and those with no dependents. Many large manufacturers implemented 20 percent reductions in pay, and unions, which had flexed their muscles in a series of 1919 strikes, had little leverage during this crisis. Plant shutdowns and cutbacks were common. Akron, Ohio, which had thrived during World War I, experienced an exodus of almost 50,000 rubber workers (Goldberg 1999, 73). Meanwhile, employees of American Woolen Company in Lawrence, Massachusetts, faced a two-month plant shutdown, and when the factory's doors reopened, its workweek had been cut from five days to four. This represented one of the deepest recessions in the nation's history and yet it was surprisingly short. Improvements in productivity helped the nation emerge from the economic abyss. Soon, people were back at work with money in their pockets, and assembly lines were again humming along in the race to increase productivity. Innovation and prosperity remained part of the American environment through most of the decade—until disaster struck.

Electricity Reshapes Manufacturing

As electricity became the predominant form of energy used in factories during the 1920s, electrical power drove the financial growth of manufacturing throughout the decade. By 1929, electricity powered 70 percent of American industry, and its expanded use made it possible to more than double manufacturing's output between 1919 and 1929 (Dumenil 1995, 59). Although electricity was not a new product in this decade, the nation produced more hydroelectric power between 1920 and 1930 than it had in all preceding years. Moreover, oil found in Oklahoma, Texas, and California powered electric generators, motors, and transmission lines, thus lowering the price of electricity. At the decade's end, the United States was generating more electrical power than the rest of the world combined.

Use of electricity to replace steam and coal as the primary fuel sources in manufacturing made it easier for factory owners to streamline the production process. When the century began, complicated machinery had connected steam-driven machines to power sources, but small electric motors made that unnecessary. Electricity also enabled factories to increase efficiency by driving control mechanisms, such as flow meters, temperature gauges, and shut-off devices. Electric power made the conveyor belts on Henry Ford's assembly lines purr and enabled him to set a benchmark on October 23, 1925, when he rolled a completed automobile off the assembly line every 10 seconds. It also improved the efficiency of petroleum production. And it had profound effects on the production of chemicals, steel, rubber, and paper products. Electricity represented such a step up in terms of technology that factory owners replaced more than 40 percent of functioning steam engines between 1919 and 1927 (Leuchtenburg 1993, 179). Thanks largely to electricity, the average hourly output per manufacturing employee increased by 72 percent between 1919 and 1929 (Dumenil 1995, 59). Investments in new factories and equipment almost doubled during the same period.

Labor Unions Suffer Setbacks

The peak of labor union membership in the 1920s occurred in the decade's first year. Afterward labor unions' strength diminished. A tough business strategy known as "the open shop campaign" was largely responsible for this change; however, unions also struggled under the weight of a pro-business political atmosphere, antiunion court rulings, and expanded business efforts to benefit employees, thus making organized labor superfluous. All of these factors limited union efforts to establish a foothold in mass production industries. Open-shop organizations existed in 240 cities in 1920. The effort to keep unions out of manufacturing facilities took many forms. Employers blacklisted union sympathizers, adopted "yellow-dog contracts" that required new employees to give up the right to unionize, and in some cases moved factories into areas that were not hospitable to unions, such as the South. (This last practice was known as "the runaway shop.") Automobile manufacturers were among the fiercest proponents of the open shop. And because the American Federation of Labor (AFL) represented skilled craftsmen, its resources had no impact on the unskilled laborers who manned the assembly lines of large manufacturers. The garment industry used the runaway shop strategy, moving operations from New York to northeastern Pennsylvania. Textile companies moved many jobs to the South, closing down operations in New England.

The year 1922 represented the decade's busiest period for strikes. The first big walkout was a textile workers' strike in New England, which management and labor ended through compromise. A cause for greater concern was the long and bloody walkout of 600,000 coal workers. Beginning April 1, one mining company hired strikebreakers to do strip mining in Herrin, Illinois, and employed armed private detectives to protect them. Little is known of the particulars, but in response to militant protest by workers, private detectives killed three strikers. In retaliation, union members slit the throats of some scabs and gruesomely forced others to crawl into a cemetery where they were shot. The coal strike ended with an agreement that froze wages at 1920 levels. The settlement also omitted some mining operations from the contract, which allowed the owners to cast out union members.

The Great Railroad Strike of 1922 caused significant interference with railroad transportation at a time when trains were an important means of transportation for raw materials as well as factory products. Some workers were unhappy with new work rules and wage cuts instituted by private owners who reclaimed control over the railroads after a period of federalization during World War I. On July 1, 400,000 railroad shop workers walked off their jobs. President Warren G. Harding believed that the overlapping coal and rail strikes threatened the national economy, so he sought legal intervention. Less than three months after the strike had begun, a federal court injunction ordered workers to stop any activity that might bolster the walkout. The strikers abandoned their protest and returned to work without winning any concessions. Within all industries, there were an average of 34 strikes per year from 1920 to 1925 and only 18 per year from 1926 to 1930. This compared with an average of about 100 per year in 1916–1921 (Dumenil 1995, 63). Coal company strikes were scattered throughout the decade, and in 1929, textile workers, the majority of whom were women, launched a strike in Elizabethton, Tennessee. However, none of these later actions caused widespread effects.

The Supreme Court also acted to weaken the labor movement in four rulings that reduced the effectiveness of union boycotts, limited the government's ability to regulate child labor, made it easier for employers to win injunctions against pickets, and labeled a government-established minimum wage a violation of employers' freedom to draw up contracts. Moreover, the AFL's own shortsightedness affected union growth adversely. Reluctance to accept African American members limited the federation's opportunity to expand. Also, the AFL lost some of its appeal because it openly opposed some government aid to workers. As the decade drew to a close, total union membership had plummeted by almost a million workers.

American Inventions of the 1920s

While mass production changed the pace of American work, inventors continued to create new products for the 20th century. Listed below are some items introduced in the 1920s.

Tommy gun	Submachine gun invented by General John T. Thompson in 1920.
Band-Aid	Adhesive bandage produced in 1921 by Earle Dickson, an employee of Johnson & Johnson.
Polygraph	Lie detector created by University of California medical student John Larson in 1921.
Traffic signal	T-shaped stop-and-go device conceptualized by Garrett Morgan in 1923.
Dynamic loudspeaker	Model for all voice projection systems patented by two General Electric researchers, Chester W. Rice and Edward Washburn Kellogg, in 1924.
Liquid fuel rockets	Projectiles designed by Robert Goddard in 1925.
Can opener	Serrated edge added to manual can opener by the Star Can Company of San Francisco in 1925.
Quartz crystal watch	Highly accurate timing mechanism created by Warren Morrison during work at Bell Telephone Laboratories in 1927.
Television transmission	First signal sent in 1927 was a dollar sign composed of horizontal lines using dissector tube. Created by Philo Farnsworth.
Bubble gum	Pink Dubble Bubble gum created by Walter Diemer in 1928.
Electric shaver	Grooming aid patented by U.S. Army Lt. Col. Jacob Schick in 1928.
Car radio	Device refined in 1929 by Paul Galvin, which consumers added to existing cars.
Television system	Cathode ray tube called the kinescope developed by Vladimir Zworykin while working for RCA in 1929.

Henry Ford's Model A, shown here in the production process, exemplified the drive toward greater use of mass production in this decade. (Bettmann/Corbis)

Auto Industry Leads the Way

The automobile industry spearheaded the spread of mass production through practical advances and appeals to consumers. From Henry Ford's introduction of the assembly line in 1914 onward, auto manufacturers continued to dazzle consumers with their accomplishments. In 1929, they produced 4.8 million vehicles, a huge leap from 4,000 in 1900 (Dumenil 1995, 58). As production grew, manufacturers moved beyond the simplicity of cars like the basic black Model T, which boasted only four basic parts. Changes to the car were both mechanical and cosmetic. Early automobiles had an exterior covering of paint and varnish. Then oven-dried enamels became more common; however, most cars remained black because producing color finishes was expensive. An accidental discovery in a DuPont laboratory in 1920 led to development of a substance called Duco, which offered brilliant color without great expense. Other changes were on the way. General Motors' K Model Chevrolet, introduced in 1925, was a long sedan with amenities such as automatic windshield wipers. Hudson introduced its sporty Essex at about the same time. In that single year, Henry Ford watched his share of the market fall from 54 to 45 percent.

Two years later, Ford did what might have been unthinkable to a less resourceful man: He shut down his plant for an entire year, laying off 10,000 workers. While the plant doors were closed, he prepared the factory changes necessary to produce the new Model A. Then he invested $1.3 million in advertising his new product. When the Model A debuted on showroom floors in late 1927, an eager public lined up to see it and ordered 500,000 cars based solely on the Ford's reputation and the car's appearance. The factory produced 6,400 Model-As a day in 1928, and within a year Ford was back on top in sales (Parrish 1992, 45). Meanwhile, at General Motors (GM) a new business philosophy was taking over. Under the leadership of Alfred P. Sloan Jr., GM adopted the premise that sales could be sustained by convincing drivers to abandon their old cars in favor of new models. While Ford concentrated on providing a single cheap model, GM fared better by establishing different lines of automobiles to suit consumers' tastes.

The six major automakers—Ford, General Motors, Hudson, Studebaker, Chrysler, and Packard—employed 7 percent of all manufacturing workers in 1929 (Parrish 1992, 40). Glass, steel, and rubber producers, who made automobile components, necessarily grew with the auto industry. Asphalt and concrete companies also prospered because automobile owners wanted to travel on smoother roads. Filling stations, repair shops, motels, and tourist camps also sprang up to serve motorists.

Henry Ford's River Rouge Plant

The River Rouge Plant in Dearborn, Michigan, is clear evidence of Henry Ford's bold approach to manufacturing. By the mid-1920s, the plant was "easily the greatest industrial domain in the world," according to historian David L. Lewis (National Park Service). Just south of Detroit, the factory was virtually a city in itself. When construction ended in 1928, it contained 120 miles of conveyor belts and more than 15 million square feet of floor space. Its power plant generated enough electricity to serve a Detroit-sized city, and the site had its own railroad with 16 locomotives and 100 miles of track. River Rouge had no residents, but at its peak 100,000 people worked there (Henry Ford Museum). With construction already under way when the decade began, tractors became the first vehicles to roll off the assembly line in 1921. Six years later Ford moved the last automobile assembly line from his old Highland Park factory to River Rouge. The site housed steel and glass furnaces, plate-glass rollers, ore docks, and plants to produce radiators, transmissions, tires, frames, and assemblies. In 1927, the company achieved the first ore-to-assembly production of an automobile. "Machinery is the new Messiah," Ford once declared (Leuchtenburg 1993, 187).

Scientific Management and the White-Collar Boom

Increasing adoption of engineer Frederick W. Taylor's scientific management strategies led to new common practices in the way industries functioned in the 1920s. The system, which was based on Taylor's time-motion studies done with a stopwatch, led managers to take away a great deal of workers' autonomy.

Instead of working at their own pace, workers were given detailed instructions on exactly what they should do and how fast they should do it. Taylor's ideas had their biggest impact in factories, but some office and retail managers also adapted the process to their use. In most factories, managers allowed machines to set the pace of operations, which forced employees to work faster. Managers in the textile industry ordered employees to operate more machinery, a system they called the "stretch-out." As factory workers faced regimentation, demand for white-collar workers grew because companies began to place more emphasis on other areas of the operation. Salaried managers stood atop the industrial career ladder, and it was their job to make sure that efficiencies in the factory provided a foundation for growth in other facets of the business. As attention turned toward marketing, advertising, and distribution, companies created more white-collar positions. Some of these workers earned enough to make a place for themselves in the middle class. However, many were low-paid clerks or secretaries who served as support staff to managers.

Welfare Capitalism

During this era, the largest mass-production operations began reaching out to employees by offering services to make them feel happier and more secure. Keeping employees satisfied obviously contributed to a healthy work atmosphere, but employers also hoped their strategic generosity would make labor unions obsolete. The practice of labor capitalism became widespread in the biggest companies during the early 1920s although it had been first introduced a decade earlier. One common practice was the establishment of a "company union." This organization enabled workers to choose representatives to express their ideas and voice their complaints in an environment controlled by the company. Businesses also offered an array of benefits, including life insurance, profit sharing, pensions, and employee sports activities. Companies such as Goodyear, General Electric, AT&T, Procter & Gamble, Bethlehem Steel, and International Harvester were foremost in establishing these programs. However, only a small percentage of American workers had the opportunity to benefit from these initiatives. In 1928, just 1 million workers could participate in stock-ownership plans, and only 6 million received coverage from company life insurance programs.

Mass Production Transforms Life in the United States

As it raised the standard of living, mass production transformed much of the nation both inside and outside the factory gates. With new opportunities came new expectations and new challenges. The drive toward efficiency changed the workplace by adding to both white- and blue-collar sectors and creating a greater divide between those two worlds. As more blue-collar workers were able to eke out a decent existence, some white-collar workers rejoiced at their admission to the middle class. Mass production and the economic boom of the 1920s bolstered a huge imbalance between rich and poor. Five percent of American families received one-third of all income (Dumenil 1995, 306). While the rich enjoyed the finest products an industrial society could provide, workers lived in crowded tenements. To make ends meet, members of the working class put 2 million of their children to work before they had reached the age of 15.

In the decade's probusiness climate, politicians as well as ordinary Americans supported the factory lords whose success had materially transformed their worlds by generating a consumer economy. The success of industrial leaders turned them into icons of the American dream. When asked to choose the greatest man in history, college students in a 1920s poll ranked Henry Ford third, behind Jesus Christ and Napoleon (Parrish 1992, 39). Calvin Coolidge, who served as president for more than half of the decade, was proud to help the wealthy through low taxes, scanty regulation, and high tariffs that made it impossible for consumers to buy cheap foreign-made products. "The man who builds a factory builds a temple," he once said (Dumenil 1995, 31). Manufacturers also contributed to the entrenchment of urban ghettoes. The availability of unskilled work outside the rural South led to a hastening of African American migration, for some, out of the former slave states and, for others, into urban areas within the South. In addition, uneducated immigrants crowded into areas where they could get jobs without learning a craft. While the jobs offered new opportunities, most of them did not pay well and did not provide opportunities for upward mobility within manufacturing companies. Consequently, these workers could not afford to leave the dreary tenement neighborhoods of America's cities.

Finally, manufacturers' efforts to be cost-efficient may have nourished the seeds of the Great Depression: Because factory workers did not earn enough to buy all of the products rolling off the assembly lines, consumers became more dependent on credit. Overproduction also led to lower prices and laid the groundwork for the economic disaster. Markets for automobiles and construction began to demonstrate an end to the boom as early as 1925. In the ballyhoo of raucous prosperity, the product surpluses that spawned the 1920–1921 recession were quickly forgotten; however, those days of high inventories, skyrocketing unemployment, and low wages had offered Americans a taste of what was to come after the 1929 stock market crash.

TOUGH TIMES FOR FARMERS

Decline in the 1920s

Independent American farmers, once at the heart of the U.S. economy, found themselves greatly marginalized in the 1920s. In a rapidly urbanizing nation with

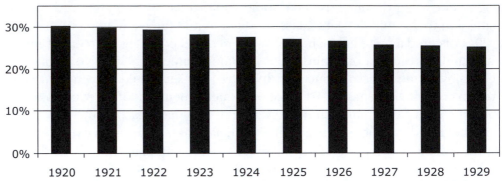

Figure 1.2 *Farm Population in the U.S. in the 1920s (percent of entire population).*
Source: *United States Bureau of the Census.*

an economy now driven by manufacturing, farmers struggled to achieve prosperity. While the automobile and the radio linked urban Americans to one another, many farmers lived in isolation. Electricity brought light to factories and
urban homes, but without electrical lines to connect far-flung farms, the people
of rural America knew the darkness of night and dodged the shadows of obsolescence. The 1920s were difficult years in agriculture, particularly for small
family-owned farms. There is some debate about whether their experience represented a true depression, but it is clear that many farmers felt the desperation
of economic collapse before the Great Depression swathed the nation in de-
spair. Like some manufacturers, farm owners experienced production surpluses.
However, farmers had few employees to dismiss, and often they could not afford
new machinery that might have enabled them to achieve more efficient production and prosperity. Farmers also faced capricious assaults from Mother Nature. Widespread insect infestations wiped out entire crops. Two opposite and
equally devastating weather-related conditions—drought and flooding—also
stymied small farmers' best efforts to flourish.

One thing was clear: agriculture needed to bolster its political clout. Before
mass production had seized the public imagination and business had become
a near-obsession among politicians, farmers in the late 19th century had rallied
behind the Populist Party and put agrarian problems in the national spotlight.
Those days were gone. Already many farmers and farm workers had accepted
defeat, leaving their farms behind to seek their fortunes in American cities. Many
of those who once might have supported the farmers' cause now were working on assembly lines and living in tenement buildings. Despite the nation's new
priorities, farmers and their allies were neither silent nor helpless in the 1920s.
Members of the newly formed congressional farm bloc, made up of lawmakers
from agricultural states, began pushing for legislation to help their constituents
in 1921, and the group achieved some success, particularly early in the decade.
Nevertheless, the bloc's best efforts could not turn Americans' attention away

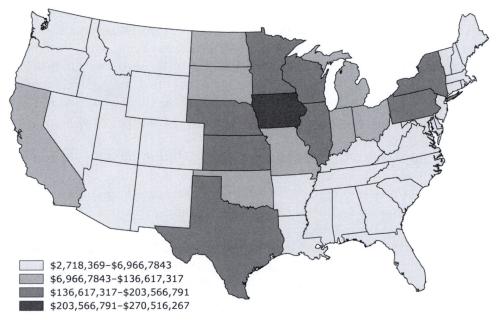

$2,718,369–$6,966,7843
$6,966,7843–$136,617,317
$136,617,317–$203,566,791
$203,566,791–$270,516,267

Map 1.2 *Total Value of Implements and Machinery by State in 1930*

from the manufacturing behemoth that seemed to promise a bright future far away from the farm.

What small farmers really wanted was aggressive government action to support agriculture, both financially and politically. In an atmosphere that eschewed government intervention in business operations, farmers' pleas for extensive and expensive federal assistance often fell on deaf ears. Giving farmers money to compensate for surplus crops struck a strangely discordant tone in the minds of those who revered capitalism in its purest form. The small farmers could not count capitalism as an ally. As their operations faltered, larger agribusinesses demonstrated their economic potential. These ventures could be run like sophisticated businesses and could prosper by adopting some of the mechanical creations and the underlying philosophies of mass production.

Overproduction and Agricultural Collapse

Early in the 1920s, farmers and manufacturers shared a common problem: an inventory of surplus products resulting from expanded production during World War I's booming export years. For manufacturers, new products and innovative use of machinery offered a way out of the recession of 1920–1921; however, farmers never fully recovered because an overabundance of crops led to sharp price cuts. Consequently, many farmers never had an opportunity to partake in the decade's spree of prosperity. Agricultural surpluses became the top farm issue of the 1920s. At the urging of the federal government, farmers had used more acreage for wartime production so that they could supplement European crops. During the war, many farmers had added fixed costs while expanding production. After the war, they felt trapped: their fixed costs remained, but there was no longer a market for their expanded production. The supply simply exceeded demand, and American consumers, who wanted to use hard-earned dollars to buy the new status symbols of the decade, had no interest in subsidizing farmers by paying higher prices.

America was home to 6.4 million farms in 1920 (Growing a Nation), and on most of those farms, hopelessness rose as crop prices sank. In short, European farmers had returned to work and decimated the finances of the American farmers who had made up for their crop shortages during World War I. A decline in farm income was inevitable, and that plunge prevented small farmers from saving enough money to invest in new technology. Cotton prices dropped to 20 cents a pound from a dollar a pound in 1920–1921, and it took 60 bushels of corn to buy a ton of coal in 1921, whereas only 6 bushels of corn had bought that amount of coal just two years earlier (Goldberg 1999, 57). Hampered by large debts, they also faced competition from imported goods, including Argentine beef and Egyptian cotton. These harsh realities set the stage for declines in the farm population, in overall farm income, and in the total value of farm property during the decade. Although poor farmers were hard-pressed to purchase the innovations provided by mass production, the new industrial revolution did touch their lives. Truckers began to take over the job of delivering fresh produce to market, and even in rural areas, movie houses began to spring up.

Depression or Not?

Most historians have labeled the entire period of 1921–1940 as a time of agricultural depression. For example, historian Arthur S. Link stated, "The most important domestic problem in the 1920s was the agricultural depression that began in the summer and fall of 1920 and continued intermittently until 1935" (Link 1955, 263). Louis M. Hacker recounted the economic collapse early in the 1920s by writing that although "the greater part of the economy recovered by 1922 and was enjoying the unprecedented prosperity of the golden 1920s, agriculture remained depressed. By 1929, the farmer was worse off than he had been not only ten years earlier but indeed twenty years earlier" (Hacker 1947, 1077). However, questions have been raised about whether that across-the-board designation is accurate. The conclusion that farmers faced a depression in the 1920s is based on aggregate figures collected by the Department of Agriculture, but accounting historian H. Thomas Johnson has argued more recently that the extent of economic distress in American agriculture may have been exaggerated. He contends that the gap between farm and nonfarm income in the 1920s was not as great as others have suggested. At the heart of his argument is the belief that the hardest-hit farmers were those who capitalized on increased earnings during World War I and raised their fixed costs. He points out that those farmers who entered the 1920s with the same fixed costs they had before the war are missing from most historians' analysis of the period because they are lost in a deluge of aggregate numbers (Johnson 1985). Later historians have characterized the 1920s as a period in which farming became more of a business and when traditional farmers' ties to the soil weakened.

Natural Disasters

Natural phenomena, beginning with the Arkansas River flood of 1920, worsened the collapse of American farming in the 1920s. A series of unforeseeable events across the United States destroyed crops and, in some cases, devastated entire farms. Significant insect infestations destroyed or reduced many farmers' crops over the course of the decade. The boll weevil, which first entered the United States in Texas, was destroying cotton crops as far north as the Carolinas. The Mexican bean beetle, as its name suggests, is native to Mexico and also to the southwestern United States. However, it was discovered in Alabama in 1920 and subsequently spread to other states. The European corn borer, which is extremely destructive to both field corn and sweet corn, was first spotted in the United States in the 1920s. All of these pests caused short-term reductions in overall production and were extremely harmful to the economic lives of individual farmers. Moreover, recurring scattered droughts parched much of the nation's farmland in the 1920s, lowering production for many farmers. California, for example, reported drought-like conditions in part or all of the state in 1917–1921, 1922–1926, and 1928–1937 (Paulson et al. 1991). In other words, California farmers experienced only one completely drought-free year in the entire decade.

The biggest natural catastrophe for farmers in this decade was the result of too much, rather than too little, water. Deluges in the early months of 1927 combined with a huge snowmelt in the Rocky Mountains to cause massive flooding in the Mississippi River Valley. Overflowing rivers and streams poured water across farmland and glutted the rising Mississippi. The mighty river crested unexpectedly early from Cairo, Ohio, to New Orleans. At Baton Rouge, it rose to 47 feet. Despite reassuring words from the Army Corps of Engineers, residents worried that levees might not hold, so they braved the storms to reinforce them with thousands of sandbags.

The break came on April 27 near Greenville, Mississippi. Rampaging floodwaters picked up houses, livestock, and trees, carrying them away and redrawing the landscape. An estimated 700,000 people lost everything they owned; a thousand more lost their lives. New Orleans's business leaders convinced Louisiana's governor to spare the Big Easy by giving his approval to destroy levees

Refugees from vast 1927 flooding in the Mississippi River Valley stand in a refugee camp in Vicksburg National Military Park. (Library of Congress)

downriver with dynamite. That decision dispatched floodwaters on a path of destruction through rural Louisiana, where thousands saw their world disappear under a river of hell. Despite pleas for disaster aid from six governors, a wary Calvin Coolidge refused to visit the area of destruction. He did name Herbert Hoover to head a Mississippi Flood Committee that was given wartime powers to aid the suffering thousands. As many as 35,000 people took part in relief efforts, and Hoover distributed $50 million drawn from the American Red Cross and other sources. At first, planes and boats spotted and rescued survivors. Then about 350,000 refugees were transported to camps in seven states where the survivors lived in tent cities that were racially segregated. Adding nightmare upon nightmare, whites reportedly assaulted African Americans in the camps and forced some to work at gunpoint (Miller 2003, 344–347).

Farmers and New Technology

Technology and mass production transfigured much of American life in the 1920s, but many small farmers were not able to take advantage of the goods produced on the assembly line or in the laboratory. These innovations had the potential to offer farmers the same kind of increased efficiency that redefined manufacturing, but small farmers seemed to live just beyond the reach of modernization. For many farmers, costs made new machinery unattainable, and the typically remote locations of small farms made the extension of electrical lines, phone lines, and paved roads impractical.

Initially many could not afford tractors or trucks. The combination of low crop prices and high fixed costs left many small farmers with little flexibility. Nevertheless, the cheap tractor eventually had a dramatic impact in the 1920s by reducing the amount of time needed per acre to plow fields, plant seeds, and reap crops. In addition, by eliminating the need to feed and keep horses and mules, the tractor expanded the available acreage for cash crops. In cotton country, experimentation was leading the way to mechanization. In 1926, a cotton stripper was introduced for farmers in high plains areas. It stripped the entire cotton boll off the plant. International Harvester was experimenting with cotton pickers that would remove the cotton from the boll without damaging the plant, although a successful mass-produced machine would not emerge until after World War II. The first hybrid seed-corn company was organized in 1926, and in the same year an experimental grain that was resistant to stem rot, CERES wheat (named for Crop Environment Resource Synthesis), became available. In addition, farmers enjoyed expanded access to synthetic fertilizers. After World War I, the synthetic fertilizer industry took over factories once used to produce synthetic nitrates and ammonia for explosives. This bolstered the industry and offered farmers new options.

For those small farmers who could afford to buy some or all of these scientific wonders, new productivity was possible. However, two basic problems still remained: the existence of a crop surplus and a continuing struggle to cover fixed costs. Large operations, conversely, found that the innovations of the 1920s offered the opportunity for prosperous agribusiness. Many small farmers could not keep up with the growing costs of operating a small farm, but like manufacturers, agribusinesses achieved savings by using technology on a large scale. With their profits, they purchased the latest technological advances and improved their yield per acre, which widened their share of the market.

The Farm Bloc

Beginning in 1921, a group of lawmakers set out to improve the conditions facing farmers. Arthur Capper of Kansas and William Kenyon of Iowa led the coalition of mostly Western and Southern legislators who became known as the farm bloc. Working as a bipartisan effort in both houses of Congress and with the support of Warren G. Harding's activist Secretary of Agriculture Henry C. Wallace, this group pushed through several important pieces of legislation that attacked

Mexican Workers' Role in Texas Agribusiness

Agribusiness showed remarkable growth in Texas during the 1920s, and one reason for that burgeoning success was the availability of a cheap Mexican work force.
Large operations were dependent on the undemanding and mobile workers who
crossed the border to earn their wages; however, small farmers, tenant farmers,
and American farm laborers felt threatened by the influx of workers from Mexico.
Mexican immigration jumped to 487,775 from just 173,663 in the previous decade
(Montejano 1999, 173). This phenomenon heightened the anxieties of some Texans who feared that these workers would change their communities and their
state irrevocably. A San Antonio congressman accused the big growers of not
thinking "beyond the next cotton crop" and predicted that the immigrants would
be a threat to Texans' safety and way of life.

Probusiness forces in the nation's capital supported the growers by excluding
Mexico from the many nations that faced new restrictions on immigration during
this period. A sociologist who interviewed 44 farmers found 33 thought Mexican
laborers gave Texas agriculture a boost (Montejano 1999, 175). The exceptions
were tenant farmers, many of whom claimed that Mexican workers were ineffi-
cient. These farmers had good reason to fear that their landlords would reclaim
their land and use Mexicans to cultivate it. One West Texas grower said that
without the Mexican workers, "the laboring class of white people, what there is,
would demand their own wages and without doing half the labor the Mexican
does" (Montejano 1999, 175). Big growers also claimed Mexicans were valuable
as consumers of American-made products. Ultimately, farm labor in Texas became
identified as "Mexican work," an occupation that was too demeaning for white
Texans. One ranch manager concluded, "The Americans can usually get something
better, for example, filling station work. My brother took $1 a day there rather
than $1.50 from my father on the farm" (Montejano 1999, 180).

farmers' many problems from different angles. The goals of the Packers and
Stockyards Act of 1921 were to maintain competition among meat packers
and establish public control over the rates charged by commission merchants
and stockyards. The Grain Futures Act of 1921 gave the secretary of agriculture
regulatory power over grain exchanges. And the Capper–Volstead Act of 1922
exempted rapidly growing farm cooperatives from antitrust laws.

The farm bloc with Capper as its leader officially ceased to exist in 1923; however, the push for legislation to aid farmers did not end. The decade's biggest
and most controversial piece of agricultural legislation was the McNary–Haugen
Farm Relief Bill, which would have formed a Federal Farm Board to buy surplus crops and either hold them off the market or sell them overseas. More than
any other proposal, this legislation reached the heart of farmers' concerns and
embraced the solution they advocated most strongly. Some felt that fixed costs

made it impossible for small farmers to operate profitably without some kind of government support. With backing from the agricultural supporters, the bill won congressional approval in two consecutive years—1927 and 1928—but Coolidge, who did not believe the federal government should interfere with commerce, vetoed it in both years. The bill, which would have encouraged overproduction, was flawed, but Coolidge offered no plan of his own.

Many Abandon Farm Life

Census figures show that more than a million people left American farms during the 1920s. This marked a dramatic change from the previous decade when about 100,000 Americans had quit farming. In 1920, the agricultural community made up 30.1 percent of the nation's population; by 1929, only 25.2 percent of Americans were farmers. The total value of American farms dropped from $78.4 million in 1920 to $57.7 million in 1929. Land was abandoned too: farmers faced with surpluses left 13 million acres of cropland untended between 1919 and 1924 alone. The farm exodus reflected an array of negative factors. At the same time, the total value of farm products was cut in half. Farmers' real purchasing power and their net income dipped by 25 percent (Parrish 1992, 83). As a group, farmers claimed only 9 percent of the national income in 1929, compared to 16 percent in 1919. At the decade's end, growers of staple crops faced the same threat of overproduction that had contributed to their difficulties in 1920. Per-bale cotton prices had dropped from $1.76 to 85 cents over 10 years, while wheat opened the decade at $2.19 per bushel and ended it at $1.04 (Leuchtenburg 1993, 100).

Among those leaving rural areas in large numbers were African Americans. As wage laborers, sharecroppers, or tenant farmers, they were especially vulnerable to destitution if they remained in the rural South. Many older African Americans were trapped in arrangements that bordered on slavery because of debt agreements with landowners; this was not an appealing future for younger workers who could join the unskilled labor pool in urban areas of the North. There also were new job options closer to home for farmers in the South. Large corporations were beginning an invasion of the former Confederacy for factory locations where they believed labor agitation was unlikely. Textile jobs in small towns and cities provided more security than farm work.

There were a few new trends that affected farming favorably and offered hope for the coming years. Milk production jumped by one third between 1919 and 1926, and ice cream sales took a 45 percent increase. Agribusinesses were able to stake out new territory because of new public attention to nutrition: Nineteen commercial operations were able to nearly double the acreage profitably set aside for vegetables (Allen 2000, 138). In addition, new prospects for agricultural goods could be seen in the development of frozen foods such as ice

Farm workers pile hay on a wagon in 1927. (Library of Congress)

cream. Clarence Birdseye invented packaging for frozen foods in 1923, and frozen meat, fruit, and vegetables would be marketed in the first year of the next decade. The philosophy developed by the hard-working members of the farm bloc was not dead. Much of it would bear fruit in the 1930s. Franklin Roosevelt's New Deal incorporated many of the ideas that had foundered under the more conservative leadership of Republican presidents Harding, Coolidge, and Hoover. A variety of federal programs benefited farmers through direct aid and projects such as the Rural Electrification Administration, which welcomed them into the mass culture.

AFRICAN AMERICAN WORKERS' GAINS AND LOSSES

In Search of a Better Chance

For African Americans the mass production revolution of the 1920s did not offer a realistic expectation of prosperity. Whether they lived in the North or the South, most African Americans found themselves competing for the least appealing jobs. Their work tended to be physical in nature, offered little or no opportunity for

Table 1.1. African American Population Growth between 1920 and 1930

Cities	1920	1930	Growth Rate (percent)
New York	152,467	327,706	114.9
Chicago	109,458	233,903	113.7
Philadelphia	134,229	219,599	63.6
Baltimore	108,322	142,106	31.2
Detroit	40,838	120,066	194.0
Atlanta	62,796	90,075	43.4

Source: United States Bureau of the Census.

advancement, and paid very little. In the rural South, African Americans traditionally worked as sharecroppers, tenant farmers, or wage laborers—workers who were not slaves but who had little to show for their independence. In a rigidly segregated society, their existence was grim, and their income was paltry. They lived in poverty and under the threat of violence in a region where the lynching of a black man remained a crime that often went unpunished. Making matters worse for these agricultural workers was a nationwide decline in farm prices. Many white men were struggling to maintain small family farms as they confronted declining income and high levels of debt. A farmer's problems carried risks for his employees. He could lose his entire operation or be forced to release his employees. Also looming in the shadows was the possibility that a farmer somehow might find the money to buy machines that could replace human workers.

As the United States left behind its agrarian roots and turned into an increasingly industrialized society, the outlook for African Americans in the South actually worsened. They were educated in segregated schools that offered limited learning opportunities, and many left school early to earn what little money they could. As a result, a significant proportion of African Americans in the South never achieved literacy. And even in the competition for unskilled and semiskilled jobs, literacy had become an important prerequisite.

In search of a better life, thousands of African Americans left the South every year in search of work. Most moved to urban areas in the Northeast or Midwest. Generally, the migrants were young, without deep roots in the South. In their new locations, they hoped to acquire unskilled factory jobs that paid more than they could earn as wage laborers in the South. Factories did hire African Americans, and some treated them equitably. However, African Americans usually found themselves in the least appealing jobs. Once they got a job, migrants learned that most of the apparently higher income would be consumed in the cost of a place to live. Crowded, unhealthy apartments were overpriced, so African American workers surrendered their income for the privilege of living in a slum. Moreover, to earn a paycheck, African Americans often worked in

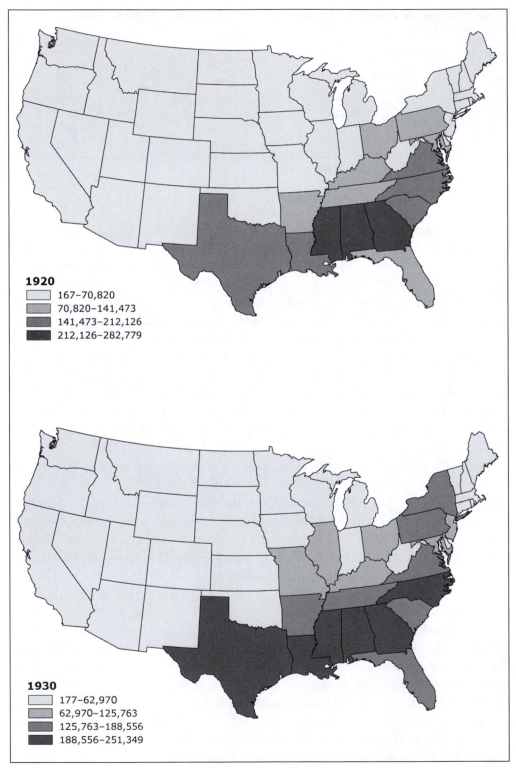

1920
- 167–70,820
- 70,820–141,473
- 141,473–212,126
- 212,126–282,779

1930
- 177–62,970
- 62,970–125,763
- 125,763–188,556
- 188,556–251,349

Map 1.3 *Male African American Population in 1920 versus 1930*

unhealthy or dangerous conditions. Those African Americans who did become skilled laborers found that they were usually not welcome in labor unions. Sometimes, unions set up African American "affiliates," but at the bargaining table, African American workers had little representation. Often when companies had to lay off workers, African Americans were the first to go. African Americans discovered that jobs outside the South offered an escape from both farm labor and the legalized segregation preserved through the Jim Crow laws of Southern states. However, they also found that the assembly line did not lead to the Promised Land.

Participation in World War I Raised Hopes

African Americans entered the 1920s with optimism about reaping some benefits in the aftermath of World War I. More than 300,000 African American men served in the U.S. military's segregated units during the war, and military experience had given them new exposure to areas of the United States and other countries where dark skin was not a trigger for violence or suppression. Thousands more bolstered the booming industrial economy by moving to the North and taking on jobs in factories manufacturing defense goods and other products. As the 1920s began, those who still lived in the South read good news in the *Chicago Defender* and other African American newspapers: Great work opportunities could be found in Northern cities where African American children could get a decent education and African American adults could establish good homes without the constant threat of violence. After boll weevils devastated cotton crops in the South, many thought the move represented a risk worth taking. Young African American men in particular tended to make the leap and look for work either in Southern cities or, more probably, in the urban centers of the Northeast and Midwest. In the South, there was little hope for a better life, although some Southern factory jobs were a notch above sharecropping or tenant farming. In the North, with industry booming and jobs multiplying, the prospects seemed more promising.

African American Life in the South

Most African Americans lived in the South in the 1920s, and like their slave ancestors, they lived restricted lives. For the most part, they were limited to agricultural work, domestic work, or menial, low-paying jobs in industry. They could not vote or move about the community freely without the threat of violence. In agriculture, most African Americans labored as cotton sharecroppers, who worked on farms for a share of the overall income. Generally, a sharecropper spent his life in debt to the planter who employed him. The planters provided certain goods to sharecroppers without itemizing the cost. Then, when

*African American workers pick peanuts on a farm in Terrell County, Georgia, in
1929. (U.S. Department of Agriculture)*

the planter received payment for his crop, he often told his sharecroppers that
instead of drawing a profit, they had sunk deeper in his debt.

Farm life was difficult for African Americans, and statistics show that the number of African American farm operators dropped by more than 40,000 in the
1920s (Smith and Horton 1995, 128). Meanwhile, the size of the average African
American farmer's operation decreased by 2.2 percent while the average white
farmer's operation grew by 10.3 percent in acreage (Smith and Horton, 80).

Some African Americans moved to Southern cities where they competed
with whites for jobs as street cleaners, tradesmen, or truck drivers. Often African
Americans in the urban South were restricted to segregated neighborhoods,
and they lived in houses without electricity or indoor plumbing. In textile and
tobacco factories, these African Americans could find only menial and tedious
jobs. Whether they lived in rural or urban areas, African American children in
the South generally received a poor education. A 1921 survey of teachers in segregated schools for African American children showed that most teachers had
only a high school diploma, and teachers without high school diplomas outnumbered those with college degrees. As a result, it was quite possible to attend
one of these inferior schools for years without achieving the literacy necessary

for career advancement. This offered little hope for future generations. By the end of the 1920s, the South had lost a total of 750,000 African Americans (Dumenil 1995, 285).

Northern Reality versus Expectations

The African American population of the North almost doubled in the 1920s, reaching a total of 1,355,789 (Smith and Horton 1995, 1634). Northern cities were not equipped to handle such massive growth, and industries were not expanding at an adequate rate to absorb such a heavy influx of would-be employees. Their legal rights expanded when they left the South behind, but white American racism was not isolated in that region. Consequently, migrants faced an emotional roller coaster when they reached their new homes.

In Chicago, for example, cheering crowds often greeted trains arriving with new migrants, according to the *Chicago Defender.* Nonetheless, migrants had difficulty finding jobs and enjoyed little job security, especially after 1924. In fact, the number of unemployed African American workers increased during the decade. All of the news was not bad: many African Americans rode out the 1920–1921 recession by working as strikebreakers during a meatpackers' strike that opened up about 5,000 jobs (Canaan 2001, 152). As a result, African Americans were able to make inroads in meat packing plants and slaughterhouses, often taking skilled jobs that offered a brighter future; however, working conditions sometimes caused debilitating illness or injuries. By 1926, so many African American Chicagoans were unemployed and destitute that a new shelter was opened to house them. Many of the newly unemployed were railroad employees who had been laid off. The following year, the Wabash Avenue YMCA reported that there were 150 applicants for every 100 jobs (Canaan 2001, 153). Many workers, including those in the food industries, faced seasonal layoffs. There also was little progress in African American workers' pay during the 1920s. For unskilled men, $17 a week was typical. Semiskilled men made 50 cents an hour (Canaan 2001, 156). The flood of new workers from the South worsened overall conditions for workers by increasing the pool of workers beyond the market's demands.

In general, areas outside the South fell short of expectations in their racial attitudes too. Non-Southern states did give migrants the newfound right to vote; however, African American migrants who found good jobs soon discovered that there was little hope of advancement because of their skin color. Immigrants had a higher likelihood of being promoted. Available housing for African Americans in cities outside of the South usually was filthy, substandard, crowded, and expensive. As a result, some desperate families threw "rent parties," charging admission for gatherings with food and dancing. Because unions often excluded blacks, African Americans had trouble getting into skilled work, and even when they did, they lacked the collective bargaining clout of union members. With few exceptions, the only African Americans with representation in dealings with their employers were those who worked for huge manufacturers that offered welfare capitalism and established a company union through which employees could express grievances. Moreover, schools in cities like Indianapolis and Cincinnati were segregated just like the Southern schools many migrants had attended. Some Northern hospitals also segregated patients by race.

Racial Violence

Race relations in the United States were fragile as the 1920s began. There had been more than 20 race riots in the previous year, and as African Americans increasingly chose to move to the urban areas outside the former states of the Confederacy, open racial hostility sometimes accompanied them like a silent stowaway. Changes in population because of the influx of African Americans created new points of tension in communities accustomed to a more homogeneous population. In addition, the South did not easily give up its long history of racial violence. African Americans might have felt empowered by service in World War I, but some white citizens felt the need to use violence as a means of reinforcing control. Violence rattled both the North and the South. More than 200 African Americans reportedly were lynched in 1920–1925 alone. This brand of vigilante capital punishment continued through the decade, and although lynchings were more common in the South, they were not isolated to that region. In a noteworthy case, a mob in Duluth, Minnesota, lynched three accused rapists in June 1920. Afterward, many African Americans left the town. Also in 1920, whites killed African Americans trying to vote in Ocoee, Florida, and a similar attack on a group of African American women occurred in Birmingham, Alabama, in 1926. Whites also burned the entire African American community in Rosewood, Florida, in 1923.

The worst violence of the decade occurred in 1921 in Tulsa, Oklahoma, after a white elevator operator reported that an African American man had molested her. Police imprisoned the accused man, and an angry white mob quickly gathered in the streets seeking to lynch him. Armed African Americans, including some veterans, confronted the white crowd, and gunfire erupted on both sides. Afterward, furious whites invaded the city's African American neighborhood, killing more than 30 African Americans and destroying both businesses and homes. African American residents managed to kill some of the intruders before most of the city's blacks fled. In Detroit white mobs responded violently to African Americans who moved into predominantly white neighborhoods. In 1925's third case of mob violence against black newcomers, a large crowd outside the home of Dr. Ossian Sweet threw rocks through the windows. Gunshots fired from the Sweet house killed a white man. As a result, Sweet was tried twice

Historians' Debate:
African Americans Migrated, but Why?

African American migrants who left the South in the 1920s had many motivations. Historians generally give economics top billing among the causes, and they are quick to acknowledge the role played by African American newspapers in the North, which reported great opportunities in factory work. However, sociologists Stewart E. Tolnay and E. M. Beck argue that white violence has been underestimated as a factor in African Americans' decision to move. In their view, mob violence may have mattered at least as much as job security. Ironically, they conclude, whites decreased their violent behavior when they realized that a black exodus could create economic problems in their own region. In Tolnay and Beck's analysis, whites had used violence as a means of controlling the black working class, and in the end, the black working class's exodus diminished the level of that violence (Tolnay and Beck 1990, 365).

Historian David J. Goldberg credits very specific economic stimuli with causing a flood of migration in 1923. First, the imposition of new restrictions on immigration offered the prospect of less competition for unskilled jobs. Second, the decision to cut U.S. Steel's workday from 12 hours to 8 signaled the creation of many new jobs that might be open to African Americans. About 68,000 African Americans left Georgia in a four-month span of that year, and 24,000 departed from South Carolina over a seven-month period (Goldberg 1999, 107). Third, cotton farmers in both states had been particularly hard hit by a boll weevil infestation that adversely affected African American farmers, sharecroppers, and tenant farmers. Labor shortages caused by that year's African American migration affected every Southern state.

for murder. The first trial ended in a mistrial. In the second, an all-white jury acquitted the physician.

Marcus Garvey

African Americans found many obstacles in their path toward economic success but few leaders with new approaches. Longtime African American spokesman Booker T. Washington stressed the merits of having patience and waiting for gradual change to improve the lot of African Americans. At the same time, W. E. B. Du Bois emphasized the need for racial unity. However, a very different set of ideas and approaches came from Marcus Garvey. A native of Jamaica, Garvey believed that blacks should exercise self-help to build political and economic power. He also was committed to overcoming European colonialism in Africa. Consequently, he urged people of African heritage to reclaim their ancestral home and even claimed the title, "provisional governor of Africa."

Garvey began his career as an activist early by starting the Universal Negro Improvement Association before he entered the United States at the age of 19 in 1916. To demonstrate to African Americans that they could succeed in business, he established several business operations and organizations. Among his ventures were the Black Cross Nurses, restaurants, a laundry, millinery shops, grocery stores, and a newspaper, *The Negro World*. His most ambitious project was the Black Star Line, a steamship company owned and operated by African Americans. In the African American middle class, Garvey found many converts, some of whom invested their hard-earned money in the ship line. The company's first ship, the SS *Yarmouth,* set sail in January 1920 en route to Havana. Two days later, the Coast Guard had to assist the ship's crew when the *Yarmouth* was found sinking just 101 miles from New York. The company failed in 1922.

Soon conflict began to surface within Garvey's organizations, and in 1922, he was charged with mail fraud. The government claimed he had used photos of a ship that the company did not own as a ploy to sell stock through the U.S. mail. A group of African American leaders appealed to officials to take quick action. In 1923, an all-white jury convicted Garvey, and he was sent to a federal penitentiary in Georgia two years later after unsuccessful appeals. Coolidge commuted his sentence in 1927, and he was deported.

African American Women's Work

African American women often found themselves relegated to the very worst jobs. Those who abandoned agricultural labor usually found domestic work whether they lived in the North or South. Frustrated and struggling to survive, they "found every door except the kitchen door closed to them," one migrant said (White 2005, 418). And domestic jobs sometimes paid as little as $1 a day. Even in urban areas, African American women faced many closed doors: While white women could find clerical and sales jobs, those avenues were closed to their African American counterparts in most cases. Furthermore, manufacturers in most cities denied them factory work. Chicago, where 21.4 percent of African American women worked for manufacturing companies in various jobs, was an exception. About 14 percent of those women worked in meatpacking houses, where many were assigned to wash fat, a messy job often performed in poorly ventilated rooms with dangerously slippery floors (Canaan 2001, 150).

In the workplace, employers generally segregated black women from white women, who often earned higher pay and had such conveniences as rest rooms. Because organized labor often discriminated against blacks, working African American women lacked the means to voice their grievances. There were small advances: the Hesperus Club of Harlem became the first female affiliate of the Brotherhood of Sleeping Car Porters in 1925. However, at a time when the average unskilled African American man earned $17 a week in Chicago's food in-

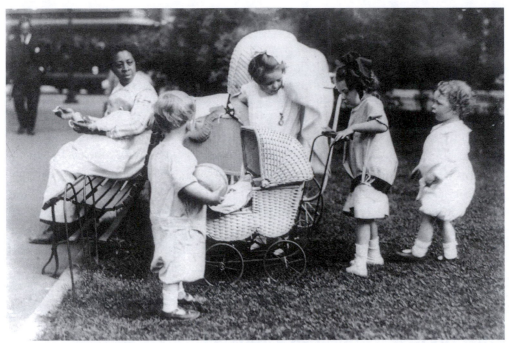

Often, the only jobs available for African American women of this era were domestic positions, and among their common chores was caring for white children, as this woman did in Washington, D.C. (Library of Congress)

dustries, African American women averaged only $15.20. In skilled positions, women earned about five cents per hour less than their male counterparts (Canaan 2001, 157). And women's wages did not rise during the 1920s. In some cases, educated African American women found opportunities that enabled them to serve their own community. Some worked as social workers or in nonprofit organizations such as the Urban League and YWCA. Others found teaching jobs. Ironically, it was easier to attain a teaching job in the South because the segregation of schools generated more openings. Often African American women filled the teaching ranks of such schools even without college diplomas. But teaching jobs were more difficult to find in the North, where standards for teachers were the same for blacks and whites.

The Auto Industry and African American Men

Many African American men found work in mass production, especially within the auto manufacturing business and the steel industry, which played an important role in the production of automobiles. In these nonunionized workplaces, blacks had a better chance of earning equal pay for equal work; however, African American men faced little chance of being promoted beyond the level of unskilled workers. Factory work did not carry as much prestige as some other jobs, such as being a Pullman railway porter or working in the U.S. Post Office; however, the industries that employed the most African American men during the 1920s were auto and steel manufacturing and meatpacking.

Auto factories hired thousands of African American men. Henry Ford, who drew disdain for his open anti-Semitism in the 1920s, aggressively sought out black men for factory jobs and allowed them to fill a variety of positions within the manufacturing process. Other auto manufacturers hired smaller numbers of blacks or put them in the least desirable factory jobs. Although treatment of African American workers varied, employment in the auto industry and spin-off industries led to the skyrocketing black population of Detroit. Blacks could find steelwork in Chicago, Cleveland, Pittsburgh, Buffalo, Gary, and Youngstown. By 1925 African American men had claimed about one-fifth of the jobs in steel manufacturing (Goldberg 1999, 109). However, managers generally assigned African American men to the most dangerous jobs, placing them around blast furnaces, open hearths, and coke ovens.

Entrepreneurs and Professionals

A small percentage of the African American community found success as entrepreneurs or professionals, generally within African American neighborhoods. In all, African Americans made up about 3.8 percent of professionals in 1920; by 1930, that figure had risen to 4.2 percent. African Americans represented 3.3 percent of the nation's retailers in 1920, and only 3.0 percent at the end of the decade (Smith and Horton 1995, 1062). However, in 1929, African Americans still owned about 25,701 retail enterprises with total sales of more than $100 million. More than one-third of African American-owned establishments sold groceries, and an additional 21 percent were restaurants. Almost 10 percent sold automotive supplies, and the others operated general stores or were retailers of apparel, lumber and building supplies, furniture and household goods, or second-hand items (Smith and Horton 1995, 257). In 1929, African Americans organized the Colored Merchants Association under the leadership of Albon Holsey. The group's aim was to establish stores and stock them by purchasing merchandise collectively. This effort was wiped out two years later by the Great Depression. In addition to selling products, African American entrepreneurs opened neighborhood businesses that offered necessary services ranging from laundering to banking.

Migration Affects Industry, Black–White Relations

By the 1920s, African Americans were playing a notable role in mass production industries, and a continuing migration from the rural South into urban areas had begun to change race relations in both urban and rural areas throughout the country. Still, in overall numbers, African Americans did not make gigantic gains in the workplace. As the Great Depression neared, African Americans had a slightly smaller share of the gainfully employed population than they claimed in 1920. Their portion of the overall workforce dropped from 11.6 percent to 11.3 percent, despite continuing growth in the black population. African Americans, who represented 9 percent of the nation's total population, made up 19 percent of the agricultural work force, down only one percentage point from a decade earlier, and most African American agricultural workers remained in the South (Smith and Horton 1995, 1062).

During the 1920s, African American lives were most heavily invested in the sector of the economy that suffered the most. More than 81 percent of African American farm workers remained tenants or sharecroppers while about 0.3 percent were employed as managers (Smith and Horton 1995, 58). The number of African American farm owners dropped from 218,612 to 181,016 nationally (Smith and Horton 1995, 128), only 18.5 percent of African American agricultural workers in 1929 (Smith and Horton 1995, 58). The majority of African American farm owners did not live well. Most experienced poverty without 20th-century conveniences. Among African American farm owners in the South, only 2,750 had telephone service; 1,712 had electric lights, and 1,160 had indoor plumbing (Smith and Horton 1995, 91). With 176,130 African American farm owners in the South, less than 2 percent had these basic amenities (Smith and Horton 1995, 58). Tenants and sharecroppers were significantly less likely to have telephones, electric lights, or indoor plumbing than African American farm owners. Clearly, for those who had stayed in the rural South, the decade offered very little real progress. As the farm economy continued its decline over the next decade, their lives would worsen with greater poverty and more mob violence.

Although thousands of African Americans migrated to get jobs in manufacturing, their share of manufacturing jobs inched up from 7 percent to 7.3 percent over the course of the 1920s (Smith and Horton 1995, 1062). In many industries employers still restricted them to the least-sought-after positions. However, African Americans in industry made some advances by acquiring skills and organizing themselves in ways that helped to compensate for the labor movement's frequent failures to include them. African American women, for the most part, remained locked into domestic work as cooks, servants, or laundresses, but the proliferation of African American neighborhoods opened up nonindustrial opportunities for urban African Americans serving their own community in the professions, in retailing, and in public service jobs. As the children of unskilled immigrants began to move their parents and themselves out of the tenements, African American workers found greater isolation in urban ghettoes. Living in an island community within a large city had at least one benefit for African Americans: it enabled them to develop a unique culture, combining the slave culture of the rural South with new urban traditions.

WOMEN IN THE WORKPLACE

Limited Opportunity

American women charged into the workforce in the 1920s and found new opportunities for employment in two arenas. The total number of women in the workforce increased by more than two million, according to the U.S. Census, and more than 10 million women, married and unmarried, had employment outside the home. By 1930, they represented 22 percent of the working population, up from 20 percent at the decade's beginning when only 8.6 million women collected wages. As new job markets opened, more positions in the workplace became identified as women's work. A monotonous routine and low pay were key components of most jobs available to female workers. Women also found little room for advancement in most careers.

Employers welcomed women workers into the new offices of industrial establishments and other businesses. As typists, telephone operators, and stenographers, they worked primarily for male managers. Their work was essential to the efficient operation of modern businesses, but its specialized quality seldom gave women an opportunity to take on more challenging work within companies. Labor unions, which wanted to protect their male membership, generally

Women work alongside men in a Washington, D.C., office, in 1925. (Library of Congress)

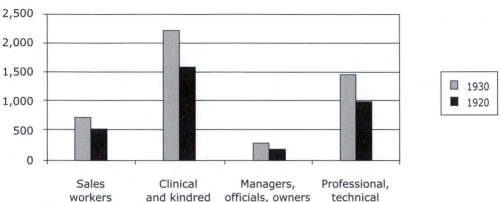

Figure 1.3 *Women in White-Collar Jobs in 1920 and 1930 (thousands).*
Source: *United States Bureau of the Census.*

did not welcome women members, and in some cases they acted to pigeon-hole women in nonunion jobs where their competence represented no threat to the men who were their cherished members. This also has been interpreted by some as a conscious means of limiting women's potential role in the industrial economy. Retailers also began hiring more women to fill sales positions. As the consumer economy of the 1920s spread, stores needed more personnel to serve eager customers with money to spend. In these years, restaurants became more willing to hire women as waitresses, often replacing men who previously held positions as waiters. Domestic work, which had always been a female domain, remained so. Positions in domestic, clerical, and sales work occupied more than half of working women in 1930. In spite of official and unofficial limits on the types of work they could do, more and more women went to work outside the home.

More than one quarter of women over the age of 16 worked in 1930. Women continued to be underrepresented in the professions. Nevertheless, they remained dominant in the feminized professional categories—nurses, schoolteachers, librarians, and social workers. The stifling routines that many female employees faced did not go unnoted in the 1920s. *Ankles Preferred,* a silent film released in 1927, centered on the life of a woman employed in the tedious job of a department store clerk. One scene shows the central character waiting eagerly for the workday to end. The image of a large clock is superimposed on her face, demonstrating the boredom that defined the work lives of many American women. The comedy traces the leading character's efforts to prove her undiscovered worth in the business world, but the film's end takes a traditional turn when she concludes beauty is her greatest asset. For women who chose to stay at home and direct their labors toward efficient maintenance of their own homes, monotony was also a factor, although new kitchen appliances added some novelty to the process.

Women's Horizons Broaden but Remain Limited

Women workers entered the 1920s with an expanding array of jobs available to them. Like African Americans, women had taken on a bigger role in the work force during World War I to replace workers in the armed services. Millions of women had worked in munitions plants or replacing men who had left home to serve in the armed services. Most of the women who took on challenging roles in wartime were working outside the home when the war began. It is therefore not surprising that many hoped to maintain their new positions. Approval of women's suffrage also raised women's hopes for greater equality. However, working women were not able to keep those jobs. The AFL claimed that women had weakened the standards of skilled labor, and one spokesman declared "the same patriotism which induced women to enter industry during the war should induce them to vacate the positions after the war" (Parrish 1992, 141). And most women went quietly.

The typical working woman was single and younger than 25. For that reason employers tended to view all women as "transient" workers who would leave when they married. This stereotype was incorrect. In 1930 29 percent of working women were married, almost double the percentage in 1900. However, only 10 percent of married women worked. (Dumenil 1995, 112–113). Almost half of women workers held jobs in the expanding and increasingly feminized ranks of clerical employees and salespeople. The 1920s brought little expansion of women's roles in traditionally male fields. Despite booming industrialization, women's share of manual labor jobs, such as those in industry, remained virtually stagnant in the 1920s. Some women found niches in manufacturing. For example, in the South, tobacco companies gave working-class white women the job of making cigars and cigarettes while African American women prepared the tobacco in dirty, smelly buildings.

Women were able to make inroads in the food service industry as waitresses. Restaurants were proliferating across the country in less formal and less expensive formats. The morality of the early 20th century made it unseemly for women to work in establishments serving alcohol; however, the institution of prohibition in 1920 removed that concern and broadened women's job opportunities. Census figures indicate that domestic work occupied about one-third of working women. African Americans and immigrants bore a disproportionately large share of this work. Almost 2 million American women performed domestic work in private homes in 1930. Fewer than a million workers remained in agriculture.

For many women who lived in households with parents or husbands, working outside the home provided a degree of autonomy. However, women's pay was consistently lower than men's. The National Industrial Conference Board reported in 1927 that the average weekly wage for a woman was $17.36, while the average wage for a man was $29.35 (Miller 2003, 255). Female salespeople earned a little more than half of their male counterparts' pay. Low wages forced many women to live with their parents, find roommates, or dwell in boarding houses.

Establishment of Women's Bureau

To address the growing role of women in the labor force, the Department of Labor established the Women's Bureau in 1920. This was an outgrowth of a World War I agency known as the Women in Industry Service. After the war, feminists argued for a permanent agency to serve working women, and Congress approved its establishment. The Women's Bureau's function, as described by law, was "to formulate standards and policies which shall promote the welfare of wage-earning women, improve their working conditions, increase their efficiency, and advance their opportunities for profitable employment" (Harvard University Open Collections Program). Clearly, the bureau's mandate did not cover expanding the breadth of women's job opportunities or guaranteeing that women received equal pay for equal work. As a result, the bureau often fell short in the eyes of feminists.

Under the leadership of Mary Anderson, the bureau focused primarily on industrial workplaces and worked to improve women's wages and working hours and eliminate health and safety threats in their work environment. It often achieved these goals by supporting protective legislation, and this angered women's rights activists who felt that women did not need special protection at work. They believed that women should work as equals to men with no special restriction on work hours or other burdens of the working world. Among the bureau's unsuccessful efforts was the 1920s drive for a minimum wage for women. Anderson's female staff included journalists, economists, social workers, and statisticians. Among them were many former activists in the Women's Trade Union League (WTUL), including Anderson. The WTUL had helped women to form labor unions in the early years of the 20th century. During the 1920s, it trained organizers and workers in summer schools. Despite the heavy infusion of labor experts on its staff, the bureau's advice to women workers was generally conservative and did not support radical economic or social change. Nevertheless, the bureau did seek to erase myths about women workers through radio broadcasts and publications. It argued forcefully against the idea that women should be paid less because they were working only to raise money for frivolous purchases. It also fought the notion that working women were transient members of the work force.

Working with the National Consumers League and the Women's Educational and Industrial Union, the bureau achieved perhaps its greatest accomplishment of the 1920s—valuable and groundbreaking research about female workers and women's work. Much of this data would lay a foundation for later programs to attack the Great Depression. Furthermore, the bureau sought to set in motion an effort to prepare women for service in industry during a future international conflict. After World War I, the Women's Bureau frequently circulated newsletters within the federal government with the intent of spurring planning for that possibility. However, its warnings were ignored, and the government remained unprepared.

Expansion of Clerical and Retail Jobs

During the 1920s, women flooded into stores and offices to fill job openings. Because women considered these jobs less demeaning than factory work, it is not surprising that the number of women in clerical jobs exceeded the number in factory work by 1930. Retail work offered fewer openings for women, but jobs in stores also attracted middle-class women and working-class women who were eager to work without dirtying their hands in a factory. Changes in the workplace created a growing need for women in clerical support in the nation's offices. In the prosperous years of the 1920s, banks, insurance agencies, industrial corporations, and other companies enlarged their office staffs to improve communication, record keeping, and overall efficiency. By the end of the 1920s, more women worked in the clerical field than in any other segment of the economy except service jobs, which included domestic workers.

Clerical work resembled the labor of the assembly line in some ways. Often there was one large office for all clerical workers. The sounds of factory machinery were missing, but with ringing telephones, clicking typewriters, and squealing file drawers, offices had the activity and atmosphere of a multi-part operation rolling noisily toward a single goal. Clerical staffers typically followed a rigid discipline that involved much repetition and subservience. As one analyst commented, a secretary "thinks *with* her employer, thinks *for* her employer, thinks *of* her employer" (Kessler-Harris 1982, 234). Most working women eventually married and left the work world behind without ever escaping this rigid environment (Freedman, 1974, 393). The increasing use of office machines, such as typewriters and adding machines, made clerical work more specialized. Inventors produced simple versions of both in the late 19th century, and in the 1920s, these became excellent tools in mass production's expansion of office work. Men sometimes started their careers in clerical jobs. In fact, in 1920, almost as many men as women were classified as clerical workers, but most male clerical workers eventually moved into other jobs. By the 1920s, the least skilled office workers—stenographers and file clerks—were almost always women. Female clerical workers seldom advanced to higher-level jobs. At best, a woman could look forward to becoming a chief bookkeeper or an executive secretary, but women almost never supervised men.

Retail jobs demonstrated an allure for young women, including those with college degrees. Some even moved from small towns to larger cities just to get retail jobs in urban department stores. The requirement for saleswomen to interact casually with customers made the boundaries of their daily routine less rigid than those found in clerical work. In addition, a sense of female unity and camaraderie helped saleswomen to maintain greater autonomy, according to historian Susan Porter Benson (Dumenil 1995, 115).

Many American-born daughters of immigrants were among those who leaped at the opportunity to get white-collar work in an office or store. They wanted to earn a living in an atmosphere that was much cleaner and healthier than the sweatshops where their mothers had labored. Because of their ethnicity, these women struggled to compete with "old stock" women, whom employers often preferred. In sales, immigrant daughters sometimes were confined to selling less expensive goods while young women from older stock sold more expensive merchandise. Similarly, immigrant daughters often were placed in the least visible clerical jobs.

Labor Unions Shun Women

American labor unions in the 1920s generally worked against the advancement of women workers rather than welcoming women into the ranks of union members. Labor leaders' statements suggest that they thought of women as temporary workers who eventually would return to their "proper place"—the home. Although more than 3 million working women could have qualified for union membership in 1927, the National Bureau of Economic Research reported that a mere 265,095 actually had joined (Miller 2003, 256). Most who had become union members worked in the garment trades. One male member of the Amalgamated Clothing Workers of America wrote that members of his union "still cherish the old theory that women are transient in industry. . . . But less and less frequently does a woman leave the industry when she marries" (Kessler-Harris 1982, 229). In other words, women were competing with men for unionized jobs, and in most cases, unions made it clear their loyalties were with the men.

In some industries, women formed their own labor organizations, but male union leaders seldom tried to build a working coalition with the women's groups. Faced with the prospect of losing support from the League of Women Voters and the Women's Trade Union League, the AFL did reach out to women in 1925 by urging that they be organized and integrated into existing unions; however, the initiative failed because union locals rejected the concept. Another reason for women's lack of union ties was an absence of unions in much of what was traditionally considered women's work—domestic work, hairdressing, teaching, and clerical work. Still, women in these fields sometimes united behind a cause. For instance, many African American domestic workers in Washington, D.C., united in refusing to wear uniforms or to take live-in positions.

Protective Laws

Beginning in the late 19th century, state laws started to protect women as a special class of workers. This legislation typically called for shorter hours. In some places, women's night work was outlawed. These laws were typically described as protecting the health and morals of female workers. The Women's Bureau supported both state and federal laws to reduce the number of hours a woman could work in a 24-hour period and to prohibit certain types of night labor. Often reform groups and consumer leagues rallied behind this legislation, just as they supported regulation of child labor. And labor unions supported protective laws because they bolstered the opportunities for male employment. In 1924, the U.S. Supreme Court upheld a New York law prohibiting women from working in restaurants between 10 p.m. and 6 a.m.

However, some women opposed protective laws, claiming that they robbed women of potential pay for working additional hours or late hours. These feminists strived to overturn the public conception that male and female workers should be treated differently. In the 1920s, the failed drive for passage of an Equal Rights Amendment, submitted to Congress in 1923, carried the potential of invalidating protective laws. Ultimately, these laws helped to channel women into the careers that were considered to be women's work. One candy company executive said, "It would not be possible for a woman to reach a more executive position because the fifty-four-hour law limited women's work in New York State" (Kessler-Harris 1982, 237).

Marital Status an Issue

The belief that working women should or would resign when they married was so entrenched in the culture of the 1920s that some cities and states fired teachers who married. In some places, these rules also applied to secretaries, librarians, and social workers. In addition, some banks and insurance companies would not hire married women. To explain these policies employers said they were setting a good example for other women. Of course, they also were limiting the chances of losing an employee to pregnancy. With married women constituting almost one-third of the female work force by the end of the decade, women often had to be creative. To draw extra income, some married women opened their homes to boarders. Others took factory jobs because child labor laws now made it impossible for their children to earn money for the family. African Americans made up a significant portion of married women in the workforce, and they usually earned a living as domestic workers. In some cases, Southern companies developed special rules for married female employees that allowed them to leave work early.

Working-Class Daughters

In working-class families, daughters—like sons—were expected to work and to allocate their income for the good of the family. In the 1920s, most of these girls left school and joined the workforce no later than the age of sixteen. In most cases, they continued working at least until they were married. And while parents expected sons to contribute only some of their pay to the family, daughters usually were required to turn over the full amount to their parents, and they were given small allowances. With the rise of the consumer economy, this double standard became less acceptable to young women in the 1920s. The children of working-class immigrant families felt even more pressure to work, and the job opportunities open to them were fewer and less pleasant.

Women pack sliced pineapple at a canning plant in Hawaii in 1928. (National Archives)

Professional Growth and Decline

By 1930, women accounted for 14 percent of all professionals in census counts. Most working women with professional jobs fell into the standard female categories—teachers, social workers, and nurses. In fact, women filled 80 percent of teaching jobs in the 1920s (Dumenil 1995, 16). During the decade, the percentage of women who were physicians actually declined because of medical school quotas. Female physicians represented only 4.4 percent of the workforce in 1930, down from 5 percent 10 years earlier. Similar declines occurred in dentistry and in science. The nation had fewer than 75 female accountants. And lawyers maintained their position as just 3 percent of the female workforce. Although about one-third of all advanced graduate degrees went to women, they filled less than 8 percent of academic jobs (Parrish 1992, 141). In 1928, *American Banker* reported that 2,000 women held executive positions in banks (Kessler-Harris 1982, 236). And women posted some gains in editorial and religious roles, too.

Important Changes Affect Women's Role in Economy

American women turned a corner in the 1920s. They did not receive equal pay for equal work or get the opportunity to match men's participation in the professions. However, like the men on assembly lines, they embraced a new role created by mass production and necessary to the operation of a complex, modern economy. For the first time women truly entered the world of business, and as they did, they unknowingly built a trap that held women captive for decades to come. Working in business, they followed the same outline, perpetuated the same routine. With little opportunity for advancement, they became unchanging fixtures in the shifting tides of the business world's high seas. Men's jobs changed to match the business realities of evolving competition and technological advancement, but women were always there typing and answering telephones, typing and answering telephones. Women's ventures into the factory and the office gave them a role in industrial life. For some it was not enough; however, others loved the work despite its restrictions. A 1926 survey of secretaries found that some liked their jobs because of the limitations: their jobs seldom interfered with their personal lives (Kessler-Harris 1982, 233). The 1920s also added retail work to the list of culturally accepted jobs for women. This field was not defined as a women-only category of work, although its low pay made it less attractive to men.

While some women explored the new frontiers in offices and retail stores, many women remained in what had been traditionally female work—teaching, nursing, and social work. As women reached the end of the 1920s, they had added clerical work to that list of traditional female work without opening doors

Historians' Debate:
Progress or Not?

The most frequently cited and probably the most widely read book about the history of the 1920s is Frederick Lewis Allen's *Only Yesterday.* An "instant history" published in 1931, it is still in print today and remains on many student reading lists. Allen's journalistic account is undeniably well written and provocative, and it remained a relatively unchallenged standard until the 1950s and 1960s when historians began questioning his treatment of various topics, including working women. Historian Roger Butterfield noted in 1957 that historians had shed little new light on the 1920s since publication of Allen's work (Noggle 1966, 300). Most notably, that there was little contention about Allen's descriptions of women's work leaves the reader with the impression that virtually all women had jobs and that even stay-at-home mothers struggled against the seductiveness of the business world by convincing themselves that their work was as important as the filing clerk's daily agenda.

With greater exploration, historians increasingly have concluded that the reality of women's lives in the 1920s may have been lost in the breeziness that made Allen's book and others so appealing. The image of the revolutionary flapper storming into the work world and striking blows for women's equality was misleading, given the limitations working women faced. A new emphasis on women's history in the 1950s and growing attention on women's status in the 1960s and 1970s cast a new light on the 1920s and stressed how much further women had to go. Still, for commentators who wrote during or immediately after the 1920s, there was clearly more than a glimmer of achievement in women's advances in the workplace. V. F. Calverton, a radical editor of *Current-History,* wrote at the end of the decade that "women's economic independence has been a far more important item in her emancipation than her political enfranchisement." Calverton noted married women's expanded role in the workforce but also acknowledged widespread discrimination against working women (Freedman 1974, 376). Charles and Mary Beard wrote in the 1930s that "women now assumed an unquestioned role in shaping the production of goods, material, humanistic, literary, and artistic" (Freedman 1974, 378). Clearly, a significant shift was perceived by contemporary commentators, although they generally agreed that feminism had stumbled after winning suffrage. Women's progress in the workforce during the 1920s was significant at that time, but as later historians began comparing those advances with true equality, their shallowness became clear.

for women to pursue jobs outside of society's definition of women's work. And most women chose to keep the most traditional women's work of all—being a wife and mother and running a household.

Biographies

A former trade union member, Mary Anderson became the first director of the Department of Labor's Women's Bureau in 1920. (Library of Congress)

Mary Anderson, 1872–1964

Women's Bureau Chief

Swedish-born Mary Anderson began her working life as a domestic worker and advanced to become a boot- and shoe-maker, trade union leader, federal factory investigator, and agency chief. In 1920, she became the first woman to work her way up to the leadership of a federal agency. Anderson was the first director of the Department of Labor's Women's Bureau, a post she held for a quarter of a century. The bureau's work began in 1918 when it was a World War I agency called the Women in Industry Service. Anderson joined the operation a year later. When the war ended, women's groups pushed for the operation to be made a permanent part of the Department of Labor, and Congress voted on June 5, 1920, to create the bureau. "As the world evolves," Anderson once said, "so too does the growing role of women who are proving their infinite capabilities in today's complex workplace, and exhibiting a new usefulness now and for the future" (U.S. Department of Labor, 1991). During her leadership of the bureau, the number of female workers more than doubled. Anderson retired in the 1940s.

Arthur Capper, 1865–1951

Senator

Arthur Capper, a Kansan and a former journalist, was elected to the United States Senate in 1918 and became a leading advocate of farmers in the 1920s. As a representative of a farm state, he was quick to recognize the problems facing U.S. agriculture when the high European demand for U.S. crops ended after World War I. Starting in May 1921, he joined Iowa senator William Kenyon in leading the newly formed "farm bloc," which attempted to support farmers by uniting farm state lawmakers in support of legislation that would ease the burdens crushing American agriculture. Among the group's successes in the early 1920s was passage of a bill sponsored by Capper. The Capper–Volstead Act of 1922, labeled by some as the "Magna Carta of Agriculture," bolstered farm cooperatives by exempting them from antitrust laws. The farm bloc blamed World War I government actions for leading farmers to overproduce and sought aggressive government moves to correct the problem. Arguing for government assistance in the form of high tariffs, Capper wrote, "Possibly those who favor protection to manufacturers and free trade to the farmer understand his situation better than he does, but there can be no question that the American farmer regards himself as a full-fledged American and as entitled to participate on an equality with all other interests in the American policy of protection of the American market" (Capper 1929, 123). Capper remained in the Senate through 1948 when he retired.

Paul Galvin, 1895–1959

Inventor and Businessman

As the founder of Motorola, Paul Galvin changed Americans' experience as listeners by introducing and mass producing car radios. These devices were not standard in cars of the 1920s, so Galvin's product had to be installed into cars after manufacturing.

After serving in the military in World War I, Galvin first entered the manufacturing sector in production of batteries. First, he joined with Edward Stewart in 1921 to establish a storage battery factory in Wisconsin. When that venture failed, he moved to Chicago and went to work as a personal secretary with the Brach Candy Company. In 1926, he again partnered with Stewart in a battery production company, but a flaw in the product doomed that effort. Galvin created the Galvin Manufacturing Corporation in 1928 with the goal of selling home radios, but he later refined the concept of car radios and made those products his primary focus. Sales reached $287,000 in 1930—the same year that he claimed the trademark Motorola. Later, he worked out an arrangement with B. F. Goodrich to sell Motorola products in the company's tire stores. Ultimately, Galvin reentered the home radio market and produced police radios, two-way radios, and televisions.

Hortense Powdermaker, 1896–1970

Labor Leader

Hortense Powdermaker pursued two careers that were unusual for women of her era. After graduating from Goucher College in 1921, she went to work in the Chicago offices of the seven-year-old Amalgamated Clothing Workers of America (ACWA). The union sprang up after leaders of the United Garment Workers tried to expel some militant locals. Because of the ACWA's militant roots, the American Federation of Labor refused to recognize it. After a short time, Powdermaker became dissatisfied with her office work, and her supervisors assigned her to lead the union's organizing efforts. This job provided her first exposure to fieldwork. In 1925, she started studying at the London School of Economics and Political Science where she enrolled in an anthropology course and decided that was the field that interested her most. She received a Ph.D. in 1928 and immediately set out for Lesu, Ireland, where she did fieldwork. Years of research resulted in a book, *Life in Lesu,* which was published in 1933. She did later fieldwork in rural Mississippi and Zambia, and during her career, she was affiliated with Yale University and Queens College in New York. She died in 1970.

A. Philip Randolph organized the Brotherhood of Sleeping Car Porters in 1925. He became an influential labor leader and civil rights advocate. (Library of Congress)

A. Philip Randolph, 1889–1979

Labor and Civil Rights Leader

A. Philip Randolph devoted much of his life to the fight for African American rights. Once called the most dangerous black man in the United States, he began as a labor leader and continued pushing for economic and civil equality throughout his long life. Born in Florida, he moved to New York City in 1911. There, he supported himself by working as a waiter, a porter, and an elevator operator while he attended the City College of New York as a night student. He embraced socialism during World War I but later decided that unionization offered the best economic protection for African American workers. At the request of a group of porters, he organized and became president of the Brotherhood of Sleeping Car Porters in 1925. The union, now known as the Brotherhood of Railway and Airline clerks, faced a difficult struggle. It received a charter from the American Federation of Labor in 1929, but the Pullman Company used many tactics to discourage the organization, including firing union members. Abortive strikes and failed arbitration sessions made the union's prospects appear bleak in its early years. However, two victories came in 1935: Under the oversight of the National Mediation Board, the union won an election to represent the employees, and the American Federation of Labor reversed an earlier decision and granted the brotherhood an international charter. Two years later, the brotherhood reached a contract agreement with the Pullman Company.

Meanwhile, Randolph's role in the black community broadened. He became first president of the National Negro Congress in 1936. This umbrella group's goal was to promote a black mass movement by drawing various African American organizations together in a joint effort. In 1941, Randolph threatened to organize a black march on Washington to demand more jobs for African Americans in the thriving defense industry that was gearing up for possible U.S. participation in World War II. Although the march never took place, Randolph's efforts apparently spurred President Franklin D. Roosevelt to issue Executive Order 8802, which required equal employment opportunities for all groups in the defense industry and in the federal government. After the war, he led a drive to desegregate the military. That crusade prompted President Harry Truman's Executive Order 9981, which demanded integration of the armed services in 1948. When the Congress of Industrial Organizations and the American Federation of Labor merged in 1955, Randolph was elected vice president. He also played a key role in the civil rights movement of the 1950s and 1960s.

Alfred P. Sloan Jr., 1875–1966

Businessman

A graduate of MIT, Alfred P. Sloan Jr. began his automotive career at a New Jersey roller bearing factory. In 1918, General Motors' William C. Durant hired him and he became a GM vice president at 43. Two years later, a shareholders' revolt ousted Durant, and Pierre du Pont took over the company's leadership and its presidency. He named Sloan as his assistant. GM badly needed reorganization, and Sloan created an entirely new structure that served the company well. He was among the first to recognize that consumers could be persuaded to trade in their old cars for new ones and that other buyers would purchase the used cars. Sloan, who became GM's president in 1923, also created a full line of cars for GM to appeal to different tastes and spending levels. By the mid-1920s, the quality of GM cars was comparable to the quality of Fords; in the long run, GM's decision to offer a line of different models proved more profitable than Ford's choice to stick with a single, almost-always-black inexpensive car. Unlike Ford, Sloan avoided the public spotlight. He became chairman of the board at GM in 1937 and served in that post until 1956 when he retired at the age of 81.

Henry C. Wallace, 1866–1924

Farmer, Publisher, Official

Henry C. Wallace was born on a small family farm near Orient, Ohio, and his agricultural roots guided the course his life would follow. He graduated from Iowa State University in 1892 with a degree in dairy science. He later joined the faculty as a professor of agriculture, but he maintained the family farm in Orient. A man of many talents, Wallace also contributed to another family business— *Wallace's Farmer*—a popular farm journal. The journal, launched in 1895, used the motto "Good farming, clear thinking, right living." It provided a mix of news, entertainment, research, and opinion. His father Henry edited the publication until his death in 1916 when Henry C. took over. At its peak in the 1920s, the journal had a circulation of 250,000 (Rodale Institute).

Wallace also helped to form the American Farm Bureau in 1920, and within a year, it had grown to become the nation's biggest agricultural organization with more than a million members. Additionally, he was a longtime president of the Cornbelt Meat Producers Association. Because of Wallace's varied credentials as an expert on farming, Republican presidential candidate Warren G. Harding consulted him during the 1920 presidential campaign. Months later, when Harding was elected president, he asked Wallace to join his cabinet as secretary of agriculture. Wallace was a progressive, which worried some Republicans; nevertheless, he won approval. In his new role, Wallace was a strong supporter of conservation, and he promoted farm relief programs. One of his primary concerns was the government's role in regulating production to match demand—an issue that was not resolved during his tenure. In 1924, Wallace died unexpectedly after surgery. His book, *Our Debt and Duty to the Farmer,* was released after his death. His son Henry A. Wallace later served as secretary of agriculture and vice president of the United States in Franklin D. Roosevelt's administration.

REFERENCES AND FURTHER READINGS

Allen, Frederick Lewis. 2000. *Only Yesterday: An Informal History of the 1920's.* New York: Perennial Classics.

Canaan, Gareth. 2001. "'Part of the Loaf': Economic Conditions of Chicago's African-American Working Class during the 1920s." *Journal of Social History* 35 (1): 147–174.

Capper, Arthur. 1929. "Farm Relief and the Tariff." *Annals of the American Academy of Political and Social Science* (January): 120–123.

Dean, John W. 2004. *Warren G. Harding.* New York: Times Books.

Dumenil, Lynn. 1995. *The Modern Temper: American Culture and Society in the 1920s*. New York: Hill and Wang.

Fass, Paul S. 1977. *The Damned and the Beautiful: American Youth in the 1920's*. Oxford: Oxford University Press.

Freedman, Estelle B. 1974. "The New Woman: Changing View of Women in the 1920s." *Journal of American History* 61 (2): 372–393.

Geospatial & Statistical Data Center. http://lewis.lib.virginia.edu (accessed June 30, 2006).

Goldberg, David. 1999. *Discontented America: The United States in the 1920s*. Baltimore: Johns Hopkins University Press.

Goodwin, E Marvin. 1990. *Black Migration in America from 1915 to 1960*. Lewiston: Edwin Mellon Press.

Green, Julie. 1994. "Working Gender: Recent Scholarship in American Labor History." *Frontiers: A Journal of Women Studies* 24 (3): 181–190.

Growing a Nation: The Story of American Agriculture. http://www.agclassroom .org (accessed June 30, 2006).

Hacker, Louis M. 1947. *The Shaping of the American Tradition*. New York: Columbia University Press.

Harrison, Alferdteen, ed. 1991. *Black Exodus: The Great Migration and the American South*. Jackson: University Press of Mississippi.

Harvard University Open Collections Program. *Women Working, 1800–1930*. "Women's Bureau." http://ocp.hul.harvard.edu/ww/organizations-bureau.html (accessed June 21, 2006).

Henry Ford Museum. History of the Rouge. http://www.thehenryford.org/ rouge/history.asp (accessed June 22, 2006).

Johnson, H. Thomas. 1985. *Agricultural Depression in the 1920s: Economic Fact or Statistical Artifact?* New York: Garland Publishing.

Kessler-Harris, Alice. 1982. *Out to Work: A History of Wage-Earning Women in the United States*. Oxford: Oxford University Press.

Kutler, Stanley I., ed. 1995. *American Perspectives: Historians on Historians*. Baltimore: Johns Hopkins University Press.

Kyvig, David E. 2002. *Daily Life in the United States 1920–1940*. Chicago: Ivan R. Dee.

Leuchtenburg, William E. 1993. *The Perils of Prosperity 1914–1932*. 2nd ed. Chicago: University of Chicago Press.

Link, Arthur S. 1955. *American Epoch: A History of the United States since the 1890s*. New York: Alfred A. Knopf.

Lorant, John H. 1967. "Technological Change in American Manufacturing during the 1920's." *The Journal of Economic History* 27 (2): 243–246.

McGraw, Thomas K. 2000. *American Business, 1920–2000: How It Worked.* Wheeling, IL: Harlan Davidson Inc.

Miller, Nathan. 2003. *New World Coming: The 1920s and the Making of Modern America.* New York: Scribner.

Montejano, David. 1999. "The 'Mexican Problem'" in *Major Problems in American History, 1920–1945,* edited by Colin Gordon, 172–185. New York: Houghton Mifflin Company.

National Park Service. Ford's River Rouge Complex. http://www.nps.gov/NR/travel/detroit/d38.htm (accessed February 22, 2008).

Noggle, Burl. 1966. "The Twenties: A New Historiographical Frontier." *Journal of American History* 53 (2): 299–314.

Parrish, Michael E. 1992. *Anxious Decades: America in Prosperity and Depression, 1920–1941.* New York: W. W. Norton & Co.

Paulson, R. W., E. B. Chase, R. S. Roberts, and D. W. Moody. 1991. "Major Floods and Droughts in California," excerpt from *National Water Summary 1988–89 —Hydrologic Events and Floods and Droughts: U.S. Geological Survey Water-Supply Paper 2375.* http://geochange.er.usgs.gov/sw/impacts/hydrology/state _fd/cawater1.html (accessed June 26, 2006).

Persons, Warren M. 1922. "The Crisis of 1920 in the United States: A Quantitative Survey." *The American Economic Review* 12 (1): 5–19.

Rodale Institute. "Good Farming, Clear Thinking, Right Living." The New Farm. http://newfarm.org/features/0904/wallacecenter/bio.shtml (accessed June 21, 2006).

Smith, Jessie Carney, and Carrell Horton. 1995. *Historical Statistics of Black America.* New York: Gale Research.

Tolnay, Stewart E. 2001. "African Americans and Immigrants in Northern Cities: The Effects of Relative Group Size on Occupational Standing in 1920." *Social Forces* 80 (2): 573–604.

Tolnay, Stewart E., and E. M. Beck. 1990. "Black Flight: Lethal Violence and the Great Migration, 1900–1930." *Social Science History* 14 (3): 347–370.

U.S. Bureau of the Census. *Historical Statistics of the United States: Colonial Times to 1970,* 1975. Washington: Department of Commerce. http://www2 .census.gov/prod2/statcomp/documents/CT1970p1–01.pdf (accessed June 30, 2006).

U.S. Department of Labor. 1991. Labor Hall of Fame Honoree. http://www.dol .gov/oasam/programs/laborhall/1991_anderson.htm (accessed December 1, 2006).

U.S. Geological Survey. http://geochange.er.usgs.gov (accessed June 30, 2006).

White, Catherine J. Curtis. 2005. "Women in the Great Migration: Economic Activity of Black and White Southern-Born Female Migrants in 1920, 1940, and 1970." *Social Science History* 29 (3): 413–455.

Mass Consumption
and Leisure

OVERVIEW

During the 1920s, the length of the average workweek for the nation's people dropped to 45 hours (Drowne and Huber 2004, 143), some 20 hours fewer than the average workweek in 1870 (Goldberg 2003, 20). This reduced workweek created more time to devote to leisure. Although prior to this time most Americans not only lacked time for leisure but also suspected idleness as a form of immorality, the 1920s marked a time of vastly increased acceptance of and interest in recreation. Elements of business culture such as mass production and machine-age technologies such as the radio, phonograph, and motion pictures combined to form new appetites for entertainment. The concept of working hard and then playing hard began to prevail among most of the country's people. As commentator Robert L. Duffus wrote of the situation in 1924, "the right to play is the final clause in the charter of democracy. The people are king—*et le roi s'amuse*" ["The people are king—and the King takes his amusement"] (Mowry 1963, 46). As Americans became more fully engaged in leisure, they explored a whole range of recreational pursuits. Because of differences in tastes and gaps in material circumstances, American patterns of leisure during the 1920s varied considerably by social class. White-collar leisure included movies, book-club reading, success literature, and rags-to-riches stories. Working-class leisure tended toward sports, amusement parks, movies, jazz clubs, and dance halls. Generally speaking, Americans of the 1920s became more favorably disposed to such things as leisure spending, recreational travel, and the notion that free time offered a way to offset work or recuperate from the rigors of everyday life. According to Lynn Dumenil, spending on leisure increased 300 percent during the 1920s (Dumenil 1995, 65).

TIMELINE

1920   A Model T automobile is finished every minute.

Eight players for the Chicago White Sox are indicted for conspiracy in "throwing" the 1919 World Series. This scandal has many referring to the team as the "Black Sox."

America's rail mileage peaks at 253,000.

Traffic lights are introduced.

The Grand Canyon National Park is dedicated on April 20.

1921   Babe Ruth hits 59 runs in one season of baseball. By 1927 he would become the highest paid player in baseball, receiving $70,000 a year.

First hamburger restaurant chain, White Castle, opens.

Charlie Chaplin's *Idle Class* opens in theaters.

Screen star Roscoe "Fatty" Arbuckle becomes engulfed in a scandal when he is arrested on manslaughter charges. Although he is later acquitted, stigma still attached to him.

Rudolph Valentino appears in *The Sheik* opening on October 31.

1922   First Technicolor film, *Tale of the Sea,* is seen in New York City. The technique, developed by Herbert T. Kalmus, would not be used widely in films released until 20 years later.

First 3-D movie is created, which requires special glasses for viewers.

Nanook of the North becomes America's first documentary film.

Hays Office begins to censor Hollywood films.

Americans suffer just fewer than 15,000 fatalities related to automobiles. By 1930, this figure would soar to more than 32,900.

1923   At their annual convention, the General Federation of Women's Clubs votes to crusade against jazz, largely based on its perceived deleterious influence on young women's morality.

Kodak offers the buying public home-movie equipment for purchase.

Singer Eddie Cantor releases, "Since Ma Is Playing Mah Jong." Millions are spent on game sets purchased in the United States.

Rin Tin Tin becomes the screen's most famous dog. Sales of dogs of his breed, the German shepherd, rise.

The Warner Brothers studio is established.

Harold Lloyd's *Safety Last* has its premiere on April 1.

Brinks unveils the first armored vans on June 9.

On October 1, the Disney Company is established.

On November 6, Jacob Schick receives a patent for an electric shaver.

1924   The premiere of Douglas Fairbanks in *The Thief of Baghdad* takes place on March 18.

On April 14, a merger of two motion picture studios creates Metro-Goldwyn-Mayer (MGM).

The ten millionth Model T leaves the assembly line June 15.

On June 28, the *Ziegfeld Follies* opens on Broadway. June 30 marks the date Will Rogers joins Broadway's *Ziegfeld Follies*.

On August 11, presidential candidates appear on newsreel for the first time.

On October 28, Harold "Red" Grange plays his first college football game.

1925   A Model T automobile is finished every ten seconds.

Ford starts manufacturing pickup trucks.

Charlie Chaplin appears in *The Gold Rush*.

On February 17, the first in-flight movie is shown: *The Lost World*.

On April 13, the first commercial air travel begins between Detroit and Chicago, sponsored by Henry Ford.

1926   Auto antifreeze is developed for the first time, which makes it easier to use vehicles year-round.

The word "documentary" makes its first appearance.

Kodak develops the first 16-mm movie film.

It is estimated that there are 32,000 speakeasies in New York City, roughly double the number of taverns operating prior to Prohibition.

On July 16, *The Son of the Sheik* premieres.

Rudolph Valentino dies on August 23 at age 31 of a perforated gastric ulcer. The public mourns and even riots over loss of a beloved celebrity.

On September 28, a Broadway adaptation of Anita Loos's novel, *Gentlemen Prefer Blondes,* featuring flapper Lorelei Lee, opens.

On October 31, magician Harry Houdini dies of peritonitis.

On November 3, entertainer Annie Oakley dies at age 66.

1927

The Lindy Hop becomes popular among the nation's dancers.

Ford comes out with the Model A, available in colors such as Niagara Blue and Violet. A related popular song proclaims "Henry's Made a Lady Out of Lizzie."

Reno, Nevada, establishes a three-month residency period for those seeking a divorce, a much shorter route than the one-year period most other localities demanded. Reno becomes the place to go for a swift dissolution of marriage.

The first Academy Awards are presented in a ceremony lasting under five minutes. These awards were not called "Oscars" until 1931.

The first commercial airline begins operation.

As the year opens, Massachusetts becomes the first state in the nation to require motorists to have auto insurance.

The Harlem Globetrotters are created.

Al Jolson appears in *The Jazz Singer,* the first full-length "talkie" motion picture, which debuted on October 6. The first dialogue spoken was "Wait a minute, wait a minute, you ain't heard nothin' yet."

On January 5, Fox Studio presents Movietone technology, in which sound and sight may be synchronized in a motion picture.

Buster Keaton's *The General* premieres on February 5.

On October 27, Fox Movietone News completes the first news film with sound.

On May 20, aviator Charles Lindbergh departs on his solo transatlantic flight. His aircraft is known as *The Spirit of St. Louis.*

June 8 is the date on which the California Association for Guidance for Producers issues a list of "don'ts" and "be carefuls" for motion pictures.

On June 13, Lindbergh is welcomed back to New York by 4 million well-wishers with a ticker-tape parade.

On August 12, Paramount premieres *Wings* with Clara Bow, the "It" girl. The film won the first Academy Award for best picture.

On November 13, a structure spanning the Hudson River, the Holland Tunnel, the first underwater auto tunnel, becomes available to motorists (all 1.8 miles of it).

1928   Walt Disney's character Mickey Mouse makes his first appearance in *Plane Crazy,* a silent parody of the Lindbergh craze.

Walt Disney's animated film, *Steamboat Willie,* introduces the sound-on-film technique to animated features, making possible synchronized sound.

Bell Labs of New York presents a demonstration of color television featuring images of roses and the American flag.

Bubble gum is invented.

On July 17–18, Amelia Earhart becomes the first woman to cross the Atlantic by air. She also conducts a solo round-trip across the United States.

On July 30, George Eastman offers the first demonstration of a color motion picture.

The first animated electric sign, known as the "zipper," appears on the Times Building in New York's Times Square on November 6.

1929   Popeye the Sailor and Tarzan appear in the comics for the first time.

Cross-country air travel becomes available for passengers.

The first residential trailer is built, although these homes on wheels will not be marketed until the 1930s.

The Museum of Modern Art opens in New York City.

Guy Lombardo sings "Auld Lang Syne" at New York's Waldorf Astoria, creating a New Year's routine.

Robert and Helen Lynd publish their sociological study of Muncie, Indiana: *Middletown.*

Construction on the Empire State Building is under way.

When the stock market crashes, *Variety*'s headline proclaims that "Wall Street Lays an Egg."

THE NEW CONSUMER CULTURE

In Search of Purchasing Power

During the late 19th century, cultural observer Thorstein Veblen coined the term "conspicuous consumption" to describe the practice of material display conducted in an attempt to wield economic status in society. By the 20th century, spending took on additional meanings. During World War I, for example, Wilson's Committee on Public Information (CPI) urged Americans to show patriotism and support for troops through their spending and investment patterns. The acqui-

A group of female models pose around a new car in a promotional photo, holding large numbers for the year 1928. The women's attire featured in this photograph depicts several fashion trends of the 1920s. The new bobbed hair styles of the era were characteristic of flapper fashion. Rayon garments and silk stockings came into high demand during the 1920s, as traditional cotton stockings were no longer considered to be in style. (Getty Images)

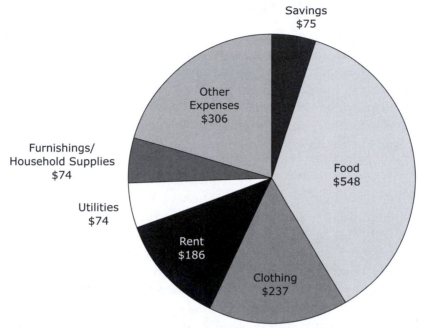

Figure 2.1 *Average Annual Budget for Working-Class Family of Five in the 1920s.*
Source: *Miller 2003, 282, based on data from Bureau of Labor Statistics.*

sition of Liberty Bonds became an act of spending to be understood as an act of national allegiance rather than ostentation.

By the 1920s, technological developments, sales techniques, and changing notions of what the modern home in America should look like created more demand for consumer goods of all kinds but especially those that involved mechanical innovations. By 1927, 220 in every 1,000 American homes had radio receivers, 450 in 1,000 had phonographs, 550 in 1,000 had automobiles, and 600 in 1,000 had telephones. While average incomes were on the rise during the 1920s, the cost of such merchandise still stretched the means of America's families. To maintain the lifestyles to which they aspired, both inside and outside the home, Americans would need to look beyond their savings to gain purchasing power.

Scholars David Desser and Garth S. Jowett refer to the years 1922 to 1929 as a "frenzy of consumption" in the United States (Desser and Jowett 2000, 85). Prosperity, easy credit, lowered inhibitions about spending, availability of new consumer goods, and heightened expectations for material comfort created a climate in which consumption became a way of life for many Americans. This outlook resulted in new expenditure patterns for life's necessities and unprecedented sales of such nonessential items as the latest fashions in clothes, appliances of convenience, and materials related to leisure, such as movie tickets, vacations, and the like.

Who Had What? The Good(s) Life

While the 1920 census helps inform a discussion of American household composition, it does not reveal everything about daily life for the nation's people. The 1920s in America witnessed shifts in the standard of living for the nation's people. Habits of thrift gave way to patterns of consumption. While there were significant disparities among social classes and cultural groups during the 1920s, the average U.S. salary rose from $1,236 per year in 1920 to $1,368 in 1930 (Drowne and Huber 2004, 294). The national per capita income, which is computed by dividing the total national income by the total population, went from $7,495 in 1919 to $8,939 in 1929 (Friedman 2004, 192). Because per capita income reckons multiple sources of revenue (such as wages, salaries, and property income) and takes account of all persons (including adults and children not employed), this figure may be an even stronger indicator than is average salary of a nation's standard of living. Consumer confidence was high, and innovation in technology provided the public with a wide array of new products and purchasing options. In particular, Americans became more willing to invest in durable goods during this decade.

The 1920s represented a time when increases to the standard of living and changing notions of what a modern American home required resulted in altered consumer patterns. For one thing, levels of service and forms of utilities available to America's households had changed. These figures varied depending upon how remote the home's location might be. Generally speaking, the larger the community, the greater the percentage of families who had the benefit of public garbage collection, piped water, stationary bathtubs, stationary kitchen sinks, gas, and electric lights. For example in 1926, 100 percent of residents in communities with over 100,000 residents had piped water in their houses and 81.5 percent had electric lights (Gregory 1995, 328). In fact, Americans went from using 57 billion kilowatt hours of electricity in 1920 to 118 billion kilowatt hours in 1929 (O'Neal, 2006, 85). Once the majority of American homes had electrical service, it became possible to market household machines and devices powered by electricity (Gregory 1995, 328). New electrical devices, such as kitchen appliances and radio receivers, could be used within these newly wired households, so the potential market for them grew. This new equipment would hasten lifestyle changes within America's homes. At this time in the United States, modern electrical appliances became associated with the good life.

Who Borrowed What?
The Growth of Consumer Credit

Credit was far from a new concept in the 1920s although it assumed new importance during this decade. Merchants and service providers sometimes extended credit directly to their customers when circumstances allowed it. In other instances, loans from banks, loan companies, and insurance companies helped Americans make ends meet.

There are many ways to account for the decade's increase in debt despite postwar prosperity. Not everyone prospered during the 1920s, and groups such as farmers suffered some major setbacks during this era. Many Americans still struggled to meet their financial obligations. In addition, a shift in perspective took place during this time. While it was once considered shameful to owe money, debt was not only common during the 1920s, it was increasingly considered acceptable to live beyond one's means.

Major Influences on Patterns of American Consumer Behavior

Several historical factors during the 1920s proved favorable to the emergence of a culture of consumption. In the period following World War I, overproduction became an issue in some industries. The postwar economy, coupled with increased efficiencies in production, forced industrialists to build a consumer base commensurate with their increased factory and plant outputs. Furthermore, with the era's development of new technologies, including additional forms of mass media, there were more forms of merchandise made available for Americans to consume. Since World War I, Americans had been encouraged to think about spending as one's patriotic duty, as representing investment in the country and its future. This consumer ethic helped to change the spending habits of the American people.

As historians such as Richard Fox and T. J. Jackson Lears have been careful to note, however, the consumer ethic was a complex phenomenon that operated on numerous levels. With rising wages and the increasing routinization of work in an industrialized society, for example, consumers tended to look elsewhere for compensating interests and pleasures. Among these benefits were what Fox called the "characteristic institutions and habits of consumer culture—the motion picture, the radio, the automobile, the weekly photo-newsmagazine, installment buying, the five-day work week, suburban living, to name a few," which helped to define the good life in modern America (Fox and Lears 1983, 103). In consumer goods, leisure, and "the merchandising of thrills," the nation's workers sought solace and self-definition (Lears 1993, 1594).

Also helping to shape consumer choices during the 1920s were several forms of "expert" guidance. According to Fox and Lears, "Consumers are not only buyers of goods but recipients of professional advice, marketing strategies, government programs, electoral choices, and advertisers' images of happiness" (Fox and Lears 1983, xii). Such voices sought during the 1920s to persuade the

A Nation of Consumers?

As early as 1933, sociologist Robert Lynd described the 1920s as a time when Americans could be said to be engaged in buying a living rather than simply earning one. "It is because so much of living must be bought in our increasingly specialized, urbanized culture that a study of consumption habits occupies a place in any study of social trends" (Lynd 1933, 857). Lynd saw the transformation of citizens into consumers as potentially injurious to the nation's values and prospects. Later social historians of the 1920s have sought, as Robert Lynd did before them, to understand the reasons behind this trend.

For instance, having assessed—and lamented—the state of American patterns of spending, saving, and investing, Robert Lynd advocated consumer literacy. He wrote, "The increase in new kinds of goods and services, the decline in home handicraft knowledge, the increased complexity of mechanical devices and fabricated commodities, new pressures on the consumer to buy, and new tensions within the consumer, make new demands for consumer literacy" (Lynd 1933, 881). Informed product selection was only part of this literacy, as Lynd envisioned it. As important as insight into merchandise was an awareness of how to live within one's means.

In recent times, scholars have attempted to strike a balance between accounts of consumerism that placed all the power with influences external to the consumer (societal forces such as marketing, advertising, and publicity) and those accounts that placed it entirely with the internal will of consumers (individual choices based upon personal preferences and independent judgments of need). Most recent research on consumerism investigates the complex relationships between societal influence and individual choice. "The study of mass culture has to be more," writes T. J. Jackson Lears, "than the study of the corporate marketing strategies embedded in mass-produced texts; the text can be a site of contested meanings, and to grasp the full range of those meanings we need to understand the audience not only as a set of social categories (the familiar litany of class, race, gender) but also as a disparate collection of individuals" (Lears 1993, 1606). The behavior of Americans during the 1920s cannot be reduced to merely the role of consumers or the buying demographics into which whole groups of Americans could be said to fall.

American public that they could be happier, more successful, and more appealing if only they made the correct purchases.

Historians of this era in American history have debated the extent of such forces for governing consumer behaviors. Initially, historical accounts tended to portray consumers as passive recipients of such advertising and marketing messages. Subsequent historians began to question this interpretation, suggesting that consumers had substantial ability to resist such forces, if only they realized the importance of their own agency. These cultural observers, sometimes called "moralists," critiqued materialism as a lifestyle and scoffed at its illusions of personal fulfillment.

Door-to-Door Sales

With the amount of concerted labor modern households required, marketers sometimes found it more effective to bring their sales force to the homemaker rather than waiting for the homemaker to visit the store. The image of the traveling salesman is an enduring one in American culture, and the 1920s helped create that effect. Door-to-door sales of small appliances and other household needs flourished during the 1920s. Aluminum cookware and vacuum cleaners were just two of the product lines that were marketed door-to-door during this era. Prominent companies in home sales included Singer, Electrolux, California Perfume Company (later renamed Avon), and the Fuller Brush Company (Friedman 2004, 198).

By 1925, Alfred C. Fuller's company employed 4,200 salesmen. These company representatives received training to be effective in interpersonal interactions with consumers. Fuller salesmen were encouraged to adopt a buoyant affect and endlessly pleasant manner. When asked how they were feeling, for example, Fuller men were to offer a customary response: "Fine and dandy" (Friedman 2004, 207). Many sales representatives joined in this cheer offensive, including Al Teetsel, the best-known salesman for Fuller and founder of the Fine and Dandy Club, an organization supporting salesmen in their efforts to optimize business through positive thinking.

A positive attitude helped set the climate for sales but was not sufficient in itself to ensure success. Household brushes represented the core of the Fuller company's product line. For Fuller "brush men," as for many door-to-door concerns, sales pivoted on the home demonstration. Salesmen needed to gain access to the house in order to model the merchandise for homemakers. Using scripts developed to appeal to homemakers, salesmen for Fuller sought to win over these consumers. The strategy involved "positive response," a technique in which the sales representative asked questions designed to elicit a reply of "yes" from prospective customers. Once the consumer was responding positively, the salesman hoped to use those elements of agreement to secure the purchase. Fuller representatives typically provided a sample of their goods, a "Handy Brush" to the client.

As such techniques suggest, the sales pitch was not merely an appeal to reason. In-home marketing of wares reflected the era's notions of psychological influence. Salesmen positioned themselves as guests in the consumer's home, where customary hospitality might be offered them. The routines used by Fuller salesmen—and other companies—sought to manipulate consumers through physical presence in the home, carefully couched scripts, and appeals to the consumer's unspoken desires for status, popularity, and personal power.

America's Department Stores

Department stores were not an invention of the 1920s. For years, such establishments had enabled customers to shop for a range of goods, from clothing to home furnishings. However, this decade was a pivotal one in the history of such stores. The country was generally prosperous, and consumers were well disposed toward buying. The availability of credit on large purchases of durable goods encouraged increases in other areas of personal spending. Although mail-order shopping had begun to claim its share of the retail market, department stores provided customers with the opportunity to examine merchandise firsthand and leave the store with purchases in hand. The nation experienced a period of retail growth, and department stores of the 1920s enticed a middle-class and upper-class clientele with merchandise displays, along with such atmospheric amenities as pipe organ music. Department stores actively advertised in area newspapers and presented their locations as palaces of consumption. Indeed, department stores operating during the 1920s were among the largest and most appealing the country had ever seen. Macy's in New York and Loren Miller and Company in Chicago were just two examples of successful department stores operating during this era.

Store owners and managers worked hard to earn the ultimate goal: loyal, life-long customers. For that reason, the department store was the place for shoppers who wanted more than just the item itself from a given purchase. At department stores, customers received the personal touch, from convenient wrapping to fulfillment of special orders. During the 1920s, Jordan Marsh fielded 2,000 such requests from customers weekly. To compete, Filene's would send a staff member out to purchase items elsewhere if the consumer's desired merchandise was not on hand in their store. This standard of customer service placed considerable burdens on workers. Betty Mindling, employee of Norton's Department Store and member of local 1250 of the Department Store Workers Union, described it in a poem, "The Shop Girl's Saga": "With a smile, we stand aimed to

Rotunda of the City of Paris Dry Goods Company in San Francisco, ca. 1920. Although most social historians examining department stores have concentrated on the flagship stores associated with major department store chains, smaller, independent stores operated across the country, as this example from San Francisco attests. (Library of Congress)

Table 2.1. Number of Sears Catalogues Distributed Each Season (Twice Annually), 1900–1929

Year	Number of Catalogues Distributed
1900	425,000
1910	2,304,000
1915	4,393,000
1920	5,133,150
1925	6,650,000
1929	7,151,000

Source: Adapted from Lynd 1933, 870.

please, / No matter how feet ache and pain; / Though selected clientele come to tease, / The show must go on—there are sales to gain" (Library of Congress, 1936–1940, 6).

With the appearance of chain stores, however, department stores faced increased competition. At first, chain stores were "poor man's stores," but during the 1920s virtually all classes of consumers could be found at five-and-ten-cent stores and grocery chains (Lynd 1933, 870). While department stores offered skilled customer service, the efficiency, standardization, and collective buying power of chains threatened to undercut their standing in the marketplace. As Edward Albert Filene, department store pioneer, put it in a December 27, 1927, speech "The Present Status and Future Prospects of Chains of Department Stores," "Mass production has made mass distribution necessary" (Filene 1927, 1). If department stores did not address the problem, chain stores would be only too happy to handle it for them. Consequently, many major department stores began chains of their own. For example, in 1922 Macy's went public and began opening branch stores across the country.

It was also during the 1920s, thanks to the growing prevalence of automobile travel, that the first shopping centers in America appeared. These clusters of retail stores shared a parking lot and customer base. Because so many consumers had automobiles available to them, such stores did not have to confine themselves to urban centers. In time, shopping centers, like chain stores before them, would threaten the economic viability of urban department stores.

Mail-Order Sales and Chain Stores

As the decade of the 1920s opened, the two giants of mail-order commerce were Montgomery Ward and Sears, Roebuck and Co. Parcel post legislation and the rise in farm income during the World War I era created the climate necessary for the success of mail-order commerce. When farm incomes went up, so typically did catalogue sales at Sears, Roebuck. In 1925, Sears and Roebuck embarked on a new venture, a chain of stores where customers could purchase catalogue goods in person. This move had been based upon the success of mail-order selling, but the new stores soon rivaled mail-order selling. Sears also invested significantly in radio, acquiring a Chicago station known as WLS for "World's Largest Store," the familiar Sears, Roebuck catalogue slogan. Among this station's offerings during the 1920s was a country music program known first as "WLS Barn Dance" and subsequently as the "National Barn Dance" and the "Grand Ole Opry" (Cox 2005, 180). This programming coincided with the close relationship Sears and Roebuck cultivated with rural Americans.

The 1920s helped launch both the concept of the chain store in retail and the premise of self-service. Chain stores conducted enough volume of business that they could buy in bulk from suppliers, thus offering savings to their customers. Chain stores also provided a predictable experience for America's consumers, even when they traveled outside their local areas. In an increasingly mobile society, shoppers appreciated the option of patronizing familiar establishments. Everything from the overall appearance of the stores to the shelf locations of particular products might—and often did—prove consistent among stores in the same chain. It took a while for chain stores to dominate the American marketplace. According to historian Susan Strasser, in 1923, two-thirds of the nation's consumers were conducting their retail business at local "mom-and-pop" establishments (Strasser 1989, 65). In the period from 1920 to 1927, however, chain-store sales volume in the United States tripled (Emmet and Jeuck 1950, 606). By the late 1920s, chain stores were becoming both more numerous and more popular with shoppers. For instance, in 1927 alone, the F. W. Woolworth Co. five-and-ten-cent chain linked 1,600 stores and took in $272 million dollars (Leinwand 2001, 36).

There is some debate concerning which American grocer was the first to implement self-service shopping. Some claim that the Alpha Beta Stores of Los Angeles, California, came first with self-service in 1912. Usually, though, researchers credit Piggly Wiggly with the innovation. With his wholesale grocery stores, Clarence Saunders of Memphis pioneered the concepts of chain stores and self-service retail. His Piggly Wiggly stores, begun in 1916, have been cited as the first such establishment to allow customers to move among stocked shelves and select their own items for purchase rather than directing a clerk behind a counter to furnish them. This approach reduced labor costs because customers selected their own purchases from among the store's shelf-displayed stock. It also increased impulse buying among consumers who became interested in additional items as they shopped. Saunders's arrangement of the stores took its inspiration from the conventions of cafeteria dining. In fact, until the term "supermarket" caught on, such stores were called "groceterias." They accomplished for grocery shopping what automats had done for dining out. Saunders placed a rail below grocery display areas, providing this surface for shopping

Table 2.2. U.S. Families Using Convenience Foods in Greater Milwaukee, 1922–1930

	Percentage of Families Using Product		
Item	1922–1923	1927–1928	1930
Canned Soup	—	89	87
Prepared Mayonnaise	54	45	55
Canned Milk	47	37	46
Packaged Soda Crackers	—	51	78
Packaged Bacon	—	27	44
Packaged Cheese	22	47	54

Source: Milwaukee Journal, Consumer Analysis, annual reports, as presented in Lynd 1933. President's Research Committee on Social Trends, Volume 2, "The People as Consumers," 877, in section spanning 857–911.

baskets just as cafeteria customers used rails to slide their trays toward the cashier. Chain stores helped even consumers on the move to maintain store loyalty. This chain went from 515 stores in 1920 to 2,500 stores in 1929 (Time-Life 1998, 79). Customers responded positively to the value and consistency of grocery shopping at chain stores.

Working to Live, Not Living to Work: The Well-Appointed Home

With the availability of new technology and appliances came increased expectations for cleanliness, efficiency, and productivity in the American home. During the 1920s, an average household required between 51 and 60 hours of labor per week on housework alone (Kyvig 2004, 66). At the same time, due to changes in immigration policy and other factors, fewer servants were available for employment within the home. With heightened standards of home care and lowered numbers of household staff on hand, American homemakers faced new domestic challenges, to which they responded in a variety of ways. Use of commercial laundries rose 57 percent during the period from 1914 to 1924 (Allen 1931, 66). Restaurant patronage tripled during this decade (Kyvig 2004, 113). The marketing of prepared, processed, and ready-to-eat foods also made an impact on the homemaker's experience. From 1914 to 1925, for example, bakery production rose 60 percent (Best 2003, 18). Similarly, the number of delicatessens went up by 40 percent from 1910 to 1920 (Best 2003, 18). Indeed, many of today's familiar merchandise brands got their start during the 1920s: Quaker Oats (1921), Wonder Bread (1921), Wheaties (1924), Rice Krispies (1928), and Peter Pan peanut butter (1928). It was at this point that brand-name recognition

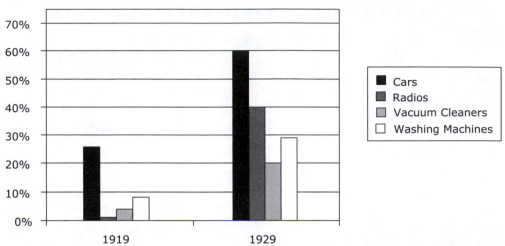

Figure 2.2 *American Ownership of Home Appliances, 1919–1929.* Source: *Adapted from Friedman 2004, 195.*

started to become a more important consideration in American retail. Even with increased reliance upon ready-to-eat foods, America's homemakers were still left with a lot of housework to perform.

For that reason, during the period following the war, industrial and military suppliers began to turn their attention to the American family and its needs. Companies like Westinghouse and General Electric began to develop merchandise for use in the home, such as kitchen appliances. These new durable goods could be marketed as aids to the American homemaker. Consequently, the decade brought a selection of new or refined modern conveniences and labor-saving devices, including washing machines, electric irons, telephones, refrigerators, fans, pop-up toasters, sewing machines, radios, and vacuum cleaners. As refrigerators and freezers were introduced to America's kitchens, perishable foods could be maintained in stores and, eventually, in home. For example, Popsicles, Good Humor bars, Klondike bars, and Eskimo Pies appeared during this decade.

Overall, both the trends in food preparation and the changes in the average American diet reflected changes in thinking about domestic life. During the 1920s, the nation's people ate less wheat and corn than during previous decades. They increased their consumption of sugar, fresh produce, and dairy products (Carter 1977, 125). Soda fountains grew in popularity and these establishments provided, among other things, an alternative to bars during Prohibition. Soft drink sales soared, increasing from 175 million cases in 1920 to 273 million cases in 1929 (Drowne and Huber 2004, 139). Americans consumed considerably more packaged and prepared foods, learned to rely upon convenience foods, and dined out more than ever before.

AUTOMOBILITY

Americans Hit the Roads

It is difficult to overstate the impact automobile travel had on American culture during the 1920s. Everything from skirt lengths to building placements reflected the frequency with which the nation's people were motoring about in automobiles. For many families, the expense of an automobile represented the household's spending—or overspending—for leisure. As William Ashdown remarked in a June 1925 piece for the *Atlantic Monthly,* "Confessions of an Automobilist," "The habit of thrift can never be acquired through so wasteful a medium as an automobile. Instead, the habit of spending must be acquired, for with the constant demand for fuel, oil, and repairs, together with the heavy depreciation, the automobile stands unique as the most extravagant piece of machinery ever devised for the pleasure of man" (quoted in Mowry 1963, 50–51). While automobiles had practical applications, their use was still chiefly recreational.

Advertisement showing a side view of a Ford sedan with four passengers and a woman getting in on the driver's side, 1923. (Library of Congress)

Table 2.3. Vehicle Registrations (Passenger Cars and Trucks) in the United States, 1919–1928

Year	Cars	Trucks
1919	6,771,174	794,372
1920	8,225,589	1,006,082
1921	9,346,195	1,118,520
1922	10,864,128	1,375,725
1923	13,479,608	1,612,569
1924	15,460,649	2,134,724
1925	17,512,638	2,441,724
1926	19,237,171	2,764,222
1927	20,230,429	2,896,886
1928	21,630,000	3,120,000

Source: Adapted from Wolman 1929, 59.

Popularity of Auto Ownership

As automobiles became less expensive to own and consumer credit became more readily available, Americans became car owners. At the beginning of the 1920s, there were only 8 million automobiles on the road. By decade's end, that number rose to 23 million (Drowne and Huber 2004, 248). Not only were automobiles a status purchase, they were increasingly being deemed a necessity of modern life. In an April 12, 1921, address, President Warren G. Harding told Congress "the motorcar has become an indispensable instrument in our political, social, and industrial life" (Flink 1975, 140). Sometimes this view involved considerable sacrifice, as William Ashdown pointed out: "Many families live on the brink of danger all the time. They are car-poor. Saving is impossible. The joy of security in the future is sacrificed for the pleasure of the moment. And with the pleasure of the moment is mingled the constant anxiety entailed by living beyond one's means" (quoted in Mowry 1963, 48). Not only was initial outlay of a car purchase difficult for some families, but also the cost of fuel, maintenance, repairs, and improvements made the burden even greater than many foresaw. The 1920s saw the invention of such auto extras as safety glass, balloon tires, automatic starters, and car radios. It seemed that there were always features of one's vehicle to fix or improve, and all at a cost.

"Ride Now, Pay Later": Purchasing on the Installment Plan

Even though automobiles were becoming more affordable, they remained beyond the reach of many of the nation's consumers until consumer credit became prevalent. Henry Ford had extended the market for automobiles by offering low-end vehicles without such "extras" as a choice of color. This approach helped control cost; the Model T retailed at $310 in 1921. Still the cost of automobile ownership remained substantial. Once Americans met their obligations for rent and insurance, approximately one out of five dollars they spent was devoted to paying off automobiles (Miller 2003, 174). General Motors built on Ford's success in making these products available to a wider segment of the nation's people by offering installment plans to their customers. The first installment finance corporation was the General Motors Acceptance Corporation (GMAC) in 1919. By 1929, there were 1,000 such companies in operation within the United States (Olney 1991, 109).

Installment buying was pioneered by automobile dealerships that used slogans involving wordplay, such as "Let us feather your nest with a little down" (Leinwand 2001, 36). Through such an arrangement, dealers sold retail contracts to a finance company to which consumers would make regular payments until the item was paid in full. For the car manufacturers, installment credit helped soften the effects of the industry's overproduction because it generated more eligible buyers. For dealers, installment plans took some of the pressure off their contact with customers because the finance companies followed through with payments. For customers, the benefit was the ability to use and enjoy an item even though they did not have sufficient resources to purchase it with cash. Customers would pay a percentage of the item's cost in cash as a down payment on the purchase. Such payments' percentages depended upon the total cost of the merchandise. In 1925, down payments on radios and phonographs were typically 25 percent, and appliances such as sewing machines and washing machines required 10 percent down. The highest down payments were demanded for automobiles, with percentages ranging from 30 to 40 percent depending upon whether the auto was new or used (Olney 1991, 113).

Historian Martha Olney provides a good example of how installment buying worked. She describes a used car with a price of $670 in 1931 that might require an initial outlay of $150. If the customer had a trade-in vehicle with a value of $100, that would leave a balance of $420. To this balance, finance charges and an insurance premium would be added, resulting in a total of $487. The buyer might then have this cost spread out across 10 monthly payments (Olney 1991, 110).

Owing to Own in America

Payment plans for vehicles became extremely popular with America's consumers, which resulted in sharp increases for automobile purchases. As the decade opened, just one in three households had a car. By 1930, four in every five American families owned an automobile (Kyvig 2004, 27). Between 60 and

70 percent of these vehicles were purchased through installment credit (Friedman 2004, 197). The upward trend in installment buying represented a change in both practice and outlook. Once freed from the belief that only cash purchases were honorable, Americans began to purchase a variety of items besides vehicles using installment credit. During the years from 1919 to 1929, consumer nonfarm credit more than doubled (Streissguth 2001, 34). By 1927, consumer debt reached approximately three billion dollars (Miller 2003, 152). Household borrowing became less stigmatized as America shifted from a culture of thrift and saving to a consumerist outlook of "buy now, pay later." Although installment buying began with the car industry, it became a popular way to purchase a variety of durable goods. Combined with postwar production, availability and acceptability of consumer credit helped clear the path for a culture of consumption in America.

Investments in Road Infrastructure

As more Americans took to the road in automobiles, road improvements and expansions became necessary. The surfaces used for horse-powered transportation no longer sufficed for the growing vehicular traffic. Gasoline and paving companies, among others, lobbied the government to extend and refine the network of all-weather streets available to America's motorists. Consequently, during the 1920s, state and government spending on road improvements was considerable. The Federal Highways Act of 1916 had already taken steps toward creating a network of hardtop roadways. The Federal Highway Act of 1921 went further, linking the nation with 10,000 miles of highway. Cities of 50,000 residents or more were linked with paved roads; gas taxes garnered each state's share of the contributing costs (Miller 2003, 190). In 1925, Route 66, "the Main Street of America," opened, providing 2,000 continuous miles of road between Chicago and Los Angeles. U.S. Highway 20 carried motorists between Massachusetts and Oregon. Other innovations, such as the Holland Tunnel, which opened in 1929 and connected New Jersey and Manhattan, made it easier to reach some destinations. Such road improvements, highway networks, and connectors made it more possible and pleasant to traverse the country by automobile.

As the interest in car travel grew, so did the number and variety of roadside services available in the United States. It was during the 1920s that many of the modern conveniences for motorists sprang up along highways and major roads. These new businesses catering to motorists included diners, hamburger stands, and drive-in restaurants. The Pig Stand in Dallas–Ft. Worth, Texas, which opened in 1921, claimed to be the first drive-in restaurant. During the same year, White Castle restaurant appeared in Wichita, Kansas, selling sacks of hamburger sandwiches for diners on the go. During the 1920s, filling stations also proliferated. The number of gas stations in America went from 12,000 in 1921 to 143,000 in 1929 (Drowne and Huber 2004, 247).

Once drivers became comfortable with the idea of trips of longer durations, roadside services started to include more conveniently located and affordably priced lodgings. Examples of such facilities included auto camps, cabin camps, and motels ("motor hotels"). The first motel appeared in San Luis Obispo, California, in 1925. By 1926, there were about 2,000 motels in America, many of which were located in popular 1920s recreation destinations such as Florida and the American West (Green 1992, 199). Motels became popular because they were less costly than hotels, and guests could park right outside the rooms where they would be staying while on the road.

Social Life Speeds up in a Car Culture

The mobility created by automobiles and an increasingly national road system helped change how Americans lived. For one thing, Americans and the regions they inhabited became better and more widely connected. The 1920s introduced the concept of the suburbs, with residents commuting to work by automobile. It was also the point at which bus transportation of school-age children became more feasible. In 1922, Morris Markin founded the Checker Cab Manufacturing Company in Kalamazoo, Michigan, and hired rides by cab became available in America's larger communities. The following year, the Hertz Drive-Ur-Self Company (later Hertz Rent-a-Car) took shape, creating the option of renting automobiles for private use. Sunday drives, road trips, and family vacations also became common during this period. All of these developments helped increase the freedom of movement Americans enjoyed.

With geographic mobility came a measure of independence. Youth, in particular, enjoyed new liberties both as drivers and passengers. With the use of cars, they could escape the scrutiny of parents and other sources of supervision. In terms of courtship rituals, parlor visits yielded to unsupervised dates often conducted with cars. During the 1920s, closed cars—those enclosed with roofs and windows—became standard, affording additional privacy to an automobile's occupants. In some cases, this meant parking, lovers' lanes, and petting, forms of physical intimacy that would not have as easily been negotiated during the prior period, when suitors paid calls to the homes of young women they fancied. Observers of the time, even those who applauded the geographic liberty cars afforded young people, fretted over the impact of such changes on morality. Such was the ambivalence of Lydia Lion Roberts in March 1926 when she wrote in the publication *American Cookery,* "Blessed be the automobile and the radio which have taken the women into the outside world and brought the world into the home. These two blessings have also brought their problems that are being earnestly discussed. What about . . . the new trio—the boy, the girl, and the automobile?" (quoted in Rose 2004, 410). Some social customs, such as courtship, would be changed forever by car culture. No one knew what all the attendant consequences of such a transformation might be, but they had reason for concern.

The increase in motor travel also had an impact on the experience of community in the United States. Americans traveled, relocated, and commuted more than had been typical in the past. As a consequence, residents of towns, cities, and suburbs became more isolated from one another. Even in places where families had lived in the same homes for generations, a greater number of community members—especially the young—no longer identified with the people who lived beside them. It became both more common and more socially acceptable for neighbors to be strangers to one another (Flink 1975, 157).

Roadside Attractions

In an era when fewer potential customers conducted all their travel on foot or by horse, the methods for engaging consumers with signage and other advertising needed to take into consideration the rate at which buses and other vehicles were moving through environments and past business establishments seeking their patronage. The 1920s introduced to the United States a variety of techniques for capturing the public's attention, from neon signs to skywriting. For example, a visitor to New York's Times Square, Broadway, or 42nd Street in 1927 was greeted with an overwhelming presentation of some $10 million worth of electric signs and billboards (Leinwand 2001, 263). While these strategies worked for urban dwellers and other consumers who daily spent time in densely populated areas, different approaches became necessary to address audiences between and beyond the nation's major cities and towns. With the increase in automobile travel and the development of a national network of paved roads during the 1920s, changes became visible along America's highways: novelty architecture and billboard advertising. These new visual elements were designed to catch the eye and hold the attention of passersby. While en route to their destinations, motorists and their passengers could glance over at a billboard or novelty building and get an immediate sense of the message it offered. For that reason, the scale of these structures had to be oversized, such as sandwich stands shaped like giant hotdogs. Similarly, to appeal to auto culture, a billboard's graphics and print needed to register quickly in the minds of viewers.

The classic example of such a roadside strategy came from the Burma-Vita Company in 1925. To promote Burma-Shave shaving cream in Minnesota, the company presented a billboard series designed to be viewed as a sequence. These signs were arranged in such a way that they could be read in their entirety from a moving vehicle. Each board featured a line of copy offered in the form of a poem: "A peach looks great / with a lot of fuzz / but man's no peach / and never was / Burma-Shave" (Miller 2003, 191). This approach was so successful in

A bulldog-shaped restaurant, Los Angeles, ca. 1920s. Novelty architecture made advertisements of commercial buildings, drawing the attention of potential customers. (Bettmann/Corbis)

generating publicity for the product that the campaign was repeated elsewhere. Roadside advertising had to match the excitement and momentum of motorized travel.

Breakdowns and Crack-Ups on the Open Road

During the 1920s, rates of automobile ownership tripled (Kyvig 2004, 27). As America acquired what historian James J. Flink called a "car culture," there was a price to pay for the freedom, mobility, and independence automobiles provided. With more automobiles on the roads, many of them operated by new drivers, motoring was something of a dangerous proposition. By 1923, the first traffic signal light appeared in New York City, a gesture toward automating the movement of automobile traffic (Miller 2003, 173). In 1927, Massachusetts became the first state to require automobile insurance to address the costs of collisions and injuries. In 1928, the first traffic circle and cloverleaf were set in place to help avert road accidents. Traffic jams, parking problems, refueling costs, insurance premiums, and auto repairs all became part of modern American life.

Table 2.4. Motor Vehicle Fatalities in the United States, 1920–1930

Year	Number of Fatalities
1920	12,500
1921	13,900
1922	15,300
1923	18,400
1924	19,400
1925	21,900
1926	23,400
1927	25,800
1928	28,000
1929	31,200
1930	32,900

Source: Adapted from Wattenberg 1976, 720 and Gregory 1995, 135.

Not only did automobility change the American way of life, it also had an impact on the American way of death. As more cars took to the roads, traffic increased, accidents became more frequent, and automobile-related deaths were more numerous. America went from 12,500 automobile fatalities in 1920 to 32,900 in 1930 (Wattenberg 1976, 720: Gregory 1995, 135; Miller 2003, 173). While automobiles had contributed in many ways to the quality of ordinary life in the United States, they nonetheless posed new road risks for drivers, passengers, and pedestrians.

TOURISM: THE NATION LEARNS TO VACATION

Family Vacations

In a board game named "Touring" marketed in the United States during the 1920s, players pretended they were taking a road trip. Game play involved many of the experiences awaiting the era's travelers, such as running out of gas or having a flat tire (Giordano 2003, 64). As the game's theme suggests, Americans were taking to the roads in unprecedented numbers. During the 1920s, tourism became a popular pastime for a greater percentage of the American public. The number of Americans who could take family vacations increased, and the tourism industry grew dramatically during this time. More salaried workers than ever were provided with two weeks of paid vacation each year, and while few members of the working class enjoyed that privilege, a growing number were permitted to take unpaid time away from work without penalty or job loss upon their return.

Auto Camping

In increasing numbers, the nation's population embarked on vacations that involved overnight stays. For these trips, car travel began to compete with rail travel. Auto camping had several features travel by rail lacked. Travel by car freed cross-country tourists from the timetables and routes prescribed by railroads. Auto travel also permitted stops at will, sightseeing as desired, and un-

Al Capone's Custom Automobile

Although most social historians focus on the 1920s' newly affordable vehicles such as the Ford Model T, there were also more extravagant automobiles on the market. Upscale cars included Packard, Pierce-Arrow, Nash, Hudson, Stanley, DeSoto, and Reo. None, however, could rival the lore surrounding the custom automobiles of gangster Al Capone. Their features are still written about, and collectors long for a glimpse of one of Capone's famous vehicles.

Cars were important tools for pick-ups, getaways, and other clandestine maneuvers in the gangster's occupation. Attacks on rival gangs and confrontations with the authorities often took place while crime figures were securely positioned within their vehicles. Therefore, it was desirable to have automobiles well suited to such situations.

Although there is some ambiguity about how many customized cars actually belonged to Al Capone, it is clear that he favored Cadillacs. A 1928 Cadillac prepared for Capone was rumored to be equipped with a speed capacity of 120 mph, 3,000 pounds of bulletproofing, a regulation police siren, and the first private installation of a police band receiver. It was also painted in the colors traditionally used by police vehicles. Of Capone's 1920 V-16 Cadillac, it is said that the owner's specifications included bullet-proof glass, portholes through which occupants might place their weapons, dent-free fenders, combination locks for security, floor openings through which one could drop roofing nails to foil vehicles in pursuit, and a mechanism in the exhaust system that permitted the car to emit a smokescreen for the same purpose.

While it is difficult to sort fact from fiction when it comes to the provenance and special features of these custom automobiles, it is clear that Capone's cars were outfitted in ways few other American consumers might require.

planned changes in itinerary. Travelers in an automobile could also select more scenic routes than typified the day's train travel. In addition, motor camping provided an alternative to restaurant meals and hotel stays while on the road. During 1922, for instance, only 1,500 of the 51,000 visitors to Yosemite National Park stayed in hotels (Aron 1999, 211). Beyond being costly, hotels, like trains, ran on schedules and routines of their own, further constraining the traveler. Furthermore, hotel staff customarily received gratuities for their services, depleting the traveler's budget. Auto campers kept their own hours, cooked their own meals, slept in their own tents, and controlled their travel costs.

Auto camping began informally, with impromptu camps set up wherever motor tourists decided to pause in their travels. Tents placed adjoining or nearby the parked automobile housed travelers overnight. This camping technique, sometimes called "gypsying," appealed to individualists who wished to come and go as they pleased. This method of auto camping was the chief one up

Lake Public Auto Camp Party, probably in or near Yellowstone Park, 1923. During the 1920s, the enthusiasm for automobiles and the growth in tourism combined to produce a new approach to vacationing, in which travelers lodged at roadside auto camps as they motored across the country. (Library of Congress)

until 1920. By the 1920s, motor tourists started to enjoy the option of established municipal camps, arranged and outfitted for the purpose. The first such location was opened in Waterloo, Wisconsin, in 1920 (Jakle 1985, 158). Such camps offered the companionship of fellow tourists as well as a range of conveniences, sometimes including drinking water, electricity, showers, restrooms, laundry tubs, and cooking facilities in a central kitchen. By 1925, there were more regulations in place to protect families of campers, and fees became usual for use of the sites. These public camps would in turn give way to slightly more formal accommodations, such as cabin camps, at which guests could find ready-made shelter and could rent such items as bed linens and mattresses. Cabin camps were especially popular in the American Southwest. In time, roadside camps would be replaced by motor courts and trailer parks, where motorists could park their vehicles on stopovers along a journey. By decade's end, tourists were improvising to develop campers on wheels or house trailers.

Popular Destinations: Santa Fe and the American West

This trend toward recreational tourism, when combined with the affordability of car travel, resulted in a rise in the number of family vacations conducted via automobile trips. The auto made it easier for vacationers to explore the country beyond the portion already accessible through rail travel.

Some vacation options enabled tourists to combine both rail and auto travel, such as the vacation packages offered for visitors to Santa Fe, New Mexico. Since 1878, the Atchison, Topeka and Santa Fe Railway Company had been transporting passengers to the American Southwest. For as many years, rail hotels, located conveniently along the railroad corridor, accommodated rail travelers. Rail service and hotels along the route helped to make locations such as Santa Fe popular leisure destinations for American vacationers. Cashing in on curiosity about Indian culture, merchants and other business owners provided tourists with entertaining but safe encounters with another way of life.

During the 1920s, riders of the Atchison, Topeka, and Santa Fe Railroad could extend the reach of the railroad by engaging ground services such as those available through the Harvey Company. With the help of Harvey's "Indian Detours," visitors to Santa Fe could participate in road tours lasting up to three days. The concept of a "detour" implied a departure from the standard tourist fare. The Harvey Company touted their trips as ventures "off the beaten path" of tourism. Escorted by Harvey guides, known as Indian Detour Couriers, Santa Fe visitors could observe what purported to be authentic Native American dances and rituals. Other companies provided similar experiences for tourists. Koshare Tours, founded in 1921, was acquired by Atchison, Topeka, and Santa Fe Rail Company in 1926, which made the partnership of rail and road travel complete.

In addition to expenditures on transportation, lodging, and tours, visitors contributed in other ways to the local economy. They often purchased trinkets that were manufactured as inexpensive versions of Native American arts and crafts. Sales of such merchandise spiked during the late 1920s, when both authentic Pueblo artifacts and affordable replicas became souvenirs for visitors to Santa Fe.

The commercialization of the region and its indigenous populations led to distorted perceptions of the American Southwest. Companies catering to tourists packaged the experience and gave middle-class visitors a nonthreatening version of Pueblo history and life. Furthermore, within such prefabricated vacations, the influences of Spanish and Mexican cultures either went unremarked or appeared in stereotypical fashion. While purporting to introduce visitors to the area's history and people, such tourist entertainments not only appropriated the area's cultural traditions but also threatened them. As culture critic Dean Mac-Cannell notes, "None of what is called 'traditional' can be anything but grave markers for tradition" (quoted in Norris 1994, 176).

However misleading such ideas about the region and its culture might be, Santa Fe emerged as one of the nation's creative centers. Santa Fe's population effectively doubled during the period from 1916 to 1930 (Tobias and Woodhouse 2001, 105). It became a haven for creative people such as poet Witter Bynner and essayist/novelist Mary Austin. Others, such as author Willa Cather, made frequent visits to the area.

Table 2.5. Visitors to America's National Parks and Forests, 1919–1930

Year	Visitors to National Parks (thousands)	Visitors to National Forests (thousands)
1919	757	
1920	920	4,833
1921	1007	
1922	1045	
1923	1281	
1924	1424	
1925	1762	15,280
1926	1942	
1927	2381	
1928	2569	
1929	2757	
1930	2775	31,905

Source: "Annual Reports of the National Park Service and Forest Service," as presented in Steiner, 1933. President's Research Committee on Social Trends, Volume 2, "Recreation and Leisure Time Activities," 920.

Popular Destinations: America's National Parks, Monuments, and Forests

The 1920s marked a time of renewed interest in intercity travel. Following the conclusion of World War I, rail travel was restored to its full service levels. In 1920, 1.2 billion Americans purchased rail tickets (Drowne and Huber 2004, 259). Train travel made it possible for Americans to move across the country and reach a variety of destinations in the West. Among these were America's national parks, monuments, and forests. The Great Northern Railway, for instance, connected visitors with Glacier National Park in Washington State. Since 1916, when President Woodrow Wilson created the National Park Service, interest in locations such as Yellowstone (Wyoming), Yosemite (California), Mt. Rainier (Washington), and Grand Canyon (Arizona) was on the rise. Set aside as a national park before the creation of the National Park Service, Yellowstone National Park celebrated its golden anniversary as a national park in 1922. National Parks throughout the nation saw increases in the number of visitors, such as Carlsbad Caverns, which went from 10,904 visitors in 1925 and 1926 to 76,822 visitors in 1928 and 1929 (Rothman 1998, 159). In fact, 1924 brought the first National Conference on Outdoor Recreation, held in Washington, D.C. Overall, visits to America's national parks rose from 198,606 in 1910 to 2.7 million in 1930 (Miller 2003, 174). In addition to national parks, other popular vacation spots included Atlantic City, New Jersey; Niagara Falls, New York; and Palm Springs, Florida.

Popular Destinations: The Nation's Living History Museums

The 1920s also witnessed a movement to create history-related tourism centers, such as living history museums. Living history museums typically consist of districts that combine historic buildings with restored or re-created cultural landscapes to create for visitors the effect of walking into an historical setting. The attempt is to accomplish the sensation of immersion in another era and its way of life, as though a time machine had transported one back through time to another place and another society. In other words, a living history museum's professionals are not content to collect, catalog, and display objects related to the American past. Rather, they seek to provide visitors with insights into what that society might have felt like to its members. Much of this effect relies upon compelling arrangements of physical space and the labors of accomplished interpreters—staff members who assume the roles of members of the historical society evoked by the museum. These first-person informants conduct characteristic work and life activities while interacting with tourists for both dramatic and educational purposes. Living history museums at Colonial Williamsburg, Greenfield Village, and Mystic Seaport and Preservation Shipyard provided another option for vacations and leisure activities during the 1920s.

Colonial Williamsburg Colonial Williamsburg, a site opened to visitors in 1926, is likely the nation's best-known living history museum. As the location name suggests, this attraction offers tourists a restoration of the 18th-century capital of Virginia during the time it was still a British Colony. Colonial Williamsburg covers 301 acres, making it the largest outdoor living history museum in the United States.

The project began as the concept of Bruton Parish Church's Rev. William Goodwin. It would not have proceeded, however, without sponsors. These donors were found through cultivation of interest from John D. Rockefeller and holders of Standard Oil wealth. With such support, it became possible to establish a private concern, the Colonial Williamsburg Foundation. The foundation made possible this rare presentation of an entire town as it might have been found during 1790.

This location may represent the culmination of the Colonial Revival movement that commenced with America's centennial in 1876. A centerpiece of Colonial Williamsburg is the restoration of Carter's Grove plantation. The property includes many structures spared from demolition as well as some reconstructed buildings. For example, in 1988, the Department of African-American Interpretations and Presentations was established. In this way, previously unseen aspects of the built environment, such as slave quarters, were reintroduced at Colonial Williamsburg.

As a living history museum, Williamsburg uses reenactors who are employees attired in period costume and performing functions associated with life in pre-Revolutionary America. The reenactors also interact with visitors through the technique of first-person dramatizations. Such embodiments of social history seek to make the experience of everyday life in Colonial America more immediate and accessible than a conventional museum display might prove. Visitors learn about the realities of daily life for early Americans, including manners, politics, religion, holidays, and family. Information is also available concerning the material world in colonial times, such as animals, gardening, tools, trades, clothing, and food.

Greenfield Village Colonial Williamsburg is not the only living history museum at which Americans receive an invitation to "let the past speak to us." At the Henry Ford Museum and Greenfield Village, visitors are afforded a perspective on American history that is both a heartfelt and curious tribute. The Dearborn, Michigan, attraction was an original concept from American inventor Henry Ford (1863–1947). With something of the reverence Walt Disney would later express for small-town America in his design of such attractions as "Main Street USA" at Disneyland, Ford sought to make Greenfield Village "America's Hometown." The building for what is now the Ford Museum, but was then called the Edison Institute, was dedicated in 1928. Ford's collection includes an unusual array of Americana, including both plainspoken objects and such items as a Revolutionary War camp bed used by George Washington and the Ford Theater balcony chair in which Abraham Lincoln was seated at the time of his assassination.

The 13-acre property around the Ford Museum first opened in 1933 and features reproductions and 80 historical structures. In something of the visual arrangement of a New England village, Ford had arranged a suite of historic districts for visitors to experience. Perhaps predictably, there was a version of Ford's first assembly plant. Because Ford so admired another American inventor, also available were re-creations of Thomas Alva Edison's residence and his Menlo Park, New Jersey, labs. Along with these areas were sites designed to recall the homes of the Wright Brothers, George Washington Carver, Noah Webster, and Robert Frost. Visitors could also see Ford's take on a William Holmes McGuffey School, in tribute to the man behind the popular readers used by American schoolchildren since 1836. Like some other living history museums, Michigan's Greenfield Village seeks to make the American past immediate by surrounding guests with the original buildings and artifacts or accurate reproductions of them.

Mystic Seaport and Historic Shipyard Mystic Seaport is another living history museum that got its start during the 1920s. Also the site of the Museum of America and the Sea, Mystic Seaport functions as a living history environment for the study of maritime lore. This facility, located on the Mystic River in Connecticut and founded in 1929, covers about 17 acres. It houses a collection of some 500 historic seafaring vessels, including the *L. A. Dunton,* the *Joseph Conrad,* and the *Charles Morgan,* the last whaling ship afloat. In the Planetarium, visitors can learn about the role of stars and constellations in water navigation. The on-site museum features artifacts such as scrimshaw and oral histories.

Like its living history counterparts Colonial Williamsburg and Greenfield Village, Mystic Seaport attempts to provide visitors with a first-hand experience of another era in America's history. With a reconstruction of a 19th-century village, Mystic tourists and schoolchildren can enter the era of wooden shipbuilding. Assisting in this process are "role players," or staff members charged with first-person dramatization of life within the historic community.

See America First: The Growth of Tourism

The 1920s became a time of dramatically increased recreational travel and tourism. Shorter work hours, higher incomes, smaller families, and the concept of the weekend all help to create an atmosphere in which vacations came within the reach of more Americans. The affordability and prevalence of automobiles changed the way Americans traveled, including while on holiday. By 1930, over 80 percent of Americans' vacation trips were conducted by car (Aron 1999, 204). Auto camps and cabin camps began to punctuate America's highways, providing free or modestly priced accommodations during multiple-day road trips. It was during this decade that automobile travel of all sorts produced a whole set of roadside business establishments. These businesses helped motorists meet daily needs while on the road and continue on their way in an efficient manner. Family vacation travel involved such popular destinations as national parks, seaside resorts, and living history museums. In general, then, tourism grew as an industry and America's families came to plan on travel as a part of their annual routines. The roads became more hospitable to all motorists, which make the distance between residences, attractions, business establishments, or even coasts seem less formidable.

VAMPS AND SHEIKS:
AMERICANS AT THE MOVIES

The Rise of Film Studios

Early motion pictures played an important role within the imaginative lives of ordinary Americans. Films presented audiences with spectacles, but more importantly, they fueled viewer fantasies of a life beyond everyday routine. A writer in the *Saturday Evening Post* characterized the experience in this way: "Before you know it you are living the story—laughing, loving, hating, struggling, winning. All the adventure, all the romance, all the excitement you lack

Table 2.6. Admissions to Spectator Amusements, 1921–1929 (millions of dollars)

Year	Movies	Other Theaters	Spectator Sports
1921	301	81	30
1923	336	146	46
1925	367	174	47
1927	526	195	48
1929	720	127	66

Source: Adapted from Streissguth 2001, 297.

in your daily life are in the Pictures. They take you completely out of yourself into a wonderful new world" (Giordano 2003, 67–68).

When the decade opened, motion pictures represented the fifth largest industry in the nation (Goldberg 2003, 20). The success of film had already hurt the businesses of live theater and vaudeville. Although some films were still being made elsewhere, during the 1920s California established itself as the center for filmmaking. The movie industry was dominated by a handful of studios, sometimes known as the "big five": RKO Pictures, Paramount, Fox Films, Warner Brothers, and Metro-Goldwyn-Mayer. These studios produced most of the films made during the 1920s, and the output was considerable. Film studios operated like movie factories, averaging 500 films each year during the 1920s. The studios also owned and controlled approximately half of the first-run movie theaters, resulting in a monopoly of sorts. Screen stars entered contracts with studios, and the studios that contracted for their services controlled the professional lives—and to an extent the private lives—of their talent. Hollywood became the hub for the era's film industry, and the star system began to make film actors and actresses famous.

Silent film actor Rudolph Valentino. Although Valentino played a variety of exotic male leads in romances for the silent screen, his most memorable character may have been the Sheik. (Library of Congress)

Rudolph Valentino, touted as "the Great Lover," was one of many matinee idols launched by American motion pictures. When he died prematurely and at the height of his fame, the tabloids had a heyday. The August 23, 1926, issue of the New York *Daily News* proclaimed

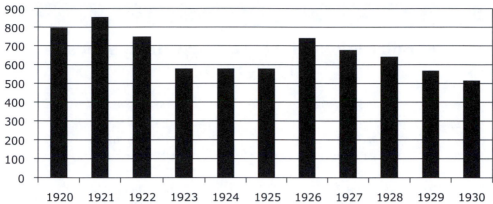

Figure 2.3 *Number of U.S. Motion Pictures Released, 1920–1930.* Source: *Adapted from Steinberg 1980, 42.*

that "the Great Director today stood ready to call Rudolph Valentino off the screen of life" (Andrist 1987, 165). Not to be outdone, a reporter for the New York *Evening Graphic* went to Campbell's Funeral Church where Valentino's remains were to be prepared for burial. While there, he posed in a coffin for a photograph, over which the paper superimposed a file picture of Valentino's head. It was published before Valentino's body could arrive at the funeral parlor (Andrist 1987, 165). Valentino's viewing was managed with a bronze-lidded coffin which rendered only his face visible, largely to deter fans seeking souvenirs. The whole response to Valentino's death was a pageant itself worthy of the screen.

The Golden Age of Silent Films

As the 1920s opened, movies were already a popular entertainment. It was the era of silent films, which often featured performers who had gotten their start in the previous era's forms of theatrical performance, rich with traditions of burlesque and variety entertainment. Numerous performers in the 1920s began in vaudeville, including singer Eddie Cantor, humorist Will Rogers, and comedian W. C. Fields. Some entertainers were more successful than others in making the transition from the stage to the screen, such as the Marx Brothers and the Three Stooges. In particular, the 1920s represented the classic era of silent comedy, including such films as Harold Lloyd's *Safety Last* (1923), Charlie Chaplin's *The Gold Rush* (1925), and Buster Keaton's *The General* (1926).

During the 1920s, attending a film often meant an experience that blended filmed entertainment with live performance. Live instruments often provided musical accompaniment to the stories told by silent films. Most frequently, this musical score came from an organ situated within the theater, such as the "Mighty

Popular Silent Movies in the United States, 1920–1929

Year	Popular Silent Films	Year	Popular Silent Films
1920	The Flapper	1925	The Charmer
	The Kid		The Gold Rush
	The Last of the Mohicans		Little Annie Rooney
	Pollyanna		The Merry Widow
	Polly with a Past		The Phantom of
	Treasure Island		the Opera
1921	Disraeli		Stella Dallas
	The Four Horsemen of	1926	Beau Geste
	the Apocalypse		Ben-Hur
	Little Lord Fauntleroy		The Black Pirate
	The Lotus Eater		Let's Get Married
	The Queen of Sheba		Son of the Sheik
	The Sheik		Sparrow
1922	Blood and Sand	1927	Flesh and the Devil
	Foolish Wives		It
	The Prisoner of Zenda		The King of Kings
	Robin Hood		Seventh Heaven
	Tess of the Storm		Sunrise
	Country		Wings
	The Young Rajah	1928	Abie's Irish Rose
1923	Bluebeard's Eighth Wife		Excess Baggage
	The Covered Wagon		Just Married
	Down to the Sea in Ships		Last Command
	The Hunchback of		Laugh, Clown,
	Notre Dame		Laugh
	The Ten Commandments		The Wind
	The Trail of the	1929	Bulldog Drummond
	Lonesome Pine		Disraeli
1924	Abraham Lincoln		The Kiss
	Forbidden Pleasure		West of Zanzibar
	Manhandled		Why Be Good
	Monsieur Beaucaire		Wild Orchid
	The Sea Hawk		
	The Thief of Bagdad		

Wurlitzer" at the Paramount Theater in Seattle, Washington. In between film presentations, audiences might see vaudeville acts or other live performances.

By 1922, weekly ticket sales topped 40 million, and that figure would more than double by the decade's end (Time-Life 1998, 80). Screen comedy favorites such as Harold Lloyd, Buster Keaton, and Charlie Chaplin delighted viewers with everything from physical comedy to social satire. Comedy was not the only form of silent film to flourish during the 1920s. Other popular pictures were such genre films as romances, mysteries, westerns, and adventures.

The 1920s witnessed such growth in movie ticket sales that entertainment entrepreneurs began to build movie palaces, exceptionally large venues that seated 1,500 or more audience members. Many of these theaters were decorated in elaborate fashion and often featured classical themes. For example, Grauman's Egyptian Theatre, which opened in 1922 and had a capacity of 1,760 seats, was designed to capitalize on the Egyptian craze surrounding the discovery of King Tut's tomb earlier that year.

Then as now, entertainment businesses relied upon the sales of refreshments and other concessions to supplement income from ticket sales. Many of the candies now associated with concession stands made their first appearances during the 1920s: Life Savers (1920), Oh Henry bars (1920), Jujyfruits (1920), Chuckles (1921), Bit-O-Honey (1924), and Twizzler's licorice (1928).

The Rise of Picture Palaces

As the motion picture industry grew, new theaters appeared across the country to display films to an eager public. Film production was brisk, with studios producing many more films each year than they do today. During the 1920s, the majority of movie theaters offered different films daily (Solomon 1980, 5). By 1927, more than 20,000 theaters operated in the United States. This was the decade during which air conditioning began to be featured within movie theaters, adding to the appeal of theater-going when the mercury outside climbed.

The 1920s was also the time during which many of the nation's historic movie theaters opened their doors. Approximately 500 of the new motion picture houses built during the 1920s were elaborate, high-capacity facilities costing more than one million dollars each (Solomon 1980, 5). Most were located in major cities, such as the Fox Theater in Atlanta, Georgia, and the Oriental Theater in Chicago, Illinois. These picture palaces brought luxury to film viewers, including live dancers and musical accompaniment to the feature films. Movie palaces were designed to dazzle audiences with elegance and extravagance. Writing in a March 1929 article for *The New Republic,* commentator Lloyd Lewis described the effect on a woman viewer in this way: "When she goes home that evening, she will perhaps clean spinach and peel onions, but for a few hours, attendants bow to her, doormen tip their hats, and a maid curtsies for her in the ladies' washroom. She bathes in elegance and dignity; she satisfies her yearning for a 'cultured' atmosphere. Even the hush that hangs over the lobbies means refinement to her: voices that have been raucous on the street drop as they drop upon entering a church. . . ." (Lewis 1929, quoted in Mowry 1963, 58–59). The experience of movie-going became a carefully scripted escape from daily life's drudgeries, and everything about the theaters of this era had been designed to enhance and sustain the opulent illusion.

The largest and perhaps the most celebrated of America's movie palaces was Samuel Lionel "Roxy" Rothafel's Roxy Theater in New York. When it was built in 1927, the Roxy cost $10,000,000 and seated 6,200. In fact, the Roxy Theater in New York was advertised in newspapers and magazines as the "Cathedral of the Motion Picture." Not only was the Roxy large and ornate, it also provided an unsurpassed standard of entertainment. It was equipped with an enormous pipe organ, a 100-voice chorus, 50 ballet dancers, and the largest permanent symphony orchestra anywhere. Its entire staff, including its theater attendants, was "drilled" in their duties by a retired Marine colonel. The grand opening of the Roxy was a major media event, attended by screen stars and other celebrities dressed in their finery. The first film shown at the Roxy was a Gloria Swanson and John Boles picture for United Artists, *The Love(s) of Sunya*.

Rothafel was far from the only impresario behind the construction of 1920s motion picture theaters. Sid Grauman was widely considered the era's master showman. Before the 1920s had even begun, Grauman had begun building impressive movie houses, such as the Million Dollar Theater, which had a 2,345-seat-capacity and opened in 1918 in Los Angeles, California. During the 1920s, Grauman added to his empire with two major palaces located on Hollywood Boulevard. The Egyptian Theatre, with 1,760 seats, opened its doors in 1922. It played host to the industry's first premiere party for Douglas Fairbanks in *Robin Hood* (1922). Grauman's Chinese Theater opened in 1927 and seated 2,258 patrons. Here, in the cement in front of Grauman's Chinese, the theater owner would invite Hollywood stars to place their footprints and handprints, starting with screen favorites Mary Pickford and Douglas Fairbanks on April 30, 1927.

Movies Widen the Viewer's World, Threaten Morality

During the early years, motion pictures were often deemed a potentially bad influence on the public, especially on the young, both in terms of the content of films and the experience of sharing a darkened theater with strangers. Films did not need to be especially lurid to excite such controversy. Even with standard movie-going fare, viewers took some of their social cues from what they saw on screen, including tips derived from watching love scenes. A generation of

America's youth imitated screen fashions and mannerisms. This was the beginning of America's fascination with film's celebrity culture, including magazines such as *Motion Picture, Photoplay,* and *Screenland.* Fans followed the publicity for their favorite stars, experienced the glamour of Hollywood vicariously, and incorporated elements of makeup, apparel, or speech in their own lives. In addition, many young viewers experimented with wooing and petting techniques demonstrated for them on film. Surveys taken in the nation's high schools suggested that the students themselves assigned some blame to immoral movies for inducing young people to do "what they should not do." Whether for good or for ill, the films were serving an instructional role. As historian Robert Sklar noted, "At the movies one could still learn how proper, wellborn, old Americans behaved, and also—what genteel culture never taught—how they misbehaved" (Sklar 1970, 18). In the movies, audiences witnessed images of a changing culture, in which the youth of America rebelled against the customs and traditions of the previous generation.

Flapper Culture, On the Screen and Off

The quintessential figure of youth rebellion during the 1920s was the flapper. Motion pictures about flappers abounded. As long as there were movie theaters accessible to them, even young people residing in the most remote or provincial areas of the country could watch the exploits of flappers and their male companions. Flappers were unruly young women who sought through their attire, outlook, and life choices to signal their refusal of their parents' values and expectations. Such women wore short skirts, bobbed their hair, used makeup, danced, drank, smoked, flirted, listened to jazz, and kept company with young men without the benefit of chaperons. With every turn, they showed a flagrant disregard for the mores and morality of mainstream America.

Although no one is certain who originated the term "flapper," it is plausible that cultural observer H. L. Mencken coined it in one of his essays in *The Smart Set* (1915). The image of the flapper pervaded popular culture, including motion pictures. For example, Louise Brooks played a flapper in *A Social Celebrity* (1926) and Clara Bow appeared as a flapper in *The Plastic Age* (1925). Psychologist G. Stanley Hall defended the flapper in a 1927 piece for *Atlantic Monthly,* proclaiming that "never since civilization began has the girl in the early teens seemed so self-sufficient and sure of herself, or made such a break with the rigid traditions of propriety and convention which have hedged her in. . . . Let us hope that she is really more innocent and healthier of mind and body because she knows and does earlier so much that was once admissible only later, if at all" (quoted in Rose 2004, 390). By 1927, however, the flapper trend had subsided. The youthful rebellion of the flapper had become co-opted, and even the Sears, Roebuck catalogue featured "flapper fashions" for girls and women.

During the 1920s, elegant motion picture theaters took the place of the old nickelodeons. While it took some time for America's theaters to catch up with film's new sound technology, by the end of the 1920s it became clear that talkies were here to stay. (National Archives)

Long after the flapper receded, however, films would continue to be held morally suspect. Critics of movie morality saw through the now-familiar ploy in which film characters would spend the bulk of the film committing misdeeds only to be set right at the film's end (Kyvig 2004, 93). Both within and beyond the film industry, concerned Americans called for restraint in film depictions of misconduct. By 1927, in an effort to clean up America's movies, Will H. Hays, working on behalf of the Motion Pictures Producers and Distributors Association, issued moral guidelines for Hollywood productions. These guidelines consisted of lists of "be carefuls" and "don'ts" to be heeded by filmmakers. In 1930, the Motion Pictures Producers and Distributors Association adopted the Hays Code. Although this code had many specific guidelines, it sought to uphold three general principles. First, "No picture shall be produced that will lower the moral standards of those who see it. Hence the sympathy of the audience should never be thrown to the side of crime, wrongdoing, evil, or sin." Second, "Correct standards of life, subject only to the requirements of drama and entertainment, shall be presented." Finally, "Law, natural or human, shall not be ridiculed, nor shall sympathy be created for its violation." It was not until the mid-1930s that the Hays Code, also known as the Production Code, found enforcement. Under the auspices of the Production Code Administration, United States films were reviewed and issued certificates of approval prior to release. For the most part, the film industry cooperated with this form of regulation to demonstrate good faith with concerned members of the American public. In the face of 1920s scandals involving figures from the film business, such as the Fatty Arbuckle murder trial, Hollywood studio executives may have felt they had little high ground on which to stand in opposition to the restrictions made by the Hays Office.

The Arrival of Talkies

Although the motion picture itself was still fairly new, technological developments achieved during the 1920s helped develop and refine the medium. During the

Fatty Arbuckle Scandal

As if there weren't enough concerns about the moral impact of motion pictures on American youth, along came the trial of one of silent comedy's giants, Roscoe Conkling "Fatty" Arbuckle. Initially, Arbuckle was a comic actor for Keystone Film Company, and he later worked for Paramount. He was a large man who played big characters for the screen, but it was his true-life misadventures that earned Arbuckle lasting public notoriety.

Arbuckle was known for his tendency toward self-indulgence. On one such occasion in 1921, he attended a party at the St. Francis Hotel in San Francisco, California. At that gathering, a female guest, Virginia Rappé, drew Arbuckle's attention. She was a young actress with whom he interacted that night, but accounts vary about the nature of their contact. In the most lurid versions of events, Arbuckle forced himself on Rappé and she died from injuries sustained while bearing Arbuckle's considerable weight. Whatever the truth of the incident, prosecutors formally charged Arbuckle with the rape and murder of Virginia Rappé. He was tried three times; the first two trials ended in a hung jury and the third trial concluded with an acquittal. While in legal terms Arbuckle's name was cleared, he would be subject to stigma for the rest of his life. At the very least, he had been guilty of impropriety; at worst, he had gone free despite committing a violent crime.

silent era in American film, motion pictures often had live musical accompaniment, typically played on the theater's organ. This music may have taken the form of a score provided for a specific film or music improvised for the occasion by an organist using stock sheet music that coincided with a particular scene's tempo and mood, whether triumph, suspense, or tragedy. As the decade continued and innovations in film emerged, owners of film venues faced decisions about whether to outfit their theaters with each new sound device. In 1926, Warner Brothers introduced Vitaphone, a sound system that was best suited for film musicals. Starting in 1927, film innovators began adding sound to silent films through a process that created "part talkies." Al Jolson's *The Jazz Singer* (1927) was the first true "talkie." Even so, the film only included three songs and fewer than 350 spoken words. The first words spoken on screen seemed auspicious: "Wait a minute, wait a minute! You ain't heard nothing yet!"

The advent of talking pictures was a mixed blessing for actors and actresses from the silent screen. As the later film musical *Singin' in the Rain* would dramatize, not all performers from the silent era made a successful transition to the "talkies." Faced with the new expectations that they speak and sing effectively on screen, some silent stars found they were not equal to the challenge. Others struggled with the shift in acting practice because the incorporation of sound in film called for less pantomime and visual storytelling.

Table 2.7. Number of U.S. Movie Theaters, 1926–1930

Year	Wired for Sound	Silent	Total
1926	—	19,489	19,489
1927	20	21,644	21,664
1928	100	22,204	22,304
1929	800	22,544	23,344
1930	8,860	14,140	23,000

Source: Adapted from Steinberg 1980, 40.

The dramatic rise in ticket sales resulting from the introduction of sound to film—nearly double previous figures—left little doubt that talking pictures would prevail. During the period from 1927 to 1929, when theaters were being reconfigured to accommodate sound technology, many motion pictures were released both as silents and talkies. By decade's end, almost all American theaters had begun to make the switch to talking pictures. As the talkies came to theaters, audience behaviors also shifted. Whereas during the silent era filmgoers spoke to one another and responded to the screen, theaters expected audiences at talkies to remain quiet so that dialogue could be heard. The result was a more passive and more introverted movie-going experience.

The Dream Machine: Transforming Leisure through Technology

Leisure helped define the decade of the 1920s in America. As a 1920 advertisement for Radiolite watches proclaimed, "There's time for work and time for play." During the 1920s, motion pictures emerged as one of the nation's most popular forms of leisure-time entertainment. Between 1920 and 1930, movie ticket sales soared from 35 million to 80 million weekly (Broer 1990, 131), growth so precipitous that many vaudeville venues were remodeled to function as movie houses. Part of the attraction was the escape movie-going offered audiences. Print advertisements for Paramount Pictures appearing in 1924, for instance, promised viewers "escape from Everydayland." This campaign's copy went on to explain that "Paramount means adventure, romance, love, comedy and thrilling experience of every kind to millions whose lives would otherwise be monotonous" (Heimann 2004, 348). Films were not merely an escape from reality, however, because screen images began to influence everyday life in America. Viewers often imitated styles and emulated behaviors portrayed on the screen. As a form of recreation, film-watching commanded an increasing share of the family budget. "Good times," as Robert Lynd explained in 1933, "have become an expected part of the routine week of family members, rather than a matter of special occasions" (Lynd, 1933, 866).

OTHER AMUSEMENTS

Leisure Time

Just as travel became a popular form of leisure during vacations, and motion pictures became a welcome escape from workaday life, Americans also found a whole range of diversions to entertain and occupy themselves when they were at play at home. Some were passing fancies while others became lasting hobbies and interests. With shorter working hours came the ability to explore such diversions as crossword puzzles, games, sports, and amusement parks.

As cultural observer Frederick Allen noted in *Only Yesterday,* "the country had bread, but it wanted circuses" (Allen 1931, 134). During the 1920s, people would have both. The consumer demand for entertainment during the 1920s was insatiable, and countless forms of amusement became available to gratify those interests.

Fads and Fancies

Several new pastimes became crazes during the 1920s. These entertainments would surface as fads, suddenly grow in popularity, and then subside. Two memorable examples of such 1920s fancies were crossword puzzles and the game of Mah Jongg. An ancient Chinese game played with carved tiles, Mah Jongg became an unexpected American craze in 1922 when it was imported and Americanized as a parlor game. The enthusiasm was not without its irony. Chinese immigration was greatly restricted at this time, but the game was still a welcome arrival, as were Chinese restaurants in America's cities during this period. Most historical accounts credit Joseph P. Babcock of the Standard Oil Company with introducing the game to the United States following a trip he made to Shanghai. He made an English language edition and received a patent for his version of the game.

Through the efforts of importers such as W. A. Hammond's Mah Jongg Sales Company of San Francisco, California, the American market flooded with cheap English-language game sets produced by Babcock's competitors, including versions manufactured for sale at five-and-ten stores. In 1923 alone, $1,500,000 worth of Mah Jong sets were imported to the United States. American factories began making them as well, including United States Playing Card, Milton Bradley, and Parker Brothers. Manufacturers frequently held exhibitions and other spectator-oriented events to support the sales of these Mah Jongg sets. Demonstration games went on in cities from Chattanooga, Tennessee, to Milwaukee, Wisconsin. The craze peaked in 1923, with formation of the Mah Jongg League of America and crooner Eddie Cantor's recording of a popular song, "Since Ma is Playing Mah Jongg" (Drowne and Huber 2004, 127). By 1924, the game was becoming less fashionable and prestigious. As journalist Helen Bullitt Lowry wrote in the August 10, 1924, issue of the *New York Times* Magazine, "For better or for worse, the game is irretrievably committed to the ways of democracy" (quoted in Rose 2004, 402).

Enthusiasm similar to that for the game of Mah Jongg surrounded the phenomenon of crossword puzzles. Crossword puzzles derived from other word-based puzzles, such as acrostics and word squares. The first published crossword puzzle, then known as a "word-cross," was designed by Arthur Wynne and appeared in the *New York World* on December 21, 1913. The first book-length collection of puzzles, however, did not appear until 1924, when Richard Simon and Max Schuster determined that the first title to be published by their new press, Simon and Schuster (albeit issued under the name Plaza Publishing Company), would be a collection of crosswords. *The Crossword Puzzle Book* cost $1.35 a copy and, in a cross-promotion with the Venus Pencil Company, came complete with a sharpened pencil. This was a highly successful debut for Simon and Schuster, which sold 40,000 copies in the first three months (Millington 1975, 11). Puzzle books were soon in great demand for commuters, hobbyists, and travelers. Specialized collections of puzzles with such common themes as celebrity, Biblical, or Yiddish clues began to circulate. The explosion of interest in crosswords also boosted sales of *Roget's Thesaurus,* a tool favored among puzzle fans. Crossword tournaments took place, such as a 1925 Harvard and Yale match held at the Hotel Roosevelt. A Broadway musical, *Puzzles of 1925,* even acknowledged the level of crossword fanaticism that peaked during that year. In addition, there were such novelty items as crossword-puzzle themed jewelry and clothing. America's crossword-puzzle craze subsided by 1926. Although people still enjoyed working the puzzles, there was no longer the same preoccupation with them.

The excitement regarding both Mah Jongg and crossword puzzles signaled that Americans had enough time on their hands to sit down and play such games or work such puzzles. While these two examples were not the only crazes of their kind during the 1920s, they were two of the most extensively documented in the popular press of the time.

Magic and the Supernatural

Another popular American avocation involved matters occult. Ever since the 19th century, curiosity about the supernatural had attracted many Americans to spiritualism. Proponents of spiritualism posited that individuals with strong spir-

Houdini is secured in a straitjacket for a performance, ca. 1920. (Library of Congress)

itual gifts, known as mediums, could use those abilities to communicate with the dead. The first wave of interest came from Civil War widows and others bereaved by the era's conflicts. World War I occasioned a resurgence of spiritualism as another generation of war survivors sought contact with their deceased loved ones.

At this time, it was typical for a spiritual medium to devote sessions with clients to séances. In conducting a séance, the medium would usually provide the customer with some physical manifestation of her or his psychic ability. Important signs could involve such phenomena as levitation of objects, rattling chains, rapping on tables, trance speaking, spirit hands, bell ringing, or slate writing; all were considered evidence that the souls of the dead were responding to the spiritual medium and trying to communicate with the living through the séance.

During his career, Houdini put many spiritualists to the test, including the Davenport Brothers, the Fox Sisters, Eusapia Palladino, and Dr. Henry Slade. By 1920, Harry Houdini had already secured national fame as a magician and escape artist, but he went on to build a reputation as a debunker of spiritualism. Houdini set out to expose fraudulent mediums by revealing how they misled their customers. To accomplish this work, Houdini often donned disguises and attended séances so he could observe the practices of suspect mediums. It was not unusual for him to attend these events in the company of a police officer or member of the press because Houdini wanted to make public the deceit and exploitation he believed underlay the "services" of spiritual mediums. As someone skilled in the arts of illusion, Houdini could readily discern the forms of subterfuge used to fool people, and he could also reproduce those feats and demonstrate them to others. To facilitate his efforts, Houdini even studied with psychic Anna Eva Fay. With his own skill and her tutelage, Houdini proved an effective debunker of spiritual mediums.

In 1922, Houdini's crusade against spiritualist fraud brought him to the attention of the editors of *Scientific American* magazine, and he served as a panel judge for a contest that challenged spiritualists to produce genuine demonstrations of their art. Two years later, Houdini published two works related to his experiences with demystifying spiritualism: *A Magician among the Spirits* and *Houdini Exposes the Tricks Used by Boston Medium "Margery."* In fact, Houdini became so adept at duplicating the effects achieved by spiritual mediums that he incorporated some elements of spiritualist sleight-of-hand in his stage shows by the mid-1920s. During 1926, he went on to testify against fortune-telling before the House of Representatives in Washington, D.C. This appearance signaled Houdini's support for an anti-fortune-telling bill, one that ultimately did not pass.

Some say that Houdini challenged spiritualism so vigorously because deep down he really wanted to find someone with a legitimate claim as a medium. One of Houdini's friends, *Sherlock Holmes* author Sir Arthur Conan Doyle, was a believer and had tried unsuccessfully to convert Houdini to spiritualism. Before his 1926 death, however, Houdini promised his wife that he would attempt to contact her from the afterlife using a special agreed-upon code. His widow hosted numerous séances but eventually declared that if Houdini could contact her he would have done so; she would no longer attempt to reach him. Houdini's debunking of spiritualism, like his stage illusions, appealed to Americans of the 1920s, who embraced amazing feats and exposés with equal energy. Magicians and mediums, after all, had a lot in common. Both relied upon the public's interest in the supernatural, both asked the public to suspend disbelief, and both simultaneously dazzled believers and entertained skeptics. Americans of the 1920s found themselves intrigued with unexplained phenomena, prompting more than a few to experiment with Ouija boards, visit psychics, or consult spiritual mediums.

Amusement Parks and Roller Coasters

During the 1920s, commercial amusements grew in popularity. By some accounts, there were some 1,500 roller coasters in operation during the 1920s (Cartmell 1987, 123). The same technology that was automating workplaces was

Patrons purchase tickets at the entrance to "Coaster Dips," the roller coaster at Glen Echo Park, Maryland, near Washington, D.C., in the 1920s. (Library of Congress)

being used to animate leisure attractions. Even as he championed the cause of leisure, commentator Robert L. Duffus revealed his ambivalence regarding the forms that leisure took in modern America. In a 1924 article for *The Independent,* he wrote, "I do not maintain that all their amusements are wholesome, nor that the excessive standardization and mechanization of work and play alike is without its dangers" (quoted in Mowry 1963, 46).

Americans appear not to have shared these reservations. Amusement parks continued to attract Americans with leisure time. In some ways, this was the golden decade for mechanical rides and roller coasters. Larger and more complex rides were set in place during the 1920s, and many involved features that had not been possible previously. "Deno's Wonder Wheel," for instance, built at Coney Island in 1920 by the Eccentric Ferris Wheel Company, weighed 400,000 pounds and stood 150 feet high and 140 feet wide. It held up to 144 riders at once. New technologies and engineering techniques developed in other ventures came to be applied in the design of amusement park attractions. The result was a whole range of thrills available at parks across the country. Examples of 1920s roller coasters include the "Bobs" at Chicago's Riverview Park, the "Blue Streak" in Poughkeepsie's Woodcliff Pleasure Park, the "Cyclone" at Fort Lee, New Jersey's Palisades Park, and the "Lightning" at Boston's Revere Beach. The "Dip-Lo-Docus," which appeared for the first time in 1923, was billed as "the Jazz Ride," and was installed in parks at locations such as Maplewood, New Jersey's Olympic Park (Cartmell 1987, 123).

Perhaps the most celebrated of all amusement complexes of this time, however, was Coney Island in Brooklyn, New York. At this location, daily attendance during the 1920s could reach 800,000 (Giordano 2003, 65). It was at Coney Island that the "Cyclone" first appeared in 1927, although it would be replicated and imitated elsewhere.

Although the amusement parks were generally designed as working- and middle-class entertainments, even celebrities visited and enjoyed them. Charlie Chaplin, Charles Lindbergh, and Al Capone were among the era's roller coaster enthusiasts.

Miniature Golf: Putters in Paradise

While conventional golfing had been played in the United States before, miniature golf first took hold of the American public during the 1920s. Although the sport had appeared in England and Scotland during the 19th century, it was not until the early 20th century that the diversion reached America. Some accounts credit resort owner Garnet Carter of Chattanooga, Tennessee, with introducing the whimsical pastime to the United States (Drowne and Huber 2004, 151). Also known as "garden golf," miniature golf became a popular family entertainment. During the 1920s, most miniature golf courses featured a garden-like setting. During the second half of the decade, courses even began to appear on Manhattan rooftops. These locations made use of a new surface introduced in 1926, cottonwood hull carpet dyed to resemble a lawn. By decade's end, the country boasted over 40,000 ready-made miniature golf courses at locations such as resorts and hotels. Still other Americans played on homemade courses in yards or parks.

Early mini-golf courses were distinctive, featuring original layouts and design elements. Such eye-catching structures as windmills and other novelty features helped give each mini-golf course its own character. Often placed alongside major roads or highways, the spectacle of a well-designed course drew both curiosity and business from passersby. As the decade unfolded, however, standardization came into play with the use of prefabricated courses. In 1929, the first franchise appeared, Tom Thumb Golf. After prefabricated courses and franchise operations began to dominate the miniature golf industry, variations among courses and their features became fewer. The enthusiasm for miniature golfing continued through the 1920s and reached its peak during the Great Depression.

Participant Sports

Many of the popular forms of recreation during the 1920s—radio, phonograph, and motion pictures, to name a few—were sedentary activities. Still, Americans did participate in more active forms of leisure, including the sport of bowling. In the United States, bowling has remained a very popular amusement, especially among members of the working and, to a lesser extent, middle classes. In the 1920s, the number of Americans participating in bowling, whether as individuals or members of bowling teams, grew dramatically. During the period from 1920 to 1930, the number of people bowling leaped from 27,000 to 219,000 (Wattenberg 1976, 400).

Perhaps the first real professional bowler, Andy Varipapa dazzled audiences for decades with his regular game play as well as with his stunts on the lanes. Varipapa was an Italian immigrant who first tried baseball and boxing but eventually settled on bowling as the sport where he would make his mark. Varipapa once said he could make a bowling ball do everything but talk; this was nearly so. He routinely bowled between 207 and 213 a game during the 1920s. In addition, Varipapa developed a variety of trick shots that he performed for the enjoyment of onlookers. In one routine, he kicked the ball down the lane but still knocked down all the lane's pins. In another well-known stunt, Varipapa, who was ambidextrous, sent two balls down the lane simultaneously to take down a 7–10 split. Always a showman, Varipapa arranged obstacles such as showgirls, guiding the ball between their feet and down the lane to the waiting pins. His antics gained the attention of Hollywood, and Varipapa appeared as himself in newsreels and several films during the 1920s, including *Sport Slants #5* (1932), *Strikes and Spares* (1934), *Set 'um Up* (1939), and *Bowling Tricks* (1948). He bowled well into his 90s, and was inducted into the American Bowling Congress Hall of Fame in 1957.

Andy Varipapa embodied the era's madcap sensibility and the public's love of spectacle. In the process, he also promoted the sport of bowling, which increased the number of Americans who could be found trying to perform Varipapa's trick shots at bowling lanes across the country.

Spectator Sports

The 1920s was a time of substantial growth in most spectator sports. Those who could not attend sporting events began to listen to matches broadcast over the radio or read the results in the sports page of the local newspaper. America's favorite pastime, baseball, provides a good example of this development. The Black Sox scandal that had surrounded the 1919 World Series clouded the game's reputation for a time, and the trials of those implicated in the incident extended into the 1920s. Still, the sport seemed to recover from this disgrace, and Americans of the 1920s turned out to watch baseball in record numbers. A 1920 rule change that prohibited pitcher alteration of the game ball through such methods as "scuffing" or "spitballs" resulted in an increase in hits and runs because the ball became easier to hit without such interference. Consequently, games become more exciting to watch, and old hitting records fell. Interest in playing the game also grew, especially among those who had previously been denied the opportunity. Since 1920s baseball remained racially segregated, this decade saw the birth of the "Negro Leagues," with the Negro National League in 1920, the Eastern Colored League in 1923, and the American Negro League in 1929. From 1924 to 1927, a Negro League World Series was conducted, parallel to the play-off process used in major league baseball. It would not be until the 1940s that an African American, Jackie Robinson, would cross the color line to play major league baseball.

During the 1920s, people in the United States celebrated their favorite sports heroes, including boxer Jack Dempsey, swimmer Johnny Weismuller, football player Harold "Red" Grange, and baseball player Babe Ruth. It was a time when such idols were idealized, and young people dreamed of achieving such athletic prowess when they became adults.

Growth of Games and Pastimes in America

During the 1920s, Americans were, in short, ready for play. Indeed, although the nation's people had always enjoyed recreation, people of the 1920s came to expect it and regard it as a right. Numerous major forms of recreation either originated in the 1920s or were extremely popular during the decade. Some of these enthusiasms were fleeting, such as goldfish-swallowing. Others, such as pogo sticks, yo-yos, and roller-skating, would become staples of youth culture and play. Leisure environments began to proliferate, including bowling alleys, amusement parks, roller coasters, and miniature golf courses. Traveling circuses enjoyed popularity as family entertainment, as did auto races. For the most part, however, a majority of the new leisure activities were sedentary and involved only a physically passive role such as viewer or listener.

BIOGRAPHIES

Joseph Park Babcock, 1893–1949

American Popularizer of Mah Jongg

Joseph Park Babcock was born in Lafayette, Indiana, in 1893. He attended Purdue University, where he earned a degree in civil engineering. Babcock entered the employ of the Standard Oil Company, occupying a post that required extensive travel to China. It was on the basis of this exposure to Chinese culture that Babcock developed a keen interest in a game he observed many Chinese people playing with small pieces known as tiles: Mah Jongg.

Joseph Babcock's fascination with the game motivated him to popularize it in the United States. In 1919, Babcock developed tiles adorned with English numerals. The following year, he created a simplified version of the game. By 1922, Babcock was involved in importing Mah Jongg sets to the United States. Babcock also published a book describing this new form of game play: *Babcock's Rules for Mah Jongg—The Red Book of Rules* (1923). In the same year that this book appeared, Babcock secured an American patent on the game name: "Mah Jongg." Through his affiliation with the Mah Jongg Sales Company of America, Joseph Babcock earned enough money to enter Yale Law School in 1924. He graduated from Yale in 1927.

Theda Bara, 1885–1955

Silent Film Actress

Born to immigrant parents residing in Cincinnati, Ohio, Bara's given name was Theodosia Burr Goodman. A performer known to audiences by her stage name, Theda Bara became a legendary star of American silent films. She made her first film in 1914, and went on to appear in more than 40 films before her retirement from motion pictures in 1926. In keeping with the era's fondness for screen fantasy, studio executives marketed Bara as an exotic princess. She played various female leads, including Cleopatra, and functioned in her films as a sex symbol. Her screen wardrobe often consisted of elaborately decorated but scanty costumes. The Hays Codes would later restrict such attire.

In the parlance of the day, Bara was termed a "vampire" or "vamp" for her seductive qualities. As the titles of some of her films suggested, Bara was frequently cast as the temptress: *The Vixen* (1916), *Salome* (1918), *The She Devil*

Both on the screen and off, film studios promoted actress Theda Bara as a mysterious and alluring figure. She often portrayed romantic characters, such as Cleopatra or the Vamp. (Library of Congress)

(1918), *The Unchastened Woman* (1925), and *Madame Mystery* (1926). Few prints of her films survive, but Bara's persona endures as a prominent figure within silent film history.

Clara Bow, 1905–1965

Actress and the "It" Girl

In many ways, Clara Bow personified the "New Woman" of the 1920s. The circumstances of the young actress's arrival in Hollywood also made her debut a media-ready story. Bow won a 1921 "Fame and Fortune" contest in which the prize was a chance to act in the 1922 motion picture *Beyond the Rainbow*. Bow's part was ultimately edited out of the film. She went on to appear in many of the decade's films, including *The Plastic Age* (1925) and *Flaming Youth,* film adaptations of novels by Percy Marks and Warner Fabian, respectively. Typically, she played the part of a flapper, the carefree and colorful young woman who flouts social and moral conventions. One of her films, *It,* gave Bow her most enduring nickname, the "It" girl. In this film, Bow plays Betty Lou Spence, a department store clerk who sets out to live by the dictates of an Elinor Glyn book about the importance of sex appeal. The clerk goes on to marry her boss at the store. Glyn called Bow the "It" girl, meaning that she had something special about her that attracted men in particular. The nickname stayed with Bow throughout her film career.

Charlie Chaplin, 1889–1977

Silent Screen Actor and Comedian

Born Charles Spencer Chaplin Jr., the actor-comedian who may well be the best-recognized star of the silent screen is known the world over as Charlie Chaplin. Chaplin's most familiar character is a role he reprised in a number of films: the tramp. This humble figure, attired in tattered and ill-fitting clothes and walking with a cane, functioned as an everyman in his films. Chaplin first appeared on stage at the age of five, performing in a music hall. He worked in early films as an actor but eventually did everything from scoring films to directing them. In 1918, Chaplin established his own motion picture studio and production company. The following year, he joined with Douglas Fairbanks, D. W. Griffith, and Mary Pickford to create United Artists, a film distribution company. Several of his most beloved films appeared during the 1920s. Examples include *The Kid* (1921) and *The Gold Rush* (1925). While many of his films incorporate social commentary, his later works, such as *Modern Times* (1936) and *The Great Dictator* (1940), were more overtly political. Chaplin's candor about his views, both on and off screen, made him a controversial figure until the 1970s, when he was honored with a star on the Hollywood walk of fame.

Walter Elias "Walt" Disney, 1901–1966

Cartoonist and Entertainer

Walt Disney was born December 5, 1901, in Chicago, Illinois. He grew up on a Missouri farm where he demonstrated a talent for and an interest in the visual arts. By the time he was in high school, Disney started attending night classes at the Academy of Fine Arts. When World War I broke out, a still-teenage Disney became a volunteer ambulance driver. He covered the vehicle with his own cartoon drawings. This decoration anticipated Disney's eventual career in visual comedy and entertainment. Upon his return, Walt found work as an advertising cartoonist in Kansas City. Meanwhile, Disney pursued his passion for animation. In 1920, he sold his first animated cartoons. He also developed a technique for creating films that commingle animation with live action. By 1923, he joined his brother, Roy Disney, in a career in comedy films. In 1928, Walt Disney devised the character that would become the most widely recognized film star in the world: Mickey Mouse. Later that year, he released the first feature-length animated musical on film: *Snow White and the Seven Dwarfs*. This film would be followed by many other successful animated features, making it possible for Disney to build a studio in California, where he began conducting business in 1940. During World War II, the Disney Studio devoted a good deal of its time to developing training films and pro-war propaganda. In 1955, Disney opened Disneyland, the first of many Disney-themed amusement parks around the world, from Tokyo to Paris. The Disney name went on to become synonymous with family entertainment throughout the world.

Gertrude Caroline Ederle, 1905–2003

Olympic Swimmer

Gertrude Ederle grew up in New York City as the daughter of a German immigrant father. Early in life, Ederle took an interest in swimming and began competing in this sport. At the 1924 Summer Olympics, Ederle took a gold medal in freestyle relay. She set quite a number of records even before attaining her most celebrated achievement, which came in 1926 when Ederle became the first woman to swim across the English Channel. This accomplishment secured her public notice.

Upon her return from this swimming triumph, Ederle became a celebrity of sorts in the United States. New Yorkers gave her a ticker-tape parade, a dance

Gertrude Ederle makes a triumphant return to New York, her hometown, after swimming the English Channel in 1926. Ederle was the first woman to swim the channel. (Library of Congress)

step was named for her, and she made personal appearances that included portraying herself in a motion picture *Swim Girl, Swim*. Ederle subsequently devoted herself to teaching deaf children to swim.

Margaret Petherbridge Farrar, 1897–1984

Crossword Puzzle Editor

As an editor with a lengthy career, Margaret Petherbridge Farrar may be best remembered for her role in building the American appetite for crossword puzzles. Farrar was a Smith College graduate who, as the 1920s dawned, worked at the *New York World* as the secretary to the magazine section editor, John O'Hara Cosgrove. Among other duties performed in this capacity, Farrar guarded against typographic errors in puzzles published by the *World*. She gradually began to function, although in an informal way, as the paper's crossword editor. Although not all newspapers approved of such puzzles, they soared in popularity with readers. Libraries even found themselves limiting the time each patron might spend using their dictionaries. Farrar edited the first book-length collection of puzzles released by Simon and Schuster in 1924, along with countless subsequent editions through 1970. The crossword expert married John Farrar in 1926, creating a dual-career family in publishing. With time, crosswords grew in respectability and began to run in the most reputable newspapers. For example, in 1942, Margaret Petherbridge Farrar became the founding editor of the notoriously challenging *New York Times* Sunday crossword puzzle. She continued in that capacity through 1969. Thanks in part to the painstaking work of individuals such as Farrar, daily crossword puzzles have appeared in newspapers since 1950.

Edward Albert Filene, 1860–1937

Retailer

Born in Salem, Massachusetts, Edward Filene went into the family business of women's wear retailing. When his father fell ill in 1882, Edward Filene assumed leadership of the Boston-based business. Along with his brother, Lincoln, Edward Filene developed that enterprise into a highly successful commercial concern. Filene's became known as an innovative retailer and employer. By many accounts, the store developed the concepts of the bargain basement, the money-back guarantee, and the charge card. Filene also established a credit union, paid vacations for all his workers, and a minimum wage for women employees (not a standard practice of the time). In addition to his role as a merchant, Filene wrote books about business practice. By the end of the 1920s, although he remained president of Filene's, Edward Filene's progressive notions rendered him suspect among more conservatively minded stockholders.

Henry Ford, 1863–1947

Engineering Pioneer, Entrepreneur, Automaker

Although he had an enjoyable childhood on the family farm, Ford felt called to pursuits that would take him away from agriculture and toward industrial technology. In 1879, he apprenticed as a machinist in Detroit and proved adept at repairing, retooling, and running machinery and instrumentation. These talents helped him land a position as an engineer with Detroit's Edison Illuminating Company, where he became Chief Engineer in 1893. This work served as a platform for Ford's own pursuits as an entrepreneur. The Ford Motor Company had its beginnings in Detroit and Highland Park. His Model T became so popular that by 1918, this vehicle accounted for nearly a 50 percent share of the American auto market. This was the kind of success Ford had envisioned for his industry. He wanted to achieve an efficient production of a solid means of transportation for the average American consumer.

Henry Ford's hometown of Dearborn, Michigan, became the site for the Ford Company's industrial complex in the 1920s. At this plant on the edge of the

Rouge River, Ford realized his mass production concepts, such as the moving assembly line. His success as a manufacturer helped transform the United States into a car culture, bringing with it a national network of highways dotted with roadside amenities. Ford did not invent the automobile, but he did help establish it as the dominant form of transportation in the United States. With his pioneering efforts in the automobile industry, Henry Ford embodied the American ideal of the self-made capitalist.

Greta Garbo, 1905–1990

Actress

Greta Garbo was born Greta Lovisa Gustafsson in Stockholm, Sweden. After her father died when Garbo was just 14, she held various jobs to help support her family. These forms of employment included work as a clerk and a model. Her first small acting parts came during the early 1920s. She found her way into the American studio system and appeared in a range of silent films playing the part of an exotic and, occasionally, dangerous beauty. Examples include *Flesh and the Devil* (1926) and *The Kiss* (1929). When talkies arrived, her first speaking part was advertised with the promotion "Garbo talks." Garbo went on to appear in many films, earning several Oscar nominations and an honorary Academy Award in 1954. The actress was known for a reclusive tendency, and was often characterized with a modified bit of dialogue from one of her films: "I want to be alone." Garbo withdrew from the industry and lived away from public scrutiny until her death in 1990. She remains an emblem of film glamour in early Hollywood.

Harold "Red" Grange, 1903–1991

Professional Football Player

Harold Grange was born in Forksville, Pennsylvania, but spent much of his youth in the vicinity of Wheaton, Illinois. He excelled in a variety of sports as a youth. After graduating high school, Grange attended the University of Illinois. While there, he was a member of the football team. His career on the field there was so distinguished that his jersey number was retired in 1925. During that same year, Grange appeared on the cover of *Time* magazine, an honor accorded to few of the nation's college seniors. As soon as he completed his last college season of football, Grange signed a contract to play halfback with the NFL's Chicago Bears.

Grange has been credited with the rise of popularity in professional football in the United States, and he was instrumental in forming the short-lived American Football League (AFL). Known as the "Galloping Ghost," a name given to him by Chicago sports writer Warren Brown, Grange continued to play professional football through 1934, at which time he retired from the sport.

Following retirement, Red Grange made personal appearances, including work as a sports commentator. Grange's life story entered print through an as-told-to autobiography, *The Red Grange Story* (1953), written in partnership with Ira Morton. Grange was inducted into the Football Hall of Fame in 1963.

Harry Houdini, 1874–1926

Illusionist and Master Magician

Born in Hungary on April 6, 1874, as Ehrich Weiss, Harry Houdini became a world-renowned master magician and illusionist. Houdini developed an early interest in performance, appearing in a home-styled circus as a youth. He resolved to become a showman and worked in vaudeville on the Orpheum Circuit. His first appearances were as a contortionist and trapeze artist. His magic act was featured at Chicago's World's Columbian Exposition in 1892. By the turn of the century, he had emerged as a popular entertainer, especially in terms of his work as an escape artist. Promotional materials depicted him locked in chains and described him as the "King of Handcuffs." Houdini went on to perform a wide range of feats, from jailbreaks to escapes from straitjackets. One of his most famous stage tricks came in 1918 when he made an elephant disappear at New York's Hippodrome Theatre. Other enthusiasms for Houdini included the history of magic, aviation, and the challenge of discrediting frauds posing as psychics and spiritualists. He hoped to be remembered after his death for his research into the world of magic. More than a parlor-trick magician, Houdini excited audiences with the mystery of his stunts and the intrigue of his escapes. The public loved seeing him free himself from the most restrictive and dangerous predicaments, perhaps providing a vicarious sense of agility, freedom, and agency. These talents became so widely recognized that by 1920, Funk and Wagnall's listed Houdini's surname as a verb.

Al Jolson, 1885–1950

Stage and Screen Actor

Born Asa Yoelson, the entertainer professionally known as Al Jolson came to the United States from Lithuania. Jolson became a vaudeville-influenced stage performer whose signatures included singing and appearance in blackface. He worked on Broadway from 1911 until 1940. He is best known for his leading role in the first "talkie" motion picture, *The Jazz Singer,* in 1927. Over the course of his career, Jolson recorded songs for several record labels, including Columbia, Brunswick, and Decca. He had hits with such tunes as "Swanee" and "Rock-a-bye Your Baby with a Dixie Melody." Jolson also appeared on radio frequently, and "The Al Jolson Show" aired from 1933 to 1949. Tributes to the performer include two popular motion pictures: *The Jolson Story* (1946) and *Jolson Sings Again* (1949).

Helen Newington Wills Moody Roark, 1905–1998

Tennis Champion and Olympic Medalist

Born in Centerville, California, Helen Wills (as she was then known) developed an early interest in athletics. Wills attended, but did not graduate from, the University of California, Berkeley. She demonstrated considerable skill in the sport of tennis, for which she became best known. Wills played in singles, doubles, and mixed doubles tennis competitions. At the 1924 Olympic Games in Paris, Wills was awarded two gold medals for tennis, which was in its last year as an Olympic sport. These medals recognized Wills's wins in both single and doubles competition.

Her many career victories in tennis made Wills a public figure. Dubbed "Queen Helen" by her detractors, Wills was reserved in demeanor both on and off the court. She was a quiet force in her sport, commanding some 31 Grand Slam titles. In 1928, she wrote and illustrated *Tennis,* a manual for those wishing to improve their game. Wills is also credited with helping to shift the court attire for women from the traditional and ungainly ankle-length skirts to more practical knee-length costumes. Wills appeared twice on the cover of *Time* magazine, first in 1926 and again in 1929. She continued to play tennis throughout most her life, and emerged as an exemplary figure in U.S. women's professional sports.

Samuel Lionel "Roxy" Rothafel, 1882–1936

Businessman and Showman

Samuel Rothafel hailed from Stillwater, Minnesota. It would not be in the Midwest's small towns but rather in the nation's cities that Rothafel would make his name. Rothafeld was a great showman of the 1920s; he came into his own as a businessman during the years of silent motion pictures. He helped establish and manage some of the most legendary theatrical venues built during this era, including the Strand, the Capitol, the Roxy, and Radio City Music Hall. As these examples suggest, Rothafel promoted movie palaces capable of delivering a rich experience for film patrons. Features such as his incorporation of multiple projectors, orchestral music synchronized to the films, and live dancers distinguished Rothafel's entertainments from more prosaic movie theaters. The Radio City Music Hall, for instance, boasted a full dance line known as the "Roxyettes," later known as the Rockettes. He was one of the figures who helped give the golden age of American film its sheen.

George Herman "Babe" Ruth, 1895–1948

Baseball Player and Record Holder

As a beloved baseball player, Babe Ruth remains one of the best-known figures in his sport's history. He debuted with the Boston Red Sox and ended his career playing with the Boston Braves, but it is for his time with the New York Yankees that Ruth is best remembered. In fact, Yankee Stadium, which opened in 1923, was nicknamed "The House That Ruth Built." Fans loved to turn out to watch him play, and he was affectionately dubbed the "Bambino" and the "Sultan of Swat." Often credited with reviving attendance at baseball games in the wake of the Black Sox scandal, Ruth excelled on the field. Newspapers followed Ruth's exploits both on and off

Legendary baseball player Babe Ruth at bat, ca. 1920. (Library of Congress)

the diamond, and it is rumored that his keen appetites for food and drink, among other indulgences, compromised his health. Ruth set numerous home-run records. His career hitting percentage still remains unparalleled. During an age of sports heroes, Babe Ruth was never surpassed. In 1969, Ruth was named the sport's Greatest Player Ever.

Rudolph Valentino, 1895–1926

Actor in Silent Films and "Talkies"

Rudolph Valentino was among the most beloved motion picture stars of the 1920s. He was a popular leading man in many silent film romances, and his appearances were especially appreciated by women viewers. Born Rodolfo Alfonso Raffaelo Piero Filiberto Guglielmi de Valentina d'Antoguolla, the Italian immigrant adopted the screen name of Rudolph Valentino and began his career in film in Hollywood in 1917. His first parts were as villains, but he is best remembered as "the Sheik," the title role of a 1921 film. Valentino emerged as the era's most exotic screen lover and reprised his most famous role in a sequel, *The Son of the Sheik,* in 1926. His career was cut short when, at age 31, he died of complications from ulcer surgery. The actor's death left viewers stricken with grief. Some 100,000 mourners stood outside Valentino's New York funeral; a near-riot occurred when some bereaved fans attempted to enter the ceremony. A second Valentino funeral was held in Hollywood, California, where he had achieved fame.

REFERENCES AND FURTHER READINGS

ABC-CLIO. 2001. *The 1920s: Teacher's Guide; A Supplemental Teaching Unit from the Records of the National Archives.* Santa Barbara, CA: ABC-CLIO.

Adler, Selig. 1968. *The Uncertain Giant, 1921–1940.* New York: Macmillan.

Allen, Frederick Lewis. 1931. *Only Yesterday.* New York: Bantam.

Andrist, Ralph, and the editors of American Heritage. 1987. *History of the 1920s and 1930s.* New York: American Heritage/Bonanza Books.

Aron, Cindy S. 1999. *Working at Play: A History of Vacations in the United States.* New York: Oxford University Press.

Belasco, Warren. 1997. *Americans on the Road: From Autocamp to Motel, 1910–1945.* Baltimore: Johns Hopkins University Press.

Benson, Susan Porter. 1986. *Counter Cultures: Saleswomen, Managers, and Customers in American Department Stores, 1890–1940.* Urbana: University of Illinois Press.

Best, Gary Dean. 2003. *The Dollar Decade: Mammon and the Machine in 1920s America.* Westport, CT: Greenwood Press/Praeger Publishers.

Bilton, Alan, and Philip H. Melling. 2004. *America in the 1920s: Literary Sources and Documents.* Mountfield, East Sussex: Helm.

Blum, Stella, ed. 1981. *Everyday Fashions of the Twenties.* New York: Dover.

Boardman, Fon Wyman, Jr. 1968. *America and the Jazz Age: A History of the 1920's.* New York: H. Z. Walck.

Borus, Daniel H., ed. 1992. *These United States: Portraits of America from the 1920s.* Ithaca: Cornell University Press.

Broer, Lawrence R., and John D. Walther, eds. 1990. *Dancing Fools and Weary Blues: The Treat Escape of the Twenties.* Bowling Green, OH: Bowling Green State University Popular Press.

Brown, Dorothy M. 1987. *Setting a Course: Women in the 1920s.* Boston: Twayne.

Butsch, Richard, ed. 1990. *For Fun and Profit: The Transformation of Leisure into Consumption.* Philadelphia: Temple University Press.

Carson, Gerald. 1986. "The Fuller Brush Man." *American Heritage Magazine* 37(5): 26–31.

Carter, Paul A. 1977. *Another Part of the Twenties.* New York: Columbia University Press.

Cartmell, Robert. 1987. *The Incredible Scream Machine: A History of the Roller Coaster.* Bowling Green, OH: Bowling Green State University Popular Press.

The Clara Bow Page. "Clara Bow." http://www.clarabow.net (accessed September 10, 2006).

Cox, Jim. 2005. *Music Radio: The Great Performers and Programs of the 1920s through the Early 1960s.* Jefferson, NC: McFarland.

Desser, David, and Garth S. Jowett, eds. 2000. *Hollywood Goes Shopping.* Minneapolis: University of Minnesota Press.

Drowne, Kathleen, and Patrick Huber. 2004. *The 1920's.* Westport, CT: Greenwood Press.

Dumenil, Lynn. 1995. *The Modern Temper: American Culture and Society in the 1920s.* New York: Hill and Wang.

Dye, Victoria E. 2005. *All Aboard for Santa Fe: Railway Promotion of the Southwest, 1890s to 1930s.* Albuquerque: University of New Mexico Press.

Emmet, Boris, and John Jeuck. 1950. *Catalogues and Counters: A History of Sears, Roebuck and Company.* Chicago: University of Chicago Press.

Filene, Edward Albert. 1927. "The Present Status and Future Prospects of Chains of Department Stores," as featured document within online exhibit for American Memory Projects, "Prosperity and Thrift: The Coolidge Era and the Consumer Economy, 1921–1929." Available at http://memory.loc.gov/ammem/coolhtml/coolhome.html (accessed on September 11, 2006).

Flanagan, Maureen A. 2006. *America Reformed: Progressives and Progressivisms, 1890s–1920s.* New York: Oxford University Press.

Flink, James. 1975. *The Car Culture.* Cambridge, MA: MIT Press.

Fox, Richard Wightman, and T. J. Jackson Lears, eds. 1983. *The Culture of Consumption: Critical Essays in American History, 1880–1980.* New York: Pantheon Books.

Freedman, Estelle B. 1974. "The New Woman: Changing View of Women in the 1920s." *Journal of American History* 61:372–393.

Friedman, Walter A. 2004. *Birth of a Salesman: The Transformation of Selling in America.* Cambridge, MA: Harvard University Press.

Fuller, Kathryn H. 1996. *At the Picture Show: Small-Town Audiences and the Creation of Movie Fan Culture.* Washington, DC: Smithsonian Institution Press.

Furnas, J. C. 1974. *Great Times: An Informal Social History of the United States, 1914–1929.* New York: Putnam.

Geocities. "Flapper Culture and Style." http://www.geocities.com/flapper_culture/ (accessed September 10, 2006).

Gewirtz, Arthur, and James J. Kolb. 2003. *Art, Glitter, and Glitz: Mainstream Playwrights and Popular Theater in 1920s America.* Westport, CT: Praeger.

Giordano, Ralph. 2003. *Fun and Games in Twentieth Century America: A Historical Guide to Leisure.* Westport, CT: Greenwood Press.

Goldberg, David J. 1999. *Discontented America: The United States in the 1920s.* Baltimore: Johns Hopkins University Press.

Goldberg, Ronald Allen. 2003. *America in the Twenties.* Syracuse, NY: Syracuse University Press.

Grant, Robert, and Joseph Katz. 1998. *The Great Trials of the Twenties: The Watershed Decade in America's Courtrooms.* Rockville Centre, NY: Sarpedon.

Green, Harvey. 1992. *The Uncertainty of Everyday Life, 1915–1945.* New York: HarperCollins.

Gregory, Ross. 1995. *Modern America, 1914 to 1945.* New York: Facts on File.

Haining, Peter. 2001. *The Classic Era of American Pulp Magazines.* Chicago: Chicago Review Press.

Hall, Ben M. 1961. *The Best Remaining Seats: The Story of the Golden Age of the Movie Palace.* New York: Bramhall House.

Hanson, Erica. 1999. *A Cultural History of the United States through the Decades: The 1920s.* San Diego: Lucent Books.

Heimann, Jim, ed. *20s: All-American Ads.* Los Angeles: Taschen, 2004.

Horowitz, Daniel. 1992. *The Morality of Spending: Attitudes toward the Consumer Society in America, 1875–1940.* Chicago: Ivan R. Dee.

Jakle, John A. 1985. *The Tourist: Travel in Twentieth-Century North America.* Lincoln: University of Nebraska Press.

Karl, Barry D. 1983. *The Uneasy State: The United States from 1915 to 1945.* Chicago: University of Chicago Press.

Kurian, George Thomas. 2001. *Datapedia of the United States, 1790–2005; America Year by Year.* Lanham, MD: Bernan Press.

Kyvig, David E. 2004. *Daily Life in the United States, 1920–1940.* Chicago: Ivan R. Dee.

Lears, T. J. Jackson. 1993. "Mass Culture and Its Critics." In *Encyclopedia of American Social History,* edited by Mary Cupiec Cayton, Elliot J. Gorn, and Peter W. Williams, 1591–1610. New York: Scribner.

Leinwand, Gerald. 2001. *1927: High Tide of the Twenties.* New York: Four Walls Eight Windows.

Lewis, Lloyd. 1929. "The Deluxe Picture Palace." *The New Republic* (March 26): 175.

Library of Congress. American Life Histories: Manuscripts from the Federal Writers' Project, 1936–1940. "Lore of Department Store Workers." Available at http://memory.loc.gov/ammem/wpaintro/wpahome.html (accessed on September 11, 2006).

Liebs, Chester. 1995. *Main Street to Miracle Mile: American Roadside Architecture*. Baltimore: Johns Hopkins University Press.

Lynd, Robert. 1933. "The People as Consumers." In President's Research Committee on Social Trends, Volume II, *Recent Social Trends in the United States*, 857–911. New York: McGraw-Hill.

MacCann, Richard Dyer. 1996. *Films of the 1920s*. Lanham, MD: Scarecrow Press.

May, Lary. 1980. *Screening out the Past: The Birth of Mass Culture and the Motion Picture Industry*. New York: Oxford University Press.

Miller, Nathan. 2003. *New World Coming: The 1920s and the Making of Modern America*. New York: Scribner.

Millington, Roger. 1975. *Crossword Puzzles: Their History and Their Cult*. Nashville: Thomas Nelson.

Mirken, Alan, ed. 1970. *1927 Edition of the Sears, Roebuck Catalogue*. New York: Bounty Books.

Mowry, George, ed. 1963. *The Twenties: Fords, Flappers, and Fanatics*. Englewood Cliffs, NJ: Prentice-Hall.

Nasaw, David. 1999. *Going Out: The Rise and Fall of Public Amusements*. Cambridge, MA: Harvard University Press.

Nash, Roderick. 1970. *The Nervous Generation: American Thought, 1917–1930*. Chicago: University of Chicago Press.

Noggle, Burl. 1974. *Into the Twenties*. Urbana: University of Illinois Press.

Norris, Scott, ed. 1994. *Discovered Country: Tourism and Survival in the American West*. Albuquerque: Stone Ladder Press.

Nye, David E. 1990. *Electrifying America: Social Meanings of a New Technology, 1880–1940*. Cambridge, MA: MIT Press.

Olney, Martha. 1991. *Buy Now, Pay Later: Advertising, Credit, and Consumer Durables in the 1920s*. Chapel Hill: University of North Carolina Press, 1991.

O'Neal, Michael J. 2006. *America in the 1920s*. New York: Facts on File.

Parrish, Michael. 1992. *Anxious Decades: America in Prosperity and Depression, 1920–1941*. New York: W. W. Norton.

Peacock, John. 1997. *The 1920s*. New York: Thames and Hudson.

Peiss, Kathy. 1998. *Hope in a Jar: The Making of American Beauty Culture*. New York: Metropolitan Books.

Pendergast, Sara, and Tom Pendergast, eds. 2002. *Bowling, Beatniks, and Bell-Bottoms: Pop Culture of Twentieth-Century America*. Detroit: UXL.

Penny Press. "Puzzles in History—The Crossword Puzzle." http://www.penny press.com/solvers/history.shtml (accessed September 10, 2006).

Pomeroy, Earl S. 1990. *In Search of the Golden West: The Tourist in Western America*. Lincoln: University of Nebraska Press.

President's Research Committee on Social Trends. 1933. *Recent Social Trends in the United States,* Volumes I and II. New York: McGraw-Hill.

Robinson, David. 1968. *Hollywood in the Twenties*. New York: A. S. Barnes.

Rose, Cynthia, ed. 2004. *American Decades: Primary Sources, 1920–1929*. New York: Gale.

Rosenberg, Emily S. 1982. *Spreading the American Dream: American Economic and Cultural Expansion, 1890–1945*. New York: Hill and Wang.

Rothman, Hal K. 1998. *Devil's Bargains: Tourism in the Twentieth-Century American West*. Lawrence: University Press of Kansas.

Sann, Paul. 1957. *The Lawless Decade: A Pictorial History of the Twenties*. New York: Crown.

Schlesinger, Arthur M., Jr. 1957. *The Crisis of the Old Order, 1919–1933*. Boston: Houghton Mifflin.

Schudson, Michael. 1991. "Delectable Materialism: Were the Critics of Consumer Culture Wrong All Along?" *The American Prospect* 5:26–35.

Scriabine, Christine Brendel. 2000. *1920s: America Enters the Modern Age*. Amawalk, NY: Jackdaw Publications.

Shaffer, Marguerite S. 2001. *See America First: Tourism and National Identity, 1880–1940*. Washington, DC: Smithsonian Institution Press.

Shannon, David. 1965. *Between the Wars: America, 1919–1941*. Boston: Houghton Mifflin.

Sklar, Robert, ed. 1970. *The Plastic Age*. New York: G. Braziller.

Solomon, Barbara H., ed. 1980. *Ain't We Got Fun? Essays, Lyrics, and Stories of the Twenties*. New York: New American Library.

Steinberg, Cobbett. 1980. *Film Facts*. New York: Facts on File.

Strasser, Susan. 1989. *Satisfaction Guaranteed: The Making of the American Mass Market*. New York: Pantheon Books.

Streissguth, Thomas. 2001. *The Roaring Twenties: An Eyewitness History*. New York: Facts on File.

Tiede, Tom. 1988. *American Tapestry: Eyewitness Accounts of the Twentieth Century*. New York: Pharos Books.

Time-Life Books. 1998. *The Jazz Age: The 20s*. Alexandria, VA: Time-Life.

Tobias, Henry J., and Charles F. Woodhouse. 2001. *Santa Fe: A Modern History, 1880–1990*. Albuquerque: University of New Mexico Press.

VanTassel-Baska, Joyce. 2003. *The 1920s in America: A Decade of Tensions.* Dubuque, IA: Kendall/Hunt.

Waller, Gregory A. 1995. *Main Street Amusements: Movies and Commercial Entertainment in a Southern City, 1896–1930.* Washington, DC: Smithsonian Institution Press.

Watson, Elwood, and Darcy Martin, eds. 2004. *"There She Is, Miss America": The Politics of Sex, Beauty, and Race in America's Most Famous Pageant.* New York: Palgrave Macmillan.

Wattenberg, Ben J. 1976. *Statistical History of the United States: From Colonial Times to the Present.* New York: Basic Books.

Weatherly, Myra. 2006. *Living in 1920s America.* Farmington Hills, MI: Greenhaven Press/Thomson Gale.

Wilson, Chris. 1991. *The Myth of Santa Fe: Creating a Modern Regional Tradition.* Albuquerque: University of New Mexico Press.

Wolman, Leo. 1929. *Recent Economic Changes in the United States.* New York: McGraw-Hill.

Wrobel, David M., and Patrick T. Long, eds. 2001. *Seeing and Being Seen: Tourism in the American West.* Lawrence: University Press of Kansas.

Yellis, Kenneth A. 1969. "Prosperity's Child: Some Thoughts on the Flapper." *American Quarterly* 21 (Spring): 44–64.

Zeitz, Joshua. 2006. *Flapper: A Madcap Story of Sex, Style, Celebrity, and the Women Who Made America Modern.* New York: Crown.

Urbanization, Politics, and Suffrage

OVERVIEW

Rapid change had profound effects on the way Americans lived and on the issues they embraced during the 1920s. Far from the nation of gentlemen farmers that Thomas Jefferson once had envisioned, the United States' success as an emerging capitalist giant changed citizens' choices about where to live and work as well as their ideas about politics and the right to vote. The year 1920 marked a pivotal moment in American history. The U.S. Census conducted that year was the first to show that more Americans lived in urban areas than in rural settings. Moreover, Americans demonstrated changing political agendas as women headed to the polls for the first time.

The great influx of immigrants in the decades immediately before and after the turn of the century had helped to transfigure America's true metropolises. These urban centers offered sights and sounds that were both wondrous and horrifying. As gleaming skyscrapers and noisy, traffic-packed streets transformed the landscapes of many American cities, new problems evolved as well, and the problems were not limited to the largest cities. In 1920, 29 million Americans lived in cities of 100,000 or more (1920s Fashion). From air pollution to entrenched political corruption, urbanization raised issues that city dwellers were forced to address. Millions of Americans were attracted to the urban job market, but not all of them chose to live within the cities, where the dark side of urbanization was most prevalent.

Urbanization led to a proliferation of suburbs, which would have been impossible without the rapidly increasing use of automobiles that marked the century's first quarter. By 1926, a Model T could be purchased for just $290, and 75 percent of cars sold were purchased through installment payments (Flink 1972, 458–461). As a result of the car's low cost and the convenience of installment payments, many working-class Americans found that they, too, could own this machine that seemed to be a vehicular representation of the American dream. By 1929, the United States had 26.7 million gasoline-powered vehicles, compared to just 2.5 million in 1915 (Pratt 1980, 41). The human-to-automobile ratio was 30:1 in 1920 Chicago; 11:1 five years later; and 8:1 in 1930, when both Seattle and Detroit had one car for every four residents. Los Angeles began the 1930s with a three to one ratio (McKelvey 1968, 62–63). Suburban enclaves expanded the population within a metropolitan area without raising population density within the city's borders. Nevertheless, people who lived in the suburbs and worked in the city often contributed to the initiation of such new problems as heavy traffic and pollution by driving cars into the city each day to get to their workplaces.

As municipal governments wrestled with problems and experimented with possible solutions, a new tension arose between urban and rural priorities. Rural voters often had strong objections to immigration while many urban dwellers were unsympathetic to farmers struggling to recover from the agricultural price collapse after the end of World War I. In some ways, urban Americans and their rural counterparts seemed to be living in different time periods because providing public utilities such as electricity, telephone, and water was much easier in urban areas. As a result, many city dwellers enjoyed all that the 20th century had to offer while many farmers seemed stuck in the 19th century.

Much of the electorate, whether urban or rural, hungered for a return to "normalcy." During World War I, the lives of American civilians had been touched in unexpected ways, including the draft, federalization of the railroads, and attempts to squelch dissension. The 1918 influenza pandemic and the Red Scare of 1919–1920 had added to a sense of instability as the 1920s began. The public desire for a return to past standards was apparent in the consecutive choices of three conservative Republicans for president as well as Republican majorities in Congress. (Though not all Republicans in Congress were conservative, most were. Moreover, Congress's overall conservatism was guaranteed by the combination of conservative Republicans and Southern Democrats, who represented some of the most conservative politicians in office.) Despite the hegemony of conservatism, the drive for change was not quite dead. The Progressive Party again nominated a strong candidate for president in 1924, and Robert La Follette's relative success bolstered regional movements for change.

Politicians' constituencies doubled in 1920 when the suffrage movement finally succeeded in winning women's right to vote. Some mistakenly believed that women's votes would fundamentally alter the nation and bring greater equality between the two sexes. These pundits anticipated that women would vote in a bloc, but they did not. Early in the decade, women had some success promoting legislation of special interest to them; however, that brief period of female influence ended when it became clear that women would not vote as a bloc. Some women were appointed or elected to public offices during the 1920s, but their service earned footnotes in political history and little more. Many women believed that getting the right to vote should be feminists' ultimate goal; however, some women continued their roles as activists. These two groups positioned themselves on different sides of a great chasm created by proposals for an Equal Rights Amendment, which would have made men and women equal under the law.

For the most part, this decade did not inspire activism or government intervention. Political machines tended to dominate big cities that were struggling to serve expanding populations, and the leaders of smaller municipalities occupied themselves with issues such as road building and establishing adequate parking for the expanding population of automobiles. The nation was leaning away from the concept of big government. For most Americans, a sense of relative security existed amidst an atmosphere of great change. When the stock market crashed in October 1929, Americans did not know where to look for help—and the federal government was similarly stymied. The financial collapse would create fundamental changes in American politics and in many citizens' attitudes about the role of the federal government.

TIMELINE

1920	As part of the Red Scare, the United States Department of Justice works with local police and deputized civilians to arrest thousands of suspected radicals on January 2 and 3.
	The League of Women Voters is founded in February.
	In May, police arrest anarchists Nicola Sacco and Bartolomeo Vanzetti for robbery and murder in a case linked to the Red Scare.
	The 19th Amendment to the Constitution is ratified in August, giving women the right to vote.
	American voters choose Republican Warren G. Harding as the new president in November. Harding, who captures 61 percent of the vote, defeats Democrat James M. Cox.
1921	Alice Robertson of Oklahoma becomes the first woman to preside over the House of Representatives in June. Her tour of duty lasts 30 minutes.

Because the United States Senate refuses to approve the Versailles Treaty, Harding signs a joint resolution in July officially ending U.S. involvement in World War I.

On Christmas Day, Harding commutes the prison sentence of Socialist leader Eugene V. Debs, who had garnered more than 900,000 votes in the 1920 presidential race despite his imprisonment.

1922   Congress approves the Cable Act, which expands protection of American women's citizenship, in September.

In October, Georgia's governor appoints Rebecca L. Fenton to be the first woman to serve in U.S. Senate.

1923   Warren G. Harding dies during a cross-country trip in August.

A day later, Calvin Coolidge is sworn in as the nation's 30th president. Coolidge's father, a notary, presides over the 2:30 a.m. ceremony.

During October, Montana senator Thomas J. Walsh reveals the results of an 18-month investigation of the Teapot Dome scandal in which Secretary of the Interior Albert Fall leased federal lands to oil companies under questionable circumstances.

The Equal Rights Amendment is introduced in Congress in December.

1924   Coolidge wins reelection, capturing 54 percent of the vote in a three-way contest.

1926   Coolidge signs the Revenue Act, decreasing the size of the federal government. This legislation, approved in February, lowers income taxes and surtaxes.

The nation's most successful Socialist leader Eugene V. Debs dies in October.

1927   The Holland Tunnel, connecting New York City with Jersey City, New Jersey, opens in November. More than 50,000 vehicles use the tunnel on its first day.

1928   Herbert Hoover beats Al Smith to win the presidency. Hoover collects 58 percent of the vote against the first Catholic nominee of a major political party.

1929   On February 14, members of Al Capone's gang kill seven rivals in Chicago's St. Valentine's Day Massacre.

Congress meets in special session in April to consider actions to address growing problems in the nation's economy.

Albert B. Fall is convicted of accepting a $100,000 bribe in the Teapot Dome scandal. He is sentenced to a year in prison and a $100,000 fine.

Hoover meets confidentially with business and labor leaders in November to discuss the October 29 stock market crash.

URBANIZATION

The Ease of City Living

As the 1920s began, urban life was becoming a larger part of the American experience. Census figures show that more than half of all Americans lived in communities defined as urban, and more than two-thirds of those lived in the nation's 58 largest cities. Nevertheless, many of those classified as urban dwellers probably would have disagreed because the Census Bureau's definition of an urban area was any community with a population of 2,500 or more. While some might quibble with the government's definition of an urban area, the Bureau of the Census's figures accurately reflected urban growth created by the settlement of immigrants, the internal migration of African Americans to areas where industrial jobs were available, and the growth of some villages into larger communities. In addition, through publishing, broadcasting, and tourism, urban areas played a bigger role in providing an intellectual framework for the nation as a whole, not only those who lived in urban areas.

Transportation played a big role in the development of urban America during this decade. Los Angeles, for example, began to sprawl across much of Southern California in the 1920s because, for the first time, citizens showed a preference for automobile travel over riding trolleys. Limitations of trolley lines had created boundaries for urban growth, but the emergence of cars as the preferred means of transportation coincided with Los Angeles's horizontal growth and a doubling of its population in the 1920s. Businesses and residents increasingly abandoned the city's center while traffic congestion became a factor of everyday life that government addressed through highway planning rather than support for public transportation. In 1923, 68 percent of the city's residents entered the downtown business district each day, but by 1931, only 52 percent traveled downtown on a daily basis (Teaford 1986, 65). Los Angeles's proliferation of highways was an exaggerated example of a change that was occurring in urban areas around the country. Automobiles spurred the growth of suburban-type communities both inside and outside cities' limits.

New York's Fifth Avenue is crowded with Ford Model Ts in this March 1920 photo.
(Library of Congress)

City life changed at a rapid pace. The percentage of residents working in blue-collar factory jobs had begun a slow decline in most cities, and more people found work in white-collar positions. Horse-drawn carriages were making way for automobiles and trucks. Office buildings were climbing toward the sky on sites where three- and four-story walkups had once stood. New York City's Holland Tunnel immediately handled about 2,000 cars per day when it opened in 1925 (McKelvey 1968, 49). Newly conceptualized tabloid newspapers and radio stations captivated a growing mass market. In densely populated areas, extending networks for electricity, telephones, and running water was much easier than it was in rural areas. As a result, city living offered luxuries that made everyday life easier and everyday work more efficient. The modernization, sophistication, and apparent prosperity of urban life gave city dwellers a sense of superiority over people in rural America; however, economic figures show that many people in urban America were eking out a meager existence.

As major cities blossomed from coast to coast, the pace of urbanization was strongest in the East; nevertheless, Los Angeles's surprisingly rapid growth broadened the sense that urbanization was, indeed, a nationwide phenomenon. Although the Western frontier had been declared closed only 30 years earlier, the West ranked second to the East in urbanization by 1920. The South and the Great

Plains still were largely rural; the scattered cities in these regions offered an escape from rural isolation without the skyscrapers of New York or the highway network of Southern California. Many Americans left their farm roots to find better jobs and higher standards of living.

Force of Urbanization Strongest in Northeast

American cities' growing magnetism was more potent in some places than in others. Throughout the decade, the Northeast was far more urbanized than the rest of the nation. Census data show that the number of people living in any community of 2,500 or greater represented about 60 percent of the total population in the Northeast in 1920. By the end of the decade, more than 70 percent of Northeasterners were urban dwellers. In the West, the urban population in 1920 was around 30 percent, but it climbed to more than 40 percent before the decade's end. The Midwest's urban population was slightly lower than the West's throughout the 1920s. And predictably, the South was the least urbanized section of the nation throughout the decade. In 1920, less than 15 percent of Southerners lived in urban areas; that percentage remained below 20 percent at decade's end. Consequently, at a time when more than 70 percent of the Northeast's population was urbanized, more than 80 percent of Southerners still lived in isolated locations or in communities of less than 2,500 people. Although 20 Southern cities had populations of more than 100,000 people, the region had no huge metropolises. This regional disparity unavoidably led to huge economic, political, and sociological differences that would remain in place for decades to come.

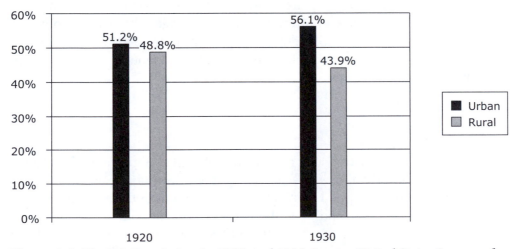

Figure 3.1 *The U.S. Population in 1920 and 1930.* Source: *United States Bureau of the Census.*

Table 3.1. Top Ten Most Populous Cities in the U.S. in 1920 and 1930

1920	*1930*
New York	New York
Chicago	Chicago
Philadelphia	Philadelphia
Detroit	Detroit
Cleveland	Los Angeles
St. Louis	Cleveland
Boston	St. Louis
Baltimore	Baltimore
Pittsburgh	Boston
Los Angeles	Pittsburgh

Source: United States Bureau of the Census.

Although most urban dwellers in 1920 lived in smaller cities and towns, the population was slowly shifting to the bigger cities. That year's census showed that New York, Chicago, and Philadelphia were home to more than 1 million people each. In Detroit, where the population had exploded because of the auto industry's phenomenal expansion, the population was just under 1 million. Los Angeles was bigger than New York in geographic area, but New York's population was 10 times as large. It is, therefore, not surprising that New York's dense population led architects and planners to view taller buildings as a means of increasing their options, especially for workplaces. Los Angeles, on the other hand, sprawled. But Los Angeles was not the only sunny city to experience dramatic population growth. Resort areas attracted many newcomers. Employees at hotels and other facilities that catered to tourists added to the permanent population, and a surging wave of resettling retirees changed the demographics of these areas. Miami's population grew 234.4 percent in the 1920s, and at least 5 of the 10 fastest-growing metropolitan areas could be identified as resort cities (McKelvey 1968, 33).

1920 Census

The 1920 census offered America a new picture of itself. The percentage of Americans who lived in urban areas rose to 51.2 percent from 45.6 percent in 1910. The rural population dropped to 48.8 from 54.4 percent in the same period. At some point between 1910 and 1920, the nation's population had become more urban than rural. Over the course of the 1920s, this trend continued, and the urban population grew to 56.1 percent of the population by 1930. The census also showed that the number of American communities with 2,500 or more

1920

- 7–1,421
- 1,421–2,835
- 2,835–4,249
- 4,249–5,664

1930

- 15,254–2,158,902
- 2,158,902–4,302,550
- 4,302,550–6,446,198
- 6,446,198–8,589,844

Map 3.1 *Urban population in 1920 and 1930*

people had risen to 2,728 from 2,269 between 1910 and 1920. This increase indicates that many of the people added to the urban rolls probably stayed in the same communities, but over the course of the decade, those villages grew into towns large enough to be classified as urban. By the decade's end, there were 3,183 communities large enough to be considered urban. The total population in 1920 was 15 percent higher than it had been a decade earlier; urban population grew by 29 percent, and the rural population by just 3.2 percent. During the 1920s, the growth rate of the overall population was 16.2 percent, with the urban population continuing to expand at a higher rate than the rural population.

Skyscrapers

In cities with confined geographic areas and growing populations, builders increasingly decided that adding vertical space was the best way to accommodate a burgeoning business community. Consequently, the 1920s was a period of significant skyscraper construction, and in some cases, the new buildings reflected the era's esthetic tastes. By 1929, one count registered a total of 377 buildings exceeding 20 stories in cities across the United States. New York City was home to 188 of these structures, and 15 of those were more than 500 feet tall (McKelvey 1968, 48). Among the most noted skyscrapers completed in the 1920s were Chicago's alabaster Wrigley Building and New York's Standard Oil Building, which had an unusual curved base. The RCA building, constructed in New York in the late 1920s, boasted a decorative crown intended to represent radio waves.

In the spirit of the age, Col. Robert R. McCormick sponsored a 1922 design competition for a new structure to house the Chicago Tribune Company. The American winner produced a now-acclaimed Gothic tower with a plain spire. However, the daring second-place entry by Finland's Eliel Saarinen attracted more attention with a mountain-like construction that gradually receded toward an undecorated top. Public reaction to the entry led Saarinen and his son Eero to move to the United States, where they found great success. Construction of New York's Chrysler Building, a fine representation of the then-popular art deco style, got under way in the 1920s. Its elaborate use of color and geometric shapes won rave reviews. Construction of the taller but more mundane Empire State Building also began; however, construction of both structures continued into the next decade. While most designers of skyscrapers did not embrace bold art deco designs, the Empire State Building and many others were topped by art deco ziggurats—pyramids with each floor smaller than the one beneath.

Suburbs

As American metropolises grew, the swiftest population expansion occurred in residential areas outside the cities' cores. Powered by the affordability of auto-

Historians' Debate: Suburbs Just for Wealthy?

Over the years, historians often have generalized about the suburbs of the 1920s, describing them as retreats for the wealthy and the white-collar workers within the middle class. However, more recent accounts have emphasized the existence of suburbs that served the working class. While blue-collar workers seldom landed in the same neighborhoods as wealthy suburbanites, many metropolitan areas offered suburban communities for members of the working class.

For example, neither the richest nor the poorest gravitated toward New York's borough of Queens, across the East River from Manhattan. However, Queens was home to both middle-class and working-class neighborhoods. It offered an escape from the frazzled pace of Manhattan, but Queens was densely populated by look-alike brick and wood-framed houses. To meet the demand for housing in Queens, builders filled farmland with row houses and six-family tenements. In blue-collar neighborhoods like Cambria Heights, homebuilders replicated plain, three-bedroom homes. Many residents were relatively recent immigrants escaping from ethnic slums. By 1920, the availability of a five-cent subway ride to Manhattan had made commuting affordable for a wide array of workers.

Blue-collar suburbs also formed a ring around Los Angeles during this period, according to historian Nancy Quam-Wickham. She noted aggressive competition among a scattering of suburbs in the southern half of the Los Angeles basin. Their goal was to attract industrial businesses as discoveries of oil contributed to growth in the local steel industry. Between 1922 and 1926, 29 of 37 new steel fabrication plants had the sole mission of serving the petroleum industry through the manufacture of pipelines, tools, and refinery equipment. Because it was unincorporated, one neighborhood, Lomita, offered working-class residents the option of saving money by growing food in small gardens or raising chickens in residential yards. The area was not exactly urban, but its location was convenient for workers because it was near Torrance, where oil had been found in 1922.

mobiles and the availability of mass transit, this burgeoning development provided nighttime sanctuaries for many urban workers. Some of these areas fell within a city's boundaries but were far removed from its business district. Others were once-separate communities swallowed by acquisitive metropolises, such as Los Angeles, which annexed 80 square miles and almost 600,000 residents during the 1920s (Tygiel 2001, 2). Some suburban areas lay outside cities and developed reputations for the kind of residents they attracted. Suburban communities like Beverly Hills maintained their glamour while others lost their exclusivity as newer, more genteel communities purloined their cachet.

The population of New York City's borough of Queens doubled during this decade. The Detroit suburb of Grosse Point Park, which stretches out along the sparkling waters of Lake St. Claire, experienced a 700 percent jump in population. The number of residents in the Cleveland suburb of Shaker Heights skyrocketed by 1,000 percent (Teaford 1986, 69). Land speculation accompanied suburbanization, especially in California and Florida. As Northerners flocked to the Miami area seeking permanent or seasonal homes, many immediately settled down in suburbs such as Palm Beach and Boca Raton. This led to a huge real estate boom that did not collapse until a 1926 hurricane ended it with a harsh splash of reality.

City life in . . .

New York

On the list of the biggest American cities, New York firmly held number one status with a population of 5.6 million. More than a million new arrivals called the city home by the end of the decade. Its nearest competitor, Chicago, was less than half as big. To many Americans, New York exemplified what was worst about urbanization—the crowding, the traffic, the noise, the dirt, the violence, and the raucous polyglot. In his 1927 book, *New York Is Not America,* Ford Madox Ford argued that the nation's largest city was entirely alien. Old-stock Americans like Ford looked down on its diverse neighborhoods and population.

Despite its unique qualities, New York has long been emblematic of the hard-driving capitalist nation, and during the 1920s, the city gained popularity as a tourist destination. Some small-town visitors liked to come to the big city, stare up at the tall buildings, and visit exotic ethnic neighborhoods where they could glimpse authentic specimens of the Chinese, Italian, and Jewish populations. As the city tried to lure visitors who might jump in their new cars and visit Gotham, Midtown Manhattan became synonymous with New York City in the minds of many Americans by 1929. At the beginning of the 1920s, the Woolworth Building in Lower Manhattan was the most heralded landmark, but by 1930, it had been overshadowed by the beautiful Chrysler building in Midtown.

Chicago

Known for its healthy job market as well as its gangsters, Chicago faced a decade of big changes in population density that led to a boom in residential construction. The rate of residential construction for buildings housing 40 or more units skyrocketed by 1,994 percent in the 1920s compared to the preceding two decades (Radford 1992, 3). Like New York, the Windy City grew upward. With 384 buildings over 10 stories high and 65 over 20 stories, the city was developing a crowded skyline (McKelvey 1968, 48). One cause of the city's population growth was the migration of African Americans from the South. Upon arrival, African Americans found crowded living conditions, but most relished the escape from Jim Crow laws. In addition, African Americans had a real opportunity to acquire city jobs in Chicago. In 1928, the South Side elected the first African American congressman from a northern city. By 1929, five representatives and one senator made up the black caucus in the state legislature. At the same time, some suburbs used zoning laws and other rules to maintain an all-white citizenry.

Atlanta

In the 1920s, Atlanta was a city caught between its past and its future. The city that William Tecumseh Sherman had burned to the ground during the Civil War was seeking a new identity. Atlanta had risen from the ashes to become the state capital in 1877, but in the 1920 census, the city ranked 33rd among American cities in population. At that time, the railroad industry was the city's largest employer. Atlanta also ranked second in candy making, producing about $5 million in candy each year (Garofalo 1976,

As the nation's second most populous city, Chicago enjoyed the advantages of urbanization and suffered from the accompanying problems. Shown here are the Temple Building and the Morrison Hotel in 1925. (Library of Congress)

189). However, Atlanta's business leaders were hungry to achieve greater industrial success by luring northern manufacturers to the city. Eager to shed the image of a city populated by idle antebellum gentlemen, the Chamber of Commerce launched the Forward Atlanta Movement in 1926. Atlanta's boosters claimed that the effort attracted more than 100 companies in its first year alone. The city's population made a healthy jump from just over 200,000 in 1920 to 260,475 in 1930, but it moved up only one spot on the list of the nation's most populous cities. The city's population included a sizeable and active African American community that could not partake in the new opportunities created by business growth.

Los Angeles

Los Angeles's urban development was unusual. A metropolis sprang up without a single dominant industry. While the city did lead the nation in filmmaking, it also ranked second in tire manufacturing and third in aviation. And in the 1920s, Los Angeles businesses were consolidating at a surprising rate, with big companies buying out smaller operators to form large corporations. However, the city's appeal went far beyond its manufacturing capacity. The film industry added glamour to its image, and its consistently warm climate was a magnet to many

Americans. The discovery of oil within the Los Angeles metropolitan area was also a boon to growth. Los Angeles was the third-fastest-growing city in 1920, and it moved up several notches over the course of the decade. In 1923, *Saturday Evening Post* correspondent Albert Atwood wrote with some consternation about the "extraordinary and almost unprecedented pouring of population, money and prosperity into one section of the country and more particularly into one city" (Tygiel 2001, 3). As it grew, the predominantly white city developed significant African American and Mexican communities as well as a small Japanese population.

Birmingham

In this era, Birmingham, Alabama, was the South's most striking example of an urban industrial area. A treasure trove of iron, coal, and limestone located near the city quickly transformed Birmingham into the region's leading steel manufacturer. The central city's population, which was 178,806 in 1920, was more than four times as large as it had been at the turn of the century. It grew by more than 45 percent in the 1920s to 259,678. The entire metropolitan area had a population of 310,054 in 1920 and grew to 431,493 in 1930 (Brownell 1972b, 22). As the decade began, the city's population included 6,084 immigrants and more than 10,000 Americans with at least one foreign parent. Blacks made up almost 40 percent of the population (Brownell 1972b, 28). A 1924 study showed that the town also had more than 106,000 industrial workers (Brownell 1972b, 26). By the decade's end, some forms of industrial production had dropped a bit. United States Steel Corporation, which bought out a Birmingham company in 1907, did not want its Southern facility to prosper at the expense of its operations in the North. If steel produced in Birmingham had cost less than steel made in Pittsburgh, many of the company's customers would have bought from Birmingham, reducing profits in the company's primary operation at Pittsburgh.

Progress Fires Grand Views of the Future

The rapidly changing urban landscape spurred the American imagination, just as the swift adoption of electricity, automobiles, telephones, and mass production widened Americans' expectations. Having absorbed so much change early in the century led many to anticipate an even grander future. After witnessing the proliferation of skyscrapers and growing dependence on subways, many city planners looked for creative ways to use the space above and below city streets. Engineer John K. Hencken proposed a 16-mile elevated highway through New York City. He hoped that this roadway would help the city avoid increasing traffic congestion. Other city planners envisioned elevated playgrounds, moving traffic platforms, and underground railway cargo service.

Harvey Wiley Corbett of New York City accurately anticipated an age when some high-rise buildings would be connected by aboveground enclosed walkways. He also predicted sidewalk bridges hundreds of feet above city streets—an idea that has become a reality on highway overpasses in some urban settings although it is not used as commonly as he expected.

In 1928 and 1929, ambitious city planners saw one of their imagined landscapes take shape in northeastern New Jersey. Designers of the suburban city of Radburn, advertised as the "Town of the Motor Age," hoped to create a pleasant environment that would allow human beings and automobiles to coexist in an attractive and safe environment. Planners used a series of super blocks to divide the city. A ring of dead-end roads led into each of the 30- to 40-acre super blocks. This design averted the frequent problem of heavy traffic passing through residential neighborhoods, where children might be playing in the streets. Pedestrian underpasses allowed people to walk from block to block without the danger of crossing a traffic-laden intersection. Radburn's plan, which included park space within the super blocks, was intended to segregate people from automotive traffic. Planners Clarence Stein and Henry Wright also wanted the city to be self-sufficient, with industrial, commercial, and residential sectors satisfying each other's needs. Built around the same time, Sunnyside Gardens in New York's Queens borough was a similarly planned community with ample green spaces. Both turned out to be too expensive for low-income residents.

Another model city of this era was Kingsport, Tennessee. This privately financed community had been incorporated in 1917 by businessmen who hoped that the 1920s would bring industries to the area. Their lures were Kingsport's strategic location, natural resources, low wages, antiunion environment, and cheap land. The developers' largest goal was to generate new business for the Carolina, Clinchfield and Ohio Railway. They hired city planners, architects, and landscapers to map out the city's physical plan, and they relied on guidance from Columbia University and the state normal school at Johnson City to establish a school system. By 1927, the town's promoters reported the addition of 10 manufacturing plants that employed 3,383 workers.

Many of these innovations sprang from the very real problems already associated with urban growth. Rapidly increasing use of automobiles facilitated development of urban areas. At the same time, cars contributed to new and unforeseen problems. In America's existing urban areas, officials found that they could no longer avoid addressing some of the negative effects of urban growth.

URBAN ISSUES

Strain on the Infrastructure

If Henry Ford had not introduced the assembly line a decade earlier, urbanization and the problems associated with it probably would not have played such a significant role in the 1920s. The same techniques that had expanded industrialization, spurred suburban growth, and enhanced the nation's increasing urbanization also accelerated problems such as traffic congestion, parking, and air pollution. There were no easy solutions in the 1920s, and many of the new urban problems of that decade remain unsolved many decades later.

Urban transportation was a key issue for most cities, and cars stood at the heart of that problem. The ever-expanding ranks of automobile owners created traffic jams that lengthened the amount of time spent on daily commutes from suburban homes to jobs in the city. The need for bridges and tunnels to accommodate auto traffic became clear during this decade, and some impressive engineering feats such as New York City's Holland Tunnel and Philadelphia's Benjamin Franklin Bridge represented efforts to ease traffic tie-ups. Cars also contributed to both air and noise pollution, and they required storage space in the form of parking lots or multistory structures. Finally, human use of these mechanical wonders killed people—pedestrians, drivers, and passengers. Automobile accidents killed 11.9 people per 100,000 Americans each year between 1918 and 1922. That number had more than doubled by 1928–1932, when traffic fatalities had reached 25.2 per 100,000 (MacLennan 1988, 234). Increasing traffic deaths led the U.S. Chamber of Commerce and the National Safety Council to organize conferences on the topic in 1924 and 1926. Moreover, cities had difficulty maintaining public transportation as an inexpensive alternative to automobiles. Equipment costs and increasing competition from automobiles made it difficult to maintain government-subsidized public transit at a time when government involvement in Americans' daily lives was shunned by many voters, especially business leaders.

Urban factories sometimes contaminated the water as well as the air. And they were sources of noise within metropolitan areas. Often these areas bordered on railroad tracks or docks, which made transportation of goods easier. Dirty factory districts and residential ghettoes represented the ugly side of city life that made so many Americans concerned about the nation's growing embrace of urbanization. Pollution clearly held health hazards—and many believed that urbanization itself threatened American lives. The mere presence of so many people in one place carried health risks. In the wake of the previous decade's influenza pandemic, Thomas Edison bemoaned the future of the crowded city. In the March 1927 issue of *Popular Science Monthly,* he predicted that "disaster must overtake us" unless cities quit "building ever taller buildings" (Leinwand 2001, 310).

Corruption of society and in city government represented a different kind of urban corrosion. While dishonesty and crime were not new, automobiles and trucks provided new prosperity to criminals, enabling gangsters to expand their empires and simplify the transportation of illegal goods. The unpopularity of Prohibition in many urban areas also gave gangsters a respectable clientele. Speakeasies, bordellos, and gambling houses found eager customers in many metropolitan areas, and as illegal activity flourished, urban gangsters gained power

With alcoholic beverages banned by Prohibition, bootleggers flourished by ignoring the law. In this 1922 photo, cases of moonshine lie alongside a wrecked car. (Library of Congress)

and handed out patronage like benevolent rulers. The new prominence of gangsters served to reinforce rural fears about cities, which some saw as dens used for the propagation of sin. Despite the voices of doom, American cities were here to stay, and so were many metropolitan problems.

Pitfalls of Urban Life

City residents often felt that they enjoyed a higher standard of living than their rural cousins; however, the advantages of urban life did not come without a cost. Although jobs within metropolitan areas often paid more than the farm jobs their parents or grandparents may have held, many urban workers just managed to make ends meet. A 1927 report from the National Industrial Conference showed that in New York City the weekly budget of an urban manual laborer was $36, while a white-collar worker typically could afford to spend $40 a week. Out of each week's pay, a white-collar worker in Brooklyn owed "ten dollars to the landlord, fifteen to the grocer, butcher and milkman, five to the clothing stores and nine to all his other creditors" (Leinwand 2001, 15–16). That left the white-collar worker with $1 per week in discretionary income. A factory worker in Queens spent a bit less to attain roughly the same standard of living—and because a manual laborer's budget was smaller, he, too, had little leeway for unexpected expenses. Given this lack of economic flexibility, finding and paying for living space often was a challenging part of the urban experience.

Ethnic neighborhoods commonly were sites of demographic transformations. As Jews, Italians, and other immigrants moved out of ghettos and settled in upwardly mobile suburbs, they were replaced by African American migrants and immigrants. With immigration restricted in the 1920s, many cities became more dependent on arriving African Americans to fill neighborhoods and take over low-level jobs. In New York, where the African American population more than doubled in the years following World War I, Harlem provided fertile ground for African American culture in the 1920s. The neighborhood was home to thousands of former farm workers from the South as well as Spanish-speaking blacks from the West Indies. By the end of the decade, Harlem boasted the nation's largest black community, with a population of 164,566 in East Harlem (McKelvey 1968, 39). If East Harlem's black population had been counted as a separate city in the 1930 census, it would have ranked as the 47th most populous urban area in the United States—just between Grand Rapids, Michigan, and Hartford, Connecticut. In the South and West, workers sometimes could find cheap homes in newly annexed districts, but many cities lacked adequate housing for the working poor. Often urbanization forced cities to adopt new policies to provide high-density, multifamily housing. While skyscrapers filled many business districts, most metropolitan apartment houses rose no higher than seven floors. Crowded tenement neighborhoods mirrored urban traffic congestion.

As with transportation issues, state legislatures hesitated to invest the state's resources in resolving problems that often were confined to urban areas. New York governor Al Smith called the state legislature into special session in 1920 because he hoped lawmakers would pass an amendment to the state constitution that would have allowed construction of homes using state housing credits. However, the legislature refused his request, instead granting a tax exemption to promote private investment in urban housing. New York's lawmakers were following a philosophy spread by Lawrence Veiller, director of the National Housing Association. He condemned subsidized housing plans in New York, Los Angeles, Boston, and Chicago because he believed that, with proper encouragement, private investment could solve urban housing problems.

Obviously, however, when workers enjoyed only $1 of discretionary income per week, they were unlikely to have the ability to pay the higher rents that almost certainly would accompany private construction of new residential buildings. The opportunity to undertake private construction of low-income housing failed to entice many businessmen because of the small likelihood that they could claim quick and sizeable profits. For many Americans, urban life offered great promise, but finding a place to live sometimes was the first difficult trial in a daily struggle to eke out a decent existence.

Urban versus Rural

In the 1920s, many Americans found themselves trapped between competing impulses. While metropolitan life and its many modern conveniences attracted popular attention, the agrarian myth pulled the nation's imagination toward the past. Historian George Edwin Mowry concluded that "social nostalgia, more of a historical force than is generally recognized, . . . explains the tenacious grip that the rural bias still had on many Americans in 1920 and the decades thereafter, when the nation had become predominately urban" (Garofalo 1976, 196). The urban–rural tug-of-war was evident in many parts of American life. Residents of metropolitan areas often exhibited contempt for their rural neighbors. The *New Yorker* magazine, which debuted in 1925, proclaimed that it was not written to appeal to "the old lady in Dubuque"; at the same time, the rurally based Methodist Board of Temperance, Prohibition, and Public Morals claimed that Broadway shows were "naked, profane, blasphemous and salacious" (Leuchtenburg 1993, 226). The urban polyglot seemed exotic and exciting to many, but largely homogenous or segregated rural white populations often saw metropolitan diversity as an alien force degrading American life. Some saw cities as windows to tomorrow; others viewed them as incubators for crime.

Historian William E. Leuchtenburg contended that existing urban–rural conflict gained new life in the 1920s as a result of internal stresses within each camp. Urban radio stations had begun touching rural lives, and many popular American novels now ended with the protagonist triumphantly setting out to pursue the bright lights of the big city. At the same time, some representatives of metropolitan life displayed sentimentality about small-town living. The hero of Sherwood Anderson's *Winesburg, Ohio* leaves for urban America, but Anderson also voiced distaste for the "filth and disorder of modern civilization" (Leuchtenburg 1993, 128). In 1929, Henry Ford, whose ingenuity helped to make Detroit a metropolis, opened Greenfield Village, a museum that reflected his affection for the small-town life of an earlier time.

Rural fears blocked efforts to consolidate metropolitan cities and counties in Seattle, St. Louis, and Cleveland. Often representation in state legislatures was disproportionately tilted toward rural interests. Some state constitutions called for reapportionment after each decennial census; however, legislatures sometimes blocked these changes. Whereas 41 Connecticut cities had five-sixths of the state's population, those cities had only one-third of legislative representatives. Detroit was home to one-third of Michigan's population but less than one-sixth of its legislators (McKelvey 1968, 62). Such disparities led some to discuss the secession of "city states." The 1928 presidential election was the first to mirror

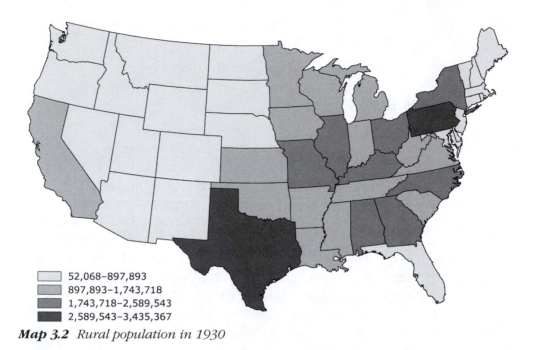

Map 3.2 *Rural population in 1930*

Legend:
- 52,068–897,893
- 897,893–1,743,718
- 1,743,718–2,589,543
- 2,589,543–3,435,367

the urban–rural rift. When native New Yorker Al Smith rose to the top of the Democratic field of candidates, the *New Republic* reported that "a representative of the unpedigreed, foreign-born, city-bred, many tongued recent arrivals on the American scene has knocked on the door and aspired seriously to the presiding seat in the national Council Chamber" (Leuchtenburg 1993, 229). Instead of climbing trees as a boy, Smith had ascended to the top of stacked crates on the city's waterfront. In addition to being a city dweller, Smith was a Catholic and an opponent of Prohibition, and for these combined sins, Protestant ministers across the nation attacked him. He lost the election to Herbert Hoover, an Iowa-born supporter of Prohibition; however, Smith made major gains for the Democratic Party among immigrant groups in urban areas.

Lawlessness in the City

Corruption in city government became a more visible problem in the 1920s. Some politicians, such as New York mayor Jimmy Walker, accepted donations from business leaders who wanted favors from the city. Elsewhere, undisguised gangsters spread the tentacles of their operations into municipal government. Many elected leaders accepted money from special interests, and the definition of corrupt behavior became blurred by the tacit acceptance of speakeasies as a part of urban American life. Boston's mayor James Curley openly believed in pursuing the "direct method" of government "even if you have to break a few laws and tear up red tape" (Teaford 1986, 51). In Indianapolis, the mayor was convicted of corrupt practices, and six city council members paid fines for accepting bribes. While political machines often violated laws, they could expect the support of first-generation immigrants who had little understanding of the American electoral system. These newcomers often traded votes for jobs or for favorable treatment from judges, police officers, and other government officials.

Beyond the involvement of money-wielding interest groups, many cities were riddled with the racketeering operations of organized crime. In racketeering schemes, gangsters coerced legitimate businesses to pay for "protection" from violence or competition. When the racketeers became successful enough to command large amounts of money, they used cash and threats to make inroads in politics. In Detroit, even Henry Ford became loosely tied to the mob through his association with Chester La Mare, head of a Sicilian bootlegging empire. When La Mare was convicted of violating Prohibition in 1927, Ford employee Harry Bennett argued that the automaker himself should supervise La Mare's rehabilitation. Eventually, Ford employed 8,000 ex-convicts as strikebreakers and thugs, whom he was supposed to be rehabilitating. Throughout the decade, two Cleveland gangs fought for dominance of an Italian neighborhood's liquor manufacturing. In San Francisco, Black Tony Parmagini controlled alcohol and narcotics trafficking, and Kansas City's John Lazia ruled gambling and bootlegging ventures.

Although mob activity occurred in many cities, it was most obvious in Chicago. In 1927, at least 91 rackets operated in the city. Among affected industries were such seemingly mundane fields as laundry, linen supply, barbers, bakers, municipal workers, and ice cream distribution. Chicago racketeering was responsible for 108 bombings and 379 slayings in a single year. And a modest businessman could order the murder of a competitor for less than $100. In many cities, political influence could be bought. To guarantee that the Chicago mob's choices won on Election Day 1924, "automobiles filled with gunmen paraded the streets. . . . Polling places were raided by armed thugs and ballots taken at the point of a gun from the hands of voters waiting to drop them in the box," according to the Illinois Crime Survey (Teaford 1986, 45). One Chicago newspaper reported that more than $1 million had been paid to the Eighteenth Ward William Hale Thompson Men's Club by promoters of prostitution, liquor, and gambling. Thompson was the city's mayor for most of the decade and enjoyed a friendship with Al Capone, who took over mob leadership in 1925. Observers said Capone ran city government from his suite at the Lexington Hotel.

Too Many Cars, Too Little Time

Increasing traffic congestion was the most frustrating problem plaguing American cities in the 1920s. "Traffic has increased several times faster than the population

New automated signals direct traffic on the streets of Washington, D.C., in 1925.
(Library of Congress)

in all our principal cities," reported a Cleveland planning consultant, Robert H. Whitter, in 1920 (McKelvey 1968, 43). Three years later, 68 of every 100 people living within a 10-mile radius of Los Angeles crowded into the central business district each day—and automobiles were the primary mode of transportation there. This human and automotive population density caused maddeningly slow traffic in places, and at the same time, the overpopulation of American road-ways led to a rising death toll from auto accidents. Some metropolitan areas merely attacked the problem by planning more roads. Los Angeles fell into this category, and so did Detroit, which owed its growth to the auto industry. In 1927, Detroit became the first city to propose a system of highways and loops to ease congestion of traffic going into and out of the downtown area. The Motor City rejected a 1929 plan for subway construction.

Other cities turned to technology to lessen congestion. In a 1922 attempt to improve traffic flow, the City of New York set up traffic signals at 26 inter-sections along Fifth Avenue and connected them in such a way that a single police officer could change them all simultaneously. After General Electric de-veloped a system in 1924 that enabled a time clock to make stop-and-go signal lights operate on a schedule, Cleveland became the first city to put the system to work, greatly reducing traffic jams. Berkeley, California, police were the first to communicate between cars using radios in 1929. This advancement, which allowed officers to confer about traffic problems from different locations, was soon embraced by other cities.

Attempting to change human behavior was another tactic. Some municipalities tried to avert congestion by banning curbside parking. Los Angeles passed a no-parking ordinance in 1920 that created a public uproar. Movie star Clara Kimball Young led a protest caravan, and the city repealed the ordinance. After years of public resistance, Chicago finally banned curb parking in 1927. Rochester, New York, was the nation's leader in efforts to improve safety on the roads. After experiencing 164 fatal accidents in 1918, the city launched a five-year effort to improve safety in the streets. This project inspired programs elsewhere under the leadership of the National Safety Council. The Good Roads Movement advocated road maintenance, highway construction, and new driving regulations.

Because drivers were reluctant to abandon their automobiles, officials in many metropolitan areas faced heightened demands to increase the number of available parking spaces. In 1926, Boston became the first city to charge motorists for parking on the street. The Pure Oil Building's garage in Chicago opened in 1926 and offered fully mechanized parking. Elevators and conveyor belts delivered cars to open spaces within the 22-story facility. Detroit opened the first large ramp public garage in 1928. As cars gained popularity, public transportation suffered; however, many urban dwellers could not afford cars. This was especially true of African Americans, so cities faced the continuing challenge of maintaining public transportation while regulating automobile travel.

Pollution

Industries and motor vehicles combined to cause noise and air pollution in cities. However, few metropolitan residents pressured local governments for pollution action because they were more concerned about traffic congestion. The possibility of abandoning automobiles or industries never received serious consideration. Chicago and Pittsburgh were among the first cities to address air pollution, a job that University of Illinois engineers called "atmospheric sanitation." Soon, New Orleans, Kansas City, and Salt Lake City also established clean-air agencies. These offices primarily urged improvement in the operation of furnaces and the abandonment of soft coal alongside the adoption of anthracite coal. In 1926, Salt Lake City became the first American metropolis to conduct a survey of air pollution, and two years later, the federal Public Health Service began checking pollution in eastern U.S. cities. It reported that pollution cut sunlight over New York by 20 to 50 percent (Environmental History Timeline). Cleveland, Cincinnati, Akron, St. Louis, Denver, New York, and Rochester adopted air-pollution programs by 1930.

Water pollution also was an issue for cities, many of which had harbor areas polluted by companies' dumping of oil, industrial waste, and sewage. Although several cities reported that water at their ports was too dangerous for swimmers and inhospitable to fish, little was done to prevent water contamination. The Supreme Court ruled in 1921 that New Jersey had a right to dump sewage in New York harbor, and the 1924 Oil Pollution Act only prohibited intentional oil discharges in ocean waters within three miles of American shores. After automakers began depending on tetraethyl lead to stop engine knocking, some scientists studied the resulting pollution. The New York Academy of Medicine proposed in 1923 that "as far as possible, vehicles propelled by power other than gasoline displace the gasoline driven public conveyances and commercial vehicles in the city" (Pratt 1980, 42–43). Nevertheless, as then–Secretary of Commerce Herbert Hoover noted, official Washington had no reason to believe the public cared about pollution and was unlikely to take serious action in the absence of a public uproar.

City Reform

In the 1920s, cities looked for ways to make government more effective and more honest. One approach was the adoption of the city manager form of government, which placed most power in the hands of an unelected manager. Cities maintained elected councils, but in many cases, they were nonpartisan. Many reformers believed that this governmental model was a panacea. By 1930, 430 municipalities had switched to this structure; however, it became clear over time that this approach worked best in small- and medium-sized cities with relatively homogeneous populations (Teaford 1986, 52). In these locales, where the manager could focus on increasing efficiency and resolving a few minor squabbles, the system succeeded; however, in large communities with greater diversity, managers were less effective. Cincinnati, Cleveland, Rochester, and Kansas City were among the largest cities to adopt this form of government, but in Cleveland and Akron, city-manager charters were repealed after only a few years. In metropolitan areas, these systems often failed because groups opposing this form of government gathered political constituencies, whereas an unelected manager had little political capital to use in mediating between powerful rival factions.

A New America in the Mirror

Urbanization changed the way Americans lived and the way they saw themselves. The proliferation of automobiles helped to make urbanization possible, but it also created aggravating problems, including traffic congestion, air and noise pollution, and human casualties. Because of the influx of new people in American urban areas, poor housing also became a persistent problem, but public sentiment against subsidized housing limited how much progress could be made. Development of ethnic neighborhoods often sprang from discrimination and poverty, but the consolidation of ethnic communities sometimes reflected a personal choice to live among people with similar cultural backgrounds. Both African American migrants and immigrant groups found that these neighborhoods helped to preserve cultures that might have been lost if the population had been totally randomized.

Among native white stock, the expansion of the white-collar middle-class jobs in urban America altered family relationships, according to some experts. Having smaller middle-class families freed children from sharing in the burdens of work and produced new emotional ties within families. In turn, these bonds of affection led parents to focus more attention on the welfare of their children. These families featured growing involvement of fathers in child care and more intense parental consideration of child-rearing literature, dietary recommendations, and educational opportunities. Historian William Leuchtenburg has noted that child-consciousness and displays of affection became characteristic of middle-class parents during the decade (Leuchtenburg 1993, 164). Miriam Van Waters, a reformer and public servant in Massachusetts, noted that nurturing of children reflected more than family togetherness: it resulted from all relations within the family (Fass 1977, 111).

Some social reformers worried that the continued growth of urban populations with large industrial workforces threatened the well-being of the cities' elderly population. Farmers could continue working and earning an income until they could no longer handle agricultural work; however, because many blue-collar industrial jobs required physical strength, reformers feared that men would lose their jobs as they aged. Professional men and managerial employees in businesses tended to remain in their jobs until around age 70, when they retired. Statistics show that almost 60 percent of all men who were 65 or over remained among the working population in 1930. Nevertheless, older men with blue-collar backgrounds sometimes found that their work options were limited. A New York agency representative reported that "at age 63 you can safely predict that the man is not going to find work unless he is willing to take a place as a watchman" (Weiler 1989, 69).

Cities faced a constant need to change and to take on new responsibilities to simplify urban life. One new problem that demanded the attention of city government was air travel. By 1928, the nation had 5,000 airfields, and it became clear that air travel also required municipal supervision (McKelvey 1968, 32). As cities began to take responsibility for air traffic, they also found that airplanes offered a new tool for city planning—aerial photography. Airborne views gave administrators new insights into their domain. Planning of highways and future developments profited from these new perspectives on urban areas, and air travel benefited from urban development that placed many potential air travelers in areas near airfields. A symbiotic relationship existed between metropolitan growth and transportation development. Housing represented a separate piece of the urban puzzle. Spurts of growth often created situations in which both transportation resources and housing were inadequate. Finding a balance was a continuing challenge of the 1920s.

POLITICS

A Changing America

American politics in the 1920s represented a mix of attitudes. Some resulted from societal change while others were spontaneous reactions to events in the previous decade. Despite the view of the lawless 1920s, conservative impulses guided much of what occurred during this era. In rural America, fear of change carried a powerful punch. As urban areas became home to the majority of the nation's population, people who lived in the countryside sought to preserve their way of life and limit the number of changes foisted upon them by industrialization and urbanization. Radical politics, resistance to Prohibition, and the encroachment of urban ideas prompted concerns among many Americans. All three represented the threat of change and, in the minds of many, the prospect of lawlessness and chaos.

The Red Scare that began the decade brought the impact of international events to America's streets. The Bolshevik revolution in the Soviet Union exacerbated existing anxieties about the possibility of a radical revolution within the United States. Although Communists and Socialists never represented a significant portion of the American population, fears of upheaval exaggerated their potential impact. Another element of American politics in this era was a negative attitude toward the federal government. During World War I, some government actions had intruded in the lives of ordinary Americans and violated the rights of individuals. This generated a popular wish for a smaller and less intrusive government. In addition, the existence of Prohibition, which was commonly flouted by many Americans, contributed to disdain toward government. The only political change many Americans wanted was a reversion to the past.

Against the backdrop of conservative politics, some elements of American politics were changing. The continuing migration of African Americans from the South added an expanding constituency within local politics in urban areas. Because these African Americans rarely had enjoyed the right to vote in the rural South, they discovered new clout as they settled in concentrated numbers within metropolitan cities in the North and West. For the first time, white urban leaders saw the African American vote as a significant constituency worth wooing, and African American politicians could hope to win some political elections in urban areas.

The push for reform that marked the century's first two decades was in a state of decline, but it was not dead. Urban issues received the attention of local reform groups, and some vestiges of late-19th-century populism still survived in the Midwest. Nevertheless, the Progressive Party as a national entity was foundering. Although Progressives did nominate Robert La Follette, a respected candidate for president in 1924, the national party demonstrated little power to challenge the two major parties. Interest groups turned their attention to lobbying as a means of winning over lawmakers. Through lobbying, groups were able to develop stronger voices in the actions of government. This kind of political involvement did not require identification with a single party and thus made it easier for interest groups to develop bipartisan support. Because literally buying political favors was not uncommon, legitimate lobbying began to evolve in the shadow of influence peddling and bribery.

Fear of Change a Powerful Force

Change-oriented anxiety played a big part in the politics of the 1920s. No one could stop the revolutions in industrialization and urbanization, and native white Americans felt that they had lost something along the way. What many sought was a return to "normalcy." They hoped to regain the kind of life they had enjoyed before World War I spurred greater government involvement in daily life. Governmental intrusions in Americans' lives included the draft, violations of individual rights, and federalization of the railroads. Some Americans also believed that the influx of immigrants from southern and eastern Europe was fundamentally altering the United States. The federal government could be scaled down and the flood of immigrants could be transformed into a trickle, but those changes would not return Americans to the slower-paced life that they now recalled with some nostalgia. Many of the unsettling alterations in American life were unavoidable results of technological change and scientific learning—and they could not be erased. Many native white Americans feared that their voices would be lost in the din of immigrant languages and that they would lose their way in the darkness of moral corruption.

As Americans absorbed societal changes, voter turnout declined. Passions ran high on many issues, but Americans apparently placed less and less value on the power of an individual vote. In presidential elections, about 60 percent of voters outside the South cast ballots in the 1920s, and just 20 percent of Southerners voted (Gilda Lerner Institute of American History). This represented a dramatic drop from the peak in election participation—1896—when 80 percent of all voters went to the polls. And the drop occurred despite the empowerment of new voters, such as women, African Americans outside the South, and naturalized immigrants. In fact, analysts have speculated that these new voters and the poor represented the majority of eligible voters who did not cast ballots.

Disputes continue over participation of women in the elections of the 1920s, but it seems clear that African Americans and immigrants made up a significant percentage of those who failed to vote in many elections. However, naturalized immigrants first demonstrated their strength as a bloc in the 1928 election when they turned out in large numbers to support Al Smith.

The drop in voting has been attributed to a variety of factors. Among them are laws that created new hurdles for third parties; a shift to at-large municipal elections that lessened the power of minority groups; the rise of appointed commissions to oversee many facets of government, and the eventual weakening of urban political machines. All of these factors reduced the power of voters to affect government action. Some also blamed the low turnout on individuals' sense of helplessness, given the new power of lobbies in Washington. When the nation headed into the 1920s, a sense of insecurity rippled through society like a tremor from an earthquake hundreds of miles away. Conquering these misgivings would not be easy, but Americans tried throughout the decade. Then, after all of the efforts to regain "normalcy," the stock market crash in late 1929 closed the door to "normalcy" and set the stage for crises looming on the American horizon.

Red Scare

The most ominous phantom that stalked through America's nightmares was the possibility that American democracy might be subverted by Communism. The 1920s began with an extension of the Red Scare, which had started in 1919, a year of great turmoil that included crippling strikes and race riots. The U.S. Department of Justice's actions in 1919—raiding the Union of Russian Workers offices and deporting about 250 suspected radicals—were just a prelude to the peak of antiradical activity that occurred in the first days of the 1920s. Attorney General Mitchell Palmer launched a series of simultaneous raids in the first three days of 1920. With the assistance of police and deputized civilians, government agents targeted homes and meeting places in more than 35 American cities. Thousands of suspected radicals, mostly Eastern Europeans, were arrested. Figures from 1920 show that the Communist Party had between 8,000 and 15,000 members whereas the Socialist party could count 11,000 members in its ranks (Leuchtenburg 1993, 125). That represented less than one tenth of 1 percent of the American population.

Protests immediately decried this violation of individual rights. The majority of those arrested were set free in a matter of weeks, although hundreds more were deported. Despite the backlash, Palmer did not end his attacks on "alien filth." He predicted a huge Communist uprising in the United States on May 1, 1920. To counter the anticipated revolution, he placed buildings under guard, gave police protection to public officials, and ordered that the entire New York

City police force of 11,000 men be placed on around-the-clock duty. However, nothing happened. New fears arose after a terrorist attack on September 16, 1920, killed 33 people and injured more than 200 when a wagon filled with bombs exploded on the corner of Broad and Wall streets in New York's financial district. Palmer blamed Bolsheviks, but Americans did not race to judgment. The worst of the Red Scare had passed by the end of 1920.

One offshoot of the Red Scare was a legal case that attracted national and international notice and remained in the headlines for much of the decade. Two immigrant anarchists, Nicola Sacco and Bartolomeo Vanzetti, faced charges that they had killed a paymaster and guard while stealing a factory payroll of $15,766 in April 1920. Neither of the Italian-born defendants had a criminal record; however, both were recognized as radicals. In a trial that displayed the defendants' anarchist beliefs as much as the details of the crime, a Massachusetts

About 12,000 protesters gather in New York's Union Square to condemn the convictions and planned executions of Nicola Sacco and Bartolomeo Vanzetti in August 1927. Both men were executed later that month. (Underwood & Underwood/Corbis)

jury convicted them on July 14, 1921. That verdict was challenged in a series of court motions that uncovered striking evidence that a local gang was responsible for the robbery and murders. A man even confessed to committing the crimes; however, Sacco and Vanzetti never got a new trial. They were sentenced to death April 9, 1927. The case created outrage in the United States and abroad. In many places, liberals joined anarchists, communists, and socialists in condemning the convictions based on a weak criminal case. Protests occurred in the streets of Paris, Mexico City, London, and Buenos Aires. Nevertheless, the state of Massachusetts executed Sacco and Vanzetti in the electric chair August 23, 1927.

African American Politics

Although African Americans still represented less than one-quarter of the population of all urban areas outside the South, the migration of African Americans to the North and West gave African Americans their first real taste of political power. Although they often continued to experience discrimination and segregation in other facets of their lives, they could vote, send their children to integrated schools, and patronize hotels, restaurants, and beaches. Suburbs often placed restrictions on African American residency, but by the 1920s it was impossible for many white urban politicians to overlook the potential power of African Americans. In some cities, growing power brought change. Cleveland African Americans were ineligible for internships or nurses' training in the city hospital until African Americans won 3 of 25 council seats. Chicago African Americans turned to Oscar DePriest for help. He had been a county commissioner, a city councilman, and the first African American elected to Congress by a Northern city. African Americans had helped to put Republican mayor William H. Thompson in power, and now they sought favors with the help of his friend, DePriest. Thompson gave African Americans more city posts than any of his predecessors had. African Americans composed 6 percent of Chicago's population, but they held 14 percent of jobs in the city law department (Teaford 1986, 58).

Lynching of African Americans remained a common practice in the South, and throughout the 1920s, the 90,000-member National Association for the Advancement of Colored People (NAACP) attempted to protect Southern African Americans by convincing Congress to pass antilynching legislation. Nevertheless, no bill passed both houses of Congress. After race riots in the summer of 1925, Detroit's mayor named an interracial council under the leadership of theologian Reinhold Niebuhr. The panel concluded that the most troublesome problem in Detroit was overcrowding resulting from an 800 percent growth of the African American population over the preceding 10 years (McKelvey 1968, 69). As a result, the committee insisted that discrimination in housing had to end.

The Last Gasp of Progressivism

Progressives did not wield great power in the 1920s; however, the reform movement was not dead. Many Progressives still battled to cripple monopolies and protect people hurt by industrialization. In the 1922 election, Progressives defeated some conservatives for congressional seats. As a result, Congress had 36 members who identified themselves as Progressives. After that election, the Conference for Progressive Political Action, formed in that year, developed serious aspirations for a renewal of the progressive spirit. The group hoped to assemble an alliance of liberals, intellectuals, unionists, agrarians, and socialists by putting together a platform and seeking grassroots support. Some members favored putting forward a third party in the presidential election of 1924; however, others did not. At a convention in Cleveland in July 1924, Senator Robert La Follette received the Progressive presidential nomination, but the party had no slate of state and local candidates. La Follette, often labeled as "Red" by his

Senator Robert La Follette, the Progressive candidate for president, addresses a group of women in Washington, D.C., in 1924. (Library of Congress)

opponents, managed to get the endorsement of the American Federation of Labor and attracted 16.6 percent of the vote. The defeat represented the last serious effort for a strong left-wing, pro-labor party in the 1920s. However, it is worth noting that from 1921 to 1925, Progressive senator George Norris was able to successfully block efforts by the Harding and Coolidge administrations to turn over the Muscle Shoals power production facility to a private corporation, and by the end of the decade Congress twice approved progressive legislation to establish the Tennessee Valley Authority. In both cases, the bill was vetoed.

Lobbying

During the 1920s, the number of lobbyists ballooned, and they increasingly became public advocates rather than back-door opportunists. Originally, lobbyists had represented corporations and acted informally. However, beginning in World War I, a new type of lobbyist took on a larger role in the governmental process, and these lobbyists became even more common in the 1920s. The Wilson administration's World War I propaganda machine had demonstrated the power of strategically planned campaigns to sway public opinion and elected officials. The new decade brought expansion of professional lobbying on behalf of voluntary associations. The jobs of these "legislative agents" were institution-alized as a formal part of the groups they represented. (The term *lobbyist* had taken on bad connotations, so the new breed of advocates sought unsuccess-fully to institute a new name as well.) What struck Americans most was the increasing number of these advocates. "The lobbyists were so thick they were constantly falling over one another," according to one 1920s observation (Du-menil 1995, 40). Despite observations about the expansion of lobbyist activity, lobbyists were not required to register in the 1920s, so there is no precise in-formation about how many legitimate lobbyists worked in the nation's capital.

The Progressive movement, which had lost momentum, had nonetheless pro-vided an impetus for lobbying to reform government and to provide a counter-balance to widespread efforts to promote the interests of businesses. The growing emergence of interest groups representing individuals in business and in civic affairs contributed to group efforts to influence public policy. Organi-zations representing the interests of business, farming, and women scored some important lobbying successes. Lobbying on behalf of labor unions typically failed in these years of declining support for organized labor. The rise of lobbyists concerned some Americans who believed that they were dominating Washing-ton and disenfranchising American individuals. They asserted that political mi-nority groups, such as prohibitionists, were wielding undue power in Congress. In response to public dismay about the spread of lobbying, Congress launched investigations. The clearest complaint to emerge about lobbyists was that they sometimes worked in secret.

Antigovernment Passion

Opponents of blossoming power in the federal government struggled in the 1920s to seize power from bureaucrats and return it to the hands of the individual. Antigovernment forces voiced outrage about regulatory boards, bills intended to protect women and children in the workplace, federal highway programs, agricultural extension, Prohibition, and women's suffrage. They viewed these intrusive actions as unfair and unwarranted efforts to violate individual rights. Although these forces were often conservative in nature, they saw danger in the government's actions against leftists in the Red Scare as well. Such clear viola-tions of the Constitution heightened fears about Washington imposing a way of life on unwilling Americans.

One leader of this campaign was Senator William E. Borah, who opposed any expansion of federal bureaucratic clout. Borah, a maverick Republican from Idaho, joined the effort to kill a bill that would have established a federal de-partment of education. If a state hoped to get federal appropriations from this new department, the proposed legislation mandated schooling for all children aged 7 to 14 for at least 24 weeks of the year. The department, which would have been an Americanizing tool, would have required that English be the primary language in school. The bill's backers argued that state and local governments were not spending enough on education. Borah spoke for many when he wrote that the "remorseless urge of centralization, the insatiable maw of bureaucracy are depriving more and more the people of all voice, all rights touching home and hearthstone, of family and neighbor. There is not a practice, custom, or habit but must soon be censored from Washington" (Dumenil 1995, 27).

Conservatism

Conservative concerns were showcased in a number of ways during the 1920s. Support for Prohibition, the Red Scare, and scattered censorship programs displayed Americans' concerns about maintaining morality and democracy. The election of three conservative Republican presidents also demonstrated public efforts to maintain the status quo or even to turn back the clock. Warren G. Harding won by a landslide in 1920. After he died in office and was replaced by Calvin Coolidge, the new president won reelection. And in 1928, Herbert Hoover captured the White House by a significant margin. None of the three was a reformer; all were pro-business, and all promised less government intervention in American life. Republicans also maintained majorities in both houses of Congress throughout the decade, with the GOP's margin in the House exceeding 100 seats after the 1928 election.

Of course, there were some progressives among Republican lawmakers, and conservatism was not limited to the Republican Party. Just as both parties included reformers, conservatism also was bipartisan. Lawmakers from the South, who typically were Democrats, often supported extreme conservatism, particularly on matters of race. The combination of largely conservative Republican majorities plus Democratic conservatives in the South and elsewhere solidified the conservatives' hold on Congress.

Table 3.2. Presidential Elections of the 1920s

Year	Candidates	Party Affiliation	Results
1920	WARREN G. HARDING	Republican	16,152,200 (60.4%)
	James M. Cox	Democrat	9,147,353 (34.2%)
	Eugene V. Debs	Socialist	919,799 (3.4%)
1924	CALVIN COOLIDGE	Republican	15,725,016 (54.0%)
	John W. Davis	Democrat	8,385,586 (28.8%)
	Robert M. La Follette	Progressive	4,822,856 (16.6%)
1928	HERBERT HOOVER	Republican	21,392,190 (58.2%)
	Al Smith	Democrat	15,016,443 (40.9%)

Progress and Anxiety Arrive Arm in Arm

The 1920s represented an era in which anxieties about big government, immigrants, and radicals drove much of the nation's political activity. These issues generally did not affect the everyday lives of Americans; nevertheless, they somehow captivated the American imagination and acted as looming threats to national ideals. These apprehensions reflected conflicting fears about the American future. To one group, individualism and nonconformism were threats. Many native white Americans feared that the diversity that existed among exotic immigrants and radicals would usurp control of the culture and remake the United States. In the other group, Americans saw governmental control and standardization as a threat to individualism. In both cases, something precious was in jeopardy.

Because of these differing apprehensions, ideas sometimes divided the conservatives who dominated this era and who shared a common impulse to preserve American culture and rights. For instance, the battle for a department of education created battle lines between two sets of conservatives: Americanizers backed the bill because they feared a loss of power for native whites. States' rights advocates, elitist conservatives, antigovernment forces, and the Catholic Church opposed it because they feared that federal efforts might homogenize education and eliminate local and individual choice. Many Americans feared that individualism would be lost in a cookie-cutter culture of look-alike and act-alike Americans.

It is impossible to measure how much current events affected American fears. Although the Wilson administration's abuses of individual rights had begun during World War I, it was not until 1920 that opposition was sufficiently loud to bring a change in administration policies. In wartime, Americans often accept drastic government actions that would be treated as outrageous abuses of power in times of peace. Consequently, as the war receded from American thoughts, wholesale raids of civilian homes in the Red Scare became more worrisome to typical citizens. Even right-wing opponents of communism demonstrated heightened anxieties because of the government's actions.

During the presidential administrations that followed, there was little danger of government overstepping its bounds except in occasional efforts to bolster business—an activity that could be found in government at all levels. Harding, Coolidge, and Hoover all were disinclined to launch big crusades or to expand governmental power—and that suited the temperament of American voters. Harding's administration became remembered for the secretary of interior's acceptance of bribes and for Harding's own alleged sexual misbehavior; however, for the most part, these presidents remained popular until it became clear that an economic cataclysm was at hand.

During the 1920s, most Americans experienced a sense of economic stability as the standard of living rose. Predictably, the accepted pro-business approach to governing did not foster policies that would help Americans in need. And there was little federal infrastructure in place to help impoverished Americans when the Depression began in 1929. Development of broad national programs would require a revolution in American political thought and a redefinition of government's role in the lives of individual Americans.

WOMEN'S SUFFRAGE

More American Voters

The long fight for women's suffrage ended in August 1920 when Tennessee became the 36th state (out of 48) to ratify the amendment, which Congress had approved more than a year earlier. Some states previously had given women the right to vote, but the decades-long battle finally extended voting rights to almost all women. The lone exceptions were most African American women in the South, who faced a variety of obstacles to voting, including poll taxes and literacy tests. Because the fight for suffrage and the eventual victory took place

Chairman Alice Paul and other officers of the National Woman's Party stand in front of the organization's Washington, D.C., headquarters holding a banner that features a quote from Susan B. Anthony. (Library of Congress)

against the backdrop of significant world and national events, it seemed to mark the beginning of an era. Given the upheaval of 1919, this period was colored by a sense of incredible potential for good and bad, and suffrage promised another dramatic change—expansion of the electorate by 100 percent.

Some tradition-bound women opposed the suffrage amendment. However, many more united behind the banner of suffrage, which raised expectations about women as a voting bloc and the possibility of a broader women's movement. We can now see that the suffrage crusade was surprisingly single-minded in identifying its goal and generally conservative in its approach to American life. Most suffragists simply wanted women to have the right to vote. Their feminist goals ended there because they supported the existing gender roles in the United States and wanted to preserve them. There is some debate about women's voter turnout in 1920, when they first exercised the right to vote; nevertheless, it is clear that the women generally voted independently and not as a bloc. Recognition of their new status as voters and the possibility that they might unite on certain causes gave women additional clout to push for reform legislation to improve the lives of women and children for a brief time in the early 1920s. Various groups that catered to women continued to make their voices heard on certain issues, but they lacked the unity required to bring about significant change.

Even before the amendment won congressional approval, the so-called women's movement had splintered. Many middle-class women had left the National American Woman Suffrage Association to establish a group of their own, the National Woman's Party. In time, some members of this group pushed for another amendment, the Equal Rights Amendment, which was intended to clarify the equality of men and women in all facets of life. This campaign created a greater rift among women activists because its approval would invalidate laws that protected women, such as measures to limit women's working hours. For the most part, protective laws were the product of hard work by female activists who believed that members of their gender required special treatment. Understandably, women who had invested time and effort in winning approval of these measures were reticent about giving up the few hard-earned privileges that working women enjoyed. The Equal Rights Amendment never had a chance of passage in the 1920s, but its goal again fired the imaginations of feminists 50 years later.

Long Battle Ends with Voting Rights

By the time women got the right to vote, the women's suffrage movement was more than half a century old. The women who went to the polls to vote for Warren G. Harding, James E. Cox, or Eugene V. Debs were living out the dreams of those who had attended the first women's rights conference in Seneca Falls,

New York, in 1848. Twenty-one years after that first meeting, women were disappointed when the 15th Amendment to the Constitution gave African American men the right to vote but did not welcome women into the electorate. Their struggle for voting rights gained new fire in the reform-minded Progressive era. In 1920, as women awaited final approval of their voting rights, the women's movement already had suffered a major schism resulting from different tactical approaches toward winning suffrage. The National American Woman Suffrage Association (NAWSA) had used lobbying to solicit support for the amendment; however, the National Women's Party (NWP) had employed civil disobedience to generate publicity for the movement's goals. Sometimes after NWP protesters were arrested, they began hunger strikes in jail to attract public attention when they were force-fed. In states where women already had the right to vote, the NWP had raised the threat of toppling whichever party then dominated a state if the amendment was not ratified by the state legislature. The rupture in the women's movement only worsened during the 1920s.

Most women in the suffrage movement were white and held sufficient wealth to fall into the middle class. Although African American women, too, fought for the chance to vote in some states, they were not welcomed into the leading women's groups. In some cases, African American women were excluded because of simple racism; in others, exclusion resulted from white women's fears that involvement of African American women would increase Southern opposition to the amendment. While awaiting ratification of the amendment by two thirds of the states, many of the chief organizers of the suffrage movement united to form the League of Women Voters in early 1920. With the expectation that women would receive the right to vote by the end of the year, women launched the new organization under the leadership of Carrie Chapman Catt. The League chose to be nonpartisan. Its goals were to encourage women to vote, to educate voters of all kinds, and to promote social reform at all levels of government.

Members of ten women's voluntary organizations also launched the Women's Joint Congressional Committee in 1920. The committee was intended to serve as a central operation to act as a funnel for all legislative proposals promoted by national women's organizations. Included among its causes were disarmament, expansion of federal assistance for public schools, and regulations that provided extra protection for women in the workplace. As the league took shape, no one was certain how women would use their new right.

Women Go to the Polls

Most American women had their first opportunity to vote for president in 1920, and it has been estimated that women contributed at least one-third of the votes that created a landslide for Warren G. Harding. In his inaugural address March 4,

1921, Harding acknowledged women's contribution to the electoral process, saying, "With the nationwide induction of womanhood into our political life, we may count upon her intuitions, her refinements, her intelligence, and her influence to exalt the social order. We count upon her exercise of the full privileges and the performance of the duties of citizenship to speed the attainment of the highest state" (Beasley 2002, 90). Despite the League of Women Voters' efforts to encourage high turnout among women, original estimates showed a low turnout among female voters. There were women who spoke out against female voting and urged other women to stay at home on Election Day. Some were traditionalists while others simply thought women should avoid dirtying their hands in a corrupt political process.

The simple truth is that there was no means of counting women voters in 1920. Public opinion polling had not yet begun, and there was no exit polling at voting places. Only one state—Illinois—kept a separate count of women's votes. Illinois' records showed that women voted more heavily for the Republican ticket than men did. Findings also indicated that only 47 percent of women voted, while 74 percent of men cast ballots. For many years, Illinois was assumed to be typical, and analysts bemoaned low turnout among women. However, more recent studies have concluded that Illinois was atypical. Voter turnout among men was declining as women joined the ranks of voters, and although men were more likely to vote than women, the differences between the genders were not as dramatic as initial figures seemed to suggest.

The Equal Rights Amendment

Disappointed by the limitations of suffrage, the National Woman's Party wrote the Equal Rights Amendment, which was introduced in Congress in December 1923. Working under the leadership of Alice Paul, the NWP hoped to mandate equal treatment of men and women under the law. The amendment's advocates railed against continuing legal inequality in many states. This disparity was manifested in women's exclusion from juries, their inability to execute contracts, married women's limited property rights, and lower pay for women. When initially discussed in 1921, the Equal Rights Amendment, according to the NWP leadership, would not invalidate existing legislation for the protection of women. However, that position changed and ERA backers voiced disdain for protective legislation, which treated women like a population that required extra help. This created a huge new rift among female activists because many felt that it was essential to maintain hard-won protective legislation. Florence Kelley's National Consumers League, Ethel Smith's Women's Trade Union League, and Maud Wood Park's League of Women Voters all voiced opposition to the ERA. Because the NWP was an elite organization with little experience in generating grassroots support, its chances of winning approval for the ERA were small without the full support of other women's groups. Creating further damage to its cause, the NWP continued its policy of excluding African American women and representatives of labor organizations. The push for passage of the ERA predictably foundered.

Successes and Failures in Congress

In the early 1920s, women achieved legislative success on a few important issues. These triumphs represented new clout at a time when male politicians anticipated the potential power of women acting as a voting bloc. In 1921, Congress passed the Sheppard–Towner Act, designed by U.S. Children's Bureau chief Julia Lathrop, which set out to curtail the nation's high infant mortality rate. Each year, more than 200,000 American babies died before reaching their first birthdays, and 20,000 women lost their lives in childbirth. The bureau found a link between poverty and infant mortality. In families with annual incomes of $450 or less, 1 baby in 6 died. The ratio declined to 1 baby in 10 for families with incomes between $650 and $850. And among households with annual incomes of $1,250, only 1 in 16 died. The League of Women Voters had urged all political parties to endorse action on this issue in their 1920 platforms, and the Democratic, Socialist, Prohibitionist, and Farm-Labor parties did just that. Although the Republican platform did not support the proposal, the party's presidential candidate, Harding, voiced his support in October 1920. With Harding's help, the bill won approval, but some members of Congress referred to it as the "new fad appropriation." The Sheppard–Towner Act granted federal aid to finance traveling nurses, to provide personnel for clinics, and to offer other prenatal services. Kelley, a longtime supporter of protective legislation for women and children and a supporter of African American rights, said, "Of all the activities in which I have shared during more than forty years of striving, none is, I am convinced, of such fundamental importance as the Sheppard-Towner Act" (Lemons 1969, 778). A year later, women achieved a second triumph with congressional passage of the Married Women's Independent Citizens' Act, popularly known as the Cable Act. This legislation ended a long practice that stripped away the citizenship rights of American women who married noncitizens. Despite the Cable Act, a woman continued to surrender her citizenship if she married an alien unable to achieve citizenship—most often a Japanese man.

After those two successes, women found that their voices were seldom heard by lawmakers in Congress. Although the Sheppard–Towner Act was expanded to include Hawaii in 1924 and its funding was extended in 1926, the measure was repealed in mid-1929. By that time, 45 states had participated, 2 states had established programs on their own, and other states had the ability to extend the services without federal aid. In Congress, male legislators had seen that women were not acting as a unified bloc, and therefore, lobbyists for women's organizations wielded less clout. Feminists also faced disappointment about the small number of women willing to step forward and seek public office. Like African Americans, women needed elected representatives to draw public attention to their causes. Some observers began to question the value of women's long battle for suffrage. "Is Woman Suffrage Failing?" one magazine asked.

The Broader Women's Movement

The women's movement did not die with the achievement of suffrage or with the great split caused by the Equal Rights Amendment. Differing views about women's current condition and their desired future continued to surface. While some women devoted much of their energy to clarifying their positions for and against the Equal Rights Amendment, other points of view emerged. Author Charlotte Perkins Gilman stressed the need for a wider campaign to restructure households in such a way that patriarchy disappeared. Her 1915 short story, "Herland," had offered a blueprint for a utopian all-female culture. Late in the decade, as some women's groups continued to seek protective legislation for children, the NWP turned its attention to the international battle for equality and joined with foreign organizations pushing to end protective legislation and acquire true equality. With allies in Europe and South America, the NWP began seeking declarations of female equality in international treaties. Although the NWP stressed women's equality to men and their capability to achieve as much as men, Julie Lathrop and Frances Perkins, both of whom were social reformers, emphasized the differences that they believed made women special. They also proclaimed that women were morally superior to men and that they possessed maternal instincts that gave them special insights.

Evolution of Gender Roles Continues

Suffrage represented a hard-fought first victory in the struggle of American women to gain equal rights. It had not been easy because divisions among women had been clear before, during, and after the height of the suffrage movement. One problem was indifference or rejection of women's rights by many women. This was particularly true in the immigrant population because women who had grown into adulthood within patriarchal pre-industrial cultures often continued to see the family as an economic unit under the leadership of a man. Many of these women remained politically passive after suffrage was gained, thus limiting the influence of women as a group.

The suffrage struggle itself had revealed much about attitudes toward gender in the United States. Some supporters had claimed that women had higher moral standards than men and that their votes would preserve the American family by closing down bars and houses of prostitution. Others had argued that women

How Vital Is Suffrage?

For many years, female reformers had made suffrage the central issue in the quest for women's rights. However, once women gained the vote, they quickly began to question its value, and some women immediately turned their attention to action that would expand women's rights. Like the women of that era, historians have debated how important the battle for suffrage was as an element in women's history.

Eleanor Flexnor's 1959 book, *Century of Struggle,* was heralded as providing great insight into the evolution of gender consciousness among American women. In her groundbreaking 1963 work, *The Feminine Mystique,* the outspoken Betty Friedan called Flexnor's book a "definitive history of the woman's rights movement in the United States" (Lasser 1995, 117). However, historians now question the breadth of Flexnor's work as women in the 1920s questioned the value of their votes. Subsequent women historians have minimized the importance of the suffrage movement and its success. Casting doubt on the worth of the electoral process, these authors combined the techniques of social history with the ideals of late-20th-century feminism. In the 1970s, these historians focused more attention on women's lives and on gender roles. Later, following the lead of Carroll Smith-Rosenberg, historians began to give closer examination to women's private lives and to their experiences apart from their relationships with men.

The battle for suffrage and its creation of greater gender awareness among women have become marginal topics in new histories of women as historians increasingly have put personal lives under a microscope. Among 573 doctoral dissertations cited in the *Journal of American History* between March 1995 and March 2005, a mere 33 had any connection with suffrage history (Baker 2006). Nevertheless, some late-20th-century works have expanded on Flexnor's work, which remains a respected piece of historical scholarship.

would be the best advocates for policies to protect children. In reality, women voters often followed the lead of their fathers or their husbands, and they did not prove moral superiority at the polls. Nevertheless, women of the 1920s made a place for themselves in the process. About 145 women had won seats in 38 state legislatures by 1928, according to figures compiled by the League of Women Voters (Parrish 1992, 142). In addition, both Democrats and Republicans had welcomed women onto their state and national committees. There were two women in the House of Representatives, and two had been elected governor to fill places vacated by their spouses' deaths.

At the decade's close, the League of Women Voters had chapters in 45 states as well as Hawaii and the District of Columbia. Among the league's many causes during these years was promotion of the city-manager form of municipal government. In its first 10 years, the organization reported that it had helped to

In the first decade when American women enjoyed the universal right to vote, three female members of Congress stand on the steps of the Capitol. Left to right, they are Alice Robertson (R-Okla.), Mae Ella Nolan (R-Calif.), and Winifred Huck (R-Ill.). (Library of Congress)

obtain passage of 22 state statutes on children's working hours and 39 state laws intended to protect dependent, delinquent, and handicapped children. And the League was not alone in its efforts. In Virginia, local women had united to support legislation that protected children, and the legislature approved 18 of their 24 proposals Women also began a tentative entrance into the civil rights struggle. In 1920, at a Memphis meeting of Southern church members, more than 90 white women listened in awe as 1 of 4 black participants described her violent ouster from a Pullman car on her way to the gathering. The group immediately founded the Woman's Department of the Commission on Inter-racial Cooperation. Also when the League of Women Voters set up a Committee on Negro Problems in each state with an African American population higher than 15 percent, members from eight Southern states cast aside racism and joined their states' committees (Scott 1964, 309).

Some women remained apathetic, and as a group, they lost the power they initially claimed when viewed as a voting bloc. However, the 1920s provided a solid starting place for women among the electorate.

BIOGRAPHIES

Emily Newell Blair, 1877–1951

Democratic Party Official

Emily Newell Blair stood at the forefront of efforts to involve women in American politics. In the wake of a sweeping Republican victory across the nation in 1920, she accepted an invitation to map out plans for drawing women into the Democratic Party. Just a year after joining the Democratic Party in 1920, she was a member of the Democratic National Committee. Known for her role in the suffrage fight and her actions in the League of Women Voters, Blair also wrote for *Ladies' Home Journal* and *Green Book*. She was also a member of the Council of National Defense during World War I and later authored an "interpretive report" about its efforts. Although she helped to found Missouri's chapter of the nonpartisan League of Women Voters, Blair encouraged women to choose a political party and take a partisan stance.

Blair's decision to back the Democrats arose in part from her respect for President Woodrow Wilson. Furthermore, her husband and her father were both Democrats. Despite her family ties to the party, she was described as "a Democrat from principle and conviction rather than environment and tradition" when she was nominated for the committee (Anderson 1999, 111). Blair helped to organize a nationwide network of Democratic women's clubs. To get the ball rolling in each locale, she provided a set of bylaws as well as a list of topics for discussion. She had set up 1,000 clubs by the 1922 elections and almost 3,000 by Election Day 1924. The Democrats suffered another devastating loss in that year, and as the party reorganized its operations, much of the paperwork generated by Blair's work with women was discarded.

She was an original member of the Women's National Democratic Club in Washington and was its president in 1928 after resigning from the Democratic National Committee. Blair also wrote a political column for *Good Housekeeping* from 1926 to 1934.

Albert B. Fall, 1861–1944

Teapot Dome Participant

Albert B. Fall, who served as secretary of the interior for two years, holds the dubious distinction of being the first presidential cabinet member to serve time in prison. After Warren G. Harding's death, Fall's Teapot Dome case and allegations of sexual misconduct by Harding himself became synonymous with an atmosphere of political corruption within the government. Although the once-popular Harding escaped major scandals during his presidency, his reputation suffered with the public after he died. Fall's crime helped to make Harding the subject of derision in popular culture.

After supporting Harding's run for the presidency in 1920, Fall joined his cabinet in 1921. The New Mexican's downfall resulted from his management of the nation's oil reserves. During his last year

Albert B. Fall, secretary of the interior in the Harding administration, stood at the center of the Teapot Dome scandal. (Library of Congress)

in office, Woodrow Wilson had assigned responsibility for the reserves to the secretary of the navy, who was a conservationist. However, when Harding took office and asked his appointees to provide ideas about making the government more efficient, both Fall and Secretary of the Navy Edwin Denby proposed an executive order granting Fall authority over the reserves. Harding followed their recommendation, issuing the executive order May 31, 1921.

Within less than a year, word leaked that Fall had leased reserves to private oil companies that provided processed oil for the U.S. Navy. Among the affected oil fields were Elk Hills and Buena Vista in California, and Teapot Dome in Wyoming. Conservationists rallied, urging Congress to investigate use of the reserves. After a Senate committee recommended a probe, Harding sought to squelch inquiries by sending Congress a statement that he had been consulted about the leases and had given them his "entire approval." Nevertheless, hearings began in October 1923, two months after Harding died. Fall resigned in the same year. The investigation, led by Democratic senator Thomas J. Walsh, eventually uncovered a payment of $100,000 from one oilman to Fall. Walsh also uncovered Fall's service as lawyer to another oilman who profited from a lease. In 1929, Fall was tried and convicted of accepting a bribe. He served nine months in prison and paid a $100,000 fine.

Freda Kirchwey, 1893–1976

Radical Writer and Editor

Freda Kirchwey enjoyed a long career as a feminist and radical political writer. Following in the footsteps of her pacifist and pro-union father, she supported various left-wing causes while helping to mold the weekly magazine *The Nation*. Kirchwey worked for *The Nation* for more than 30 years. She began working there in 1918 as a writer and then became the magazine's managing editor in 1922. As the managing editor, she commissioned articles from a wide array of the era's most famous writers, including Charlotte Perkins Gilman, Bertrand Russell, and H. L. Mencken. As a writer, she supported the Bolshevik regime in Russia and celebrated advances by women. She told readers that she looked forward to a time "when women shall have found their sea legs and the impressive activities of advancing women of today will seem like the earnest and awkward yet somehow promising movements of a land lubber on his first day out" (Alpern 1987, 60). She also endorsed Margaret Sanger's birth control crusade.

Kirchwey joined the unsuccessful campaign to block the executions of Bartolomeo Vanzetti and Nicola Sacco, anarchist Italian immigrants who had been convicted of committing a 1920 robbery and murder. She wrote: "We've hardly talked about it—but every time we got within range of a newspaper we've rushed to it hoping, without any real hope that some miracle of mercy would have descended on the governor or someone else. It was hard to sleep through some of these nights. And everywhere we went—from Paris and Berlin to Heil-genblut in the Austrian Tyrol—people talked about it with horror and a complete inability to understand" (Alpern 1987, 75–76). She became editor of the magazine in 1933 and held that job until 1955. During World War II, she was a fierce advocate of U.S. action to rescue Europe's Jewish population, and she supported a close alliance with the Soviet Union.

Robert La Follette, 1855–1925

Progressive Leader

Identified as a Republican during most of his political career, Wisconsin senator Robert La Follette led the Progressive Party's last big foray into national politics during the 1920s. La Follette, who began his career as a grassroots reformer at the turn of the century, was the Progressive candidate for president in 1924. First elected to the U.S. Senate in 1905, La Follette was a maverick lawmaker who faced a difficult reelection campaign in 1922. Many voters aggressively opposed him because he had voted against a declaration of war in World War I and had remained a stubborn opponent of the conflict. He attacked war profiteering, opposed the Red Scare, and supported a pardon for Socialist leader Eugene V. Debs. Political advisers urged La Follette to abandon these causes and make his reelection fight while standing on middle ground. In March 1921, he gave a speech in the Wisconsin assembly chamber that was intended to unveil the new and more politically correct "Fighting Bob" La Follette. However, when La Follette took the podium, he declared his continued opposition to the war. In 1922, he recaptured his seat by a wide margin.

The National Convention of the Conference for Progressive Political Action nominated La Follette for president in July 1924. He maintained a career-long push against monopolies and opposed discrimination on either racial or religious grounds. He won the support of the Socialist Party as well as many farmers, unionists, women, and African Americans. La Follette's opponents were Republican president Calvin Coolidge and Democrat John W. Davis. Coolidge won with almost 16 million votes; Davis drew more than 8 million; and La Follette surprised pundits by capturing nearly 5 million votes. Although his defeat marked the end of national Progressive Party activity in the 1920s, La Follette is credited with bringing new life to regional left-wing organizations, including populist efforts in the upper Midwest and New York's American Labor Party.

Garrett Morgan, 1877–1963

Inventor

African American businessman and inventor Garrett Morgan found success in the world of manufacturing despite prejudice. The son of former slaves, Morgan was among the first to file a U.S. patent for a traffic signal. The prosperous Morgan was driving his car one day in Cleveland when he developed the idea for a T-shaped traffic signal in 1923. It had three positions: one-way go, one-way stop, all-directional stop. Cities and towns across the United States used his hand-cranked signal. The General Electric Corporation eventually bought the rights to Morgan's invention, and later GE improved on the signal so that it was controlled by a time clock rather than a human being.

This was not Garrett's only invention. He also received a patent for a Safety Hood and Smoke Protector in 1914, and two years later he used a gas mask that he had created to save 32 men trapped after an explosion in a tunnel beneath Lake Erie. Many fire departments requested Garrett's gas masks and the U.S. Army used a refined version during World War I.

Al Smith, 1873–1944

First Catholic Presidential Nominee

Al Smith is known for being the first Catholic nominated for president by a major political party. For many voters outside America's large cities, the man who had served as New York's governor for most of the 1920s also represented the vices attached to the nation's growing urbanization. As a Democratic social reformer,

New York governor Alfred E. Smith, a Democrat, became the first Catholic to win a major party's nomination for the U.S. presidency in 1928. (Library of Congress)

Smith was New York's governor for four terms—first from 1919 to 1921 and again from 1923 to 1929. In the 1920 election, Smith's reelection bid had been thwarted by a nationwide Republican landslide. As governor, one of his goals was to improve both the efficiency and the effectiveness of state government. He appointed women and minorities to state offices and spearheaded efforts to bolster state laws concerning child labor, women's labor, women's pensions, and workers' compensation. He also successfully led a reorganization of state government, a push for public housing, and an expansion of state parks. At the same time, he cut state taxes. As the state's leading Democrat, he found the power to break his ties to the Tammany Hall political machine, which had launched his career as a state assemblyman in 1903.

Smith vied to be the Democratic presidential candidate in 1924. Franklin Delano Roosevelt delivered his nominating speech, and in it, he labeled the governor as "the Happy Warrior of the political battlefield." However, after meeting considerable anti-Catholic sentiment at the convention, Smith withdrew his candidacy. Four years later, he won the nomination and campaigned fiercely against the Republican candidate Herbert Hoover. Most voters turned against Smith because of his Catholicism, his urban roots, or his anti-Prohibition stand. Hoover won 58 percent of the vote. Smith, who was shocked by the ferocity of anti-Catholic sentiments, never served in public office again.

Jimmy Walker, 1881–1936

New York City Mayor

Known as the "Nightclub Mayor," Jimmy Walker ruled New York from 1926 until 1932. The light-hearted Walker was seen as an opposing force to self-righteous reformers. He spent many hours in the nightclubs of West 42nd Street, where New Yorkers were free to ignore the preaching of Prohibitionists and others who sought to regulate American morals. During Prohibition, these nightclubs were actually speakeasies, of which New York reportedly had 32,000 when Walker was elected mayor in the autumn of 1925. During his tenure, Walker was most popular for opposing a seven-cent increase in subway fares in 1928 and 1929. Widely known for his lack of prejudice against African Americans and other minorities, Walker was a descendant of the Irish working class. While he was mayor, he ended a Harlem Hospital regulation that banned employment of African American doctors. And when he greeted pilot Charles Lindbergh after his successful nonstop solo flight to Paris in 1927, Walker was among the few politicians who felt no need to praise Lindbergh's Nordic ancestry.

Often described as dapper and debonair, Walker shunned Victorian morality. He was married; nevertheless, he liked to visit the city's night spots with a showgirl on his arm. Eventually, he left his wife for the beautiful Betty Compton. "It's Jim Walker's life I'm living. It's not [unsuccessful 1929 challenger Fiorello] La Guardia's life, nor Benjamin Franklin's life, nor [prohibitionist] Carry Nation's life," he asserted (Douglas 1995, 12). The former Democratic state senator had championed a bill that made it legal for New Yorkers to take part in post-church entertainment on Sundays. These events included movies, boxing matches, and baseball games. For many who labored long hours, having an opportunity to take part in such events on Sundays was a blessing, and they praised Jimmy Walker for making it possible. After the stock market crash, however, Walker's high life contrasted too sharply with the daily realities of joblessness and poverty. He faced charges that his administration was riddled with corruption and went into European exile in September 1932.

REFERENCES AND FURTHER READINGS

Allen, Frederick Lewis. 2000. *Only Yesterday: An Informal History of the 1920's.* New York: Perennial Classics.

Alpern, Sara. 1987. *Freda Kirchwey: A Woman of The Nation.* Cambridge, MA: Harvard University Press.

Alpern, Sara, and Dale Baum. 1985. "Female Ballots: The Impact of the Nineteenth Amendment. *Journal of Interdisciplinary History* 16 (1): 43–67.

Anderson, Kathryn. 1999. "Evolution of a Partisan." In *We Have Come to Stay: American Women and Political Parties, 1880–1960,* edited by Melanie Gustafson, Elisabeth Israels Perry, and Kristie Miller, 109–117. Albuquerque: University of New Mexico Press.

Baker, Jean H. 2006. "Getting Right with Women's Suffrage." *Journal of the Gilded Age and Progressive Era* 5 (1): 7–18. Available at http://www.history cooperative.org (accessed December 16, 2006).

Beasley, Vanessa B. 2002. "Engendering Democratic Change: How Three U.S. Presidents Discussed Female Suffrage." *Rhetoric & Public Affairs* 5 (1): 79–103.

Blake, Angela M. 2006. *How New York Became American.* Baltimore: Johns Hopkins University Press.

Boyer, Paul S. 1963. "Boston Book Censorship in the Twenties." *American Quarterly* 15 (1): 3–24.

Brownell, Blaine A. 1972a. "A Symbol of Modernity: Attitudes toward the Automobile in Southern Cities in the 1920s." *American Quarterly* 24 (1): 20–44.

Brownell, Blaine A. 1972b. "Birmingham, Alabama: New South City in the 1920s." *Journal of Southern History* 38 (1): 21–48.

Cott, Nancy. 1984. "Feminist Politics in the 1920s: The National Woman's Party." *Journal of American History* 71 (1): 43–68.

Dean, John W. 2004. *Warren G. Harding.* New York: Times Books.

Degler, Carl N. 1964. "American Political Parties and the Rise of the City: An Interpretation." *Journal of American History* 51 (1): 41–59.

Douglas, Ann. 1995. *Terrible Honesty: Mongrel Manhattan in the 1920s.* New York: Farrar, Strauss and Giroux.

Dumenil, Lynn. 1990. "'The Insatiable Maw of Bureaucracy': Antistatism and Education Reform in the 1920s." *Journal of American History* 77 (2): 499–524.

Dumenil, Lynn. 1995. *The Modern Temper: American Culture and Society in the 1920s.* New York: Hill and Wang.

Eagles, Charles W. 1989. "Congressional Voting in the 1920s: A Test of Urban-Rural Conflict." *Journal of American History* 76 (2): 528–534.

Environmental History Timeline. http://www.radford.edu/~wkovarik/envhist/ 6twenties.html (accessed August 10, 2006).

Fass, Paul S. 1977. *The Damned and the Beautiful: American Youth in the 1920's.* Oxford: Oxford University Press.

Flink, James J. 1972. "Three Stages of American Automobile Consciousness." *American Quarterly* 24 (4): 451–473.

Foster, Mark S. 1975. "The Model-T, the Hard Sell, and Los Angeles's Urban Growth: The Decentralization of Los Angeles during the 1920s." *Pacific Historical Review* 44 (4): 459–484.

Freedman, Estelle B. 1974. "The New Woman: Changing View of Women in the 1920s." *Journal of American History* 61 (2): 372–393.

Gardasco, Francesco, and Rocco G. Galationo. 1970. "Ethnic Displacement in the Interstitial Community." *Phylon* 31 (3): 302–312.

Garofalo, Charles Paul. 1976. "The Sons of Henry Grady: Atlanta Boosters in the 1920s." *Journal of Southern History* 42 (2): 187–204.

Gilda Lerner Institute of American History. *History Now.* http://www.historynow .org (accessed August 14, 2006).

Goldberg, David. 1999. *Discontented America: The United States in the 1920s.* Baltimore: Johns Hopkins University Press.

The History of Woman's Suffrage in America. http://www.historychannel.com/ exhibits/woman/main.html (accessed August 5, 2006).

Kirschner, Don S. 1970. *City and Country: Rural Responses to Urbanization in the 1920s.* Westport, CT: Greenwood Publishing.

Kyvig, David E. 2002. *Daily Life in the United States 1920–1940.* Chicago: Ivan R. Dee.

Lasser, Carol. 1995. "Century of Struggle, Decades of Revision: A Retrospective on Eleanor Flexnor's Suffrage History." In *American Perspectives: Historians on Historians,* edited by Stanley Kutler, 117–126. Baltimore: Johns Hopkins University Press.

Leinwand, Gerald. 2001. *1927: High Tide of the Twenties.* New York: Four Walls Eight Windows.

Lemons, J. Stanley. 1969. "The Sheppard-Towner Act: Progressivism in the 1920s." *Journal of American History* 55 (4): 776–786.

Leuchtenburg, William E. 1993. *The Perils of Prosperity 1914–1932.* 2nd ed. Chicago: University of Chicago Press.

MacLennan, Carol A. 1988. "From Accident to Crash: The Auto Industry and the Politics of Injury." *Medical Anthropology Quarterly,* Health and Industry Series, 2 (3): 233–250.

McKelvey, Blake. 1968. *The Emergence of Metropolitan America, 1915–1966.* New Brunswick, NJ: Rutgers University Press.

Mowry, George Edwin. 1968. *The Urban Nation, 1920–1960.* New York: Hill and Wang.

National Parks Service. "Al Smith." *Eleanor Roosevelt National Historic Site.* http://www.nps.gov/elro/glossary/smith-al.htm (accessed August 5, 2006).

1920s Fashion. *Enotes.* http://history.enotes.com/1920-fashion-american-decades/architecture-urbanization-philosophy (accessed August 7, 2006).

Parrish, Michael E. 1992. *Anxious Decades: America in Prosperity and Depression, 1920–1941.* New York: W. W. Norton & Co.

Pratt, Joseph A. 1980. "Letting the Grandchildren Do It: Environmental Planning during the Ascent of Oil as a Major Energy Source," *Public Historian* 2 (4): 28–61.

Quam-Wickham, Nancy. 1999. "'Another World': Work, Home, and Autonomy in Blue-Collar Suburbs." In *Metropolis in the Making: Los Angeles in the 1920s,* edited by Tom Sitton and William Deverell, 123–141. Berkeley: University of California Press.

Radford, Gail. 1992. "New Building and Investment Patterns in 1920s Chicago." *Social Science History* 16 (1): 1–21.

Scott, Anne Firor. 1964. "After Suffrage: Southern Women in the Twenties." *Journal of Southern History* 30 (3): 298–318.

Teaford, Jon C. 1986. *The Twentieth-Century American City: Problems, Promise, and Reality.* Baltimore: Johns Hopkins University Press.

Tygiel, Jules. 2001. "Metropolis in the Making: Los Angeles in the 1920s." In *Metropolis in the Making: Los Angeles in the 1920s,* edited by Tom Sitton and William Deverell, 1–10. Berkeley: University of California Press.

United States Bureau of the Census. *Historical Statistics of the United States: Colonial Times to 1970.* Washington, DC: Department of Commerce, 1975. Available at http://www2.census.gov/prod2/statcomp/documents/CT1970p1–01.pdf (accessed June 30, 2006).

Weiler, N. Sue. 1989. "Industrial Scrap Heap: Employment Patterns and Change for the Aged in the 1920s." *Social Science History* 13 (1): 65–88.

All That Jazz: Radio, Magazines, and Mass Communication

OVERVIEW

The youth culture of the 1920s found vivid expression in its use of "slanguage" or slang. Terms such as "swanky," "whoopee," and "heebie-jeebies" demonstrate the playful approach to language and the pleasure taken in the sound of human speech. Whatever objects or concepts preoccupied Americans during the 1920s surfaced in the era's slang. In an age of Prohibition, for instance, alcohol became "hooch," "rot gut," or "coffin varnish." Even the decade's accolades reflected the era's whimsical turn of phrase; what was praiseworthy was the "cat's meow," the "gnat's whistle," the "butterfly's boots," the "bee's knees," or the "elephant's eyebrows." These elements of colloquial speech became shorthand for communicating with others during the 1920s in the United States.

Also helping to define and document the Jazz Age were a number of forms of mass communication. According to Stuart Chase, during the 1920s, 35 million Americans read newspapers or tabloids each day, 30 million listened to radio programming each night, 50 million went to the movies weekly, and 15 million read popular magazines each month (Best 2003, 121). In fact, by some estimates, one-fourth of the nation's income was expended each year on amusements such as movies, radios, phonographs, candy, chewing gum, and tobacco (Best 2003, 123). Such practices became habits for the public, and as they did Americans coming of age during this time came to regard the mass media as a usual part of their lives.

TIMELINE

1920   The League of Women Voters is formed.

First short-wave radio connection was created.

Parents' Magazine begins publication.

Encyclopaedia Britannica, Inc., is chartered.

More than half the nation's homes have electricity.

U.S. illiteracy rate falls to 6 percent, an all-time low.

Palmer raids continue with searches of workplaces and residences suspected of involvement in the "Red Menace."

KDKA, a Westinghouse station in Pittsburgh, transmits the first commercial radio broadcast. The broadcast goes past midnight.

The American Civil Liberties Union is established.

The 18th Amendment takes effect on January 16, making Prohibition the law of the land.

In March, WGI of Boston claims the first regularly scheduled radio broadcasts.

Sacco and Vanzetti are arrested on May 5 and charged with murder and robbery.

Starting on August 20, Detroit radio station SMK offers a daily variety show, *Tonight's Dinner.*

On August 26, the 19th Amendment, granting women the vote, is ratified.

1921   Bessie Smith records her first album.

On January 13, the 1920 census report is released.

The U.S. divorce rate reaches double the comparable figure for the nation during 1896.

Skywriting appears as a practice.

The first "play-by-play" call of a baseball game broadcast over the radio is accomplished by KDKA of Pittsburgh.

The first radio broadcast of a sporting event, a boxing match, takes place on April 11.

The Emergency Quota Act passes on May 19, which attempts to restrict immigration to the United States to 358,000 persons per year.

The first radio coverage of the baseball World Series occurs on October 5.

On November 21, the first burial takes place at Arlington Cemetery's Tomb of the Unknown Soldier.

1922

The first radio advertisement is broadcast. The rate is $100 for 10 minutes of airtime.

The first issue of *Opportunity,* publication of the National Urban League, appears.

The first portable radio is sold.

Muzak is developed.

The Lincoln Memorial is dedicated with ceremony in the District of Columbia.

Fifty-three African Americans are lynched.

F. Scott Fitzgerald's *Tales of the Jazz Age* is published.

Emily Post publishes her bestseller book on manners, *Etiquette in Society, in Business, in Politics, and at Home.*

The first Miss America, Margaret Gorman of the District of Columbia, is crowned.

King Tut's tomb is discovered by Egyptologists George Carnarvon and Howard Carter, ushering in an enthusiasm for Egyptian motifs, as expressed in Grauman's Egyptian Theater.

Reader's Digest delivers its first issue on February 5.

On October 9, RUR (Rossum's Universal Robots) opens in New York City, introducing the words "robot" and "automaton" into popular parlance.

1923

Dance marathons become popular, including as a spectator sport. Alma Cummings dances for 27 hours in a dance marathon held at New York's Audubon Ballroom.

Composer George Gershwin debuts "Rhapsody in Blue" with the Paul Whiteman Orchestra in a New York performance.

Bessie Smith records "Down Hearted Blues."

Neon signs appear.

On March 23, Frank Silver and Irving Conn release "Yes, We Have No Bananas."

During June, Jelly Roll Morton first records for Paramount Records in Chicago.

On June 12, Harry Houdini escapes a straitjacket suspended and inverted some 40 feet in the air in New York City.

The comic strip "Moon Mullins" appears for the first time on June 19.

On July 17, the first racially mixed recording session takes place. Jelly Roll Morton and the New Orleans Rhythm Kings record "Mr. Jelly Lord."

The first transatlantic radio broadcast links England and the United States on November 25.

On December 6, Calvin Coolidge's address to the joint session of Congress is broadcast by radio, the first such broadcast of a presidential address.

1924   Simon and Schuster release the first book-length collection of crossword puzzles. It is during this same year that the *New York Times* begins to feature a daily crossword.

Eveready Hour becomes the first sponsored radio program, using a variety format to combine drama, poetry, comedy, and music.

Wheaties cereal is first touted as the "Breakfast of Champions."

George Gershwin composes his jazz-influenced "Rhapsody in Blue."

On January 1, more than 2,500,000 radios are in place in American homes. There were 5,000 or fewer such receivers in 1920.

The first gas chamber execution takes place on February 8.

On March 4, Claydon Sunny publishes "Happy Birthday to You."

On August 5, "Little Orphan Annie" by Harold Gray makes its first appearance as a comic strip.

Nathan "Babe" Leopold and Richard "Dickie" Loeb confess to the May 21 murder of Bobby Franks, age 14. Despite a defense from Clarence Darrow, they are found guilty on September 10.

The first Macy's Thanksgiving Day Parade takes place in New York City.

1925   The first Arthur Murray dance studio opens in New York City.

John B. Watson publishes *Behaviorism*.

The Goodyear Blimp takes flight as an advertising method.

The Smith Family becomes radio's first soap opera.

Al Capone presides over Chicago's thriving bootlegging operations.

The National Spelling Bee is initiated by the Louisville *Courier-Journal,* later sponsored by Scripps-Howard.

Alain Locke publishes *The New Negro,* a celebration of the arts movement known as the Harlem Renaissance.

Louis "Satchmo" Armstrong forms the Hot Five in Chicago.

On February 21, the first issue of *The New Yorker* appears.

The Scopes trial begins after John T. Scopes was arrested on May 5 for teaching schoolchildren evolution.

Forty thousand Klansmen march on Washington, D.C., on August 8.

On August 14, Mt. Rushmore is proposed.

Saturday evening broadcasts of *WSM Barn Dance* (later the *Grand Ole Opry*) begin from Nashville on November 28.

1926   Harry Scherman's Book-of-the-Month Club, a reading subscription service, begins. On April 16, the first selections are announced: *Lolly Willowes* and *Loving Huntsman.*

Burma-Shave sets in place its memorable roadside billboard campaign.

Jelly Roll Morton records with the Red Hot Peppers in Chicago. They lay down tracks including "Doctor Jazz" and "Black Bottom Stomp."

First advertising jingle, for Wheaties breakfast cereal, airs on radio.

Gertrude Ederle swims the English Channel in 14 hours, 31 minutes.

RCA, GE, and Westinghouse establish the National Broadcasting Company (NBC).

Martha Graham's first New York performance takes place.

Blind Lemon Jefferson records his first blues record for Paramount Records in Chicago in May (*Long Lonesome Blues*).

Automatic volume control becomes available on some radio models.

Walt Disney Studios opens on February 8.

On March 26, the first lip-reading tournament takes place.

1927   The Literary Guild begins its book club.

The Federal Radio Control Act is ratified on February 23, establishing the Federal Radio Commission. This body helps regulate the young medium's wavelengths, allocations, licenses, and the like. The commission affirms that the airwaves belong to the public. At this point, there are approximately 681 radio stations in the United States.

April 27 marks the first public display of a television image.

On September 14, dancer Isadora Duncan dies by strangulation when her scarf becomes entangled in an automobile wheel.

1928   Amelia Earhart becomes the first woman to fly across the Atlantic Ocean.

The Archive of Folk Culture is established at the Library of Congress.

The teletype machine enters use.

Radio stations voluntarily halt ads during "family hour."

General Electric presents a 3-by-4-inch screen television. The first sells for $75.

Ruth Snyder gets the electric chair at Sing Sing Prison on January 12.

1929   The first car radio, designed by William Lear, becomes available to motorists.

The Columbia Broadcasting System (CBS) is founded.

On February 14, the "St. Valentine's Day Massacre" results in seven deaths in a Chicago garage.

On June 27, Bell Labs provides the first color television prototype.

WHO OWNED THE AIRWAVES?
RADIO BROADCASTING IN THE 1920s

The Strength of Radio

On November 2, 1920, using a 100-watt transmitter, station KDKA of Pittsburgh made the first official radio broadcast, furnishing listeners with the results of the presidential election. The transmission went past midnight. From that point on, radio would become a major medium for communication in the United States. As a form of mass culture, radio had a distinctive strength; it transcended the

Atwater Kent stands by a radio while others listen, in the Hamilton Hotel, Washington, D.C. Kent operated one of the largest radio manufacturers of the time. (Library of Congress)

literacy barrier among its listeners. Writing in 1927 about the booming new medium, cultural observer Silas Bent noted that "even more readily than the Sunday rotogravure section or the tabloid picture paper, it reached the illiterate as well as the literate. If it is easier to look at pictures than read, how much easier to listen!" (Bent 1927, 296).

Although radio communication had been used in military contexts before, civilian radio came into its own during the 1920s, both as a form of communication and as entertainment. Technological refinements made it possible and affordable for ordinary Americans to place a radio in their homes. As Figure 4.1 suggests, sales in radio equipment grew steadily during the 1920s. At first, consumers had to put together their own crystal sets. Later, they could purchase ready-made radio sets. By Christmas of 1922, advertisements suggested radios as appropriate holiday gifts. At the time, store-bought radios were encased in wood to form cabinets that resembled home furnishings. Although the radio blended in with the living room furniture, it widened listeners' worlds by exposing them to entertainments previously unknown to them. As one advertisement slogan of the day put it, "Aladdin had his lamp; you have the Melco Supreme" (Mordden 1978, 214).

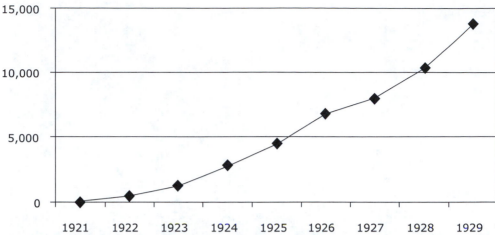

Figure 4.1 *American Families with Radios (in thousands), 1922–1930.* Source: *Adapted from Kurian 2001, 153; and Streissguth 2001, 397.*

Early Radio Programming

Radio broadcasting began in the evenings and then moved into daytime. In the beginning, radio programming reflected a fairly wide range of broadcasting objectives. For the most part, music and talk dominated the decade's radio programs. Early on, many cultural observers expressed a hope that radio could edify and uplift listeners. In 1921, station KYW was devoted to bringing the Chicago opera season to the public (MacDonald 1979, 10). The first years of radio placed a heavy emphasis on classical music, which contributed significantly to the popularity of symphonic music, both live and recorded. Radio programming also featured talk shows, such as help-line programs and programs that provided household hints and recipes. CBS offered "The American School of the Air," educational programming for children. Some churches aired their sermons or services for those who could not attend worship in person. Universities and colleges frequently acquired stations that they used to broadcast content they deemed in the public interest. Even newspapers established radio stations in the hope that it would enhance their coverage of current events and expand their print audiences.

Although first touted as a way to inform the public, radio emerged as a popular pleasure. Programming developed in response to the nation's desire for leisure-time enjoyment. Musical programming proved among the most successful ventures of early radio. For those whose residences were too remote to attend concerts and for those who could not afford a phonograph or a supply of the latest tunes, radio proved a steady supplier of new music for the listening public. Although some forms of music, such as the "race records" of artists Bessie Smith, Ethel Waters, and Ma Rainey, got little radio play while others, such as orchestral music, benefited greatly. It would not be long before the economic potential of music radio as a commercial medium became apparent. By 1922, American Society of Composers, Authors, and Publishers (ASCAP) lawyers began to seek annual fees for airing recorded music on the radio. Radio's use of recording music was so effective that the sale of phonographs and phonograph records dropped dramatically during the 1920s, ending the decade at about one twentieth the level of sales in 1920 (Green 1992, 197).

Commercial Radio Begins

Radio advertising began gradually with sponsored programs, often with shows named after the sponsors. The same companies that had transformed life within the American home—Westinghouse, General Electric (GE), and American Telephone and Telegraph (AT&T)—were frequent sponsors of radio programming. In December 1923, station WEAF debuted the *Eveready Hour,* which proved a model of sorts for sponsored variety programming on radio. Others, such as *The Chase and Sanborn Hour* and *The Fleischmann's Yeast Hour,* launched shortly thereafter. The latter featured vocalist Rudy Vallee, whom cultural observer H. L. Mencken deemed "catnip to women." Such sponsorship arrangements afforded advertisers more than promotional time; they also enjoyed a measure of creative control. For example, advertising agencies—not the radio stations or networks—hired on-air talent. As the decade unfolded, direct advertisements started to appear on the radio such as daytime programming ads targeting women listeners.

By the late 1920s, radio marketing became more sophisticated. In 1929, the first radio ratings system, known alternately as the Cooperative Analysis of Broadcasting (CAB) or the Crossley Ratings, helped radio stations and sponsors determine how many listeners each radio program attracted.

In time, radio advertising became the object of satire. In a poem that appeared in a March 1920 issue of *Radio Revue,* titled "Sponsoritis," the author mocked the degree to which radio had become infected with advertising: "Dame nature has a 'funny' way / Of spoiling our enjoyment / For everyone who lives today / Has his or her annoyment; / And each disease beneath the sun / Has diff'rent germs to bite us / Now RADIO's developed one— / They call it 'SPONSORITIS'" (Smulyan 1993, 1838).

Radio Finds Its Audience(s)

During the period from 1921 to 1929, radio sales went from $2 million to $600 million (Time-Life 1998, 77). Radio had 30 million regular listeners in the United States by 1927 (Solomon 1980, 6). Radio shared a variety of musical genres with

As they became accustomed to the properties of microphone equipment used in radio broadcast, announcers developed a style for engaging home listeners in a more personal and appealing way. (Library of Congress)

America's listening public but was most helpful to classical, country, and jazz. As radio took hold, phonograph and records sales dropped.

The strengths and limitations of the medium also shaped singing styles of the era. For instance, to optimize the sound of live singing's transmission over the radio, the style called "crooning" came into fashion. The mellow approach of the crooner did not exceed the capacity of the microphones in use during the 1920s and sounded pleasing when played on home receivers. Singers such as Kate Smith, Bing Crosby, and Rudy Vallee typify this singing style. Much of the time, however, musical programs on radio featured recorded music, available on the day's phonograph records.

In addition to showcasing music and other forms of talent, radio covered some of the major news stories and special events of the 1920s. In 1927, 50 stations in some 24 states carried an all-day tribute to "Lucky Lindy" (aviator Charles Lindbergh), which was held in the District of Columbia. As announcers became accustomed to the properties of microphone equipment used in radio broadcast, they developed a style for engaging home listeners in a more personal and engaging way. In fact, observers sometimes blamed radio for the demise of many

Amos 'n' Andy

Some breakout radio programs achieved unusual levels of popularity. Among the most popular programs during this era was NBC's comedy serial, *Amos 'n' Andy*. In 1929, this comedy team enjoyed a 60 percent share of the American radio audience (MacDonald 1979, 27).

Amos and Andy, two fictional African American characters portrayed by white performers, were migrants from Atlanta, Georgia, to the south side of Chicago. Together, they ran the Fresh Air Cab Company. Amos, played by Freeman Gosden, was a family man. Andy, portrayed by Charles J. Carroll, was the part of the duo most likely to commit a misstep that would launch one of their adventures. These characterizations derived from the minstrel tradition and the burnt-cork practices of vaudeville. The voices used to portray Amos and Andy were the auditory equivalent of blackface, steeped in racial stereotypes. Dialect humor was a prominent feature of the vocal characterizations, and Amos's and Andy's colloquialisms, such as "check and double check" and "holy mackerel!," proved memorable for the show's listeners.

The public reaction to *Amos 'n' Andy* was unprecedented. These 10-minute scripts became so important to the listening public that four Charlotte, North Carolina, factory owners assented to adjust the end-time on the work shift by 15 minutes to accommodate worker interest in the comedy routines of Amos and Andy (Solomon 1980, 122). According to some accounts, even President Hoover arranged his schedule to listen to the program (Mordden 1978, 217).

The popularity of the program translated into success for its commercial sponsors. The primary backing for *Amos 'n' Andy* was provided by Pepsodent toothpaste and Campbell's soup. During the period that Pepsodent advertised on the program, they experienced a 300 percent jump in sales (Mowry 1963, 65).

That white actors wrote and performed the scripts, along with the fact that representations of African Americans were anything but flattering, did stir up controversy. Still, the radio show continued for many years, and versions of the program appeared subsequently on both film and television. TV episodes of *Amos 'n' Andy* appeared in syndication through 1966.

daily and local newspapers of the era. According to historian Harvey Green, radio's popularity played a part in the discontinuation of over 200 dailies during the 1920s (Green 1992, 198).

In the second half of the 1920s, national radio networks began to operate. NBC was first, and CBS followed in 1928. On February 23, 1927, Congress passed the Federal Radio Act, setting in place the first federal regulations for the new medium. This piece of legislation established the Federal Radio Commission to help oversee licensing and wavelength allocation and to ensure that radio stations operated in the public interest.

Table 4.1. Number of Radio Sets in Use and Annual Radio Sales in the United States, 1922–1927

Year	Radio Sets in Use	Total Annual Sales*
1922	60,000	$60,000,000
1923	1,500,000	$136,000,000
1924	3,000,000	$358,000,000
1925	4,000,000	$430,000,000
1926	5,000,000	$506,000,000
1927	6,000,000	$446,550,000

*Total annual sales figures include radio sets, parts, and accessories.

Source: Department of Commerce data as presented in Wolman 1929, 58.

By the end of the 1920s, a range of radio news presentations and entertainment was in place, capable of combining the wishes of the listening public with the sponsor's need to reach potential customers. Entertainment included dramas, mysteries, and detective stories. Soap operas, so-called because detergent or soap manufacturers sponsored the programs, also pleased listeners. Taken together, radio's various forms of broadcast programming gathered America's families beside their home radio receivers listening to the same radio content. Writing for *Collier's* magazine in June 1922, journalist Stanley Frost remarked on this unifying experience: "It is achieving the task of making us feel together, think together, live together" (quoted in Douglas 2004, 76).

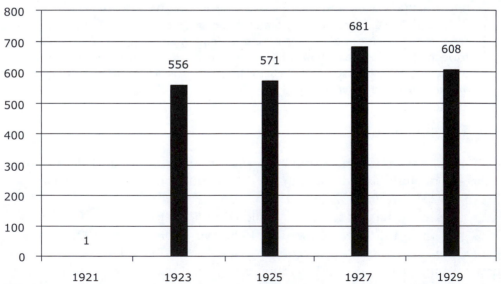

Figure 4.2 *Number of American Radio Broadcast Stations, 1921–1930.* Source: *Adapted from Kurian 2001, 300, and Streissguth 2001, 397.*

Radio Unites Its Listeners

The radio was not just another appealing consumer item to purchase for the American home. The rise of radio programming brought together its listeners. Families huddled around the receiver and shared radio programs, both with each other and with listeners across the nation. As historian Susan J. Douglas notes, radio proved a "mode of communication reliant on storytelling, listening, and group memory" (Douglas 2004, 29). Radio narratives, often presented in serial form, involved audience members in shared and ongoing storytelling experience. By 1930, fully one-third of people in the United States, approximately 12 million families, listened regularly to radio programming. In fact, radio became so successful with American audiences that it began to hurt sales of rival forms of leisure activity, such as sheet music, live theater, daily newspapers, and phonographs.

During the period from 1922 to 1927, the nation's number of radio households grew 25-fold (Balk 2006, 42). As radios became a common household item, they had something of a democratizing effect. Americans from different regions, backgrounds, and circumstances could listen to the same radio programs and features. This shared experience brought the media lives of Americans closer together, even if the rest of their lives remained separated by privilege or other distancing differences.

POPULAR MUSIC AND DANCE

Tunes That Have Endured

Among the indelible images of the 1920s is that of a flapper dancing the Charleston. Music and dance helped define the decade, and both were key to the era's popular culture.

During the 1920s, popular songs reflected current events and timely themes. For example, Prohibition inspired such tunes as "If I Meet the Guy Who Made This Country Dry" and "It's the Smart Little Feller Who Stocked up His Cellar (That's Getting the Beautiful Girls)" (Drowne and Huber 2004, 15). Record sales displaced sheet music sales as the indicator of music's popularity. In 1928, *Blll-board* magazine began to publish its charts, lists of the nation's best-selling musical records.

Musical fads, such as the brief craze for the ukulele and Hawaiian themes, helped define the decade, but this period also produced many enduring favorites of American music. The 1920s represented an exceptionally strong chapter in the history of American song-writing. George Gershwin, Ira Gershwin, Oscar Hammerstein, Lorenz Hart, Jerome Kern, Cole Porter, and Richard Rodgers all penned popular tunes during the 1920s.

Hit Songs in the United States, 1920–1929

Year	Popular Hit Song	Year	Popular Hit Song
1920	"I'll Be with You in Apple Blossom Time"	1924	"Amapola"
	"Look for the Silver Lining"		"Charley My Boy"
	"Mary"		"Deep in My Heart, Dear"
	"Rose of Washington Square"		"Fascinating Rhythm"
	"That Old Irish Mother of Mine"		"I'll See You in My Dreams"
	"When My Baby Smiles at Me"		"The Man I Love"
1921	"Ain't We Got Fun"		"Rose Marie"
	"April Showers"		"Tea for Two"
	"I'm Just Wild about Harry"	1925	"Always"
	"Ma—He's Making Eyes at Me"		"Cecelia"
	"Say It with Music"		"Dinah"
	"Second Hand Rose"		"Drifting and Dreaming"
1922	"Carolina in the Morning"		"Five Foot Two, Eyes of Blue"
	"Chicago (That Toddling Town)"		"I'm Sitting on Top of the World"
	"Do It Again"		"Moonlight and Roses"
	"Georgia"		"Sleepy Time Gal"
	"I Wish I Could Shimmy Like My Sister Kate"		"Sweet Georgia Brown"
	"Three o'Clock in the Morning"		"Yes Sir, That's My Baby"
	"Way Down Yonder in New Orleans"		"If You Knew Susie (Like I Know Susie)"
1923	"Charleston (Runnin' Wild)"	1926	"Are You Lonesome Tonight?"
	"I Cried For You"		"Baby Face"
	"It Ain't Gonna Rain No More"		"The Birth of the Blues"
	"Mexicali Rose"		"Breezin' Along with the Breeze"
	"Swingin' Down the Lane"		"Bye, Bye, Blackbird"
	"That Old Gang of Mine"		"Gimme a Little Kiss, Will Ya Huh?"
	"Who's Sorry Now"		"Someone to Watch Over Me"
			"When Day Is Done"
		1927	"The Best Things in Life Are Free"
			"Blue Skies"
			"Can't Help Loving Dat Man"

Hit Songs in the United States, 1920–1929, Continued

Year	Popular Hit Song	Year	Popular Hit Song
	"Make Believe"	1929	"Happy Days Are Here Again"
	"My Heart Stood Still"		"Honeysuckle Rose"
	"Ol' Man River"		"I'll Always Be in Love with You"
	"Side by Side"		
	"The Song Is Ended, but the Memory Lingers On"		"I've Got a Feeling I'm Falling"
	"Why Do I Love You?"		"Louise"
1928	"Button Up Your Overcoat"		"More Than You Know"
			"Singin' in the Rain"
	"Carolina Moon"		"Stardust"
	"I'll Get By"		"With a Song in my Heart"
	"I Wanna Be Loved by You"		
	"Let's Do It"		"You Do Something to Me"
	"Let's Misbehave"		
	"Makin' Whoopee"		
	"Marie"		
	"When You're Smiling"		

When seeking to engage the American public, singers of the 1920s were not limited to live performance. Phonograph recordings, radio performances, and film scores all helped reach a wider national musical audience. In responding to the acoustic strengths and limitations of the era's technology, many of the era's vocalists employed an intimate style of song delivery known as "crooning."

Dancing, too, played a crucial role in defining popular culture of the 1920s. Changing tastes in dance steps helped pave the way for popular dance instruction. Marathon dancing came into fashion at this time, and Americans embraced their outrageous pageantry of excess.

Dance Halls, Night Clubs, and Speakeasies

With electrification and associated new amenities such as air-conditioning, after-dark events became more readily available to America's night owls. Patrons listened to live music, ate, danced, and—where bootleg alcohol was available—drank.

Nightlife became more important as cities and areas within cities such as Harlem grew. In rural areas, roadhouses played the role that nightclubs did in the cities. During the 1920s, nightclubs sometimes took the form of speakeasies, illegal establishments where alcohol was served during Prohibition. In 1929, New York boasted over 32,000 speakeasies. Among the more colorful speakeasy hosts was Mary Louise Cecilia Guinan, better known as "Texas Guinan." She grew up as a Texas cowgirl and then went on to a career as an entertainer in the circus, on the vaudeville stage, and in Hollywood. During Prohibition, Guinan became a speakeasy host and performer at such clubs as the 300 Club. Her wisecracking ways endeared her to audiences, and she became known for her signature greeting to patrons: "Hello, Sucker!"

Jazz

Some contend that jazz represents the nation's greatest contribution to the history of music. Jazz bore the influences of existing musical traditions, such as ragtime, blues, and African musical forms. At the same time, however, jazz provided a unique sound and new form of musical expression. With its emphases on syncopation, improvisation, and fluidity of form, this lively musical mode rebelled from the structures and disciplines associated with earlier orchestral music in America. Jazz provided a thoroughly modern genre, and it transformed the way Americans played, danced to, and thought about music. Musician and bandleader Paul Whiteman may have best articulated the sense in which jazz music conveyed the spirit of the times. Writing in the *New York Times* in 1927, Whiteman remarked, "What is jazz? Is it art, a disease, a manner, or a dance? Has it any musical value? After twelve years of jazz I don't know. . . . In this country especially, the rhythm of machine, the over-rapid expansion of a great country endowed with tremendous natural energies and wealth have brought about a pace and scale of living unparalleled in history. Is it any wonder that the popular music of this land should reflect these modes of living?" (quoted in Leinwand 2001, 269).

Many accounts trace the origin of jazz music to New Orleans, Louisiana. In the Storyville district of New Orleans, musicians who had been trained in various musical traditions performed in bars, clubs, and other entertainment establishments. Storyville had a rather colorful history that included an active brothel trade. In 1917, the Storyville district was closed, purportedly to protect the health of U.S. sailors. As a result, a whole cadre of musicians found themselves displaced. They ventured to other cities, often those located in the Northern states, and in the process, these musicians disseminated jazz modes of composition and techniques of performance. Cities such as Chicago and New York became new centers for jazz music.

Several other factors also helped raise the popularity of jazz music in the United States. Prohibition helped create a captive audience for jazz in speakeasies and other underground settings where bootleg alcohol was served. Jazz was also helped by the arrival of civilian radio, which familiarized more listeners with the genre. Finally, George Gershwin's jazz-influenced composition "Rhapsody in Blue" debuted in 1923, which helped to confer some measure of respectability on the form.

Because jazz was the music of rebellion and because it had become linked with illicit activities of the Storyville district, jazz found its detractors during the 1920s. For instance, in 1923, at their annual convention, the General Federation of Women's Clubs voted to launch a crusade against jazz. In the popular press, articles with such titles as "Does Jazz put the Sin in Syncopation?" questioned the influence the growing popularity of jazz in America might have, especially on the nation's youth. As Anne Shaw Faulkner wrote in the *Ladies' Home Journal* in

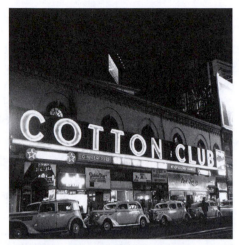

As jazz musicians ventured to Northern cities during the 1920s, new regions of the country got the opportunity to experience live jazz performances in dance clubs and night clubs. (Michael Ochs Archives/ Getty Images)

1921, "We have all been taught to believe that 'music soothes the savage breast,' but we have never stopped to consider that an entirely different type of music might invoke savage instincts" (Faulkner 1921, 16). In some ways, this taboo quality in itself helped promote jazz music to those who wished to challenge the standards and strictures of mainstream society. Just as John Held Jr.'s illustrations featured women as "Jazz Babies," America was home to a new generation that was ready for musical decadence and unruly expression.

Stepping Out: Popular Dances of the 1920s

During the 1920s, dancing was a widely popular diversion. Older steps, like the waltz and the polka, gave way to modern dances such as the shimmy and the Charleston. Dance halls, some of which could accommodate thousands of patrons, appeared in most of the nation's cities. Examples included Boston's Raymor, Chicago's Trianon, Cleveland's Crystal Slipper, Detroit's Greyston, Hollywood's Palladium, Los Angeles's Palomar, and New York's Savoy Ballroom and Roseland. In 1924, admissions to Chicago and New York dance halls exceeded six million (Giordano 2003, 64).

More than the sound of music and the smell of smoke wafted out of dance clubs in the 1920s; social dances such as the Collegiate, Breakaway, and Raccoon spread out of the clubs and became popular across the nation. First the

Foxtrot arrived, deemed racy because partners danced cheek to cheek. The Charleston was a quick-stepping modification of the Foxtrot featured in dance contests but was often banned for its physicality. The Shimmy, Black Bottom, and Varsity Drag followed as popular variations on the Charleston. Most of these dances had roots in African American cultural and musical traditions, including the blues. Both because these dances were linked with illegal drinking and because of the gyrations the steps involved, modern dances were regarded with suspicion by Middle America. The morality of such dances was questioned, and young people were cautioned against the effects of such movements in public.

Still, motion pictures somehow managed to help popularize or maintain such crazes. In the case of the "Charleston," Joan Crawford's freewheeling character in the 1928 *Our Dancing Daughters* and its sequel, *Our Modern Maidens,* drank, kissed, and danced the Charleston. Late in the decade, dances such as the Lindy Hop caught on; movements from these dances would eventually evolve into the swing dancing of the 1930s and 1940s.

The Age of Dance Marathons

Contests of almost any kind—from spelling to lip-reading—were held during the 1920s. Dance contests, especially those featuring new steps like the Charleston, were very popular. The 1920s was also a time in which Americans became preoccupied with setting new world records. In a 1928 talk marathon, for example, the winning contestant lasted 81 hours 45 minutes. There were pie-eating, coffee-drinking, and even spitting-for-distance contests.

It was during this decade that dance marathons became popular nationwide. These dancers were celebrated less for their technique than for their persistence. Participants would receive contestant numbers, which they would wear on their backs as they paired off for dancing. In most cases, dancers would be permitted a certain number of minutes of break each hour. During breaks, contestants could rest or attend to other needs before returning to the dance floor. During the craze for such events, dance marathons employed a variety of staff, including floor judges, trainers, nurses, masters of ceremonies, and some 20,000 promoters.

Even small cities and towns might boast dance marathons. In addition to attracting participants who vied for cash and other prizes, the marathons also emerged as widely attended spectator events. Crowds enjoyed the combination of athleticism and theatricality marathons delivered. Audience-pleasing moves, such as speeding up the music, also became a part of the routine. Eventually, admission fees were charged to audience members. The competition among marathons, or "dance derbies," as they were sometimes called, led to hyperbolic promotions. In 1928, for example, a marathon held at Madison Square Garden was billed as the "Dance Derby of the Century."

Marathon dancers, April 20, 1923. (Library of Congress)

In the beginning, these events had more fanfare than structure. During the early years of marathon dancing, 1923 to 1928, the emphasis was on entertainment. Dance marathons had few regulations and each marathon had different informal understandings about what rules apply to participants. There was no uniform standard by which to compare the results of one marathon to another. As a consequence, new records were constantly being set. In the early years, dancers might switch partners over the course of a marathon. Later on, it became more usual to remain with the same partner throughout an event and compete as a team.

The sport of dance marathons had its own celebrities, such as Mary "Hercules" Promitis of Pittsburgh, so nicknamed for her dancing prowess. Few marathon dancers, however, could rival 32-year-old Alma Cummings, who rose to prominence through her performance in the era's marathons. A dance teacher by profession, Cummings danced for 27 consecutive hours in a March 1923 marathon conducted at New York City's Audubon Ballroom. In accomplishing this feat, she went through six partners and seven pairs of dancing shoes.

Over time, marathons became endurance contests; a 1928 marathon event was suspended after 482 hours of dancing. They became strange pageants reminiscent of theories of social Darwinism in which only the strong survive. In fact, one of the dance marathon promoters, Hall J. Ross, became the first president of the National Endurance Amusement Association (NEAA). Endurance characterized later marathons held from 1929 to 1934. At least three deaths were attributed to the dance marathons, including the fatal collapse of Homer Morehouse in 1923 after 87 hours of dancing.

As a marathon unfolded, the public enjoyed cheering on their favorites and watching the exhaustion of the dancers. Experiences of this kind inspired Horace McCoy's book, *The Shoot Horses, Don't They?* as well as the film of the same name. The enthusiasm for dance marathons met the fate of many such entertainments of this era. The sensation surrounding dance marathons continued into the 1930s when it eventually waned in popularity. Dance marathons gave way to other spectator-oriented diversions, such as roller derbies.

"Ain't We Got Fun": Music and the Popular Imagination

Both music and dance proved integral to the distinctive leisure patterns of America during the 1920s. Whether heard live, via phonograph, or on the radio, a variety of musical genres thrived during this decade. Orchestral and country music benefited from the advent of commercial radio, which exposed larger audiences to their performers. Jazz music grew both in terms of yield and in respectability. Popular songs such as "Ain't We Got Fun" (1921), "Yes! We Have No Bananas" (1923), "My Blue Heaven" (1927), and "Makin' Whoopee" (1928) conveyed the light-hearted and animated feeling of the era's music. These lively tunes suited the dance steps commonly enjoyed during the 1920s, and some songs introduced their own new dances, such as the Charleston and the Black Bottom. Along with other contests conducted during the 1920s, dance marathons flourished, with participants vying for prizes and spectators paying for the privilege of watching the spectacle. Those who wished to learn new or traditional dance steps had the opportunity to do so either by attending lessons at dance studios or by enrolling in correspondence courses that enabled them to learn at home. It was during this decade that Arthur Murray built a successful dance instruction business, with footprint diagrams for home learners and studios for in-person instruction; his first franchise opened in 1925 in New York City. While many of the new entertainments of the 1920s, such as motion pictures, rendered Americans passive, music and dance helped keep people moving. Whether playing instruments or trying the latest step, the nation could find both active and passive musical enjoyments.

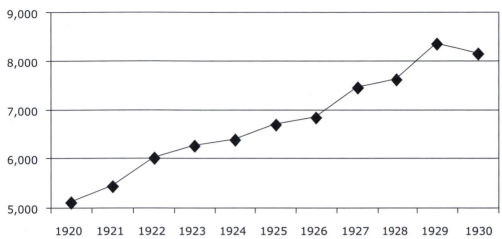

Figure 4.3 *New Books Published in the United States, 1920–1930.* Source: *Bureau of the Census,* Statistical Abstract of the United States, *1947, 499, as presented in Gregory 1995, 155.*

POPULAR READING

Rising Literacy Rates

During the 1920s, youth completed more years of schooling than before, and literacy rates in America were on the rise. While the percentage of the nation's population found to be illiterate in 1920 was 6 percent, by 1930 that figure had dropped to 4.3 percent (Gregory 1995, 302). Rising literacy rates meant that a wider audience for print materials was possible. As a result, popular reading options expanded greatly during this decade. Between 5,000 and 9,000 books were published annually in the United States at this time. America's average household expenditure on books during the period from 1922 to 1929 was $9.02 (Radway 1997, 190). In addition to books, America's consumers had other reading choices, such as conventional newspapers, tabloid papers, pulp fiction, comic books, and magazines. All of these categories enjoyed growth in circulation in the 1920s, and American readers began to "vote" on their favorites with their purchases.

The Book-of-the-Month Club

One notable development in popular reading during the 1920s was the subscription book club, a new form of mail-order retail. Harry Scherman, a writer, advertiser, and bookseller, helped develop the Little Leather Library, a series of

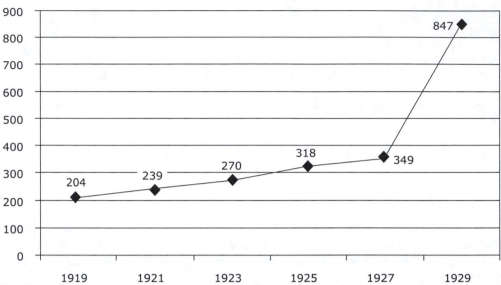

Figure 4.4 *Personal Consumption Expenditures in the United States for Books, Maps, Magazines, Newspapers, and Sheet Music, 1919–1929 (in millions of dollars).* Source: *Adapted from Wattenberg 1976, 401, and Gregory 1995, 338.*

classic titles available for the home. Scherman referred to these volumes as "furniture books" because they were visually appealing, and people bought them—at least in part—to display them to impress houseguests and visitors. This project evolved into a more enduring and lucrative venture for Scherman, the Book-of-the-Month Club (BMOC).

The Book-of-the-Month Club was an innovation in book marketing. Like the Little Leather Library, BMOC addressed a sales and distribution problem: the lack of bookstores in many portions of the country. The club played on the notion of a magazine subscription, but instead of supplying issues of a periodical the BMOC, as its title suggests, sent out monthly book-length works. It offered a different option than the Little Leather Library because it focused not on classics but on the latest in book publishing. BMOC was a subscription service that delivered to members a monthly book for an open-ended duration of time. In this way, customers could maintain an ongoing relationship as readers. Rather than collecting volumes in a finite series of classics, BOMC customers could look forward to a continuous supply of new titles and authors. As a subscription service, BOMC represented a new approach to book sales, creating a marketing circuit. A block of customers would ensure, through their membership in BOMC, return business and a foreseeable demand for the club's books. BOMC began somewhat modestly with 4,750 subscribers but secured 46,539 regular customers by the end of its first year (Radway 1997, 188). By 1929, BMOC boasted over 110,000 members.

Best-selling Fiction and Nonfiction Books, 1920–1929

Year	Fiction	Nonfiction
1920	Zane Grey	Philip Gibbs
	The Man of the Forest	*Now It Can Be Told*
1921	Sinclair Lewis	H. G. Wells
	Main Street	*The Outline of History*
1922	A. S. M. Hutchinson	H. G. Wells
	If Winter Comes	*The Outline of History*
1923	Gertrude Atherton	Emily Post
	Black Oxen	*Etiquette*
1924	Edna Ferber	Lulu Hunt Peters
	So Big	*Diet and Health*
1925	A. Hamilton Gibbs	Lulu Hunt Peters
	Soundings	*Diet and Health*
1926	John Erskine	Bruce Barton
	The Private Life of Helen of Troy	*The Man Nobody Knows*
1927	Sinclair Lewis	Will Durant
	Elmer Gantry	*The Story of Philosophy*
1928	Thornton Wilder	André Maurois
	The Bridge of San Luis Rey	*Disraeli*
1929	Erich Maria Remarque	Ernest Dimnet
	All Quiet on the Western Front	*The Art of Thinking*

Scherman's BOMC tapped into at least two strong consumer desires. First, by configuring the business as a club, BOMC created a sense of belonging for its customers. Second, by guiding readers and conferring status to specific works featured, BOMC appealed to customers' aspirations to being discerning readers of noteworthy works. Of course, the more successful BOMC became, the more powerful its influence over publishing. A committee of authors and critics was charged with identifying books to include within the club's list. In choosing which titles would be offered and which would be elevated as featured monthly book selections, BOMC's committee functioned as publishing gatekeepers and so could make or break the sales figures for a new book. Because BOMC sought to appeal to the greatest possible number of customers (and offend the fewest customers), the resulting book choices were safe and predictably middlebrow. Seen in retrospect, it is remarkable how consistently book clubs overlooked the work of figures now associated with the era, such as F. Scott Fitzgerald, John Dos Passos, D. H. Lawrence, James Joyce, and John Steinbeck.

BOMC would later be joined by other club-based book merchandising entities, such as the Literary Guild. Just as BOMC borrowed the concept of magazine subscription for its book club, the Literary Guild paralleled the also new Theatre Guild and so took its cues from the concept of the season ticket. Founded by Samuel W. Craig in 1927, the Literary Guild struck a bargain with customers; if they paid an annual fee, they would receive what amounted to a 50 percent discount on the usual bookstore prices.

Etiquette and Advice Literature

Etiquette and advice literature are never more important in American life than during times of brisk change. During the 1920s, such books were bestsellers. Whether moralists or modernists, American readers wanted to know how to speak, behave, and respond appropriately. Experts were only too happy to oblige.

Perhaps the best-known American etiquette expert, Emily Post, published her major book-length works on etiquette during the 1920s. They would go through countless editions and revisions as subsequent generations turned to Post as an authority on manners and gracious living. Part of Post's message had to do with convincing American readers that etiquette was not an outmoded art. While some aspects of etiquette might require updating for the 1920s, Post wanted her readers to understand the continued relevance of good manners and the knowledge of how to achieve them. In a passage whose overtones suggest Post's uneasiness about the increasing diversity of the U.S. population, she wrote: "America, too, has her ancient manners to remember and respect; but in the assimilation of new peoples into her economic and social organism, more pressing concerns take up nearly all her time" (Post 1922, xv). It was important to Post that Americans, both young and old, continue to cultivate good taste and right conduct.

In this effort, Post faced considerable challenges. To many Americans, especially the young, manners seemed hopelessly old-fashioned and stuffy. Post tried to counter this impression by inflecting her prose with contemporary references, as when she asserted, "Manners are like clothes, and those mirroring the fashions of today are necessarily short and scant and—*bobbed!*" (Post 1922, 683). Nonetheless, Post maintained that some of the old ways were still the best. For instance, she lamented the decline in the use of chaperones on youth excursions. For Post, such shifts in custom threatened the innocence of American youth and the purity of social encounters. "Good taste," Post wrote, "may not make men or women really virtuous, but it will often save them from what theologians call 'occasions of sin'" (Post 1922, xv). Predictably, public displays of affections (sometimes called "petting") and other dating trends were wholly unacceptable to Post.

Post also warned American readers against lapses in taste when it came to furnishing the home. In a time of economic abundance and plentiful consumer goods, Post tried to tame America's acquisitive impulses in favor of restraint in furnishing and decorating. Even she knew this was not easy to do. She observed, "Never in the recollection of any one now living has it been so easy to surround oneself with lovely belongings. Each year's achievement seems to stride beyond that of the year before in producing woodwork, iron-work, glass, stone, print, paint and textile that is lovelier and lovelier. One cannot go into the shops or pass their windows on the streets without being impressed with the ever-growing taste of their display. Nor can one look into the magazines devoted to gardens and houses and house-furnishings and fail to appreciate the increasing wealth of the beautiful in environment" (Post 1922, 683).

Emily Post was the foremost etiquette expert and columnist in the United States from the 1920s to the 1960s. Post is credited with establishing the foundation of American manners. (Library of Congress)

What Emily Post did for American private life Dale Carnegie sought to do with the nation's professional behavior. Carnegie conducted lecture tours during the 1920s, primarily on the theme "Six Ways to Make People Like You." The content of these talks would later be refined into Carnegie's memorable book, *How to Win Friends and Influence People*. Although Carnegie's focus was on success in business rather than rectitude in manners, his concepts were equally prescriptive to those of Emily Post. He encouraged the American public to approach interpersonal contact with the outlook of a salesman, always seeking to maintain a positive impression in the minds of others. By holding in mind some basic principles of sales, such as the notion that people like to be addressed by their names, the American who wishes to be successful can improve his or her business standing.

Therefore, although the 1920s—sometimes called the "lawless decade"—might appear to lack moral order and clear behavior standards, figures such as Emily Post and Dale Carnegie provided their readers with guidance in both private and public affairs. Such messages helped people navigate a society where mores were challenged and conventions were questioned.

Table 4.2. U.S. Periodical Circulations by Category, 1920–1930

Periodical	Circulation (thousands)		
	1920	*1925*	*1930*
Popular Scientific	879	1,186	1,243
National Geographic	743	983	1,300
Women's Magazines	12,701	15,050	18,676
News/Opinion Magazines	6,951	8,255	10,552
Business/Industrial	887	1,227	1,255
Social Science	354	298	276

Source: President's Research Committee on Social Trends 1933, 385.

Magazines for the Masses

As social historian J. C. Furnas put it, "the cliché 1920's—as opposed to the actual ones—were created by the printed word and show business, two media swollen since 1910 into respectively the movies and million-circulation periodicals" (Furnas, 367). Approximately 4,500 periodicals were published during 1925, and together they sold 180 million copies each issue (Kyvig 2004, 190). Most high-circulation magazines that appeared during the 1920s addressed members of the middle class, or those who wished to be. New titles included *Reader's Digest* (1922), *Time* (1923), *Better Homes and Gardens* (1924), and *The New Yorker* (1925). Other magazine favorites among American readers included *Scribner's, Collier's Weekly, Good Housekeeping, Ladies' Home Journal, National Geographic, The Saturday Evening Post,* and *Vanity Fair. The Saturday Evening Post* featured illustrations from artist Norman Rockwell and fiction from contributing authors such as F. Scott Fitzgerald, who garnered $4,000 for each story that appeared. At this time, *The Saturday Evening Post* enjoyed a circulation of 2.5 million. Some 60 percent of its contents consisted of advertising, with each full black and white ad costing $6,000 per run (Leinwand 2001, 10). To honor the sensibilities of its middle-class readership, the magazine declined all advertisements for cigarettes and alcohol. During this era, magazines were sufficiently popular that publishers could successfully target a specific audience of readers, such as women, or focus on a narrow topic, such as *Your Car.*

NEWS AND NEWS REELS

Unifying the Readership

Although the number of different newspapers available during the 1920s dropped, the circulation of American newspapers increased significantly during the decade.

Table 4.3. Number of Newspapers and Levels of Circulation, Daily and Sunday Papers, 1920–1930

| Year | Daily | | Sunday | |
	Number	Circulation	Number	Circulation
1920	2,042	27,790,656	522	17,083,604
1922	2,033	29,780,328	546	19,712,874
1924	2,014	32,999,437	539	22,219,646
1926	2,001	36,001,803	545	24,435,192
1928	1,939	37,972,488	522	25,771,588
1930	1,942	39,589,172	521	26,413,047

Source: Bureau of the Census, *Historical Statistics of the United States, Colonial Times to 1957,* p. 500, as presented in Gregory 1995, 156.

By some estimates, national circulation doubled from 1919 to 1929, reaching 40 million copies (Leinwand 2001, 249). New aspects of the newspaper industry such as syndication and wire services began to make the format of newspapers more uniform and the content more standardized. Americans also started to receive their news from new sources in addition to the traditional daily newspaper: the tabloid, the radio, and the newsreel. Gradually, the nation's news reporters and photographers began to address themselves to a national rather than local readership. While newspapers had always created the illusion of a community of readers, during the 1920s that sense became more of a reality during the 1920s. Newspaper readers from different walks of life and with distinct perspectives followed the same stories and reacted to the same columnists. These changes in newspaper production had a democratizing effect, linking readers across the nation.

Newspaper readers of the 1920s came to expect a variety of sections in the paper, including editorials, household hints, lovelorn advice, cartoons, health reporting, gossip columns, and—of course—some news. This era also marked the appearance of the sports section, where readers could follow the seasons of their favorite teams and sports

Barefooted newsboy poses in a studio holding up a newspaper with the headline "Lindy Arrives at Dayton," ca. 1927. (Library of Congress)

figures. Although comic strips had appeared in America's newspapers since the 1890s, the 1920s introduced strips, characters, and storylines befitting the era's new concerns. Although some of the technological developments of the 1920s such as radio and motion pictures competed with the newspapers for the American public's time, money, and attention, newspapers continued to increase their sales and their impact.

Gossip Columnists

In an age of "jazz journalism" filled with photographs and tabloid-style stories, gossip columnists played an important part in the reading lives of Americans. Figures such as Walter Winchell, Ed Sullivan, Louella Parsons, and Hedda Hopper became something like celebrities themselves as they reported on Hollywood news and celebrity culture. Often, these columnists had previous ties to the entertainment industry. Some had been performers themselves prior to publishing their columns. Louella Parsons was a motion picture scriptwriter. Hedda Hopper was a former actress. Walter Winchell had participated in vaudeville troupes. Ed Sullivan had served as a theater columnist. All four knew the world about which they wrote. Winchell and Parsons proved especially influential during the 1920s.

Walter Winchell entered journalism in the 1920s and worked first as a Broadway columnist. As he transitioned to gossip, he entered the realm of tabloids. He wrote first for the *Graphic* and later for the *Daily Mirror,* where he served from 1929 to 1963. Winchell commanded attention with his distinctive style of reportage. His columns were informally and crisply written. His "Drop Dead List" became notorious, and he was known for timeless witticisms such as "nothing recedes like success."

Louella Parsons wrote columns for a variety of papers, including the *Chicago Record-Herald,* the *New York Morning Telegraph,* the *New York American,* and the *Los Angeles Examiner.* Parsons was infamous for her ability to discover the secrets of screen stars. She worked for Hearst-owned publications for many years until, during the 1920s, her place of eminence was successfully challenged by Hedda Hopper, an acquaintance and professional rival.

At first, newspaper owners and tabloid editors did not put much stock in the gossip columns appearing in their publications. Entertainment did not qualify as hard news, but as readers began to respond to arts and celebrity content within these periodicals, it was clear that gossip columns were here to stay. Leading gossip columnists vied for popularity, just as they competed for exclusive interviews and "scoops" (first reports) of celebrity news. They became tastemakers as well as reporters, and the entertainment community sought to curry their favor. During the late 1920s and early 1930s, columnists Winchell,

The Funny Papers

The comics section became one of the most widely read portions of the news-paper during the 1920s. A vast majority of America's children, along with a healthy number of adults, followed closely the adventures of their favorite characters, both in daily comic strips and the Sunday edition's "funny papers." It was during the 1920s that many comic strip characters first appeared, such as Moon Mullins, Popeye the Sailor, and Little Orphan Annie.

The comic strips of the 1920s often reflected modern life and its travails. For instance, "Gasoline Alley" played on the era's preoccupation with automobiles and machinery. "Winnie Winkle," also known as "Winnie Winkle the Breadwinner," touched on the subject of changing roles for women. Both strips addressed middle-class white audiences and spoke to the challenges of everyday living.

Parsons, and others broadcast their own radio shows devoted to the latest news about high society and celebrity culture. They also made cameo appearances in motion pictures in which they appeared as themselves.

Tabloids

Although then, as now, tabloids lacked the respectability of traditional news-papers, they should not be overlooked in an assessment of American reading patterns during the 1920s. In fact, tabloids often outstripped conventional pa-pers in terms of their circulations. They were reader-friendly publications that targeted a mass audience.

The first tabloids appeared in 1919, such as Bernarr Macfadden's *True Story* and Joseph Medill Patterson's *Daily News,* and flourished during the next decade. These publications used a smaller page format than regular newspapers and proportions designed for the convenience of commuters who wished to read in subways, on buses, and on trains. Tabloids featured larger type than other newspapers, and relied to a greater degree upon photographs and illustrations for their news content.

Tabloids also differed from previous papers in terms of the way they pre-sented the news. The tabloid press emerged at a time when the audience for sensational reporting was on the rise. Readers of tabloids could count on more direct and daring stories, which often detailed improprieties, conducted exposés, or featured confessional material. Tales of sex, sports, morality, murder, and notoriety dominated the tabloid's pages, and tabloids started to be called "scan-dal sheets" because of the prurient interests they tapped. There is a saying in journalism that "if it bleeds it leads," meaning that the story with the strongest visceral reaction for audience members becomes the most important to feature; tabloids of the 1920s put that premise to the test.

Other successful tabloids in the United States during this era included William Randolph Hearst's *Daily Mirror* and Bernarr Macfadden's *Evening Graphic*. The *Evening Graphic,* sometimes dubbed "The Pornographic" for its sensationalism, went further than most in terms of pressing the limits of editorial restraint and public taste. Tabloids competed vigorously for first or exclusive coverage of the stories of the day, and by 1925, the *Daily News* had more than one million readers.

Entertainment, rather than hard news, occupied the editorial center for America's early tabloids. Given the emphasis on titillating stories, tabloids thrived on the misfortunes of others, especially if misdeeds or celebrities were involved in those tales. Items describing love triangles and features such as "beauty secrets of the stars" were typical. Tabloids incorporated such elements as a crime beat, pictorials, gossip columns, and syndicated features designed to gratify the curiosity of their readers. These publications paid their informants, and staff members sometimes engaged in questionable practices in order to sell papers. For instance, the 1920s was the era of the "composograph," a photographic print produced through the layering or piecing of several different negatives. This technique could create misleading impressions by combining people and events to manipulate visual images.

However, even an unaltered tabloid photograph could excite controversy. A landmark of sorts in the history of 1920s tabloids came on January 13, 1928, when photographer Tom Howard secured a camera under his clothes and smuggled it into the location where a prisoner with a death sentence, Ruth Snyder, was due to be dispatched. Once inside, Howard took a photograph of the very moment of Snyder's electrocution. Ruth Snyder and her lover, Judd Gray, had been tried for the March 19, 1927, bludgeoning death of Snyder's husband, a magazine editor from Queens, Long Island. Their story later formed the inspiration for the James Cain film *Double Indemnity*. The graphic photograph of Snyder's death, the first such execution of a woman in New York State, appeared on the cover of a tabloid on January 13, 1928, the first such image to reach the American public. The accompanying headline was brutally direct: "Dead!" The photo and the measures taken to acquire it raised questions about the appropriate limits of the tabloid press.

As this incident underscored, visual content was of paramount importance to tabloid sales. By 1930, approximately 25 percent of the *Daily News* consisted of sensational and eye-catching photographs. Even when motion pictures were being asked to tame their stories and imagery, tabloids endured no such curtailments. After all, it was more difficult to censor real-life events than dramatic portrayals.

Bobbed Hair Fugitive

One of the more sensational crime stories of 1920s America involved a woman who became known to the nation's public as the "Bobbed Hair Bandit." Because her name remained unknown, the suspect was so dubbed because of her modern cropped coif. The popular press followed this story closely and reported on its developments often. The accounts centered on Celia Cooney, a laundress living and working in Brooklyn, New York. In 1924, when Cooney discovered that she was pregnant, she started to worry that she and her husband, Ed, could not provide the level of financial support she deemed essential for a good start in life for the baby. Purportedly as a means to address the problem, the Cooneys began to rob area groceries and drugstores to supplement their $30 per week combined income. With the funds thus acquired, Celia and Ed Cooney traded in their single room for a new apartment. They also purchased items for the expected baby and indulgences for themselves.

The press seized upon the idea of a brazen woman robber, especially one who staged hold-ups while wearing fashionable hats and nestling a baby automatic, her preferred firearm, inside her fur coat. This interest was fueled by the couple's hubris. For instance, when another woman was falsely arrested for the crimes, Celia Cooney herself sent the arresting officers a scolding note. Authorities struggled to identify and capture the "Bobbed Hair Bandit" while the press scoffed at their failure to do so. Meanwhile, the duo had fled south to Florida, where their baby died just days after birth.

Four months after the Cooney robberies began, Celia and Ed found themselves in custody and aboard a train returning to New York where they were to face trial. Accounts of the capture and surrounding details fascinated readers, and tycoon William Randolph Hearst paid $1,000 for a ghostwritten memoir of Celia Cooney's experiences. Perhaps most striking about the tale was the extent to which Cooney, herself an avid fan of detective stories and pulp magazines, had been acting out scenarios from the fiction she read. Her life imitated popular art, and her exploits in turn filled the pages of true crime publications.

"Lucky Lindy"

Early aviators Amelia Earhart and Charles Lindbergh were among the most upbeat figures to be followed closely by the popular press. Lindbergh's flight was embraced as a national triumph and was celebrated in many ways, including parades and other tributes. Crooner Rudy Vallee sang a song in the pilot's honor entitled "Lucky Lindy." In addition, a popular dance called the "Lindy hop" came into fashion. Lindbergh then served as an advisor to airlines while commercial flight was developing.

Col. Charles A. Lindbergh rides up lower Broadway in an open car next to Mayor James J. Walker during a ticker-tape parade in New York City, 1927. (Library of Congress)

Some readers expressed relief that the positive news of Lindbergh's success provided a change of pace from the violence and scandal that so often filled the newspapers and tabloids. In fact, Mary B. Mullett, writing in October 1927 for *The American Magazine,* said that one of the greatest benefits of Lindbergh's story was its displacement of sordid tabloid stories with upbeat news. By celebrating the aviator's success so lavishly, Americans created positive stories for the tabloid press to report. She writes, "There wouldn't have been much to write about, if there had been no public demonstrations, no parades, dinners, receptions; no tidal wave of letters and telegrams; no truck-loads of gifts; no reams of poetry; no songs; no cheers and shouts; no smiles of pride; no tears of joy; no thrill of possessing, in him, our dream of what *we* really and truly want to be!" (quoted in Mowry 1963, 81–82).

Lindbergh would reenter the public eye in 1932, but for more tragic reasons. His two-year-old child with his wife, also a licensed pilot, disappeared from the family home. The kidnapping was described in the press as the crime of the century. It was in part a consequence of this tragedy that kidnapping became designated a federal crime in the United States.

Real to Reel: America's Newsreels

Newsreels were short films, usually just 10 minutes in length, aired prior to feature attractions at movie theaters. They first appeared before the American public in 1911. The period from 1920 to 1947 marked the height of newsreel production, with approximately 90 percent of the nation's theaters presenting newsreels to their audiences (Fielding 1972, 132–133).

Although newsreels recounted the news stories of the time, they were intended more for audience entertainment than for public information. Newsreels began as filler on the theatrical program and were presented alongside coming attractions, cartoons, and short-subject films on such topics as popular travel destinations. By the end of the 1920s, there were five main companies providing newsreels to America's movie palaces.

The movie studios played an important part in the emergence of newsreels as a popular form. Their interest was less journalistic than commercial. For that reason, newsreels often concentrated on content that would now be described as "human interest" stories. Curious inventions, film premieres, sports highlights, fashions, and fads were standard fare for the newsreel viewer. Therefore, while newsreels also included serious stories, the emphasis was on the sensational. For this reason, a saying of the time described newsreels as "a series of catastrophes ended with a fashion show" (Grubin 1988).

Without television to provide direct feeds of news reports and accompanying footage, the American public looked to makers of newsreels to serve as their eyes and ears. Because the reels had to be produced and delivered in a timely fashion, teams had to work quickly to meet their twice-weekly deadlines, typically on Mondays and Thursdays. For special events, the deadlines could be even tighter. Footage of the Harding inaugural was on screen in New York theaters within six hours after he had taken the oath of office. Crews became competitive in their efforts to cover key stories, and some resorted to subterfuge to land the best footage.

Newsreels were somewhat formulaic in construction; legitimate news stories, unusual stunts, and profiles of amusing figures combined to form a 10-minute presentation. Newsreels might feature segments about floods, hurricanes, strikes, riots, or combat, or they might celebrate celebrities or such sports heroes as the "Sultan of Swat," baseball player Babe Ruth. Interspersed with these pieces would be accounts of unusual events, such as a couple conducting an underwater wedding, or daredevils, such as an acrobat hanging from a trapeze suspended beneath a blimp.

While there were many companies producing newsreels at some point during the 1920s, the major producers were Paramount News, Pathé News, Universal News, Hearst Metrotone News, and Fox Movietone News. The impact of newsreels was so significant that when looking for modern forms to emulate in his experimental writing, modernist author John Dos Passos looked to the newsreel for inspiration. In his fiction trilogy *U.S.A.*, Dos Passos paid tribute to the form by incorporating sections he called "newsreels" that approximated their spectacular effects on an audience.

News as It Happens:
An Appetite for the Latest

Taken together, the newspaper, tabloid, and newsreel of the 1920s not only created an audience with an appetite for the latest story but they also became increasingly adept at delivering that news faster than had been possible in previous years. From the ideological to the idiosyncratic, reports of the day reached the American consumer through a system of mass media that was now national, and sometimes international, in its reach. This increased expectation of immediacy in journalism posed new challenges for competition, accuracy, and ethical practice. Furthermore, news outlets continued to struggle to balance their work in the public interest with the demands of making a profit, or at least meeting costs. With newsreels routinely produced under the auspices of movie studios and with newspapers and tabloids fueled by advertising, the emergence of mass culture cleared the way for an explosion of marketing. Many familiar forms of promotion—such as commercially conducted contests, sponsorship of feature presentations, product placements, publicity stunts, and sales tie-ins—came into use during the 1920s. New forms of advertising, public relations, and publicity would achieve prominence during this decade.

ADVERTISING EVERYTHING

Selling to America

From the promotion of the sale of Liberty Bonds and the home front propaganda in support of American troops fighting in World War I, it was a small step to the aggressive methods of modern advertising. Advertising was hardly an invention of the 1920s, but it achieved new prominence during this era. At the time, a writer for the Kansas City *Journal-Post* expressed it well when he asserted that "advertising and mass production are the twin cylinders that keep the motor of modern business in motion" (Time-Life 1998, 84). In fact, spending on advertising increased dramatically, with an increase from $1.409 billion in 1919 to $2.987 billion in 1929 (Friedman 2004, 196). According to reporter Stuart Chase, writing for *The New Republic* in August 1925, "of the 2,600,000 tons of newsprint pulp consumed annually, well over 1,500,000 tons goes into advertising" (quoted in Mowry 1963, 16). Even literary figures such as Dorothy Parker and F. Scott Fitzgerald tried their hands at writing advertising copy. With characteristic wit,

Parker pitched women's intimate apparel with the slogan, "Brevity is the soul of lingerie" (Miller 2003, 1511). Print ads continued to dominate the industry, but other forms of advertising were also introduced during this decade. Between 40 and 75 percent of the content of newspaper pages were devoted to advertising, and at least 80 percent of mail received during the 1920s consisted of advertisements (Best 2003, 33).

The 1920s was also a time of transformation of methods within advertising. In the past, ads had taken the form of announcements and emphasized factual information about the product itself as a strategy for boosting sales. The 1920s went beyond this form of advertisement-as-notice to experiment with new strategies and formats for promoting sales. Ads published during this time focused as much on influencing public attitudes as they did on the products themselves. Newspaper and magazine ads grew in size, often assuming full pages of the publication. Such publications also featured a high percentage of advertising between their covers. For instance, the April 1926 issue of the *Ladies' Home Journal,* their largest ever, boasted 270 pages in total; 162 of those pages consisted of advertising content. Whereas newspaper advertising doubled during the period since 1916, magazine advertising soared 600 percent (Marchand 1985, 7).

New approaches to advertising in use during the 1920s were varied. In general, there was an increased interest in polling and market research as clues to consumer attitudes and their sources. Advertisers hoped not only to discover areas of consumer demand but also to

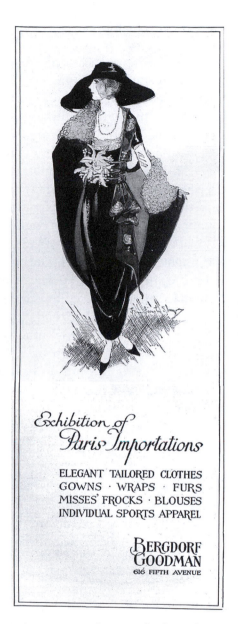

*Advertisement for Bergdorf Goodman announcing an exhibition of the latest fashion imports from Paris. (*Country Life, *March 1920)*

shape them. Testimonial ads sought to capture the popular imagination by presenting the praise for an item by celebrities and other public figures. Expert warnings and endorsements became more usual in 1920s advertising, with physicians and other respected authorities offering guidance to readers of advertisements. When presenting products and services, the era's ads made every effort to portray items as modern and up-to-date rather than traditional and old-fashioned. Sloganeering became common, and the 1920s produced many enduring examples, including the perennial slogan for Camel cigarettes, "I'd walk a mile for a camel," first seen in ads during 1921. Advertising tie-ins to popular characters and licensing of such products was also on the rise. One such instance was the marketing of Buster Brown shoes for children, named for a cartoon character that appeared in the Sunday comics section (Gordon 1998, 49). The late 1920s also marked the beginning of youth-oriented advertising, which targeted those who might become life-long customers. During the 1920s, style obsolescence also came into play. In an era of ready-to-wear clothing and other forms of ready-made merchandise, it became possible to market the latest fashions and favorites to a wide audience of American consumers.

Perhaps most noteworthy among the changing world of 1920s advertising was the dramatic growth in the use of social science theory and research to inform advertising appeals and practices. For instance, John B. Watson was a psychologist who coined the term "behaviorism." At the University of Chicago, he studied the possibilities for conditioning of emotional reactions in human subjects. Watson went on to become an adman with the J. Walter Thomson Agency where he worked on campaigns for products such as Pond's cold cream.

Buying Beauty

During the 1920s, advertising campaigns invited consumers to define themselves with and through their product purchases. Self-definition increasingly became associated in the pages of advertisements and in the minds of consumers with specific products and brand names. Advertisements attempted to link consumer goods to desired human attributes, implying that by buying the item advertised, a consumer could also acquire that personal characteristic. Nowhere is this approach to advertising more dramatic than in the marketing of cosmetics.

It was in the 1920s that respectable women started consuming their share of cosmetics, which were even promoted as part of the freedom women might exercise now that they had the vote. While previously makeup had been associated with the "painted ladies," during the 1920s American women—especially the young women—began wearing makeup on a regular basis. During 1927, 50 percent of American women over eighteen used rouge; 73 percent, toilet water;

75 percent, perfume; and 90 percent, face powder (Leinwand 2001, 194). The enthusiasm was such that novelist Dorothy Speare, author of *Dancers in the Dark,* wrote of the era's "intoxication of rouge" (Allen 1931, 52).

Although it was still considered in questionable taste to apply rouge or lipstick in public, makeup became more acceptable to the general buying public. As a result, the manufacture of cosmetics grew dramatically during this decade. To be precise, according to historian Gary Dean Best, "the cosmetics industry reported at the end of the 1920s that American women were using annually 4,000 tons of powder and enough lipstick to reach 'from Chicago to Los Angeles by way of San Francisco,' plus '52,500 tons of cleansing cream, 26,250 tons of skin lotion, 19,100 tons of complexion soap, 17,500 tons of nourishing cream, 8,750 tons of foundation cream, 6,562 tons of bath powder and 2,375 tons of rouge'" (Best 2003, 48). The "New Woman" became the new customer for a whole range of beauty products marketed for self-improvement. Even "Scarface"—gangster Al Capone—was said to use powder to improve his physical appearance.

By decade's end, the United States had 40,000 beauty shops in operation, up from just 5,000 in 1920 (Dumenil 1995, 141). Some attributed the shift in attitude and practice to the influence of motion pictures in which actresses from Louise Brooks to Mary Pickford appeared in heavy makeup regardless of the characters they played. In fact, there were often product tie-ins with films, and some of the makeup people from the movies, such as Max Factor, would eventually bring their products to the general public. In any case, American women became increasingly comfortable with wearing cosmetics during this period, and the trend would continue. An era of what scholar Kathy Peiss called "normative femininity" was under way (Peiss 1998, 135).

Testimonials

One extremely popular advertising technique in use during the 1920s was the personal testimonial for an advertised product. Society people and figures from the entertainment world were popular choices to feature for such endorsements. Film star Constance Talmadge was a favorite among advertisers, completing hundreds of endorsements. She was not alone, however; figures from Douglas Fairbanks to George Gershwin pitched products. Others were more reluctant to make advertising endorsements. Charles Lindbergh refused many advertising offers before agreeing to lend his name to a campaign for Bulova watches.

One of the most telling stories about celebrity endorsements involves Will Rogers and Bull Durham tobacco. The company was so keen to receive an endorsement from Rogers to appear in newspapers and magazines that they gave him control of the advertising copy. In return, Rogers wrote the following: "I know people are going to say: 'What do you think of Will Rogers writing and endorsing Bull Durham? That's where you're wrong. I am not endorsing it. I never smoked any tobacco in my life, not even Bull Durham'" (Segrave 2005a, 17). With his signature wit, Rogers discovered a way to appear in an ad without lending his name to a product. Ever the humorist, Will Rogers made sure the light-hearted joke was on Bull Durham.

A similar incident with celebrity testimonials involved aviator Amelia Earhart. When adman H. S. Gardner pursued Earhart for a cigarette endorsement, she accepted the money. Subsequently, while donating $1,500 of the earnings to an expedition to the Antarctic, Earhart explained to the press that it was in fact her male colleagues, not she, who indulged in smoking during the transatlantic flight (Segrave 2005b, 18).

Of course, there are other risks involved in the use of testimonials. If the celebrities providing the endorsements lose popularity, become implicated in misconduct, or become otherwise unsuitable for purposes of publicity, their testimonials may lose value or even damage the reputation of the product advertised. The only way to associate a product with a personal image without incurring such reputation risks was to create icons who could serve as brand image-makers. Betty Crocker and the Jolly Green Giant were just two of the imaginary figures devised in the 1920s to stand for a company's line of wares. These faux spokespeople ensured that misbehavior would not compromise the corporate image. Of course, as the cultural climate changed, some of these images required updating; Betty Crocker, for instance, has undergone several "makeovers." Other corporate advertising icons of the 1920s—Rastus for Cream of Wheat and Aunt Jemima for pancake syrup, for example—have since come into question for stereotypical and demeaning portrayals of African Americans. An even safer approach to testimonials was the generic endorsement, such as the 1924 advertising campaign that proclaimed Wheaties cereal the "Breakfast of Champions" (Miller 2003, 152).

Shopping as Social Insurance

In the 1920s, it became increasingly common for advertisements to appeal to the consumer's fears and insecurities in order to sell a product. This negative approach targeted human imperfections and offered solutions to everyday problems. Items related to personal hygiene, such as deodorants and gargles, lent themselves especially well to this approach. Even product names, such as "Odor-o-no," made clear the nature of the dilemma an item addressed.

Probably the most famous advertising campaign of this kind was used to sell Listerine mouthwash. The Lambert Pharmaceutical Company developed a 1922 campaign to boost sales of Listerine. Borrowing a term for bad breath used in a British medical journal, the advertisers warned against the horrors of "halitosis." One such advertisement narrated the story of Marvin, whose bad breath

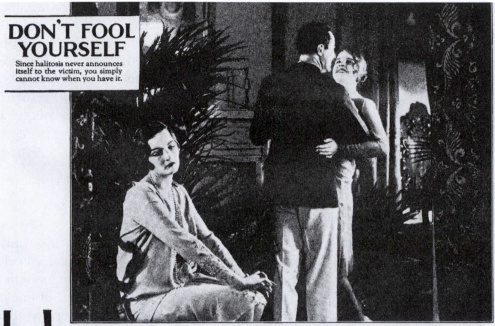

DON'T FOOL YOURSELF
Since halitosis never announces itself to the victim, you simply cannot know when you have it.

Halitosis makes

It is unexcusable . . . can be instantly remedied

you unpopular

No matter how charming you may be or how fond of you your friends are, you cannot expect them to put up with halitosis (unpleasant breath) forever. They may be nice to you—but it is an effort.

Don't fool yourself that you never have halitosis as do so many self-assured people who constantly offend this way.

Read the facts in the lower right hand corner and you will see that your chance of escape is slight. Nor should you count on being able to detect this ailment in yourself. Halitosis doesn't announce itself. You are seldom aware you have it.

Recognizing these truths, nice people end any chance of offending by systematically rinsing the mouth with Listerine. Every morning.

Every night. And between times when necessary, especially before meeting others.

Keep a bottle handy in home and office for this purpose.

Listerine ends halitosis instantly. Being antiseptic, it strikes at its commonest cause—fermentation in the oral cavity. Then, being a powerful deodorant, it destroys the odors themselves.

If you have any doubt of Listerine's powerful deodorant properties, make this test: Rub a slice of onion on your hand. Then apply Listerine clear. Immediately, every trace of onion odor is gone. Even the strong odor of fish yields to it. Lambert Pharmacal Company, St. Louis, Mo., U.S.A.

The new baby—
LISTERINE SHAVING CREAM
—you've got a treat ahead of you.
TRY IT

READ THE FACTS
⅓ had halitosis

68 hairdressers state that about every third woman, many of them from the wealthy classes, is halitoxic. Who should know better than they?

LISTERINE
The safe antiseptic

[1928]

Advertisement for Listerine appeals to the consumer's fears of unpopularity, 1928. (Bettmann/Corbis)

represents "the damning, unforgivable, social fault." Although he has wealth, charm, and ability, Marvin does not realize that halitosis is compromising his chances for success. Many of these embedded narratives hinged on the notion that a person with an odor problem is often the last to know because others are reluctant to call attention to the issue. The scare approach worked. By 1928, Lambert had an ad budget of $5 million a year. Ads based on self-improvement, especially those that provided cautionary tales to consumers, became frequent during the 1920s.

New Uses for Familiar Products: Marketing Fleischmann's Yeast

The story of Fleischmann's Yeast during the 1920s offers a marketer's case-study in product repositioning. Charles Fleischmann, a Viennese immigrant, developed this yeast to produce a fresher and more efficient leavening agent for home baking. Early advertising for his yeast cakes concentrated on the value of bread in one's diet. By promoting bread consumption, Fleischmann's company also sought to increase their yeast sales. Fortunes shifted for Fleischmann when America's households moved away from the custom of home-baked goods, instead favoring the convenience of bakery wares. Once offering a product used chiefly by baking homemakers, the yeast manufacturer had to get creative about sales as the nation's families made the transition to a heavier reliance on store-bought foods. Fleischmann tried to cash in on the era's concern for health, and so advertised their yeast cakes as a health supplement. In his yeast-for-health campaign, Fleischmann modified the approach to consumers by recommending eating a cake and a half three times each day for the prospect of more robust health. Although yeast had been used before in the treatment of various health conditions, including regularity, Fleischman adopted this strategy to survive a cultural shift away from home baking that threatened their American market. The Fleischmann Company made extensive use of newspaper and magazine advertising, and increased sales 130 percent between 1923 and 1926 (Gordon 1999, 100).

New Markets for Familiar Products: Selling Cigarettes to American Women

In the late 1920s, tobacco manufacturers began to address women as a promising new customer base, using ad campaigns in magazines and other publicity ploys to recruit women as potential smokers. For instance, Lucky Strike cigarette advertisements carried testimonials from women who were already public figures, such as actress Constance Talmadge and aviator Amelia Earhart. Such campaigns helped boost Lucky Strike earnings from $12 million in 1926 to $40 million in 1930 (Drowne and Huber 2004, 53).

Changing American outlooks toward women smokers, however, was not an easy matter. In part, the problem of selling cigarettes to U.S. women was cultural; traditionally, it was not considered proper for women to smoke. Detractors argued that smoking was unseemly for women and was particularly ill suited to their roles as mothers. In addition, women were warned against the unfortunate effects smoking might have upon their appearance, such as facial wrinkles and yellow teeth. They were also cautioned that a smoking habit would coarsen one's speaking and singing voices, another perceived factor in feminine appeal. As late as 1929, the August issue of *Good Housekeeping* featured a piece by author and politician Allan Louis Benson lamenting the unflattering effects of smoking on American womanhood.

Yet, it was more than a matter of custom that kept U.S. women from smoking freely. In 1920, tobacco use was still widely regarded as a moral threat to the nation's women. Opponents of the era's "smokes for women" efforts speculated that smoking among America's women would lead to other forms of transgressive behavior, such as drinking and petting. Historian Allan M. Brandt cites the claims of numerous antismoking campaigners that women, unlike their male counterparts, would be constitutionally incapable of practicing moderation in their tobacco intake. The moral argument about women smokers was clear. If women could not be trusted to exercise restraint in smoking, and smoking lowered resistance to other forms of temptation such as alcohol and sex, then what would become of feminine ideals of image and conduct if American women began to smoke openly? It was on this basis that anticigarette activists attempted to censor from motion pictures any depictions of women that appeared to portray smoking as a respectable habit for female characters.

Predictably, tobacco manufacturers and merchants sought to challenge these efforts. Nonetheless, the tobacco industry faced a major challenge in persuading a new market of women smokers. The negative connotations of women and smoking remained a disincentive to buying and smoking cigarettes. Although some of America's women were smoking, most did not wish to make a show of it. They smoked indoors and in private, not out in public where they could be observed smoking.

The situation called for the tobacco industry to identify an inventive advertising approach to selling cigarettes to women. While representing the American Tobacco Company in 1929, renowned publicist Edward L. Bernays, working in consultation with a psychoanalyst, devised a ploy to reduce the social stigma associated with women smoking. Bernays determined that he could best accomplish that task by recruiting women to smoke while marching in one of the most public situations, New York's Easter Parade down Fifth Avenue. He also enlisted the help of feminist Ruth Hale, who signed newspaper advertisements in support of the effort. Within this media event, Bernays borrowed from the language

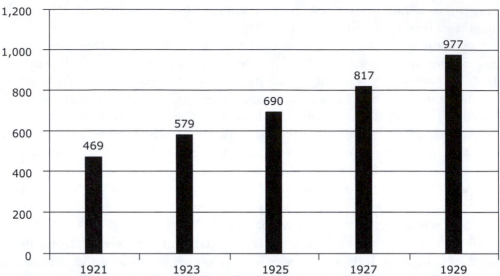

Figure 4.5 *Consumption of Cigarettes in the United States, 1921–1929 (in millions).*
Source: *Adapted from Bureau of the Census,* Statistical Abstract of the United States,
1951, 776; Gregory 1995, 335.

and rhetoric of women's suffrage to call cigarettes women's "torches of free-dom." Telegrams sent to his women marchers scripted their message for any interviews or interactions with the press at the parade. This script declared, "In the interests of equality of the sexes and to fight another sex taboo, I and other young women will light another torch of freedom by smoking cigarettes while strolling on Fifth Avenue Easter Sunday" (Tye 1992, 28–29). Bernays garnered free publicity with this staged event. Because the promotion was not confined to a single brand of cigarette as an advertisement might be, it helped sell many different brands to women. By linking "smokes for women" to the suffragettes' historic struggle for the franchise, Bernays tapped into women's desires to demonstrate independence from men's expectations.

In a sense, a right for women had been won. After the 1920s, women would no longer needed to fear arrest on charges such as "disturbing the peace" or "disorderly conduct" for lighting up cigarettes on city streets. Along with this right, however, women smokers soon commanded their share of tobacco's health and financial disadvantages. Women no longer needed to hide their cig-arettes, but neither could they hide from the effects of smoking on their bodies or pocketbooks. Advertising techniques such as Bernays's "torches of freedom" publicity stunt helped make smokers of America's women. In the course of his own career in public relations, Edward L. Bernays worked on both sides of the antismoking issue, representing tobacco and health initiatives.

How Many U.S. Women Smoked during the 1920s?

As the decade of the 1920s opened, the tobacco industry was experiencing robust sales. In the years from 1918 to 1928, cigarette production more than doubled (Allen 1931, 77). During World War I, for example, cigarettes proved a convenient item for soldiers who wished to smoke and soon were included within their government-supplied rations, which resulted in many new cigarette smokers among America's men. Even though estimated sales to women had more than doubled in the years from 1923 to 1929, they reportedly comprised only 12 percent of the American market for cigarettes (Best 2003, 28; Tye 1992, 24).

In part as a consequence of industry marketing directed to both U.S. women and men, more women—even "nice girls"—began to smoke in public during the 1920s. In the slang of the day, smokers no longer had to conceal their "coffin nails." According to historian Gary Dean Best, "*Good Housekeeping* noted in 1929 that the production of cigarettes had doubled in the 1920s—from 53 million to 106 million—and found much of the increase attributable to the rise in female smoking, especially by young women" (Best 2003, 27–28). In fact, the campaigns to win over American women to smoking were so successful that temperance groups formed to oppose the consumption of alcohol developed a parallel effort to counter smoking.

Cultural observers at the time and since have engaged in debates about the larger significance of this 1920s shift in both marketing and sales of cigarettes to women. Although the idea of women smoking outdoors and in public spaces did not lose all of its stigma during the 1920s, by decade's end it became more common for women to smoke in restaurants, at theaters, and on modes of public transportation. In fact, as early as 1925, George MacAdam wrote a commentary in the pages of the *New York Times* in which he lamented that the last male sanctuary, the railroad smoking car, would soon be lost to the country's more permissive outlook regarding women smokers.

Some historians, while noting the shift in the implied customer base within U.S. cigarette advertising during the 1920s, question just how closely this change in promotional strategies correlated with changes in women's behavior. For instance, Kerry Segrave points out just how difficult it is to arrive at reliable measures of women's market share in the nation's cigarette industry at this point in history. The nation's women still had good reason to mask their tobacco use by smoking only in private. Furthermore, women may not have been the ones to purchase all the products they consumed. Consequently, women may have been responsible for a greater share of the nation's growth in cigarette consumption, either before or during the decade of the 1920s, than the era's sales statistics can accurately record. Even though it may not be possible to present definitive counts of women smokers in 1920s America, the shift from surreptitious to defiant cigarette use by women represented a dramatic redefinition of female smoking practices.

THE RISE OF PUBLIC RELATIONS

Behind the Scenes

Observers were not entirely seduced by the era's advertising. In fact, these tactics would be the target of a lampoon magazine begun in 1931, *Ballyhoo* (Colin 1999, 106). "Ballyhoo" was the era's popular term to describe stories that combined human interest with sensationalism, and "Ballyhooligans" kept quite busy during the 1920s. The voice at work in such stories resembled the carnival barker demanding audience attention.

As the decade's advertising became more prevalent and more aggressive, another kindred industry emerged: the field of public relations. While advertising concentrated on direct sales, publicity set out to promote a brand name and to create good will with the public. The rise of public relations created employment for a host of people such as press agents and publicists. These public relations experts provided their services to individuals, products, companies, and corporations. They endeavored to increase the visibility of clients, goods, and services. Although sales might be the long-range goal of such efforts, the immediate objective was to gain public exposure and recognition.

Most public relations experts ascribed to the theory that consumers operate on the basis of a combination of instincts and unconscious motivations (Ewen 1996, 39). These experts likened the American public to a crowd or even a herd, together exhibiting a mob mentality. For this reason, public relations leaders sought ways that public opinion might be shaped, influenced, and even controlled. Many publicists advanced notions of social psychology as the foundation for their recommendations. In addition, most public relations experts attested to the power of symbols in the formation of public opinion.

The Publicity Stunt

To capture the public's attention, publicists frequently turned to elaborate promotions, stunts, or hoaxes. Some say that 19th-century showman P. T. Barnum originated the publicity stunt, but it outlived him as a strategy for generating an audience and manipulating public opinion. The silent film classic *Safety Last* (1923) offers a dramatization of such efforts. The protagonist, portrayed by comedian Harold Lloyd, leaves his home for a job in the city as a department store clerk. He convinces the store manager to participate in a scheme in which the store will award $1,000 to anyone who can attract more customers. Tapping into one of the common promotional stunts of the day, Lloyd's character secures the services of a "human fly" to captivate the public by climbing the store's exterior. When the "fly" runs afoul with the law, Lloyd himself must scale the building, which he does to comic effect. As this cinematic example illustrates, commercial competition produced some outrageous approaches to marketing.

Public relations campaigns often appealed to the era's enthusiasm for fads, novelties, and extravagant stunts. Publicity experts tied their efforts to existing public interests, such as aviation. In 1923, a candy company dropped Baby Ruth candy bars from a plane over Pittsburgh, Pennsylvania, each outfitted with a miniature parachute. Other publicity stunts involved flying banners from the tail of planes. Former war pilots and film stuntmen became barnstormers and performed stunts or transported daredevils such as wing walkers and parachute jumpers. These "flying circuses" entertained onlookers with their feats of daring, such as playing tennis or golf atop a plane's wings while airborne. It was also during the 1920s that skywriting and neon signs first appeared.

Seekers of publicity also sponsored contests of various sorts. Eating con-

Fearless Freddie, a Hollywood stunt man, clings to a rope ladder slung from a plane, about to drop into an automobile below, November 10, 1921. (Library of Congress)

tests were one technique. Ideally, these events showcased products and promoted their consumption. Singer held a search for the 100 oldest home sewing machines of any brand and offered to replace them with new Singer machines (Carter 1977, 135). Other promotions involved pageantry, such as parades and public displays. It was in 1924 that Macy's department store began its tradition of Thanksgiving Day parades, which was held annually to help launch the Christmas shopping season and to showcase toys in particular.

Some publicity efforts sought to capitalize on the popularity of celebrities such as film stars. Members of the public appeared in contests to locate celebrity look-alikes for such screen figures as Jackie Coogan. For instance, the Liberty Theater in Bellingham, Washington, held a Charlie Chaplin look-alike contest in 1921 in conjunction with the premiere of Chaplin's film *The Idle Class*. These events could create interest in a film's presentation and generate publicity for the theater at the same time.

The movie industry itself was actively involved in publicity for their studios, stars, and films. In fact, most motion picture studios had "exploitation" departments charged with promoting their studio name, stars, and films. One such venture, and one that persists to this day, was the casting of star handprints and footprints in cement outside Grauman's Chinese Theater, a movie palace located on Hollywood Boulevard. Among the first silent film stars to participate in these photo opportunities were Douglas Fairbanks, Harold Lloyd, Gloria Swanson, Tom Mix, and Mary Pickford. Others honored outside Grauman's Chinese included Charlie Chaplin, Norma Shearer, and Constance Talmadge. Sometimes the ritual would be modified to reflect the star at the center of the tribute. For instance, Al Jolson's fame for singing on bended knee in such films as *The Jazz Singer* led to him immortalize his kneeprints in Grauman's cement. The site became a popular tourist attraction, and theater customers and tourists alike enjoyed comparing their own hands and feet to imprints of their favorite film stars.

The Miss America Pageant

The 1920s was a decade preoccupied with contests of various sorts. The first Miss America Pageant was held on September 8, 1921. The event began as a contrivance to increase Atlantic City tourist trade after Labor Day. Such contests were not unique at seaside resorts at the time, but the Miss America Pageant conferred a more wholesome image on the figure of the bathing beauty. Then, as now, celebrities served as judges. Illustrator John Held Jr. and artist/illustrator Norman Rockwell both judged Miss America Pageants.

Norma Smallwood, Miss America 1926, with her hair attached to electric permanent wave equipment. (Library of Congress)

In that first year, there were only 8 contestants for the title. By 1924, the number of candidates rose to 83. The first holder of the crown was Margaret Gorman. She was fair-haired, had blue eyes, and was just 16 when she won the title. Gorman was 5 foot 1 inch tall, weighed 108 pounds, and her measurements were 30–25–32. She bore some physical resemblance to screen star Mary Pickford.

Culture critics have had a lot to say about the Miss America Pageant. One of the more interesting critiques belongs to Elwood Watson and Darcy Martin, who view it as a reaction against flapper culture. They contend that, "by consistently selecting the contestant who least resembled a 'flapper' or 'new woman,' the pageants of the 1920s promoted a standardized and retrograde ideal of womanhood and sent important messages to women and men across the country" (Watson and Martin 2004, 32).

Watson and Martin regard the pageant as a modern form of propaganda intended to reinforce traditional values of long hair, youth, feminine innocence, and domesticity (Watson and Martin 2004, 45). In fact, they suggest that the banner sashes worn by Miss America contests made a mockery of the ones worn by suffragettes in women's rights marches. In any case, the Miss America Pageant has proven to be a successful promotional event that continues to be held annually, although it no longer calls Atlantic City, New Jersey, home.

Putting the Right Spin on It: The Father of PR

During the 1920s, public relations emerged as a field of expertise. Press agents, publicists, and consultants found a wide variety of ways in which to meet the needs of their clients. These efforts included promotions, stunts, hoaxes, planted stories in the press, and media events. No one, however, was better known in the realm of 1920s publicity than the so-called Father of Public Relations, Edward L. Bernays. Between 1917 and 1925, 28 books on the subject were published, where only 8 such titles were published prior to that period (Cutlip 1994, 107). Bernays, a pioneer of public relations, authored two of those books: *Crystallizing Public Opinion* (1923) and *Propaganda* (1928). These publications helped make Bernays a familiar name in the area of publicity. He became closely associated with the notion that public opinion could be managed, even engineered through the use of public relations.

Edward Bernays opened his agency in New York in June 1919 and billed himself as a "public relations counsel." This phrasing represented an attempt to confer respectability on the work, which suggested that it was comparable to the professions of law, accounting, and engineering. Because of the frequency with which he was called upon to define what he meant by the term "public relations counsel," Bernays took out a 1927 advertisement. In it, he explained that "a counsel on public relations directs, advises upon and supervises those activities of his client which affect or interest the public. He interprets the client to the public, and the public to his client" (Cutlip 1994, 181). In the 1920s, Bernays established his reputation in the relatively new endeavor known as public relations. Whatever the client's problem, Bernays displayed an uncommon ability to address the issue through the application of his own distinctive public relations techniques. In work for the United Fruit Company, he established bananas as health food. At a moment in history during which the speed and convenience of the continental breakfast threatened to draw American consumers away from the traditional hot morning meal, for example, Benays nonetheless served the needs of Beech Nut Packing Company through a campaign that marshalled the authority of physicians to restore bacon as part of a healthy breakfast. Bernays was especially well known for his ability to identify and shift buying practices. For instance, in an era when women were getting "bobs," short haircuts asso-

Flagpole Sitting

The 1920s also introduced publicity stunts involving novelties of one sort or another. The most memorable among these may be flagpole sitting. Usually hired by businesses seeking splashy promotions, flagpole sitters would climb atop the flagpoles at the top of tall buildings and would remain there for hours at a time. These stunts attracted both onlookers and press coverage, which in turn created publicity for movie theater openings or other events. The best known of America's flagpole sitters was Alvin "Shipwreck" Kelly, who started his career in flagpole sitting in 1924. Kelly was a film stuntman who was paid handsomely, rumored at $100 an hour, to sit atop flagpoles for extended periods of time. An accomplished flagpole sitter, Kelly displayed his prowess at this feat at various locations. In 1927, Kelly spent 7 days, 13 hours, and 13 minutes perched atop the flagpole of a 13-story St. Louis building. He positioned himself on an 8-inch disk and secured his footing with stirrups. In 1929, he spent 29 days on a flagpole in Baltimore. The following year, he lasted 49 days on an Atlantic City flagpole. Part of the showmanship involved arrangements by which Kelly passed the time engaged in such activities as drinking coffee, shaving, and receiving manicures. In all, Kelly spent over 20,000 hours poised above various building flagpoles. He ultimately married one of his fans, who he learned had defended him against one of his detractors.

Kelly's feats inspired a host of others to try flagpole sitting but none achieved his prominence. Even youth got involved in the craze. Avon Foreman of Baltimore, age 15, set out to break the juvenile record for flagpole sitting. Since no such record seemed to exist, Foreman remained on the flagpole for 10 days, 10 hours, 10 minutes, and 10 seconds, calling that the new juvenile record for flagpole sitting. Foreman had many imitators among her peers, and some sustained injuries or became ill in their attempts to beat the juvenile record she had set.

ciated with flapper fashion, Bernays represented the Venida Hair Net Company. Despite the fact that hair nets had been associated chiefly with long hairstyles, which were no longer the fashion during the 1920s, Bernays boosted Venida's sales by ensuring that hairnets became standard for sanitation in workplaces such as in food preparation.

Bernays was the force behind a legendary 1924 campaign for Proctor and Gamble's Ivory Soap. At his suggestion, Ivory Soap sponsored soap carving contests and displays with the hope that audience members would become more favorably disposed toward the product. Bernays intended that "children, the enemies of soap, would be conditioned to enjoy using Ivory" (Tye 1992, 56). This "National Soap Sculpture" contest gained popularity throughout the nation and across age categories. The concept was a simple one. Soap was a good sculpting alternative; it was generally cheaper than wax or other sculpting materials, and because children were encouraged to wash with any remnants of their work, there was no waste involved in the process. Entrants to the Ivory Soap contest produced soap replicas of the Empire State Building, likenesses of public figures such as Charles Lindbergh, and a variety of other sculptures. Winners received prizes for their efforts. During the first year of the contest, the first-place winner received a soap carving miniature of Macy's first department store. The contest continued for 15 years, and while some scholars dispute the claim that 23 million schoolchildren were sculpting soap in school, there is no question that many American youth became involved in the contests. The soap-carving contest strategy became a case study within the field of public relations for several reasons. First, it embodied the trend toward youth marketing by targeting children as a market of potential life-long consumers of the product. Second, it demonstrated the era's fascination with contests of all kinds. And third, it proposed a new hobby use for a product that had previously been regarded as having one basic purpose.

In another effective public relations campaign, Bernays worked with Lucky Strike cigarettes. The company provided him with a slogan—"Reach for a Lucky instead of a Sweet"—that Bernays parlayed into a successful public relations strategy. The "father of spin" originated the phrase "A moment in the mouth and ten years upon the hips" in service of the idea of substituting smoking for eating sweets. He placed this saying in such magazines as *Life* and the *New Yorker*. He secured statements from famous figures and authorities to support the idea of cigarettes as a healthful alternative to dessert. One such testimonial came from dancer and dance instructor Arthur Murray, who attested that "dancers today, when tempted to overindulge at the punch bowl or the buffet, reach for a cigarette instead" (Tye 1992, 25). Bernays also involved dancers from the Ziegfeld Follies, who signed a pledge to smoke rather than overeat (Tye 1992, 27). The very success of the Bernays ploy had candy and sweet manufacturers in a furor because it endangered their sales to promote the sale of Lucky Strike cigarettes.

In 1929, General Electric and Westinghouse approached Bernays about a promotional event to commemorate the 50th anniversary of Thomas Alva Edison's invention of the incandescent light. This elaborate celebration, dubbed "Light's Golden Jubilee," involved many of Bernays's signature techniques, such as the use of celebrities (Marie Curie and Thomas Edison, among others) and letter-writing campaigns featuring big names (such as President Henry Ford and Herbert Hoover). As the decade closed, Edward Bernays bolstered his reputation as a "PR man" with this corporate-sponsored media event.

Few, if any, can rival Bernays as a prominent figure within public relations during the 1920s. Among the clients who retained Bernays as a public relations consultant were many of the most prominent corporate entities and concerns in the nation: General Electric (GE), General Motors (GM), Columbia Broadcasting System (CBS), National Broadcasting Company (NBC), *Good Housekeeping, Ladies' Home Journal, The New Republic, Time,* F. W. Woolworth, R. H. Macy, and the Great Atlantic and Pacific Tea Co. (A&P). Through his attempts to enhance the public image of his profession, Bernays even conducted public relations on behalf of public relations. His most effective campaign of all, however, might have been his own efforts to be hailed as the nation's greatest publicist.

BIOGRAPHIES

Frederick Lewis Allen, 1890–1954

Journalist, Magazine Editor, Author

Frederick Allen was born in Boston. He received his undergraduate degree from Harvard College in 1912 and a master's degree from the same institution the following year. After a short stint as a teacher, Allen became assistant editor for *Atlantic Monthly* in 1914. Two years later, he assumed the role of managing editor for *The Century*. In 1923, Allen joined the staff at *Harper's,* an affiliation that lasted the rest of his life. In 1941, he became editor-in-chief.

In addition to his role as a journalist, Allen had an abiding interest in American history. This avocation positioned him to write numerous popular book-length works on U.S. history and culture, including *Only Yesterday* (1931), *Since Yesterday* (1940), and *The Big Change* (1952). *Only Yesterday,* subtitled *An Informal History of the 1920s,* represented Allen's portrait of everyday life in America during this pivotal decade. Long before social history became a recognized form of academic inquiry, the work of writers such as Frederick Allen demonstrated how compelling popular histories could be. Allen's accounts of the experiences of ordinary Americans both informed and entertained his readers.

Josephine Baker, 1906–1975

Performer and Actress

Josephine Baker was born Freda Josephine McDonald. She grew up in St. Louis, Missouri, where it became clear early in her life that entertainment was Baker's calling. She began this path as a street performer but later launched a career as a dancer on the vaudeville and Broadway stages. Baker joined the cast of the very successful Sissie and Blake production of the musical "Shuffle Along." After that, she performed at New York's Plantation Club.

It was in France, however, that Baker rose to fame as an entertainer during the 1920s. She appeared at such venues as the Théâtre des Champs-Élysées and the Folies Bergère, earning wide acclaim for her dancing. At the latter theater, she appeared in a skirt fashioned from sixteen bananas, a signature look that subsequent performers would often imitate. Baker also has several film appearances to her credit, including *Siren of the Tropics* (1927), *Zou-Zou* (1934), and *Princess Tam Tam* (1935). Baker became widely known for her dancing, comedic talents, exotic beauty, and risqué costumes. She was also fond of animals, particularly her leopard, Chiquita.

Baker attempted to return to perform in the United States with an ill-fated appearance with the Ziegfeld Follies but could not match her experience of celebrity in France. In America, she contended with forms of racial prejudice not encountered on the Paris stage. Baker devoted the latter portion of her life to causes such as civil rights and cross-race adoption.

Josephine Baker, a young dancer from New York City's Harlem neighborhood, was the star attraction in the 1920s at the Folies Bergère in Paris. (Library of Congress)

Bruce Barton, 1886–1967

Advertiser, Author

Bruce Barton began his relationship to the press as a youth selling newspapers. Upon graduating from Amherst College, Barton worked with newspapers and magazines. He eventually established himself as assistant sales manager in the New York office of *Collier's* magazine, where he was also involved in the advertising department. In time, Barton became a partner in an advertising firm, Batten, Barton, Durstine, and Osborn, whose clients included U.S. Steel, General Electric, and General Motors. Barton devised the fictional character Betty Crocker for the purposes of advertising baking products. Bruce Barton had a successful career, including work as a writer, advertising executive, and congressman. He is best remembered, however, as the author of *The Man Who Nobody Knows* (1925), in which he portrayed Jesus Christ as a highly effective salesman. Barton commingles business and religion in the novel, describing Christ as, among other things, "the most popular dinner guest in Jerusalem!" (Rose 2004, 537). Barton's book remained a bestseller for two years. In 1926, Barton followed up with a second book, this time about the Bible: *The Book Nobody Knows.* Barton became a popularizer of the Gospel of Wealth movement, which regarded wealth as a sign of God's blessing and poverty as a sure sign of the poor person's failings.

Amelia Mary Earhart, 1897–1937

Aviator

As a pioneer of aviation and a female pilot, Amelia Mary Earhart became an American cultural hero. Earhart was born on July 24, 1897, in Kansas. Hers was an affluent family, and she enjoyed many privileges as a consequence. Earhart trained as a nurse's aide and worked in a military hospital until 1918. The next year, she began conducting medical studies. It was in 1920, after she left her pre-med program, that Earhart took her first flight. Following a 10-minute biplane excursion, Earhart vowed to learn to fly for herself. Toward that end, she began lessons with Anita Snook, an aviator. Eventually, Earhart acquired a plane of her own, which she named *The Canary*. She became involved in the field of aviation and established herself as one of the field's female pioneers. Earhart became active in the National Aeronautic Association and invested in an aviation company. In 1927, Earhart was approached about becoming the first woman to make a transatlantic flight. Earhart embraced the challenge and so was nicknamed "Lady Lindy" after the famed aviator Charles Lindbergh. Although she was a passenger rather than a pilot on this particular journey, Earhart found herself at the center of a media frenzy. She gave many lectures and interviews for the benefit of a curious and admiring public. Earhart piloted a solo flight across the Atlantic on May 30, 1932. She also flew the first trans-Pacific flight, departing Hawaii and landing in California, before traveling on to Washington, D.C. In 1935, she began to attempt a record-breaking flight around the world. In 1937, Earhart's plane went down off the coast of Howland Island. The circumstances of the crash were unknown, and although searches of the area were conducted, Earhart's body was never found. The mystery of Amelia Mary Earhart's disappearance resulted in intrigue and a number of unconfirmed sightings of the aviation hero.

Francis Scott Key Fitzgerald, 1896–1940

Author

Possibly the best-known American fiction writer of the 1920s, F. Scott Fitzgerald began his life modestly in St. Paul, Minnesota. Fitzgerald attended Princeton University for several years before enlisting in the army. While stationed in Alabama, he met Zelda Sayre, with whom he began a romance. They would eventually marry and have a daughter, Scottie. A number of Fitzgerald's works of the 1920s have been said to be drawn, at least in part, from his own life experiences with Zelda and Scottie. Between their indulgent lifestyle and the costs of Zelda's care for mental illness, the young family struggled to stay together and make ends meet. Fitzgerald wrote short stories and novels. His prose was spare, but his literary style was still rich with imagery and nuance. The most widely read of the author's works published during the 1920s is *The Great Gatsby* (1925), a story of a mysterious and wealthy individual, a character many believe to be based on the life of bootlegger George Remus. Other Fitzgerald books published during the 1920s include *This Side of Paradise* (1920), *The Beautiful and the Damned* (1922), *Flappers and Philosophers* (1922), *Tales of the Jazz Age* (1923), *The Vegetable* (1923), and *All the Sad Young Men* (1926). In addition, Fitzgerald published short stories in periodicals such as *The Saturday Evening Post, Women's Home Companion,* and *Redbook.* In tales such as "Bernice Bobs Her Hair," Fitzgerald captures the tension between traditional and modern ways experienced by America's youth. Fitzgerald became a memorable chronicler of the 1920s.

John Held Jr., 1889–1958

Illustrator, Graphic Designer, Advertiser

John Held Jr. was a self-taught artist whose career as an illustrator was quite active during the 1920s. He illustrated such books as F. Scott Fitzgerald's *Tales of the Jazz Age.* Held began selling his cartoon-like drawings to magazines such as *Life* in 1904. By the late 1920s, Held's pictures had been published in periodicals including *Look, Harper's Bazaar, Life, Cosmopolitan, Motion Picture Classic, Vanity Fair,* and *The New Yorker.* In fact, his drawings for magazine covers and advertisements were so popular that it is said that Held could name his own price. With his knack for graphic design, Held commanded such advertising accounts as Packard automobiles, Van Heusen shirts, and Planter's peanuts. His images of lanky figures engaged in recreation and occasional misbehavior are so endearingly rendered that they have become iconic depictions of the 1920s in America. Among his best-known works are pictures of flappers, young women who found their pleasure in flouting cultural conventions and social mores. In Held's drawings, they dance, smoke, pet, and climb behind the wheel of roadsters. The men in these images, whether young or old, appear to struggle to keep up with the era's "new woman," whose interests were in fast living and the enjoyment of the moment.

Held also created line drawings that resembled maps of the United States and its cities using landmarks befitting the era's emerging consumer culture. The maps are dotted with gas stations, hot dog stands, and drug stores. Held's whimsical turn of mind and his knack for parody resulted in a body of work that is still immediately recognizable to American viewers; whether or not they know Held's name, they know his pictures.

Langston Hughes, 1902–1967

Writer

Hughes was born James Mercer Langston Hughes, in Joplin, Missouri, on February 1, 1902. As a boy, Hughes became infatuated with books and reading, a

Langston Hughes, African American writer best known for his work during the Harlem Renaissance (1902–1967). (Library of Congress)

portent of his chosen field of writing. He attended Columbia University and Lincoln University. Although Hughes became best known for his poetry, he was also an accomplished playwright, editor, fiction writer, screenwriter, translator, and correspondent. His career spanned the period from the Harlem Renaissance of the 1920s to the Black Arts Movement of the 1960s. Nine of his early poems appeared in Alain Locke's landmark collection of Harlem Renaissance writings, *The New Negro* (1925). His poems spoke forthrightly to the human condition and the realities of racism. Hughes frequently incorporated in his writings aspects of African American folk culture, most notably elements derived from jazz, gospel, and blues music. His poems include "The Negro Speaks of Rivers," "Jazzonia," "The Weary Blues," and "Negro Dancer." Late in his life, Hughes edited numerous books, including *The Book of Negro Humor* (1966) and *The Book of Negro Folklore* (1955), which he coedited with Arna Bontemps. Hughes died on May 22, 1967, in New York City. As one of the most illustrious African American writers, Langston Hughes helped make visible, enduring, and influential the traditions of a historically disenfranchised population.

Charles Augustus Lindbergh, 1902–1974

Aviator

Charles A. Lindbergh was born in Detroit, Michigan, on February 4, 1902, the son of a congressman. He grew up fascinated with technology and air travel. As a young man, Lindbergh attended an army flying school and worked as an airmail pilot. When he wanted to enter a competition for the first nonstop flight between New York City and Paris, Lindbergh secured the sponsorship of a group of St. Louis businessmen. With their help, he acquired a $10,000 Curtis–Wright aircraft with a nine-cylinder engine. In honor of his sponsors, Lindbergh dubbed it *The Spirit of St. Louis*. In his autobiography, *We*, Charles Lindbergh describes the sensational reception awaiting him in Paris. The crowd's din made speech impossible, and he was carried about by the well-wishers until a diversion could free him from their attentions. Returning from Paris triumphant, the aviator was celebrated with 1,800 tons of ticker tape in a New York parade welcoming him back to the United States. After his record-breaking feats as a pilot, Lindbergh traveled widely to discuss aviation and promote air travel. He remained a celebrity for the rest of his life. In tribute, for example, a popular dance, the "Lindy Hop," was named after him. Lindbergh drew additional praise for his restraint in fielding requests for commercial endorsements and testimonial ads.

Alain Le Roy Locke, 1886–1954

Philosopher, Writer, Editor, Critic, and Educator

As a philosopher, writer, editor, critic, and educator, Alain Le Roy Locke opened new pathways for African Americans as he celebrated their cultural traditions. Locke was born September 13, 1886, in Philadelphia, Pennsylvania. He graduated from Harvard University in 1917. He became the first African American to receive the Rhodes Scholarship, with which he studied literature at Oxford University. Upon his return, Locke earned a Ph.D. in philosophy from Harvard University. Locke became known for his concept of the "New Negro," a term for African Americans who embraced their racial and cultural identities and used that legacy to fuel their strivings for personal and collective advancement. In 1925, Locke edited, contributed to, and published a pivotal book, *The New Negro,* that collected writings by a variety of African American authors of the day, such as Langston Hughes, Countee Cullen, Jean Toomer, and Claude McKay. With this and other efforts he became a proponent of a "talented tenth" theory, which relied upon the most gifted African Americans to lead the way to racial uplift and understanding. Locke did his part by becoming a professor of philosophy at Howard University in Washington, D.C., where he served from 1918 until 1953. Locke died in 1954 in New York City. As a civil rights leader and tastemaker, Alain Locke made visible a host of African American writers and artists, particularly those of the Harlem Renaissance.

Jelly Roll Morton, 1890–1941

Entertainer, Jazz Musician

Born Ferdinand Joseph Lamothe, this New Orleans entertainer went on to an illustrious career as a jazz musician. "Morton" was an Anglicized version of his stepfather's name, Mouton. Morton came to the public's attention as a pianist in New Orleans's famous Storyville District where he was influenced by both blues and Creole musical traditions. Over the course of his lifetime, Morton performed both as a piano soloist and with numerous jazz bands, most notably the Red Hot Peppers. He made his first commercial recording in 1923 and in 1926 began a contract with Victor Records. Morton's original compositions included the "Black Bottom Stomp," "Kansas City Stomp," "Mister Jelly Lord," and "The

Original Jelly-Roll Blues." Late in life, Jelly Roll Morton became the subject of oral histories conducted by Library of Congress folklorist Alan Lomax. For his own musical contributions and for his impact on later musical forms, such as rhythm and blues and rock and roll, Morton was inducted into the Rock and Roll Hall of Fame.

Arthur Murray, 1895–1991

Dance Instructor and Entrepreneur

Born to poor Austrian immigrants in New York City, Moses Teichman (later known as Arthur Murray) was shy and awkward until he learned to dance at age 14. He honed these skills in dance halls and dance contests until he became a dance instructor. Arthur Murray would study business at Georgia Tech, but he applied his business skills chiefly to the dance world. Murray met his wife in 1925 when she was an audience member at a radio broadcast of his dance lessons. In time, he developed an entrepreneurial model for teaching dance via the mail. Through the use of dance-step diagrams, Murray demonstrated to more than half a million mail-order clients the step sequences for popular dances. Subsequently, he established a franchise of dance instructors trained to deliver Murray's dance lessons. In the late 1930s, he went on to open a chain of dance studios where face-to-face dance instruction could be conducted personally. Murray's methods made him a popular figure in the dance world, and his famous customers included Eleanor Roosevelt and Jack Dempsey.

Emily Price Post, 1872–1960

Author, Syndicated Columnist, Etiquette Expert

Born to affluence, Emily Post first learned etiquette by practicing it with her family and by attending Miss Graham's finishing school. Early in her career, Post wrote works of fiction. These titles include *Flight of the Moth* (1904), *Purple and Fine Linen* (1906), *Woven in the Tapestry* (1908), *The Title Market* (1909), and *The Eagle's Feather* (1910). Post wrote syndicated columns on etiquette for newspapers and advice features for magazines such as *Harper's, Scribner's,* and *Good Housekeeping.* In addition, Post appeared on numerous radio broadcasts, especially during the 1930s. In 1946, she founded the Emily Post Institute for the Study of Gracious Living, the center that would be her legacy. Post is best known for her books on the subject of manners and proper conduct. For example, her 1922 work *Etiquette in Business, in Politics, and at Home,* sold millions of copies and went through dozens of printings. She endeavored to provide her audience with a clearer sense of taste and decorum. Her areas of special interest include travel, architecture, and interior design as expressions of gracious living. Emily Post remains one of the nation's best-known experts on etiquette in everyday life.

Norman Rockwell, 1894–1978

Artist and Illustrator

As one of the nation's best-known artists/illustrators, Norman Rockwell created images that have taken on iconic importance within the American imagination. He achieved this status by providing cover pictures for many mass-market magazines in the United States, including *St. Nicholas Magazine, Life, Look, Literary Digest, Leslie's, People's Popular Life,* and *Boys' Life.* His name is especially closely associated with the *The Saturday Evening Post,* a periodical which made frequent use of Rockwell's services as an illustrator and featured more than 300 of his illustrations in its cover over four decades. Known for nostalgic images of the American past, Rockwell captured recognizable experiences in family history and memorable moments in the nation's history. During the 1940s, Rockwell completed a series of four images inspired by Franklin Delano Roosevelt's reference to four principles for universal rights—Freedom from Want, Freedom of Speech, Freedom to Worship, and Freedom from Fear. Other later illustrations, such as "The Problem We All Live With," supported civil rights by illustrating young Ruby Bridges, a child involved in the school integration controversy, accompanied by federal marshals as she enters her new school. In addition, the White House commissioned Norman Rockwell to create portraits of numerous American presidents, from Eisenhower to Nixon. For his tender depictions of American life, Rockwell received the Presidential Medal of Freedom in 1977.

Will Rogers, 1879–1935

Satirist and Entertainer

Will Rogers was born in Oklahoma to parents who were both part Cherokee. Having learned how to use a lasso while growing up on a cattle ranch, Rogers began his career doing trick roping demonstrations in "Wild West" shows. His skills and rapport with the audience led to the vaudeville circuit and Broadway, where he appeared in such shows as Ziegfeld's Follies. There were also film appearances in *The Ropin' Fool* (1921) and *The Cowboy Sheik* (1924). Rogers developed his comedic abilities, which endeared him to audiences and led to Rogers's signature satire often involving political and topical commentary. He wrote syndicated weekly columns and daily short items ("Will Rogers Says") from the 1920s and 1930s. Rogers also appeared as a guest, and later a star, on radio shows. Rogers eventually received two stars on the Hollywood Walk of Fame, one for film and one for radio. Known widely as the "Cowboy Philosopher," Will Rogers offered quips that are still quoted, such as his famous line,

Will Rogers was a widely loved American folk hero simply because he was always his "natchell self." He had a flair for commenting on current events in a way that was both funny and critical, usually while performing some of his many cowboy tricks. (Library of Congress)

"I never met a man I didn't like." Rogers had an unassuming persona that permitted him to speak the truth about the phenomena he witnessed without seeming arrogant. "All I know," Rogers would explain, "is what I read in the papers." For that candor and homespun charm, the American public embraced him.

Bessie Smith, 1894–1937

Performer, Blues Musician

Orphaned at age nine, Bessie Smith became a street performer to help support herself and the other children left behind. As she matured, Smith embarked on a career as an entertainer. Among other engagements, she sang and danced in a show with Ma Rainey. As a female African American performer, Smith had to contend with both racism and sexism in order to launch a musical career. She signed with Columbia Records in 1923 and became a blues headliner on the theater circuit. Her hits included "Down Hearted Blues." She later appeared on film. Smith's last recordings before dying from complications of injuries she sustained in an automobile accident were on the Okeh label.

REFERENCES AND FURTHER READINGS

ABC-CLIO. 2001. *The 1920s: Teacher's Guide; A Supplemental Teaching Unit from the Records of the National Archives.* Santa Barbara, CA: ABC-CLIO.

Allen, Frederick Lewis. 1931. *Only Yesterday.* New York: Bantam.

Archer, Gleason L. 1971. *History of Radio to 1926.* New York: Arno.

Balk, Alfred. 2006. *The Rise of Radio: From Marconi through the Golden Age.* Jefferson, NC: McFarland and Co., Inc.

Banks, Ann, ed. 1980. *First Person America.* New York: Random House.

Barnouw, Erik. 1966. *A History of Broadcasting in the United States.* New York: Oxford University Press.

Bent, Silas. 1927. *Ballyhoo: The Voice of the Press*. New York: Boni and Liveright.

Benton, Megan. 1997. "'Too Many Books': Book Ownership and Cultural Identity in the 1920s." *American Quarterly* 49 (2): 268–297.

Bessie, Simon Michael. 1938. *Jazz Journalism: The Story of Tabloid Newspapers*. New York: Dutton.

Best, Gary Dean. 2003. *The Dollar Decade: Mammon and the Machine in 1920s America*. Westport, CT: Greenwood Press/Praeger Publishers.

Botshon, Lisa, and Meredith Goldsmith. 2003. *Middlebrow Moderns: Popular American Women Writers of the 1920s*. Boston: Northeastern University Press.

Bowen, Ezra, and the editors of Time-Life Books. 1969. *This Fabulous Century: 1920–1930*. New York: Time.

Braeman, John, Robert H. Bremner, and David Brody, eds. 1968. *Change and Continuity in Twentieth Century America: The 1920's*. Columbus: Ohio State University Press.

Brandt, Allan M. 2007. *The Cigarette Century: The Rise, Fall, and Deadly Persistence of the Product That Defined America*. New York: Basic Books.

Brass-Nickel Touring Region AACA. "Potpourri: Slang of the 1920s." http://local.aaca.org/bntc/slang/slang.htm (accessed September 10, 2006).

Calabria, Frank M. 1976. "The Dance Marathon Craze." *Journal of Popular Culture* 10 (Summer): 54–69.

Carter, Paul A. 1977. *Another Part of the Twenties*. New York: Columbia University Press.

Cayton, Mary Kupiec, Elliott J. Gorn, and Peter W. Williams, eds. 1993. *Encyclopedia of American Social History*. New York: Scribner.

Clarke, Donald. 1995. *The Rise and Fall of Popular Music*. New York: St. Martin's Press.

Colin, Gordon, ed. 1999. *Major Problems in American History, 1920–1945*. New York: Houghton Mifflin.

Covert, Catherine, and John D. Stevens, eds. 1984. *Mass Media between the Wars: Perceptions of Cultural Tension, 1918–1941*. Syracuse, NY: Syracuse University Press.

Cutlip, Scott. 1994. *The Unseen Power, Public Relations: A History*. Hillsdale, NJ: Erlbaum Associates.

Douglas, George H. 1987. *The Early Days of Radio Broadcasting*. Jefferson, NC: McFarland.

Douglas, Susan J. 2004. *Listening In: Radio and the American Imagination*. Minneapolis: University of Minnesota Press.

Drowne, Kathleen, and Patrick Huber. 2004. *The 1920's*. Westport, CT: Greenwood Press.

Dumenil, Lynn. 1995. *The Modern Temper: America in the 1920s*. New York: Hill and Wang.

Duncombe, Stephen, and Andrew Mattson. 2006. *The Bobbed Hair Bandit: A True Story of Crime and Celebrity in 1920s New York*. New York: New York University Press, 2006.

Dunning, John. 1998. *On the Air: The Encyclopedia of Old-Time Radio*. New York: Oxford University Press.

Earthlink. "Internet Guide to Jazz Age Slang." http://home.earthlink.net/~dlarkins/slang-pg.htm (accessed September 10, 2006).

Ely, Melvin. 1991. *The Adventures of Amos 'n' Andy: A Social History of an American Phenomenon*. New York: Free Press.

Ewen, Stuart. 1996. *PR! A Social History of Spin*. New York: Basic Books.

Ewen, Stuart, and Elizabeth Ewen. 1992. *Channels of Desire: Mass Images and the Shaping of American Consciousness*. Minneapolis: University of Minnesota Press.

Faulkner, Anne Shaw. 1921. "Does Jazz Put the Sin in Syncopation?" *Ladies' Home Journal,* August, 16–34.

Fielding, Raymond. 1972. *The American Newsreel, 1911–1967*. Norman: University of Oklahoma Press.

Fox, Stephen. 1984. *The Mirror Makers: A History of American Advertising and Its Creators*. New York: Vintage.

Friedman, Walter A. 2004. *Birth of a Salesman: The Transformation of Selling in America*. Cambridge, MA: Harvard University Press.

Fuhrman, Candace Jacobson. 1989. *Publicity Stunt! Great Staged Events That Made the News*. San Francisco: Chronicle Books.

Furnas, J. C. 1974. *Great Times: An Informal Social History of the United States, 1914–1929*. New York: Putnam.

Gabler, Neil. 1994. *Winchell: Gossip, Power and the Culture of Celebrity*. New York: Knopf.

Giordano, Ralph. 2003. *Fun and Games in Twentieth Century America: A Historical Guide to Leisure*. Westport, CT: Greenwood Press.

Gordon, Ian. 1998. *Comic Strips and Consumer Culture, 1890–1945*. Washington, DC: Smithsonian Institution Press.

Grant, Robert, and Joseph Katz. 1998. *The Great Trials of the Twenties: The Watershed Decade in America's Courtrooms*. Rockville Centre, NY: Sarpedon.

Green, Harvey. 1992. *The Uncertainty of Everyday Life, 1915–1945*. New York: HarperCollins, 1992.

Gregory, Ross. 1995. *Modern America, 1914 to 1945*. New York: Facts on File.

Grubin, David, dir. 1988. "The Reel World of News" (videorecording). Washington, DC: PBS Video.

Hardt, Hanno. *In the Company of Media: Cultural Constructions of Communication, 1920s–1930s*. Boulder, CO: Westview Press, 2000.

Heimann, Jim, ed. 2004. *20s: All-American Ads*. Los Angeles: Taschen.

Hilmes, Michele. 1997. *Radio Voices: American Broadcasting, 1922–1952*. Minneapolis: University of Minnesota Press.

Hoy, Suellen. 1995. *Chasing Dirt: The American Pursuit of Cleanliness*. New York: Oxford University Press.

Jazz Babies. "Texas Guinan's Culture Club." www.jazzbabies.com/flash/index .html (accessed September 10, 2006).

Kenney, William Howland. 1999. *Recorded Music in American Life: The Phonograph and Popular Memory, 1890–1945*. New York: Oxford University Press.

Kluger, Richard. 1996. *Ashes to Ashes: America's Hundred-Year Cigarette War, the Public Health, and the Unabashed Triumph of Philip Morris*. New York: Alfred A. Knopf.

Kurian, George Thomas. 2001. *Datapedia of the United States, 1790–2005: America Year by Year*. Lanham, MD: Bernan Press.

Kyvig, Danid E. 2004. *Daily Life in the United States, 1920–1940*. Chicago: Ivan R. Dee.

Lears, Jackson. 1994. *Fables of Abundance: A Cultural History of Advertising in America*. New York: Basic Books.

Lehman, Harvey C., and Paul Witty. 1927. "The Compensatory Function of the Sunday Funny Paper." *Journal of Applied Psychology* 11 (June): 202–211.

Leinwand, Gerald. 2001. *1927: High Tide of the Twenties*. New York: Four Walls Eight Windows.

Leuchtenburg, William E. 1993. *The Perils of Prosperity 1914–1932*. 2nd ed. Chicago: University of Chicago Press.

Levine, Lawrence. 1988. *Highbrow/Lowbrow: The Emergence of Cultural Hierarchy in America*. Cambridge, MA: Harvard University Press.

Levine, Lawrence. 1993. *The Unpredictable Past: Explorations in American Cultural History*. New York: Oxford University Press.

Lewis, Thomas S. W. 1991. *Empire of the Air: The Men Who Made Radio*. New York: HarperColllins.

Lindop, Edmund. 2007. *America in the 1920s*. Minneapolis: Twenty-First Century Books.

MacDonald, J. Fred. 1979. *Don't Touch That Dial! Radio Programming in American Life, 1920–1960*. Chicago: Nelson-Hall.

Marchand, Roland. 1985. *Advertising the American Dream: Making Way for Modernity, 1920–1940*. Berkeley: University of California Press.

Martin, Carol. 1994. *Dance Marathons: Performing American Culture in the 1920s and 1930s*. Jackson: University of Mississippi Press.

McCoy, Donald. 1973. *Coming of Age: The United States during the 1920's and 1930's*. Baltimore: Penguin Books.

McCutcheon, Marc. 1995. *The Writer's Guide to Everyday Life from Prohibition Through World War II*. Cincinnati: Writer's Digest Books.

Miller, Nathan. 2003. *New World Coming: The 1920s and the Making of Modern America*. New York: Scribner.

Mordden, Ethan. 1978. *That Jazz! An Idiosyncratic Social History of the American Twenties*. New York: Putnam.

Mowry, George. 1963. *The Twenties: Fords, Flappers, and Fanatics*. Englewood Cliffs, NJ: Prentice-Hall.

Ogren, Kathy J. 1989. *The Jazz Revolution: Twenties America and the Meaning of Jazz*. New York: Oxford University Press.

Peiss, Kathy. 1998. *Hope in a Jar: the Making of American Beauty Culture*. New York: Metropolitan Books.

Perrett, Geoffrey. 1982. *America in the Twenties: A History*. New York: Simon and Shuster.

Pietrusza, David. 1998. *Roaring Twenties*. Detroit: Gale Group.

Pittsburgh State University. "Jazz Age Culture." http://faculty.pittstate.edu/~knichols/jazzage.html (accessed September 10, 2006).

Plesur, Milton, ed. 1969. *The 1920s: Problems and Paradoxes*. Boston: Allyn and Bacon.

Post, Emily. 1922. *Etiquette in Society, in Business, in Politics, and at Home*. New York: Funk and Wagnalls.

President's Research Committee on Social Trends. 1933. *Recent Social Trends in the United States*, Volumes I and II. New York: McGraw-Hill.

Radway, Janice. 1997. *A Feeling for Books: The Book-of-the-Month Club, Literary Taste, and Middle-Class Desire*. Chapel Hill: University of North Carolina Press.

Robinson, Frank M. 1998. *Pulp Fiction: The Art of Fiction Magazines*. Portland, OR: Collectors Press.

Rose, Cynthia, ed. 2004. *American Decades: Primary Sources, 1920–1929*. New York: Gale.

Segrave, Kerry. 2005a. *Endorsements in Advertising: A Social History*. Jefferson, NC: McFarland and Co.

Segrave, Kerry. 2005b. *Women and Smoking in America, 1880–1950*. Jefferson, NC: McFarland and Co.

Smith, Page. 1986. *Redeeming the Time: A People's History of the 1920s and the New Deal*. New York: McGraw-Hill.

Smulyan, Susan. 1993. "Radio." In *Encyclopedia of American Social History,* edited by Mary Cupiec Cayton, Elliot J. Gorn, and Peter W. Williams, 1847–1858. New York: Scribner.

Smulyan, Susan. 1994. *Selling Radio: The Commercialization of American Broadcasting, 1920–1934*. Washington, DC: Smithsonian Institution Press.

Solomon, Barbara H., ed. 1980. *Ain't We Got Fun? Essays, Lyrics, and Stories of the Twenties*. New York: New American Library.

Stearns, Peter, and Jan Lewis, eds. 1998. *An Emotional History of the United States*. New York: New York University Press.

Stevenson, Elizabeth. 1998. *Babbitts and Bohemians: From the Great War to the Great Depression*. New Brunswick, NJ: Transaction Publishers.

Streissguth, Thomas. 2001. *The Roaring Twenties: An Eyewitness History*. New York: Facts on File.

Time-Life Books. 1998. *The Jazz Age: The 20s*. Alexandria, VA: Time-Life.

Tye, Larry. 1992. *The Father of Spin: Edward L. Bernays and the Birth of Public Relations*. New York: Crown.

Vinikas, Vincent. 1982. *Soft Soap, Hard Sell: American Hygiene in an Age of Advertisement*. Ames: Iowa State University Press.

Wallace, Aurora. 2005. *Newspapers and the Making of Modern America: A History*. Westport, CT: Greenwood Press.

Watson, Elwood, and Darcy Martin, eds. 2004. *"There She Is, Miss America": The Politics of Sex, Beauty, and Race in America's Most Famous Pageant*. New York: Palgrave Macmillan.

Wattenberg, Ben J. 1976. *Statistical History of the United States: From Colonial Times to the Present*. New York: Basic Books.

Weinstein, Irving. 1970. *Shattered Decade, 1919–1929*. New York: Charles Scribner's Sons.

Wilson, Edmund, 1975. *The Twenties: From Notebooks and Diaries of the Period,* ed. Leon Edel. New York: Farrar, Straus and Giroux.

Wolman, Leo. 1929 *Recent Economic Changes in the United States,* Volume 1. New York: McGraw-Hill.

Yancey, Diane. 2002. *Life during the Roaring Twenties*. Detroit: Gale Group.

American or Un-American?

OVERVIEW

Many events in American history have centered on a single issue—what is American and what is not. The 1920s served as a testing ground for many ideas about Americanism. Cultural leaders from the left and the right sought during these years to identify both American and un-American ideas, people, and lifestyles. For instance, is a Scottish Presbyterian more American than a Russian Jew? Is it more American to conform to the majority's lifestyle or to honor one's own roots? Is it more American to have purely Nordic ancestors or to spring from a gene pool that represents the diversity of the nation? What qualities are typical for an American? This chapter will examine those questions and their impact on the 1920s.

Perhaps more than any other issue in the 1920s, immigration policy became a reflection of white native-born Americans' doubts and fears. Citizens of the United States sometimes had voiced pride in the nation's status as a land of immigrants, but the rising tide of new settlers between 1890 and 1920 threatened to eliminate the dominance of native-born whites. For many people born in the United States, that was an unacceptable prospect. They feared the chaos of clashing cultures and the loss of power that might accompany it. In sheer numbers, the new wave of immigration was breathtaking. The latest throng of immigrants, mostly from Eastern or Southern Europe, contributed almost 20 million people to the United States between 1880 and 1930 (*Historical Statistics of the United States*). Newcomers represented between 13 and 15 percent of the total population during the years between 1860 and 1920 (Gibson and Lennon 1999). Fears of revolution crept into American thought because many of the latest immigrants came from nations associated with radical political philosophies. Add to that religious anxiety: many immigrants were Catholics or Jews—not Protestants. And often because of their large numbers and their tight-knit ethnic cultures, these new arrivals seemed disinclined to relinquish their distinctive lifestyles and embrace Americanization. As a result, many Americans and their representatives in Congress agreed: the flood should be reduced to a trickle, and preference should be given to the earlier immigrant groups whose ancestors had shown a willingness to let their own cultural heritages melt away so that they could become "American."

As the industrial economy of the 1920s thrived, many cities struggled to absorb new populations; in most cases, this process generated a drive to "Americanize" the new immigrants. Los Angeles provides an interesting example of how the process worked and of how it failed. As the city doubled its population in the 1920s and joined the list of leading American metropolises, members of the white majority saw their city transformed by nearby oil discoveries, expanded manufacturing, Hollywood's new and profitable motion-picture industry, and an influx of working-class people, who included Mexicans, African Americans, and Japanese.

In the face of so much change, the "natives," who were overwhelmingly white Anglo-Saxon Protestants, began to fortify their position by attempting to control minority groups through the process of Americanization. Mexicans attracted the most attention. Because they were willing to perform hard labor cheaply, the business community welcomed them, but there was a catch: Almost without exception, Mexicans made less money than whites, and yet Americanization efforts pushed them to emulate the middle class, people whose lifestyle lay beyond the reach of Mexican laborers. Some well-intentioned reform efforts produced improvements in the lives of Mexican immigrants. Other groups showed more interest in identifying and marginalizing potentially subversive specters casting shadows on the prosperous landscape of their boomtown.

Eugenicists worked throughout the nation to promote the importance of genetic knowledge and careful planning to protect Americans who were creatures of the "best" gene pool. These activists believed that heredity—not environment—was the most important factor in determining a person's abilities. And they contended that science had proven the superiority of one race—white people of Northern and Western European ancestry. These crusaders considered it vital to encourage reproduction among the "superior" race and to discourage procreation among "inferior" human beings. In most states, the first step was the institutionalization and segregation of people designated as feeble-minded or mentally ill. Some states later chose to sterilize many of these inmates. Not surprisingly, whites often judged minorities to have more mental defects than Caucasians, and as a result, minority groups tended to have high representation among those who were institutionalized. Eugenicists also supported restrictions on immigration to hamper growth within the "inferior" population.

The social sciences experienced significant growth during this era when Americans struggled to define themselves. The new social scientists focused increasing attention on what characterized average Americans as individuals and on how diverse groups interacted. In the process, they examined many of the toughest issues of the 1920s, including changes in American work life and interplay between ethnic groups. Sociology and anthropology, with a sprinkling of Freud's ideas about psychoanalysis, opened the eyes of interested Americans. In the process, social scientists revealed many truths about Americans and their culture. As they attempted to leave behind old fixations about racial superiority, these new professionals redirected their analysis to determine what forces shaped Americans both culturally and socially.

There has always been a certain tension between defining American identity and honoring the nation's emphasis on individuality and diversity. Over the years, this ongoing tug of war has itself become a facet of American identity. By the end of the 1920s, many Americans defined what it meant to be American by simply looking in the mirror. Old-stock Americans were wary of those who did not look or act like them. Frightened members of the American majority tried to quash ethnic differences. In the process, already-rigid ideas about ethnic groups hardened. Anxious native-born whites divided and subdivided the nation's inhabitants into small groups of acceptable and unacceptable human beings. And yet, all were expected to embrace the same culture.

Anything else would have seemed un-American.

TIMELINE

1920	In May, Mississippi becomes the last state in the Deep South to authorize eugenically segregated public institutions for the "mentally unfit."
	The Better America Foundation, which promotes "Americanization" of immigrants, is incorporated in Los Angeles.
	Henry Ford begins his anti-Semitic campaign in the *Dearborn Independent*. He devotes 91 consecutive issues to the topic and requires Ford dealers to buy the newspaper.
1921	Republican president Warren G. Harding signs an emergency bill establishing quotas for immigration in May.
1922	The United States Supreme Court rejects the arguments made by attorneys for Takao Ozawa, who sought U.S. citizenship despite his Japanese heritage.

1924   One-time eugenicist Herbert Spencer Jennings addresses a U.S. House committee in June. His testimony contradicts data that showed immigrants from northern and western Europe were superior to other Europeans.

Virginia lawmakers approve the Racial Integrity Act, which forbids mixed marriages and seeks means to monitor births and ascertain when a child of mixed parentage is born.

After years of debate on the subject of increasing immigration restrictions, the Congress approves the National Origins Act, which calls for quotas based on a nationality's population in the United States in 1890.

1925   A subcommittee of the American Eugenics Society recommends in July that immigrants be asked to prove they come from "sound family stock."

1926   The American Eugenics Society conducts a contest for the best sermon promoting eugenics; a Minneapolis minister wins in July.

1927   Six of the nation's leading eugenicists send a "Memorial on Immigration Quotas: To the President, the Senate, and the House of Representatives." In it they express the urgent need to limit immigration from Latin America.

The United States Supreme Court supports a Virginia law calling for involuntary sterilization of people with "mental defects."

In July, Henry Ford retracts all attacks on Jews in the *Dearborn Independent*.

1929   Robert and Helen Lynd's sociological study of Muncie, Indiana —*Middletown: A Study in Contemporary American Culture*—is published.

Republican president Herbert Hoover approves new quotas for enforcement of the National Origins Act.

IMMIGRATION

No Welcome Mat at the Door

The enormous wave of immigration in the years leading up to 1920 overwhelmed many white native-born Americans. There were single years in which more than a million immigrants came to the United States on a quest for jobs,

Immigrants undergo physical examinations at Ellis Island, New York, in 1923.
(National Archives)

freedom, and stability. Many of the new arrivals could not speak English, and as they squeezed into America's already-crowded urban areas, they profoundly altered neighborhoods and communities through transplantation of their native cultures.

To many Americans, these immigrants seemed more foreign than their predecessors. Most immigrants in previous years had arrived from Northern and Western Europe, Canada, and China, but during this period, a large portion of the immigrants came from Eastern and Southern Europe. Immigration from Eastern Europe, the Baltic states, and what would later be the European part of the Soviet Union climbed from almost 36,000 in 1890 to a high of about 295,000 in 1907, when these immigrants made up almost one-third of all immigrants. The annual arrival of immigrants from Southern Europe similarly had risen from about 56,000 in 1890 to more than 338,000 in 1914, when they represented more than one-fourth of all arrivals (*Historical Statistics of the United States*). Japanese immigration figures never soared to such heights. Only about 111,000 settled in the United States, mostly on the West Coast (Dumenil 1995, 263). Despite their small numbers, they generated even heavier opposition because they were not white.

And while the majority of the American population was Protestant, many of these immigrants were not. Both Catholics and Jews arrived in significant numbers. The consequent negative response of many Americans was not unprecedented. When Irish Catholics had poured into the United States in the middle of the 19th century, they had accepted low wages, and therefore, they had become a threat to the white working class. In the wake of that immigration, many Americans had embraced the nativist belief that the interests of native-born Americans should outweigh the needs of new arrivals; added to that belief was blatant religious prejudice in many cases. In the early part of the 20th century, nativism found new life. To anxious Americans, many of the new immigrants surging into the United States like a human flood seemed content to wash away American culture and replace it with their own. The possibility that American identity might be lost in the onslaught of foreign languages, customs, and ideas worried many native-born Americans.

The first effort to tighten immigration regulations was a 1917 bill requiring immigrants to prove literacy in at least one language. Swept by postwar nativist fervor and a more cool-headed conservatism, Congress overrode a veto by President Woodrow Wilson. Then, in 1921 and 1924, presidents Warren G. Harding and Calvin Coolidge signed more far-reaching legislation that dramatically cut immigration and established quotas favoring the immigrant groups that reached the United States before 1890. In these turbulent years, the United States was undergoing dramatic industrial and cultural change, and as uneasiness mounted, many native-born Americans turned their attention to the "outsiders" among them. Not all restrictionists could be defined as nativists; some were merely cautious conservatives. Nevertheless, for many, the drive to limit immigration was nothing less than an impassioned cause.

Flood of Immigration Heightens Anxiety

In 1920, wary Americans feared that immigrants might change the American way of life. The "melting pot" metaphor was quickly losing whatever validity it ever had. The white population's unwillingness to let the African American population melt into the larger whole had diminished the concept. And many new immigrants seemed too strange to dissolve into the dominant culture. Their histories—flight from persecution, revolutions, and poor living conditions—were unimportant to many native-born whites, who looked at the hordes of immigrants and saw invaders. As the new decade began, the most recent immigrants made their homes in the urban areas of America, and in some cities, immigrants represented as much as 40 to 50 percent of the population (Goldberg 1999, 141). Many newcomers settled wherever they entered the United States—Boston, Philadelphia, or New York. Others traveled a short distance to smaller cities such as Providence, Newark, and Camden. Some traveled greater distances within the United States to join large populations of their countrymen in cities like Detroit, Cleveland, and Pittsburgh.

When members of one nationality settled in significant numbers within a specific neighborhood or community, they found that they could preserve their native culture and language. Italians nestled in South Philadelphia; Jews dominated New York's East Side. Some lived in places where being able to speak English was not a necessary survival skill. And for immigrants who expected to return to their homelands, adapting to American culture seemed unnecessary. With their diverse languages, foods, religions, and customs, the new arrivals seemed exotic—and frightening—to many Americans. Dramatic changes in the population ignited new fears and rekindled old prejudices. For example, some Americans, including industrial hero Henry Ford, responded to the influx of eastern European Jews with heightened anti-Semitism. Jews were not new to America; they had been in the first European colonies planted on American shores. And there had been a significant migration of "German" Jews from Central Europe in the mid-19th century. However, many of those early immigrants had embraced the flexible precepts of Reform Judaism, which made assimilation easier. Most of the latest immigrants, who greatly outnumbered native-born Jews, were Orthodox Jews, whose dress and lifestyle set them apart. They lived in densely populated tenement houses within Jewish ghettos; the men wore long beards and yarmulkes; they ate only kosher food; and they often spoke Yiddish. These Jews brought with them the culture of tightly knit communities in Europe, and wandering into their neighborhood was like stepping onto the streets of Warsaw or Budapest.

Many citizens of the United States resented any immigrants who transformed pieces of America rather than transforming themselves to fit into the jigsaw puzzle of American culture. Italian Catholics raised many of the same concerns as Eastern European Jews. They did not disappear into the greater population; instead, they established their own little nation within the larger nation. Like Jews, Italians faced discrimination. They often were the targets of anti-Catholic literature, and some employers refused to hire them.

Adding to general anxieties about differences between the new immigrants and Americans was the relatively new scientific focus on eugenics. Charles B. Davenport, a nationally known eugenicist, was the first to suggest that Ellis Island immigrants should undergo Alfred Binet's intelligence tests. This experiment, which began in 1912, showed lower intelligence among the new immigrants, but other experts disputed the findings, pointing out that some questions reflected a cultural bias. Nevertheless, many Americans believed that this new immigrant population might dilute American strength and intelligence. Those views were supported by academics in eugenics and other fields. In his book *Races and Immigrants in America,* political economist John R. Commons argued that "peasants" and "Catholic Europe" had become "almost a distinct race, drained of those superior qualities which are the foundation of a democratic republic" (quoted in Goldberg 1999, 144).

The Red Scare of 1919 and 1920 also exacerbated concerns about the possibility that radicals might come from abroad with Communist, Socialist, or Anarchist agendas to contaminate American democracy. Many Eastern European

**Table 5.1. Occupation of Immigrants Arriving
to the United States in 1920**

Occupation	
Professional/technical	10,540
Farmers/farm managers	12,192
Managers/officials/proprietors	9,654
Clerical/sales	14,054
Craftsmen/foremen	55,991
Household workers	37,197
Service workers	18,487
Farm workers/foremen	15,257
Other laborers	83,496
No occupation	173,133
TOTAL	430,001

Source: U.S. Census Bureau.

nations were known for their radicalism, and Jews often were identified with radical causes. In the wake of such massive immigration from what were considered "tainted" lands, native-born Americans, both white and black, believed that they had to be diligent to preserve parts of American life that they held dear. All of these forces—emotional unease, religious prejudice, economic competition,

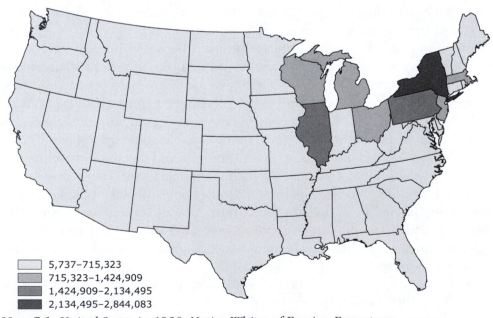

5,737–715,323
715,323–1,424,909
1,424,909–2,134,495
2,134,495–2,844,083

Map 5.1 *United States in 1920: Native Whites of Foreign Parentage*

and politicized fear—contributed to an atmosphere in which restrictions on immigration seemed not only logical but also essential to many Americans.

Emergency Immigration Act of 1921

Often driven by passion as much as politics, the crusade to limit immigration generated new zeal as the new decade began. Opponents of immigration feared that poverty-stricken Europeans would land on America's doorstep as soon as recovery from the war began. In 1919, they were surprised when the number of immigrants returning to their homelands exceeded the number seeking admission to the United States. This unexpected event resulted from a simple postwar reality: most ships traveling from Europe to the United States that year were filled with U.S. troops returning home from the war. However, in 1920, immigration picked up steam again, with more than 50,000 arriving in each month from June to December (Goldberg 1999, 151). Among them were many Jews trying to escape pogroms in Poland and armed conflict in the Ukraine.

A longtime leader of restrictionists was Senator Henry Cabot Lodge, a Republican from Massachusetts who also was the majority leader of the Senate. The aristocratic Lodge had begun expressing concerns about rising immigration almost as soon as he entered the Senate in 1893. With his support, laws requiring literacy tests had been passed three times. Each time, a different president had vetoed the legislation, but Congress enacted the third bill by overriding Wilson's veto. In 1920, Lodge's long struggle to cut immigration was ready to bear fruit. Albert Johnson, a Republican lawmaker from Washington, took command of the drive toward restrictionism in the House. Unlike Lodge, who was careful not to offend Irish immigrants in his constituency, Johnson demonstrated open distaste toward immigrants. Antagonism toward the Japanese in his home state added fire to his determination, and eugenicists were among his friends.

Immigration opponents saw an opportunity in the recession of 1920–1921: Americans, who were fearful about keeping their jobs and their incomes, easily could see immigrants as potential threats to their livelihoods. The literacy test, which required immigrants to read 40 words in any language, had not lived up to expectations. Immigration opponents once had believed that 30–40 percent of Slavs and half of Italians were illiterate, even in their native tongues; however, they had been wrong. Restrictionists made an appeal for swift action because of the expected inundation of the United States by European immigrants. The House wanted to ban all immigration, but Congress passed a bill that cut immigration to "3 percent of the number of foreign-born of each nationality," according to the 1910 census. Rejecting an exemption for religious and political refugees, lawmakers also put a cap of 357,803 on the total number of immigrants who could be admitted per year. Congress later extended the law's term from one year to three. The quota system reduced the number of immigration slots available to Southern and Eastern Europeans, and at the same time, it allocated more than half of the available openings to the earlier immigrant groups.

The National Origins Act of 1924

The emergency legislation decelerated the flow of immigrants into the United States; however, some of the legislation's details created logistical problems. For instance, the law said that no nation could exceed 20 percent of its quota in a single month, so ships began contending with one another to be the first to reach Ellis Island's immigration processing center early on the first day of each month. A trip back to Europe awaited any potential immigrants whose monthly quota already had been filled. Because of a fervent will to reach the United States, immigrants from Southern and Eastern Europe typically consumed their nations' quotas in the first six months of the year. When those who came later were ordered to return, trouble ensued. Armenians argued that they would be slaughtered if they were returned to Turkey, and Christian Poles attacked Polish Jews for allegedly consuming an unfair proportion of their nation's quota.

Using the chaos as camouflage for their restrictionist goals, many argued that Congress must pass new legislation before the emergency law expired in the spring of 1924. Eugenicists continued to back this cause because of their belief that too many "inferior" people were still arriving in the United States. Debate in Congress was both emotional and long-winded. Interestingly, the fiercest opponents of immigration were representatives of areas where few immigrants lived; the immigrants' proponents generally came from urban areas, densely populated by people of foreign birth. Anti-immigration forces brought eugenicists and other witnesses before Congressional committees to testify that using 1910 as the model year for determining national quotas gave an unfair advantage to the newer groups of immigrants. Instead, they argued, immigration totals for 1890 should be used.

Congress accepted this recommendation. The National Origins Act, which passed easily in both houses, used 1890 as a base year and lowered each nation's quota to 2 percent of that nationality's population in the United States for that year. It also lowered the total number of immigrants per year to 161,184. Experts predicted that Italy's allocation would plummet from 42,507 to 3,912 while the United Kingdom's previous quota of 77,342 would slide only to 62,458 (Goldberg 1999, 1660). The bill also placed a complete ban on immigration among people unable to become U.S. citizens. This portion of the bill targeted Asians in general, but it was prompted by anxieties over the West Coast's Japanese population. The Japanese government made it clear to American diplomats that the bill was an insult to Japan. The legislation also called for a further reduction in the total number of immigrants to 150,000 in 1927, when a survey to quantify national origin totals in 1920 was expected to be completed and used as the new basis for establishing quotas. Calvin Coolidge signed the National Origins Act. However, the anticipated 1927 survey results did not arrive until 1929, and Herbert Hoover approved new quotas at that time. Just to make sure the quotas properly favored the old immigrant groups, they were based on figures that omitted Japanese, Chinese, African Americans, and all residents of Hawaii and Puerto Rico.

Henry Ford's Anti-Semitism

Henry Ford was a hero to many Americans in the 1920s because of his leadership in the mass production of automobiles. He was not just an innovative planner who introduced the assembly line in American manufacturing. He also had become a corporate role model by paying his workers well to earn their loyalty. However, he garnered a different kind of fame as well. Beginning in 1920, Ford published a series of brutal attacks on "international Jews" in a newspaper he owned. He devoted 91 consecutive issues of the weekly *Dearborn* [Michigan] *Independent* to the single theme of anti-Semitism. At a time when the nation's Jewish population was growing as a result of immigration, these articles unleashed every stereotype of Jews and displayed them all in hideous detail. Articles explored Jews' supposedly depraved influence on the nation's government, its economy, and its morals.

Ordinarily, material published in a suburban Detroit weekly newspaper would not attract national attention; however, because Ford ordered all of his automobile dealers to buy the *Dearborn Independent,* the newspaper had a circulation of 700,000—even more than the *New York Daily News,* then the nation's most popular daily newspaper. Ford's dealers did not like buying the newspaper because they feared that its venomous attacks would reduce or eliminate sales to Jews and their sympathizers. However, they had no choice. Ford also compiled the articles in *The International Jew,* a publication translated into many languages. Because of this book, Ford received praise from Adolf Hitler in his political manifesto, *Mein Kampf.*

In 1922, without explanation, Ford stopped publishing anti-Semitic material in the *Dearborn Independent,* but he went on the attack again in 1924. In this second siege, he targeted a single man, Aaron Sapiro, a Jewish attorney from Chicago who organized farm cooperatives, a concept Ford opposed. Linking Sapiro to other well-known Jews, the newspaper concluded that a Jewish conspiracy was attempting to seize control of American agriculture. Sapiro fought back with a $1 million defamation lawsuit. Ford settled the case out of court by paying Sapiro about $140,000, publishing a personal apology to him, and retracting all of his varied attacks on Jews. Afterward, Ford Motor Company paid $150,000 for advertisements in Jewish newspapers and journals.

Japanese in America

About 111,000 Japanese lived in the United States in 1920, and many legal hurdles blocked their path to success in America. Most Japanese settled along the West Coast, but their numbers were too small to establish the kind of critical mass that might repel racist attacks upon them. Because they were neither black nor white, judges ruled that under existing law, it was impossible for them to become citizens. This interpretation of the law faced 25 court challenges between 1887 and 1923. The last two cases reached the United States Supreme Court. One of the two involved a Japanese businessman named Takao Ozawa,

This campaign poster reflects anti-immigration fervor by showing Uncle Sam grabbing the wrist of a Japanese person who is reaching for a map of California. The image was intended to promote the candidacy of U.S. senator James D. Phelan, a California Democrat who lost a 1920 bid for re-election. (Library of Congress)

who grew up in the United States, spoke English, attended college in California, married, and had children who automatically became Americans because they were born on American soil. However, in 1922, the court rejected his appeal, telling him that no matter how American he felt, he was not white and could not become American.

In the wake of Japanese successes in farming, California and Washington both passed alien land laws that made it impossible for people who were ineligible for citizenship to own land. Before these laws went into full effect, the Japanese already operated "458,056 acres of the very best lands in California," according to California's governor William Dennison Stephens in 1920. By working long hours and maintaining a low standard of living, Stephens reported that the Japanese controlled 80 percent of the state's tomato crop, 80 to 100 percent of the state's spinach crop, and large percentages of other crops (Stephens 1920, 153). The state's 1912 land law was strengthened in 1920.

The final indignity for the Japanese was a total ban on future immigration in the National Origins Act in 1924. This action made some Japanese take affirmative steps to protect their community. James Yoshinori Sakamoto founded the *Japanese American Courier* in Seattle and helped to bring new life to a defense organization, the Seattle Progressive Citizens League. That group later joined with other local organizations to form the national Japanese American Citizens League.

Friends and Foes

In the political climate of the 1920s, immigrants often were targets for blame—for lost jobs, low wages, sinking morals, and declining American identity. Beyond the ranks of doctrinaire nativists, there were groups that traditionally favored immigration cutbacks. Among them were labor unions, which saw immigrants as competition for American workers' jobs. At this time, the American Federation of Labor joined extremist calls for stopping all immigration. African American groups joined unions in backing restrictions in both 1921 and 1924. They, too, wanted no new contenders for precious jobs, and because most African Americans were native-born Protestants, they embraced many of the same fears about Catholics and Jews that motivated white nativists.

On the other side of the fight, immigrants found a few champions. Some were idealists who saw immigration as a part of the nation's past and its future. Often, these individuals were female reformers. The American Jewish Committee, the Liberal Immigration League, and the Foreign Language Press Association were prominent in the fight. Even a few unions with heavy Jewish memberships, such as the International Ladies Garment Workers Union, split with the American Federation of Labor (AFL) and defended immigration. Urban politicians also generally sided with immigrants. Before 1924, business interests had supported immigration as a means of guaranteeing a pool of low-wage workers. The National Association of Manufacturers was a longtime foe of restrictions, and the organization opposed the Emergency Immigration Law in 1921. Three years later, however, the business climate had changed. Immigration laws had no effect on cheap Mexican labor in the Southwest, and the continuing migration of African Americans to the North helped to broaden the available workforce in the Northeast and Midwest. As a result, business leaders did not fight the National Origins Act.

New Restrictions Alter National Identity

The immigration laws of the 1920s erased what had been a quintessentially American trait—the virtually unqualified acceptance of immigrants to America.

In a way, these laws redefined what it meant to be an American and altered the United States' image as a nation of immigrants. The law had its intended

Historians' Debate:
Were Japanese "Model Immigrants"?

Despite laws intended to restrict them, the Japanese in the United States improved their statistical economic standing over the course of the 1920s. By 1930, unskilled laborers made up a smaller percentage of the Japanese population, and a larger percentage of Japanese belonged to the middle class. The first analyses of this data tended to credit the Japanese with a miraculous achievement made possible by their standing as a "model minority." The Japanese earned praise for succeeding despite legal barriers and for achieving this feat without help from the U.S. government. In a 1978 *Journal of Economic History* article, Robert Higgs concluded that Japanese immigrants "had attained an economic position of solid middle-class dimensions" and "triumphed over racial discrimination" (Suzuki 1995, 889).

However, as American scholars focused more attention on the Japanese experience during this era, they questioned the figures used to reach this conclusion. One economist, Masao Suzuki, has concluded that the real secret to Japanese success was the high rate of return to Japan by domestic servants, farm laborers, and other unskilled workers. Between 1920 and 1940, about one-third of all Japanese in the United States returned to Japan, and unskilled workers were most likely to leave. Restrictive immigration laws left little hope of prosperity among those who did not already own land. This, according to Suzuki's analysis, skewed the figures to make it appear that more Japanese had risen to the middle class, when the apparent improvement in the middle class percentage actually reflected a reduction in the working class population.

effect on the composition of the immigrant population. In 1927, most of the immigrants were Mexican, German, Irish, English, Scotch, Scandinavian, and Hebrew. Only small numbers of Eastern and Southern Europeans were welcomed to America's shores. And, somewhat ironically, anger over the legislation drove thousands of immigrants away from the United States. Those who saw little future for themselves or their countrymen sometimes chose to return to their homelands. In 1927, 323,885 immigrated and 75,122 emigrated (Leinwand 2001, 6). Many Japanese immigrants were among those who returned home where they expected to find brighter futures.

The decline in immigration also weakened the cultural institutions that had tied former countrymen together. Clubs, newspapers, and mutual aid societies all experienced disintegration in subsequent decades because the immigrants' children had no interest in their ancestral homeland. Without a steady flow of new immigrants, many of these cultural groups died. In a way, this fulfilled the wishes of nativists, who feared that their voices would be lost in the cacophony of other languages.

The legislation, which did not limit immigration from other nations in the Americas, increased arrivals of Mexicans. About 500,000 legally moved to the United States during the 1920s, and businessmen quickly put this cheap labor force to work in both agricultural and industrial jobs (Goldberg 1999, 165). Contemporary sources also estimate that about 100,000 additional Mexicans entered the United States illegally each year. As a result, laws intended to discourage illegal immigration removed the statute of limitations on deportation, organized the Border Patrol in 1925, and made illegal entry a felony instead of a misdemeanor. The number of Mexican deportations climbed from 846 in 1920 to 8,438 a decade later (Ngai 1999, 90).

At 18.1 percent, population growth in the United States was smaller in the 1920s than it had been in any peacetime decade since the U.S. Census began in 1790. Throughout the 19th century, the population had grown by at least 20 percent in each decade, and in most decades, the growth had exceeded 30 percent. The growth rate between 1900 and 1910 had been 33.1 percent; however, the rate had been just 23.3 percent between 1910 and 1920, when World War I impeded immigration (Gibson 1992, 159). The declining rate in both decades was not solely the result of reductions in immigration: Increased attention to birth control methods early in the 20th century also contributed to lower population growth.

The most dramatic impact of immigration restrictions was their effect on Eastern European Jews. Even if the 1921 quotas had been left in place, it has been estimated that an additional 300,000 Jews would have left Eastern Europe between 1924 and 1929. With the exception of those who fled to Palestine, most of these Jews were among the six million slain in the Holocaust.

ASSIMILATION IN LOS ANGELES

Population Explosion

Los Angeles began the 1920s as a large city with 577,000 residents and ended the decade as a metropolis of 1.24 million Angelenos (Tygiel 2001, 2). The ultimate boomtown sprawled outward, swallowing 145 nearby towns and cities in a single decade. Although the city lacked the extensive industrial development found in New York, Detroit, and Pittsburgh, Los Angeles already had become an icon of mass culture as a movie-making mecca. Because of its distance from the nation's power centers, Los Angeles received migrants from other parts of the United States almost in the same way that New York accepted immigrants from distant lands. The decision to move west had shaped much of American

Los Angeles experienced rapid growth during the 1920s, and Southern California was home to many immigrant workers. This photo shows Broadway at Eighth Street. (Library of Congress)

history, and like America itself, Los Angeles typically was a chosen destination, not an accidental one.

The City of Angels had many pages of history yet to be filled. Unlike Philadelphia, which was a temporary home to George Washington and a regular stop on the Underground Railroad, Los Angeles's memory of itself was relatively short. It began as a Spanish settlement in 1781, but in 1920, the city still seemed young to its white, Anglo-Saxon, Protestant, and antiunion majority—and many residents preferred that it grow without any of the messy complications that come with change. Los Angeles's leaders labored through the 1920s to make the city appealing to industries. Many firms responded favorably to the excellent climate and an expanding central manufacturing district. The city jumped from 28th in industrial production to 9th. In the three-year period of 1925–1927, the city ranked second in the percentage increase in manufacturing value and fourth in the dollar value of input (Hise 2001, 19). And with new manufacturing came an influx of wage earners.

These were anxious years in the motion picture capital of the world. The city launched a powerful drive to Americanize immigrants and make their distinctiveness evaporate in Los Angeles's own melting pot. Some organizations sought to help immigrants by changing their living conditions; others sought to control potentially threatening population groups. Immigrants felt a tug from the left and a shove from the right as both sides attempted to make assimilation as easy as a spin of Charlie Chaplin's cane. At the end of the 1920s, Los Angeles remained predominantly Anglo, but migration had a significant impact on the city. Mexican immigrants, both legal and illegal, had crossed the border in search of jobs. And thousands of African Americans making an exodus from the Old South decided to try life out west. In addition, the city had a small East Asian community and a financially successful Jewish population. Los Angeles also contained Russian, Slav, Armenian, and Italian communities. In addition to sharing customs, members of these groups often clung to religions that increased the city's diversity. As Americanizers embraced immigrant communities, their efforts achieved mixed results. Having already decided that African Americans could not be assimilated, the city's leaders set out to limit diversity in whatever ways they could. Some newcomers were able to assimilate, but it was impossible for others.

The Americanization Drive

Americanization remained a strong force across the United States at this time. The movement had begun as a Progressive effort to help immigrants adjust to life in America by learning how proper Americans lived. Settlement houses and Americanization classes set out to assist newcomers in learning the language and understanding the customs of the United States. The Americanization effort eventually split into two distinct categories: the liberal effort to improve immigrants' manners and standards of living, and the conservative push to produce a nation in which all citizens were "100 percent American."

The latter effort sprang from the World War I era, when the need for unity and heightened patriotism offered a rallying cry to conservatives. During the war, this impulse often turned ugly, particularly in areas where large German-American communities existed. This movement also had a special resonance in the Southwest, where fears of an active Mexican alliance with Germany brought the primarily European war closer to home.

Los Angeles was home to organizations promoting both kinds of Americanization. Progressives sought to improve the health care, education, and home environments of newcomers. Often seen as do-gooders, these proponents of reform showed some respect for the contribution that immigrant cultures could make to the city, but they emphasized helping newcomers and limiting their disruptive effect on the majority population. Supporters of the "100 percent American" effort typically looked for signs of subversives and attempted to protect the native community from insidious threats. This type of crusade offered little room for preservation of ethnic traditions. Because of Mexico's nearness, these efforts had flowered in the area during the war and would grow along with the city during the 1920s.

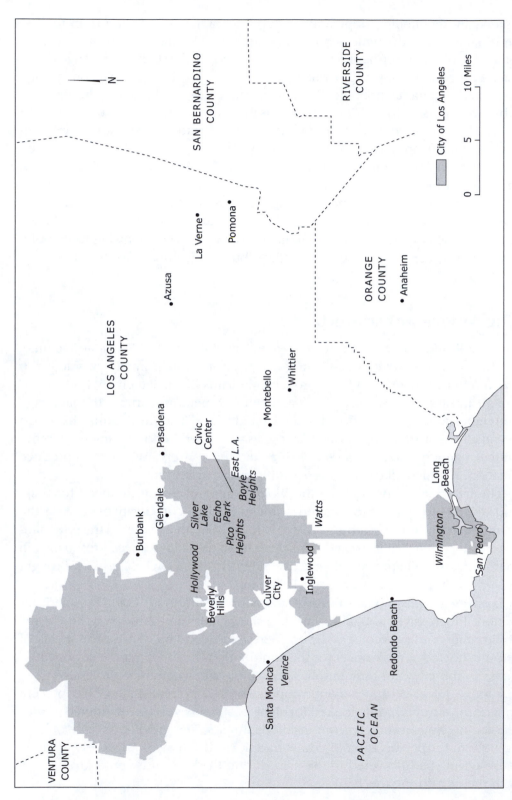

Map 5.2 *Greater Los Angeles in 1925*

Both groups of Americanizers demonstrated concern about exploitation of immigrants. In contrast to some other Americanizing cities, Los Angeles had only a low level of anti-Semitism. Even many Christian Fundamentalists, who often were suspicious of Jews, embraced a positive view of Jews. At the Bible Institute of Los Angeles, which became an influential source of education in the 1920s, students were taught that Jews were God's chosen people. While Americanization remained an active process, old prejudices still affected life in the workplace. In 1926, the National Urban League sponsored a survey of Los Angeles business owners by sociologist Charles S. Johnson. After surveying 456 companies about minority employment, Johnson chose 104 for closer study. He found that workplace expectations of minority groups sprang from impressions of where and how the ethnic groups lived. If they could get manufacturing jobs, both Mexicans and African Americans defied stereotypes through industriousness and the ability to accomplish varied tasks (Hise 2001, 22–23). By the end of the decade, more than 25 percent of the city's workers were employed in industry, and many were members of minority groups (Tygiel 2001, 3). Because of its position as a distant outpost of the East's industrial culture, Los Angeles was unusual in its cultural concerns as well as its population mix. However, in many ways, its Americanization efforts resembled those made in other cities.

Better America Federation

The Better America Federation (BAF), formed in 1920, was an outgrowth of the Commercial Federation of Los Angeles, a World War I "100 Percent American" organization. The Commercial Federation had a history of using surveillance to control suspected radicals. Like other Americanizing groups of its type, the BAF sponsored patriotic events, instruction about the U.S. Constitution, and opposition to forces it identified as potentially threatening groups, such as Communists and the radical Industrial Workers of the World (IWW). This kind of crusade often used intimidation to achieve its goals and became more coercive than voluntary. Among the aims embraced by the BAF at its inception was reawakening "in America a realization of the responsibilities of citizenship" and "a more general and intelligent acceptance of those responsibilities" (Deverell 2001, 280).

The organization's members were required to voice strict allegiance to the U.S. Constitution. Antiunionism also was one of the organization's most deeply held philosophies. The BAF opposed class consciousness and believed that Communism had given birth to progressive-era election reforms, including the voter initiative, the referendum, and recall elections. The organization, which was amply financed by Los Angeles's elite, also rejected compulsory education beyond the age of 14. As a part of its "open shop" approach to work life, it promoted the six-day workweek while rejecting minimum wages. Many of the BAF's activities were shrouded in secrecy. Los Angeles historian Carey McWilliams described the federation's less public activities, writing that the BAF employed a "host of spies, stool pigeons and informers to disrupt trade unions, to provoke violence, and to ferret out the reds" (Tygiel 2001, 5–6).

Brutal Rupture among Americanizers

Education was central to the Americanization effort, both within the BAF and among Progressives. In 1923, Los Angeles's Board of Education election widened the schism between the two groups, revealing wide disagreements about the strategies of Americanization. The BAF considered the schools as a primary battleground and set out to remove any suggestion of what it considered to be radicalism within the school system. In a March 1921 newsletter, it proclaimed that "a school board in America is no place for a socialist or a radical . . . and yet they do creep in" (Deverell 2001, 281). In the election of 1923, a Progressive Americanizer, the Rev. G. Bromley Oxnam, sought a position on the board. Oxnam, a Methodist minister at the Church of All Nations, was already known for his belief that bolstering the standard of living and health care of Mexicans would be a huge first step in Americanization. As early as 1920, he had written in his diary, "The BAF thinks me dangerous" (Deverell 2001, 283).

In the school board race, he favored pay raises for teachers, and both the *Los Angeles Times* and the BAF labeled him as a treacherous reformer. The conservative Sons of the Revolution, which had ties to the BAF, sent out a six-question survey to each of the school board candidates, and one of Oxnam's answers created a furor. The survey asked whether American history should be written or taught "from the viewpoint of America ahead of all other countries, yet not unfair to other countries." Oxnam responded by stating "it should be an established policy that both sides of all questions, political, industrial, economic, shall be looked into in a thoroughgoing manner" (Deverell 2001, 286).

From that moment forward, Oxnam faced scathing attacks from both the *Times* and the BAF. They accused him of being an ally of the IWW and keeping a radical library. Even after he left Los Angeles in the late 1920s to become president of DePauw University in Indiana, the attacks continued. By the end of the decade, Oxnam's Church of All Nations demonstrated success by improving living conditions and health care for immigrants. Infant mortality rates were cut by more than 50 percent in the Mexican community. In addition, Oxnam's own writings had expanded native-born Americans' understanding of the new arrivals. The BAF's achievements are more difficult to gauge because the organization often labored in secret. It is clear that the group skillfully used propaganda to smear the reputations of men like Oxnam and Simon J. Lubin, head of the California Commission of Immigration in Housing, one of the state agencies intended to promote Americanization. Like Oxnam, Lubin was accused of ties to the IWW. Undoubtedly, the BAF contributed to the still-powerful strain of right-wing politics in southern California.

Star of Ethiopia

When white Californians set out to Americanize new migrants to Los Angeles, African Americans were not invited to the party. White leaders had no expectation that blacks could be fully assimilated, and while they launched programs to help African Americans, these efforts did not attempt to alter black culture. Perhaps because of this hands-off policy, African Americans sought to celebrate their own unique heritage and culture. In Los Angeles, the effort took shape in a presentation of W. E. B. Du Bois's pageant, *The Star of Ethiopia,* in 1925. The production had been a great success when previously presented in New York, Philadelphia, and Washington. It portrayed the long history of Africans and African Americans. African American composers provided its musical score. The spectacle required the involvement of hundreds of volunteers who acted as extras in the cast. Younger members of the NAACP had originated the idea of presenting *The Star of Ethiopia.* Nonetheless, when Du Bois sent an aide to run the project and when the state's leading black newspaper criticized the production as a "highbrow" effort to attract publicity, younger NAACP members decided to boycott the presentation, which made it impossible to fill all of the roles in the cast. Moreover, the number of tickets sold was not adequate to cover the production's costs.

The Star of Ethiopia controversy brought to light generational splits within Los Angeles's African American community. Younger members of the NAACP refused to accept the African American's status as an outsider in Los Angeles. As college-educated intellectuals, they saw themselves as "the New Negro" and planned to succeed, no matter what impediments white society threw in their path. Also, this contretemps revealed how the city's individualistic character often impeded community boosterism.

Great Migration from Mexico

An increased migration of Mexicans to the United States occurred during the 1920s because Mexicans wanted jobs in the expanding Southwestern economy and they wanted to escape the aftereffects of the 10-year Mexican Revolution, which ended in 1920. Some came as farm workers eager to take part in blossoming agribusiness; others sought to join the urban working class. Many immigrants worked in both economies. In Los Angeles, most Mexicans made their homes near factories but remained reasonably close to farming areas so they could split their labor if necessary.

Mexican workers Inez Gonzalez, Francisco Gonzalez, and Pedro Castro talk in front of Castro's home in "La Fabrica" neighborhood of Anaheim, California. (Courtesy Anaheim Public Library)

Americanizers, often working through churches or libraries, touched the lives of many Mexicans. "In general, the united purpose of all denominations doing work among the Mexicans is to spread the spirit of Christ through personal commitment and devotion to him, and to raise the standards socially, educationally and morally among Mexican people," said a report of the Los Angeles Commission on Religion (Monroy 1983, 448). Protestant churches worked most persistently to win over Mexicans, most of whom were nominal Catholics. The Catholic Church, on the other hand, gave the immigrants little attention. The church's policy was to set up separate national parishes for Mexicans in large cities like Los Angeles rather than integrating them into predominantly white churches.

Many well-intentioned reformers feared the rapid growth of the Mexican population. One said, "According to present tendencies the time is not far distant when every other child in the elementary schools is Mexican" (Monroy 1983, 449). Progressives worried and wondered whether Mexicans could be assimilated. They launched efforts to train Mexican women in "economical house management" and their husbands in "thrift, gardening, and the principles of American government." The community directed Mexican youths toward vocational edu-

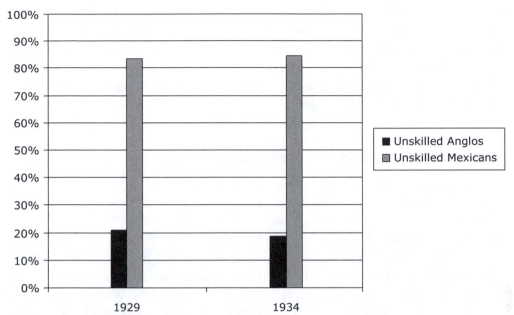

Figure 5.1 *Comparison of Unskilled Anglos and Mexican Workers in 1929 and 1934.*
Source: *Adapted from Monroy 1983, 439.*

cation. "Girls should be trained to become neat and efficient house servants,"
one source said (Monroy 1983, 450). Even the most liberal reformers seldom
saw Mexicans rising above the working class. By 1930, Mexicans made up 13.5
percent of Los Angeles County's population, but they were surprisingly reticent
about seeking American citizenship (Monroy 1983, 437). Some Mexican-born
retailers claimed they would lose their ethnic clientele if they became American
citizens. Others planned to return to Mexico.

Segregated City

While some Angelenos were attempting to Americanize new groups in the city,
local governments helped to maintain segregated housing through the 1920s.
Developers sometimes ousted Mexican settlements to make way for small, newly
constructed Anglo neighborhoods near factories. Some suburban areas also had
zoning regulations that served as an invisible barrier to nonwhites who might
want to live there. (The issue of whether Mexicans were white was the subject
of some debate.)

In Los Angeles itself, segregation through restrictive real estate covenants actually escalated in the first half of the decade. These covenants, which affected
almost every area of the city, sometimes explicitly excluded Jews, Italians, and
Mexicans as well as African Americans. The neighboring cities of Beverly Hills,

Inglewood, Glendale, Montebello, and Azusa also maintained lily-white populations by using similar covenants. Furthermore, most industrial plant operators attempted to minimize race mixing in the workplace through formal and informal practices to guarantee segregation. This effort helped to define the work sphere of African Americans in many plants. Typically, they were organized into crews with clearly defined duties.

Antiunionism Meets Social Darwinism

When they set out to attract new businesses or branch operations of established firms, Los Angeles business leaders used the city's antiunion atmosphere as well as its favorable climate as selling points. The Los Angeles Chamber of Commerce and the Merchants and Manufacturers Association also believed that workers who came to Los Angeles would be products of natural selection. Their logic was simple: if workers had the wisdom and ambition to abandon their old world in the East and move into Los Angeles's open shop work atmosphere, then surely, they must be among the nation's most efficient workers. A *Wall Street Journal* editorial backed up this thinking: "If the best American types are attracted to municipalities where the 'American Plan' [open shop] prevails, it follows that the process of selection set up diminishes the grade of citizenry in closed shop cities" (Davis 2001, 115). As the leading antiunion city and as the major city with the lowest population of Eastern and Southern European immigrants, Los Angeles would triumph, its leaders believed, by avoiding what they considered to be cultural and biological decline in the crowded cities of the East and Midwest.

Assimilation Efforts Achieve Limited Success

Los Angeles's efforts to assimilate its new residents, like Americanization projects elsewhere, faltered because of conflicting goals and hidden agendas. Some citizens made honest efforts to help new arrivals for moral reasons, but even church-based attempts to convert Mexicans into Protestants often were the products of fear—not faith. Americanization efforts could claim some clear-cut successes, including improved health care for Mexicans, but no sweeping changes.

The lack of diversity in Los Angeles at the turn of the century, when it was one of the three most homogeneous communities west of the Mississippi, probably contributed to the limited success of assimilation efforts in the 1920s. At the same time that churches, schools, and libraries tried to Americanize new residents, decisions to segregate urban and suburban neighborhoods undercut any sense that the newcomers could become equal participants in the life of the metropolis. Mexicans and African Americans typically received the lowest-paying jobs, and even the most liberal of Progressives seemed to believe that was ap-

Historians' Debate:
Immigration and Americanization

Americanization was a popular cause in the 1920s, but the issue of how foreigners become Americans has been a topic for debate since 1782 when Hector St. John de Crevecoeur published *Letters from an American Farmer*. De Crevecoeur saw Americans as a new race. He believed that Europeans cast off Old World connections when they adapted to American culture. In addition, he contended that immigrants' assimilation was both swift and simple, and that Americanization equaled emancipation.

This theory of easy assimilation contributed to the quest for Americanization. Progressive Americanizers clearly believed that their efforts could facilitate the process and make it a positive experience for new immigrants. The "100 percent American" organizations found frustration with the difficulties encountered in the transformation of new groups. In the 1920s, sociologists at the University of Chicago responded to Americanization efforts by uncovering a far more painful process of adaptation to American life that was driven by unstoppable social and economic processes. A decade later, historian Oscar Handlin began adding to the understanding of immigrants' difficult departures from their native lands and their equally difficult adjustments to new cultural mandates.

Historians in the 1960s brought new attention to repatriation among unsettled immigrants. Frank Thistlewaite estimated that one-third of European immigrants between 1821 and 1924 returned to their homelands. Other historians argued that many immigrants viewed their resettlement in America as a search for a new job, not a new homeland. And they contended that ethnic identities enriched American cultures. Some also argued that Americanization efforts had acted only as negative forces in immigrant history. In the 1970s, Herbert Gutman voiced the opinion that the type of Americanization efforts carried out in the 1920s really aimed at achieving an acceptance of capitalism. In 1990, Lawrence H. Fuchs argued that there really was no conflict between preservation of immigrants' ethnic groups and Americanization. He concluded that immigrants were welcome to keep their ancestral cultures and religions as long as they also demonstrated a willingness to act as Americans by "embracing the founding myths and participating in the political life of the nation" (Gerstle 1997, 539). Without accepting any historian's position as the "last word" on this subject, the debate itself has illuminated facets of immigration that made it impossible for Americanization to achieve complete success.

propriate. In fact, Mexicans and blacks faced discrimination in every segment of their lives, from segregated workplaces to segregated churches.

Rather than embracing American culture in the 1920s, Mexicans celebrated their own roots by establishing their own afternoon and evening schools "to inspire in the students a powerful love for our country . . . they are taught . . .

Spanish, national history, patriotic readings, stories of our heroes, [and] Mexican music" (Monroy 2001, 175). This represented the "Mexicanization" of the immigrants' children, some of whom were United States citizens by virtue of birth on American soil. Despite the Anglos' best efforts, the city's progress toward development of an ethnically diverse community was unstoppable. In addition to Mexicans, African Americans, and Jews, the city was home to Asians who brought Hinduism, Bahá'í Faith, Confucianism, Taoism, and Buddhism into the broader culture. These Eastern religions attracted the attention of many Anglos during the 1920s.

At the end of the decade, the city of Los Angeles was on its way to becoming one of the most diverse cities in the nation. The number of African Americans jumped from 15,579 in 1920 to 38,894 in 1930. Similarly, the number of Mexicans had risen from 21,598 to 97,000. In 1930, Los Angeles exceeded every American city except one—Baltimore—in the percentage of nonwhites in the population (Tygiel 2001, 2).

Not even the most idealistic Americanization project could claim that the city's minorities had been thoroughly assimilated into the overall population. Jews and Italians may have faded into the white majority, but Mexicans, Japanese, Chinese, and African Americans remained distinct groups. Efforts to transfigure Mexicans had failed to change the community's members significantly. Most religious Mexicans continued to practice a highly Mexicanized form of nominal Catholicism. Resistance to American citizenship remained strong: Most Mexicans in Los Angeles seemed satisfied with remaining migrant workers rather than becoming Mexican-Americans. They continued to leave the door open to the possibility of future repatriation.

EUGENICS

Scientific Selection

The study of eugenics in the United States sprang from a mix of scientific advancement and cultural fear. Genetics was a relatively new science, and so were Darwin's arguments for evolutionary development and survival of the fittest. In an unsettling time when immigrants inundated the United States and Americans scrambled to adjust to an economy driven by mass production, eugenics provided welcome reassurances to native-born whites that they were indeed exceptionally intelligent and hardy specimens of the human race. Leaders in the field believed that heredity, not environment, had the biggest impact on human development. And in most cases, eugenicists looked for and found what they believed to be a hierarchy of races. Not surprisingly, their pseudoscientific studies concluded that the newest immigrant groups were inferior to most native-born white Americans. Many people with deep roots in the United States welcomed this "proof" of superiority. In turn, this belief led some to fear dilution of America, both genetically and culturally, as a result of heavy migration from nations that were populated by purportedly inferior beings.

Eugenicists were serious scientists. Many held doctorates from respected universities and moved in exalted social circles. Some also taught at prestigious universities. This social status gave them greater access to American leaders than most unconventional scientists could hope to find. They used this opening to spread their beliefs across the nation and to influence public policy. Eugenicists' arguments swayed lawmakers at national and state levels. Two cases in point: they helped to convince Congress that the United States should protect itself by limiting admission of "inferior" immigrants, and they successfully promoted state laws endorsing aggressive action to reduce the number of pregnancies that might produce "mentally deficient" babies. Efforts to limit births of "defective" babies began with commitment of the mentally ill, the retarded, and the epileptic to institutions that were segregated by gender. Often the second step was to seek legislation allowing sterilization of the "mentally unfit." Specific details about authorization of these involuntary procedures varied from state to state, but sterilizations often were carried out without involvement of the inmate's family. In many states, the eugenics movement's push for legislation did not have an overtly racist component; however, in some states, eugenicists expanded their goals to include government monitoring of marriages to prevent racial mixing.

Because enforcement of eugenics mandates required legislation at the state level, centralized national organizations advised state organizations on how to achieve their goals. Various groups sprouted with a familiar cast of characters. Although men generally led these efforts, women often were the workhorses of the eugenics movement. Female activists, many of whom had received their political initiation in earlier battles against child labor and for women's suffrage, often performed the dirty work of pushing bills through state legislatures. In many cases, these were sincere reformers who believed that life would be better if human beings had a stronger genetic base. Birth control advocate Margaret Sanger was among the eugenicists' allies.

In the 1920s, birth-control advocate Margaret Sanger allied herself with eugenicists who wanted to control childbirth in a way that would guarantee the dominance of Americans from white European stock. (Library of Congress)

Leading Eugenicists of the 1920s

Eugenicism was not confined to the United States, but American writers were among the most prolific. Several American eugenicists were highly influential in the movement within the United States. They generally shared a belief in the racial superiority of people whose ancestry could be traced to a specific region of Northern and Western Europe. Their theories contributed to the sterilizations of thousands of Americans, and it was not until the mid-1920s that growing opposition to their conclusions began to weaken their stance. Examining the arguments of key leaders offers a good cross section of eugenic thought.

- Charles B. Davenport, who became an unofficial spokesman for the movement, edited a eugenics-oriented newspaper and held leadership positions in several eugenics organizations. He had a Ph.D. from Harvard and was the beneficiary of a large grant from the Carnegie Institution; however, both friends and foes accused him of having an overly simplistic scientific approach to eugenics. Davenport, who often advised state organizations on their strategies, was criticized for completely ignoring the influence of environment in human development.

- Lothrop Stoddard, who also held a Ph.D. from Harvard, took a worldwide look at racial differences in his 1920 book, *The Rising Tide of Color against White World-Supremacy,* and his 1923 volume, *The Revolt against Civilization: The Menace of the Under Man.* He believed that black, yellow, and brown races as well as "inferior Mediterraneans" threatened white supremacy around the globe. He saw Communism as a tool for minorities to achieve greater power in this contest. His books were read on many college campuses.

- Madison Grant attracted Adolf Hitler's attention by arguing that Europeans could be divided into three groups: the superior Nordics, who were a "race of soldiers, sailors, adventurers and explorers but above all, of rulers, organizers and aristocrats"; the Alpines, who lived in Central Europe and represented "sturdy and persistent stock"; and the Mediterraneans, who were, in fact, all other Europeans and were categorized as being inferior in genetic makeup (Goldberg 1999, 154). Grant worried aloud that transportation advancements would bring more inferior Europeans to America's shores. He drew the underpinning of his theories from Count J. A. de Gobineau of France, who stressed heredity's dominance over the effects of environment.

- Edward M. East, a Harvard professor, worked to convince geneticists in the early 1920s that the "harmony of the genotype" was being undermined by hybrids, which were the inevitable result of interbreeding. Unlike some of his colleagues, East acknowledged environment's role in human development. His books, *Mankind at the Crossroads,* published in 1923, and

Heredity and Human Affairs, published four years later, relied heavily on intelligence test results to back up his position on the inferiority of both hybrids and those whose ancestry could be traced to regions other than Europe's favorable zone.

Segregation and Sterilization

There were two waves of activity in the eugenics movement's campaign to segregate and sterilize "mentally unfit" individuals. The first ended as the 1920s were beginning, and the second covered the final seven years of the decade. The first sterilization period began in 1907 and continued through 1922. During that time, 18 states approved legislation that permitted the sterilization of at least 3,233 people institutionalized for mental disorders. Indiana's law served as a model for other states, thus streamlining the legislative process. Additional legislatures passed similar legislation; however, governors vetoed the bills. Lawmakers in other states approved the institutionalization and gender segregation of people with mental disorders but did not initiate the more controversial policy of involuntary sterilization. Most state governments placed their emphasis on avoiding the spread of mental retardation; however, in California, insanity received more attention. Philanthropies, which had a history of backing eugenics research, also supported the effort to win legislative approval for segregation and sterilization of people with mental problems. Among them were the Rockefeller Foundation, which eventually withdrew its support, and the Carnegie Institute.

The death knell for this period of activity sounded in 1919, when the Indiana Supreme Court overturned the law that had been used as a template for other state laws. The court dismissed the law without discussion, saying that it did not satisfy even the weakest standards of due process. Through 1921, court after court tossed out sterilization laws. The judiciary was acting to defend the weak, but judges probably also were affected by studies that cast doubt on Charles B. Davenport's theories about heredity's impact in passing along criminal tendencies.

With little delay, the Eugenics Record Office produced new and improved model legislation to correct the earlier laws' weaknesses. In 1923, involuntary sterilization bills won approval in Delaware, Oregon, Michigan, and Montana. Virginia followed a year later, and by the end of 1925, 17 states had passed legislation to make sterilization projects possible. In some states, governors blocked enforcement of the law by withholding financing for the project. The first step—placement of mentally retarded and mentally ill children and adults in gender-segregated facilities—was not terribly controversial and so was carried out in the open. However, sterilizations generated more negative responses and often seemed confined to the shadows of American awareness. Records indicate that enforcement of these laws was kept to a minimum in some states because of feared voter backlash. Nevertheless, the process continued. Minnesota, which passed a law in 1925, had sterilized only 21 people by July 1, 1926. The state sterilized 1,078 females and 202 males over the following 12 years. At this time, vasectomies carried significantly less risks than the tubal ligations necessary for women; however, female sterilizations often were more common. At least five women died nationwide after these procedures (Reilly 1991, 98).

Virginia's Racial Integrity Law

While most laws inspired by eugenicists focused on averting reproduction in what was believed to be a "mentally unfit" population, some states went a step further. After receiving a petition signed by almost 2,000 Virginians who favored legislation to preserve racial purity, the state's General Assembly approved a law in 1924 that forbade a white person from marrying a member of another race. The bill also required that the state's Bureau of Vital Statistics register and classify by race every newborn as well as much of the existing population. Supporters of the new law promoted it as a means of preserving family values. By this time, as many as 15 states had approved similar laws; however, no other state exhibited the zeal that Virginia directed toward enforcement of this law. If the state received information that a child had been born as the result of a liaison between a black person and a white person, the parents were warned that the child would be classified as nonwhite and that he or she would be relegated to the state's inferior schools for African Americans only. Of 80 cases reported, only 2 involved white men. The rest of the cases revealed the law's true target— white women accused of weakening their race by consorting with African American men. An effort in 1926 to place more attention on white men's activities did not win legislative approval. Virginia's Racial Integrity Law remained on the books until 1967, when it was struck down by the United States Supreme Court.

Buck v. Bell

Buck v. Bell, a case challenging Virginia's sterilization law, had far-reaching effects. The case involved Carrie Buck, who reportedly was a "feeble-minded woman." Buck was a young white woman who had been reared by foster parents. A relative of her foster parents had raped her, and then the family chose to have her committed to an institution for immorality. Neither she nor the baby she bore was retarded, but eugenicist Harry Laughlin argued that her immorality was "a typical picture of the low-grade moron," and the designated state board approved her sterilization in 1924, when Buck was 18. Buck subsequently appealed to the United States Supreme Court. Ruling on May 27, 1927, by an

8–1 vote, the court upheld the law. Justice Oliver Wendell Holmes wrote, "It is better for all the world, if instead of waiting to execute degenerate offspring for crime or to let them starve for their imbecility, society can prevent those who are manifestly unfit from continuing their kind" (Reilly 1991, 87). The court concluded that Buck's rights had not been violated by the law. This ruling reinvigorated the sterilization crusade. Indiana and North Dakota approved sterilization legislation in 1927, with Mississippi following in 1928. Nine additional states passed bills in 1929. During this flurry of legislative activity, bitter fights occurred in the Kentucky and New Jersey legislatures over sterilization. In New Jersey, both the League of Women Voters and the federated women's clubs backed the bill, which did not pass. In Kentucky, where the bill also failed, a senator memorably looked around at his colleagues and remarked that if such a law had been enacted 40 years earlier, "there would not be so many fools here now" (Reilly 1991, 89).

Birth Control

It may seem incongruous to imagine aggressive birth control advocate Margaret Sanger working with conservative eugenicists, but in many ways, it was a match that made sense. Many Americans viewed Sanger as a radical who was willing to encourage disobedience of laws banning birth control. She was passionate about her work—passionate enough to join an alliance with eugenicists because such an arrangement might help both movements. Birth control was an obvious answer to a problem facing eugenicists: It offered a means to deter births among unfit whites and members of inferior races. And if the eugenicists endorsed Sanger's cause, she might draw support from a previously unexpected source—conservatives.

As a result, Sanger enthusiastically jumped on the eugenics bandwagon. She argued in her 1911 book, *The Pivot of Civilization,* that "the complex problem of the feeble-minded, and the menace of the moron to human society" demonstrated "the actual harvest of reliance upon traditional morality, and upon Biblical injunction to increase and multiply a policy still taught by politician, priest and militarist" (quoted in Leon 2004, 34). Most eugenicists favored sterilization over contraception, but some were willing to consider contraception as a compromise. Eugenicists supported the opening of Sanger's first birth control clinic in New York in 1923. At that time, no foolproof contraceptive existed, but Sanger and her allies sold "feminine hygiene" products and preventive devices in black-market transactions. Eugenicists backed research aimed at producing a simple and inexpensive method of contraception, but this work primarily took place in Great Britain because the 1873 Comstock Law made contraceptive appliances illegal in the United States and banned even the exchange of contraceptive information through the mail.

The Deep South

Many women in the Deep South took part in the eugenics crusade. Often act-ing on behalf of the federated women's clubs, these women, alongside medical societies, often were the most visible lobbyists for sterilization legislation. One Mississippi newspaper reported that the state's House of Representatives had approved involuntary sterilization "amid much applause from the women in the galleries who had worked so earnestly in its behalf" (Larson 1995b, 75). By 1920, all of the Deep South states had approved laws providing gender-segregated institutionalization. Later in the decade, sterilization laws passed in every state except Louisiana. John Thomas, superintendent of the Louisiana Hospital for the Insane, argued in 1922 that "if Louisiana was to enact such a law and enforce it, within three generations insanity would, I think, be reduced by 50 percent in the state" (Larson 1995b, 44). However, the state was home to a significant number of Catholics, and the church remained firmly opposed to sterilization as interference with natural reproduction. Historian Edward J. Larson, who studied eugenics and sterilization in the Deep South, discovered that these states showed surprisingly little interest in sterilization of African Americans. Instead, the pri-mary goal was to purify the white race. He speculated that the Deep South's strict segregation and its laws against miscegenation resolved concerns about "feeble-minded" African Americans.

Universities and Eugenics

The number of colleges and universities offering eugenics studies grew dramati-cally during this era from 44 in 1914 to 376 in 1928. About 20,000 students on college campuses took part in eugenics classes (Dorr 2000, 285). The Univer-sity of Virginia hosted one of the most prominent programs. Dr. Ivey Foreman Lewis taught eugenics there from 1915 until 1953. A professor of biology and a dean at the university, Lewis believed that ancestry dominated all parts of life, even the human ability to rise to higher positions in society. Although many Southerners rejected Darwin's theory of evolution, Lewis supported it. He also taught his students that it would be easier to instill morality among genetically enhanced people. Moreover, he asserted that students could not reach beyond their innate intellectual potential, and he refused to consider the possibility that environment held importance in human development. His courses were popu-lar, drawing 185 students in 1921. By 1925, 340 students sought to enroll in his classes, although there was only room for 273 (Dorr 2000, 287).

Chicago's Psychopathic Lab

In Chicago, the Municipal Court's Psychopathic Laboratory studied people who had been deemed "mentally defective" and decided which ones were sent to

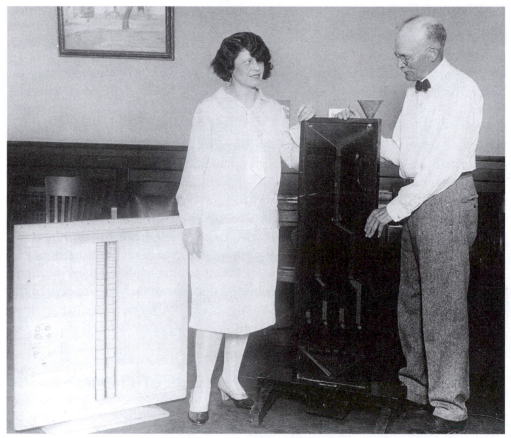

A clerk in the Chicago Psychopathic Laboratory of the city's municipal court explains a machine intended to tell parents what traits their children are likely to display. (Bettmann/Corbis)

gender-segregated institutions. William J. Hickson headed the lab, and his technique for analyzing individuals initially consisted of visual memory tests originated in Europe. He later added his own intelligence test to the process. Hickson produced a 1924 study of the occupational breakdown of 1,002 cases directed to his laboratory. Among the men, the top ten categories all encompassed unskilled workers, ranging from laborers to janitors. Only 13 professional men made the list, including 2 lawyers and 2 ministers. Among women, domestics made up one-third of the people referred to Hickson. A 1927 report showed that Hickson committed more than three-quarters of the people he evaluated. This greatly exceeded the records of the Detroit Recorder's Court, which committed 6 percent, and the Municipal Court of Philadelphia, which committed only 2 percent (Willrich 1998, 101). The state of Illinois did not sterilize inmates because the legislature consistently rejected proposed laws to allow involuntary sterilization.

Critics of Eugenics

Eugenic sterilization drew increasing opposition by the mid-1920s. The most powerful and persistent opposition came from the Catholic Church. Bishops and other church representatives often applied pressure to defeat sterilization bills, which they believed to be immoral. Some Catholics supported "positive eugenics," which promoted marriage and reproduction by "superior" people, but they opposed sterilization, which they labeled as "negative eugenics." Another key group of opponents was the burgeoning population of geneticists. Dr. Herbert Jennings at Johns Hopkins Hospital and others stepped forward and voiced disapproval of eugenicists. Although Jennings rejected the thesis that Europe could be split into "desirable" and "undesirable" zones, he did support the premise that a single pair of genes caused feeble-mindedness. He opposed sterilization because he thought it was unwise to set a legal precedent. Raymond Pearl, also at Johns Hopkins University, dismissed the eugenicists' argument that superior people breed superior children. Social scientists also joined the fight. Sociologist Lester Ward at Harvard contended that all humans were peers of the eugenicists' "aristocracy of brains." Franz Boas, the father of American anthropology, repeatedly tried to focus attention on culture rather than heredity.

Movement Erases Reproductive Rights of Thousands

More than 10,000 Americans lost the ability to have children as a result of the eugenics movement. Thousands more were institutionalized in gender-segregated facilities to prevent interaction that might lead to pregnancy. Because these people were closeted away and because they usually represented the lowest ranks of the population, we know little about their lives and how they were affected by these eugenic initiatives. However, it is worth noting that diagnoses such as "immorality" caused the institutionalization of some people who probably had no mental problems. The effects of laws to preserve racial purity are also difficult to trace beyond the likelihood that they encouraged more cautious behavior. These laws had two unspoken goals: preventing mulatto children from passing for white and stopping white women from having sexual liaisons with African American men. Because enforcement of this legislation was weak in most states where these laws existed, the impact probably was erratic. There is no evidence that any of these laws lowered the number of "mentally defective" Americans or improved the intelligence of a typical American. Although intelligence tests would become a standard part of public education in the United States, educators accepted over time that these tests often carried implicit cultural biases that made them less accurate in gauging the intelligence of minorities.

As a political phenomenon, eugenics brought women into the public sphere on an issue that could be easily feminized because women, after all, gave birth to all babies, whether geniuses or imbeciles. Many women across the country lobbied for passage of bills intended to limit births of "mentally defective" people, and they saw their participation in this effort as an extension of their previous work as reformers. However, in this case, they were attempting to reform the nature of human beings, not human society.

Within the laboratory, eugenics fell victim to new findings about heredity. Geneticist Hermann Joseph Muller discovered in 1927 that X-rays caused gene mutations and chromosome changes. This and Muller's further work on mutations cast new doubt on the belief that ancestry alone determined human qualities. More and more, scientists found environmental factors that could affect human development. However, the strongest blow to American eugenics came from Europe. The reputations of eugenicists began to diminish in the United States with the rise of the Nazi regime in Germany during the 1930s. Because Hitler and his followers preached an ideology of Aryan supremacy, few Americans wanted to be associated with these ideas. Margaret Sanger's reputation was forever soiled by her partnership with the eugenicists. The rise of the Nazis and their quick ouster of many academics probably led more American geneticists to step forward in opposition to eugenics. New disagreements arose among some geneticists who had once shied away from public statements because they lacked the means to "disprove" eugenic theories. By the close of the 1930s, eugenics no longer was considered a science.

AMERICA UNDER A MICROSCOPE

Popularity of Sociology and Anthropology

In the 1920s, Americans began systematically asking questions about themselves and about human beings in general. The social sciences reached a new level of maturity as professions and fields of study in an age when Americans struggled to grapple with the mechanistic world of mass production and the relatively new theoretical frameworks created by Charles Darwin, Sigmund Freud, and Albert Einstein. Building on earlier advances, psychologists continued efforts to refine testing of mental capacity and psychological well-being. They used test findings in efforts to help individual patients and to generate improvement in the mental health of the overall population. As Freudian theories received wider acceptance, psychoanalysis became more widely accepted.

Two new fields that truly came into their own during this decade were sociology and anthropology. Although work in both fields had begun before the turn of the century, these fields underwent dramatic changes and received new legitimacy in the 1920s. At the close of the 19th century, anthropology's reach did not extend much beyond museum walls. Evolutionary anthropologists initially were predominant. They explored racial progress since the development of human life, and they placed white culture at the apex of world civilization. Franz

Sigmund Freud's theories about psychoanalysis affected many facets of American thought in the 1920s. His tenets were often applied to other fields of study and to questions about appropriate behavior. (Library of Congress)

Boas led the effort to change and broaden anthropology's focus. With the help of students Margaret Mead and Ruth Benedict, Boas succeeded in steering anthropology away from race studies and toward cultural analyses, and by the late 1920s, the field had become professionalized. Before the 1920s, there was little consensus about the goals of sociology. Like Boas, Robert Park tried to direct his field of study away from an obsession with racial traits. Park, a prominent spokesman for the urban sociological approach that became known in the 1920s as the "Chicago school," advocated investigations of the way groups interacted. Whereas some people during this period believed that ethnic organizations were un-American, Park argued that such groups helped to crystallize individual identity. Many Americans' first taste of sociological studies came in Robert and Helen Lynd's investigation of ordinary Americans. Popular interest in their Middletown study demonstrated self-consciousness within the American population and a desire to further identify what qualified as "normal" within American culture.

Social scientists in psychology, anthropology, and sociology attracted attention by exploring sexual topics. Because many American clergymen maintained puritanical attitudes toward sex, they often found themselves in conflict with social scientists. Conservatives often viewed American acceptance of Freudian concepts, which affected all three disciplines, as evidence of imminent decline in the nation's culture and a betrayal of American ideals. Over time, these disciplines expanded beyond the bounds of academia and had an increasing impact on popular culture. Some of these new specialists reached the public at large by writing popular books in the 1920s. Also during this decade, Freud truly became a household name in middle-class homes. Simplistic forms of Freud's conclusions seeped into American culture through a variety of conduits, including word-association parlor games, child-rearing practices, and the Broadway plays of Eugene O'Neill. Without ever really understanding Freudian theory or the mechanics of sociology, many Americans adopted new concepts from the social sciences and integrated them into daily life.

New Visibility for Social Sciences

By 1920, American culture had begun to absorb the languages and the philosophies of the new social sciences. Of course, the United States was not alone in assimilating these new ideas and seeking to follow them to a deeper understanding of society. Many of the advances in social sciences were paralleled by studies made abroad, but Americans sometimes confronted these new sources of information in authentically American ways. And at times, even studies of other cultures had the goal of shedding light on society in the United States.

It would be wrong to suggest that social sciences were entirely a product of the 20th century. Early in the 19th century, weaker and less systematic forms of social science existed; however, these studies often focused strictly on the individual. As society became more complex and culture became less localized, social scientists turned their attention to the effects of group identity on individuals. For this second wave of social scientists, one of the guiding principles was the belief that individual human beings were capable of reaching the ultimate potential of their peer group. Also, many of these new specialists clung to the idea that there was a taxonomic hierarchy within the human population that needed to be understood for the sake of societal progress. Among the mid-19th century fields of study were phrenology, the study of the shape of the skull, and polygenism, which promoted the idea that the various races were created separately. Mental health care was another area of social science, and the treatment of mental problems became a controversial discipline during these years.

After the Civil War, fields of study that were new and more scientific began to affect American thought. Among them were sociology, anthropology, psychology, political science, economics, and child development. All of these fields attempted to establish professional standards to make their studies more scientific. In the early 20th century, social scientists faced the difficult tasks of delineating those standards, staking out their ground as experts, and transforming their fields of study into university disciplines. Moreover, they recognized the need to prove their worth by making new discoveries. To earn a place on college campuses, these professionals faced the difficult job of garnering public recognition and demonstrating that their pursuits were driven more by science than by preconceived and pseudoscientific notions.

It was common for the extremist, and often racist, views from within these disciplines to draw the greatest attention before the 1920s. "A man did not need to read an article or book on the biological, anthropological, psychological, or sociological aspects of race in order to participate in a race riot," concluded Thomas F. Gossett, a historian of race issues (Carter 1975, 97). Particularly after the riots of 1919, these new social scientists demonstrated the drive to transcend a fixation with race and develop serious, broadly focused fields of study in the 1920s.

The Middletown Study

When Robert and Helen Lynd set out to explore daily life in a small American city, Robert Lynd hoped that sociology could improve human life through greater understanding. The Lynds were pioneers in the use of social surveys to construct an overview of sociological interaction and community standards; however, questionnaires represented just one step in a multifaceted approach to understanding Muncie, Indiana, and its inhabitants. Their investigative methods included participation in the city's daily life, study of public records, collection of statistical data, interviews of subjects, distribution of questionnaires, and analysis of findings. Each step of the process provided information that could be used in making the other steps more productive. By careful analysis of the gathered data, the Lynds hoped to draw new insights into the lives of average Americans and to identify both typical and atypical behavior.

The study fell into six subject areas of everyday life—earning a living, making a home, preparing children for adulthood, engaging in leisure activities, partaking in religious practices, and participating in community activities. Hoping to draw a greater understanding of present behavior by making comparisons to the past, they narrowed the scope of their investigation by limiting themselves to the years between 1890 and 1924. As they began in 1924, the Lynds chose Muncie for their study because they thought an in-depth sociological study would be more meaningful in a largely homogeneous town—an approach that would generate criticism in later periods of greater multiculturalism. However, using Muncie as their Middletown, they were able to produce such a penetrating study that *Middletown: A Study in Contemporary American Culture* became a bestseller in 1929.

Through their study, the Lynds uncovered an overwhelmingly bleak sense of bewilderment and loss of community as Americans struggled to adapt to a rapidly changing world. Furthermore, to the surprise of many Americans, they found undeniable class distinctions. For more than a century, Americans had contended that class stratification was incompatible with democracy; however, by talking to the citizens of Muncie, the Lynds found clear-cut evidence of its existence. They were able to draw differentiations between a business class and a working class.

Their work produced many conclusions, including the following:

- Many products could be found in the American home in 1924 that weren't there in 1890. Among them were telephones, refrigerators, washing machines, toasters, toilets, vacuum cleaners, and furnaces.

- Automobiles, with their new privacy zones, had changed sexual relations.

- Sundays were shifting away from identification as the Sabbath and becoming more like holidays.

- Although almost everyone belonged to a church, the working class showed greater attachment to traditional religion.

- A boy who could not drive his date to a dance felt like a social outcast.

- Use of birth control methods was high among the business class, but much less prevalent in the working class.

After their initial success, the Lynds made a follow-up study, *Middletown in Transition,* in 1937. Since then, numerous scholars have descended on Muncie because the thoroughness of the Lynds' original work provided a formidable base to be used in gauging subsequent change.

The Average American

The Lynds' study of Middletown may be the most widely known study of typical Americans during the 1920s, but it is not the only one. Many social scientists devoted time and emphasis to the study of Americans. In 1927, psychologist Harry L. Hollingworth attempted to describe the average man for *The Literary Digest.* The typical man was 53 years old, weighed 150 pounds, and was five foot seven inches tall. His vocabulary consisted of about 7,500 words, and he left school in the eighth grade. He knew a bit about local geography, less about history. He had minimal knowledge about anatomy and understood even less about politics, literature, and science. The average man was likely to be either a Democratic Methodist or a Republican Baptist. He worked in skilled trades but was unlikely to have a better job than his father had. He cared more about morality than religion.

Ground-breaking anthropologist Margaret Mead poses with Samoans in a photo she mailed to colleague Ruth Benedict in 1926. Mead, who conducted a study of adolescent Samoan girls, is wearing a wedding dress woven by Makelita, last queen of Manu'a, a part of American Samoa. (Library of Congress)

Nature versus Nurture

In the 1920s, social scientists often debated the comparative strengths of natural traits and cultural characteristics. During these years, Franz Boas began to see the field of anthropology consolidating behind his theories about culture's strong impact on the development of the individual, but his position in American anthropology was soon to be eclipsed by the standing of one of his students, Margaret Mead. At the age of 23, Mead went to American Samoa. There she devoted her time to the study of adolescent girls. Boas directed her to study whether Samoan adolescent girls possessed the same "rebellious spirit" found in American girls of the same age. Thus, although she was far from home, the underlying goal of her work was to clarify a detail of American life.

Her 1929 book, *Coming of Age in Samoa,* introduced many ordinary people to the field of anthropology. The book, written to appeal to nonprofessionals, described her findings drawn from the study of 68 Samoan girls. Her conclusion was that adolescence was a much less stressful time in Samoa than it was in the United States. She contended that the homogeneity of Samoan culture enabled girls to develop into womanhood without facing as many personal choices or demands. Samoan girls also faced fewer sexual restrictions than their American counterparts, according to Mead's findings. Based on her study's results, Mead offered suggestions on how American culture could make adolescence easier for girls.

The Americanization of Freud

Sigmund Freud's beliefs about the human mind found their way into American art, anthropology, sociology, medicine, fiction, and casual conversation during the 1920s. However, it seemed that the more people talked about Freud, the more his theories became diluted. As evidence of America's downfall, a Freud detractor named Mark Sullivan cited the hundreds of American books that had been published about Freud since 1910. In the 1920s, Freud's theories were bent and mutilated to satisfy whatever people wanted to believe: repression is bad; sex is good; responsibility is meaningless when the subconscious is so powerful. Even Freud's atheism was glossed over in the interest of what he surely would have labeled a state of denial.

Social Science at Work

In the wake of Frederick Taylor's success in using scientific management to improve production on the factory floor, American business leaders in the 1920s looked for new ways to use scientific methodology to make the workplace more efficient. Through the "personnel movement," psychologists used testing to evaluate workers in various industries. One form of testing focused on measuring intelligence, another on determining which traits indicated likely success in a specific job. At a 1921 conference, psychologists were unable to agree on a definition for intelligence, thus throwing the results of intelligence tests into question. It was even more challenging for testing to identify personality factors that made a worker more likely to perform well in a specific job. After a boom in testing, many companies abandoned it between 1922 and 1925, and this movement had virtually disappeared by the last half of the decade. Tests "may help us to separate the sheep from the goats," said psychologist John B. Watson of the J. Walter Thompson advertising agency, but "they will not tell us much about the flock of sheep left from which to make our individual selections" (Baritz 1960, 73).

Americans Absorb New Views of Their Existence

Advances in the social sciences helped Americans step back and take a look at themselves. They were not the 18th-century gentlemen farmers who launched a revolution or their great-grandchildren who went to war against one another in a battle over preservation of the United States. With every passing year, they seemed to fit less neatly into any single definition—and that contributed to the stresses of the 20th century. Some could trace their families to the *Mayflower*, others began life on the other side of the ocean. Some wished all of the strange people would go back to their homelands. Others prayed in their synagogues and worried about the relatives they had left behind.

Social scientists tried to help make sense of it all by turning away from theories based on old prejudices and by using a more empirical approach. Whether the questions were big—*Was one race superior to another?*—or small—

How would a boy feel if he could not drive his date to the prom?—social scientists were there to seek the answers. Because of their expertise, these new professionals often found themselves in positions of prominence. Social scientists of all kinds stepped into roles advising leaders at all levels of government. Economists and sociologists, in particular, were on their way to becoming almost-indispensable resources at some levels of government. Psychologists also found influential work in business, advertising, mass media, charities, and, of course, universities. Human resources management's introduction in big business was still decades away, but managers were beginning to see the value of having psychological and social specialists in the workplace. The creation of many repetitive and routine jobs in the 1920s also brought psychologists into broad discussions about the meaning of work in an industrial age. Many social scientists in the 1920s tried to put theories of racial superiority behind them, but they still found uses for one of the old racist tools—standardized testing. The debate among psychologists about the value of such testing continued as the experts tried to perfect examinations for use in the schools and elsewhere. Testing advocates believed that they had great potential in preparing young people for appropriate professions.

Even dedicated professionals realized that the new social scientists needed to prove their value to solidify their status as professionals who had studied to achieve useful advanced degrees. Often their research required funding from philanthropies; therefore, it was logical to think about the marketability of research topics. Philanthropic financial support also helped to guarantee the various disciplines' futures on college campuses. It was not by accident that these fields of study emerged at a time when unsettling changes were complicating American lives. Instead, they were part of a symbiotic relationship between scientific study and the state of American culture. Some of these social sciences would become even more useful during the economic and social catastrophe of the next decade.

BIOGRAPHIES

Charles B. Davenport, 1866–1942

Geneticist and Zoologist

Charles B. Davenport, both a geneticist and zoologist, played a key role in the leadership of the eugenics campaign in the United States. Armed with a Ph.D. from Harvard University, he headed the Station for Experimental Evolution at Cold Spring Harbor, New York, which was the nation's top eugenics research facility. The Carnegie Institution financed both the station and an adjunct, the Eugenics Record Office. That office became the greatest information resource on human heredity in the United States as well as a training center for educators and social workers who wanted to learn about eugenics. For 30 years after its opening in 1910, the office also helped to bolster local eugenics groups around the United States. In addition, Davenport served as vice president of the Eugenics Committee of the United States and co-edited *Eugenical News.*

Despite the demands of supervising his expanding empire, Davenport tried to remain active in scientific research. He looked to his second-in-command at the Eugenics Record Office, Harry H. Laughlin, to handle lobbying for causes they supported, such as restrictions on immigration. Although Davenport continued trying to produce scientific research, fellow scientists sometimes criticized his work for its shallowness. He never reclaimed the academic reputation he had gained after publication of *Heredity in Relation to Eugenics* in 1911. Davenport joined five other eugenicists in a paper titled "Memorial on Immigration Quotas: To the President, the Senate, and the House of Representatives" in January 1927. The eugenicists used this communication to urge an expansion of immigration restrictions. Victories in 1921 and 1924 had limited immigration from southern and eastern Europe, Asia, and Africa; however, these eugenicists wanted to expand restrictions even more, blocking immigration from other North American and South American nations because of the potential influx of Mexicans and other Latin Americans. The low point in Davenport's career came with the 1929 publication of *Race Crossing Jamaica,* which he co-authored with Morris Steggerda. In it, the two men attempted to use measures of body size, hair type, and skin color to demonstrate racial inferiority. Experts called his approach simplistic and criticized Davenport for failing to consider the effects of culture or environment in his efforts to prove a connection between race and intelligence.

Madison Grant, 1865–1937

Eugenicist

Madison Grant, chairman of the New York Zoological Society, was one of the foremost promoters of the idea that people of Nordic ancestry had superiority over all other races. A trustee of the American Museum of Natural History, Grant wrote *The Passing of the Great Race, or the Racial Basis of European History,* which had been published in 1916 but did not attract much attention until the postwar period. In it, Grant downplayed the impact of environment in shaping human lives and instead stressed the importance of heredity. Using that framework, he was a determined advocate of using eugenics to shape society, and he endorsed sterilization of people with mental problems. Grant described World War I as "a racial tragedy." He believed that loss of life had taken a greater toll on the "blond giant than on the little brunette" (Goldberg 1999, 153).

He defined Nordics as people from Scandinavia, northern Germany, England, Scotland, Ireland, Holland, Flanders, parts of northern France, and northern Poland. He believed the weak members of the population had been eliminated

Madison Grant, chairman of the New York Zoological Society, also was a leader among eugenicists who argued that those with Nordic ancestry were superior to other races. Adolf Hitler reportedly admired Grant's work. (Courtesy of the Save the Redwoods League)

from the Nordics by the harsh environment in which they evolved. To protect the human race, he believed that the gene pool should be regulated through a rigid system. He also favored segregation of races he considered inferior and confinement of these races to ghettoes. Born in New York, Grant was a lawyer and a conservationist as well as a eugenicist. His book was translated into several languages, including German. Nazi leader Adolf Hitler once wrote to Grant that the book was his Bible.

Horace Kallen, 1882–1974

Proponent of Cultural Pluralism

Widely recognized in the social science community as the man who invented the term "cultural pluralism," Horace Kallen became one of the leading proponents of respect for the native cultures of immigrants. Kallen, a Jewish immigrant from Germany, defined cultural pluralism as the willingness to "allow for some degree of cultural diversity within the confines of a unified national experience." Rather than embracing the traditional view of a melting pot that transforms all immigrants into Americans who are palatable to the dominant culture, he opposed efforts to make immigrants conform to the behavior of the majority. As the son of an Orthodox rabbi, Kallen promoted a strong American Jewish identity, and he worked alongside fellow intellectual and literary critic Lionel Trilling in a study of American culture and the Jewish community's place in that culture.

In 1924, he published *Culture and Democracy,* an argument against pressure to eliminate the immigrants' own beliefs and traditions. Rather than being a single culture adopted by all immigrants, Kallen contended that "'American Civilization' may come to mean the perfection of the cooperative harmonies of 'European Civilization' . . . an orchestration of mankind" (Kallen 1924, 124). Each unique ethnic group was important to the richness of American culture, he argued, but he did recognize the existence of a dominant population group whose cultural behavior would have the greatest effect on the national culture. Kallen received his Ph.D. in philosophy at Harvard University under the tutelage of

William James and was classified as a pragmatist. In the late 19th century, James and others founded this wing of philosophy, which concluded that the meaning of a concept can be determined by observation of its consequences. As a professor, Kallen worked at the University of Wisconsin and the New School for Social Research. He devoted much of his life to the promotion of cultural pluralism. His last book, *Liberty, Laughter and Tears,* was published in 1968—44 years after his first. Later writers have criticized Kallen's failure in the 1920s to incorporate African Americans into his vision of cultural pluralism.

Robert Lynd, 1892–1970, and Helen Lynd, 1896–1982

Sociologists

Helen and Robert Lynd were a husband-and-wife team of sociologists who set out on a unique venture in the 1920s. As the decade began, Robert Lynd gave up a career in publishing and enrolled in the Union Theological Seminary in New York. He also participated in Columbia University courses taught by education pioneer John Dewey and economist Wesley Mitchell. One summer he undertook a church mission in a depressed Wyoming oil town called Elk Basin. Based on several articles he wrote about that community, he earned a grant to investigate and analyze the status of religion in an American small town.

This opportunity led Robert and his wife, Helen, to Muncie, Indiana, in 1924. Once they had begun gathering data for the research, the Lynds decided that they did not want to confine their study to religion. Giving up ties to their sponsor, the Lynds worked independently to produce *Middletown: A Study in Contemporary American Culture,* which was published in 1929. Helen Lynd acted as her husband's assistant on the Middletown project. She also taught at the Lincoln School in New York from 1926 to 1928. In 1929, she became a professor at Sarah Lawrence College, which was new at that time. She was one of the guiding forces in determining the college's curriculum.

Along with his wife, Helen, Robert Lynd created a classic sociological study in the 1929 book Middletown: A Study in Contemporary American Culture. *The Lynds' conclusions were based on an in-depth study of everyday life in Muncie, Indiana. (Library of Congress)*

G. Bromley Oxnam, 1891–1963

Los Angeles Pastor Who Aided Immigrants

As a minister in Los Angeles, G. Bromley Oxham sought to use social assistance to guide the city's immigrants toward assimilation with the dominant culture. In an article for *The Annals of the American Academy,* he wrote that the Mexican laborer "presents a compelling social challenge constituting at once the most serious foreign problem in Los Angeles and the city's largest Americanization opportunity" (Oxnam 1921, 130). Oxnam, pastor of the Church of All Nations, identified adult illiteracy, poor living conditions, widespread disease, and juvenile delinquency as qualities of the Mexican community that required reformation by the city's Protestant churches. Unlike some white leaders, Oxnam favored giving immigrants citizenship; in fact, he criticized Mexican workers who failed to seek it. He argued that Americanization would provide the Mexicans with new opportunities and with the ambition to enjoy a more prosperous life. Rather than seeing Americanization as a tool for controlling minorities, he considered it a weapon for reform.

As the 1920s began, Oxnam saw many opportunities for church involvement in the Mexican community. Various Protestant organizations reached out to immigrants in Los Angeles during the 1920s, but Oxnam's efforts were among the strongest. Financed by the Methodist Church, his crusade sprang from an honest desire to help the newcomers. After a disastrous run for the city's board of education in 1923, which put him at odds with more conservative Americanization groups, Oxnam continued to promote a progressive form of Americanism that would look out for minorities, whether they were children in the workforce or Mexicans trying to navigate the city's culture. However, he also faced a continuing battle to overcome his opponents' ongoing attempts to label him as a leftist. Late in life, he achieved the rank of bishop within the Methodist Church.

Takao Ozawa, 1875–?

Alien Refused Citizenship

Takao Ozawa contested the Naturalization Act of 1790, which declared that only "free white persons" were eligible for United States citizenship. The harshness of this law affected Japanese immigrants in California very deeply because the 1913 and 1920 California Alien Land Laws made it impossible for "aliens ineligible to citizenship" to own or lease land. Because many Japanese immigrants were tenant farmers, these laws eradicated their hopes for a future in the United States. Ozawa immigrated to the United States from Japan as a child. He spent his youth in California and attended the University of California at Berkeley. He later moved to Honolulu, Hawaii, which was then a United States territory. He worked for an American company there, married, and had children.

In his court battle, Ozawa argued that he was an assimilated American: "I neither drink liquor of any kind, nor smoke, nor play cards, nor gamble, nor associate with any improper person. My honesty and industriousness are well known among my Japanese and American acquaintances and friends; and I am always trying my best to conduct myself according to the Golden Rule. . . . In name, General Benedict Arnold was an American, but at heart, he was a traitor. In name, I am not an American, but at heart I am a true American" (Teel 2006). Ozawa was proud that he spoke English instead of Japanese and that he was a Christian. He simply sought the same status for himself that his children already enjoyed.

His attorney suggested that the term "free white" in the Naturalization Act had been intended to rule out immigrants of African descent and that everyone else was to be considered as white. (Native-born African Americans were made citizens in post–Civil War legislation.) However, the U.S. District Court in Hawaii rejected his plea. The case reached the U.S. Supreme Court in 1922, where a unanimous decision concluded that Ozawa was not eligible for U.S. citizenship because he was Mongolian, not Caucasian. A year later, the court upheld state laws in California and Washington that ruled out the possibility of land ownership for people ineligible for citizenship.

REFERENCES AND FURTHER READINGS

Baritz, Loren. 1960. *The Servants of Power.* Westport, CT: Greenwood Press.

Carter, Paul Allen. 1975. *The Twenties in America.* 2nd ed. Wheeling, IL: Harlan Davidson.

Chritchlow, Donald T. 1992. "Keeping the Life Stream Pure." *Reviews in American History* 20 (3): 343–349.

Cravens, Hamilton. 1985. "History of Social Sciences." *Osiris,* 2nd series, 1:183–207.

Davis, Mike. 2001. "Sunshine and the Open Shop: Ford and Darwin in 1920s Los Angeles." In *Metropolis in the Making: Los Angeles in the 1920s,* edited by Tom Sitton and William Deverell, 96–122. Berkeley: University of California Press.

Deverell, William. 2001. "My America or Yours: Americanization and the Battle for the Youth of Los Angeles." In *Metropolis in the Making: Los Angeles in the 1920s,* edited by Tom Sitton and William Deverell, 277–301. Berkeley: University of California Press.

Dorr, Gregory Michael. 2000. "Assuring America's Place in the Sun: Ivey Foreman Lewis and the Teaching of Eugenics at the University of Virginia, 1915–1953." *Journal of Southern History* 66 (2): 257–296.

Dorr, Lisa Lindquist. 1999. "Arm in Arm: Gender, Eugenics, and Virginia's Racial Integrity Acts of the 1920s." *Journal of Women's History* 11 (1): 143–166.

Dumenil, Lynn. 1995. *The Modern Temper: American Culture and Society in the 1920s.* New York: Hill and Wang.

Ellis Island Records. http://www.ellisislandimmigrants.org (accessed December 8, 2006).

Geospatial & Statistical Data Center. http://lewis.lib.virginia.edu (accessed June 30, 2006).

Gibson, Campbell J., and Emily Lennon. "Historical Statistics of the Foreign-Born Population of the United States: 1850–1990, Population Division Working Paper No. 29." U.S. Census Bureau. www.census.gov/population/www/documentation/twps0029/twps0029.html (accessed December 8, 2006).

Gerstle, Gary. 1997. "Liberty, Coercion, and the Making of Americans." *Journal of American History* 84 (2): 524–558.

Gibson, Campbell. 1992. "The Contribution of Immigration to the Growth and Ethnic Diversity of the American Population." *Proceedings of the American Philosophical Society* 136 (2): 157–175.

Glass, Bentley, and Curt Stern. 1986. "Geneticists Embattled: Their Stand against Rampant Eugenics and Racism in America during the 1920s and 1930s." *Proceedings of the American Philosophical Society* 130 (1): 130–154.

Goldberg, David. 1999. *Discontented America: The United States in the 1920s.* Baltimore: Johns Hopkins University Press.

Graham, Otis L., Jr., and Elizabeth Koed. 1993. "Americanizing the Immigrant, Past and Future: History and Implications of a Social Movement." *Public Historian* 15 (4): 24–49.

Hellwig, David J. 1981. "Black Leaders and United States Immigration Policy, 1917–1929." *Journal of Negro History* 66 (2): 110–127.

Hise, Greg. 2001. "Industry and Imaginative Geographies." In *Metropolis in the Making: Los Angeles in the 1920s,* edited by Tom Sitton and William Deverell, 13–44. Berkeley: University of California Press.

Historical Statistics of the United States: Colonial Times to 1970. 1975. Washington, D.C.: Department of Commerce. http://www2.census.gov/prod2/statcomp/documents/CT1970p1–01.pdf (accessed June 30, 2006).

Kallen, Horace. 1924. *Culture and Democracy in the United States.* New York: Boni and Liveright.

Larson, Edward J. 1995a. "'In the Finest, Most Womanly Way': Women in the Southern Eugenics Movement." *American Journal of Legal History* 39 (2): 119–147.

Larson, Edward J. 1995b. *Sex, Race, and Science.* Baltimore: Johns Hopkins University Press.

Leinwand, Gerald. 2001. *1927: High Tide of the Twenties*. New York: Four Walls Eight Windows.

Leon, Sharon M. 2004. "Hopelessly Entangled in Nordic Pre-suppositions: Catholic Participation in the American Eugenics Society in the 1920s." *Journal of the History of Medicine and Allied Sciences* 59 (1): 3–49.

Miller, Nathan. 2003. *New World Coming: The 1920s and the Making of Modern America*. New York: Scribner.

Monroy, Douglas. 1983. "Like Swallows at the Old Mission: Mexicans and the Racial Politics of Growth in Los Angeles in the Interwar Period." *Western Historical Quarterly* 14 (4): 435–458.

Monroy, Douglas. 2001. "Making Mexico in Los Angeles." *Metropolis in the Making: Los Angeles in the 1920s,* edited by Tom Sitton and William Deverell, 161–178. Berkeley: University of California Press.

Ngai, Mae M. 1999. "The Architecture of Race in American Immigration Law: A Reexamination of the Immigration Act of 1924." *Journal of American History* 86 (1): 67–92.

Noggle, Burl. 1966. "The Twenties: A New Historiographical Frontier." *Journal of American History* 53 (2): 299–314.

Ordover, Nancy. 2004. *American Eugenics*. Minneapolis: University of Minnesota Press.

Oxnam, G. Bromley. 1921. "The Mexican in Los Angeles from the Standpoint of the Religious Forces of the City." *Annals of the American Academy of Political and Social Science* 93 (January): 130–133.

Oyez. http://www.oyez.org (accessed December 8, 2006).

Parrish, Michael E. 1992. *Anxious Decades: America in Prosperity and Depression, 1920–1941*. New York: W. W. Norton & Co.

Reilly, Philip R. 1991. *The Surgical Solution*. Baltimore: Johns Hopkins University Press.

Soloway, Richard A. 1995. "The 'Perfect Contraceptive': Eugenics and Birth Control Research in Britain and America in the Interwar Years." *Journal of Contemporary History* 30 (4): 637–664.

Stephens, William Dennison. 1920. "The Governor of California on the 'Oriental Problem,' 1920." In *Major Problems in American History, 1920–1945,* edited by Colin Gordon, 153–154. New York: Houghton Mifflin Company.

Suzuki, Masao. 1995. "Success Story? Japanese Immigrant Economic Achievement and Return Migration, 1920–1930." *Journal of Economic History* 55 (4): 889–901.

Teel, Steven C. "Lessons on Judicial Interpretation: How Immigrants Takao Ozawa and Yick Wo Searched the Courts for a Place in America." Organization of

American Historians Website. http://www.oah.org/pubs/magazine/judicial/
teel.html (accessed December 8, 2006).

Tygiel, Jules. 2001. "Metropolis in the Making: Los Angeles in the 1920s." In *Metropolis in the Making: Los Angeles in the 1920s,* edited by Tom Sitton and William Deverell, 1–10. Berkeley: University of California Press.

Willrich, Michael. 1998. "The Two Percent Solution: Eugenic Jurisprudence and the Socialization of American Law, 1900–1930." *Law and History Review* 16 (1): 63–111.

Modernity and
Social Movements

Overview

The conservative climate of the 1920s played a significant role in shaping the social movements of the decade. In many ways, these movements reflected a backlash against the progressive impulse of the first two decades of the 20th century. Postwar prosperity helped usher in this conservative drift, but other factors were at play as well. The progressives strove to reform American society to protect consumers, the working classes, and the disadvantaged. It was a program that sought to create a more perfect society free of social ills and strife. That progressivism failed to deliver on these goals ensured some measure of retreat from reform; that, in the eyes of many Americans, conditions in the country actually deteriorated during the period guaranteed not just a retreat but a complete about-face. Conservative Americans also found themselves pitted against forces of modernism that threatened their vision of America. Modernists questioned many of the underlying assumptions of American society. They proposed changes in art, literature, and social mores that forced conservatives into a staunch defense of tradition that embraced religion and nativist appeals to bigotry. The bitterness of this struggle between modernists advocating change as progress and conservatives defending social traditions they viewed as representative of America made adoption of a middle ground very difficult. In many cases (evolution versus creationism, for example) reconciliation proved simply impossible. Attitudes and actions hardened as both sides came to believe they were fighting over the future course of the country. Although the traditionalists

283

eventually faltered in most of their efforts to defend an older vision of America, during the 1920s they proved remarkably resilient. The modernists may have later won the war, but the defenders of tradition won the battle during the Republican Decade.

World War I loomed large in this retreat from forward-thinking progressivism. The brutality and destruction of the conflict shattered the illusion of social progress for many. For those already wavering over the notion of progressive assistance to the underclasses, the war brought home the notion that the veneer of law and reason were very thin indeed, and if stripped away, man's barbarity quickly emerged. The wartime inflation and governmental regulation of American society also became linked with Wilson and the Progressives. A postwar economic slump and concerns over radical unrest served only to further undercut the support of the reform element. Concerned Americans began to believe that the freedoms (or, as they might have put it, mollycoddling) afforded by the liberal reforms of the Progressive Era might offer free reign to the less desirable elements of American society. The war helped nurture these sentiments in two ways: by creating prosperity and racism.

During the war, the Wilson administration hoped to bolster prowar sentiment through utilization of a massive propaganda machine. One aspect of this effort involved painting Germans as ungodly butchers bent on pillaging western Europe. This campaign led to an anti-German sentiment in the United States that reached absurd proportions. For example, the teaching of the German language and the works of German philosophers disappeared from schools and universities. The effectiveness of this propaganda proved to have lasting consequences. By giving discrimination against an alien enemy the imprimatur of the federal government, Wilson helped promote a rabidly nationalistic xenophobia that propelled both the Red Scare and the conservative social movements of the 1920s.

This racist sentiment became the foundation for a nativist sentiment typically referred to as "100 percent Americanism." These nativists embraced the notion that the only true Americans were native-born, white Protestants. Furthermore, they viewed the millions of Southern and Eastern European immigrants who entered the country during the prewar period as potential disrupters of traditional American society. The nativists believed these immigrants (who were swarthy, clannish, and overwhelmingly Catholic or Jewish) flooded into America's cities and converted urban areas into cesspools of crime, filth, and debauchery. Progressive reform, by this logic, not only encouraged these people to immigrate but also gave them ability to engage in immoral behavior after arrival. Nativists also recognized the growing significance of cities in America and determined that the power of these ethnic ghettos needed curbing. The prosperity of the 1920s helped move the country in general, as economic stability always does, toward a more conservative political climate, and it also gave more Americans the free time and income to engage in social movements. Conservative Americans found themselves challenged by the forces of modernism, and they reacted with a vengeance.

The social movements of the 1920s, therefore, possessed a fundamentally conservative nature starkly different from those of the previous decade. The progressive sentiment, however, did not completely disappear. Last vestiges of the reform movement continued to fight for liberal causes but with greatly reduced success. The final achievements of the progressive movement, in an ironic twist, hinged upon working with those with nativist dispositions. For very different reasons, "100 percent Americans" contributed to the drives that succeeded in ratifying the 18th (Prohibition) and 19th (women's suffrage) amendments to the Constitution that completed the cluster of "progressive amendments." For progressives, Prohibition meant an improvement in the quality of lives for working-class women, children, and families who long suffered from the violence and poverty associated with heavy drinking by industrial workers. Nativists saw this as a means of reducing the social vices associated with "demon rum" and the wine-loving immigrants from Southern Europe. Progressives argued that women's suffrage naturally flowed from American principles of equality and democracy. For "100 percent Americans," universal suffrage meant adding millions of old stock women to the voting rolls, women who they assumed would support conservative legislation to keep aliens and their "un-American" lifestyles at bay.

By the early 1920s, even the residual aspects of progressivism fell away. The United States developed an overwhelmingly conservative and xenophobic political culture that simply strove to eliminate the threat of "un-Americans," whom they often connected with modernism. This nativist climate spawned the most notorious social movement of the decade: the new Ku Klux Klan. The Klan exemplified "100 percent Americanism." They reviled Catholics, Jews, African Americans, immigrants, liberals, labor leaders, and advocates of all forms of modernism. With millions of members across the country, the Klan became a social and political force that helped shape politics at all levels. Their strength proved great enough to propel state legislatures toward restrictive legislation and moved the U.S. Congress to pass a series of acts curtailing immigration. The Klan's own internal problems destroyed the organization at the end of the decade but not before the hooded order left its mark on the nation.

The Klan promoted a traditional Christianity (although many members failed to live up to its tenets) that reflected a larger religious battle in the country. The same concerns about a dying American way of life also drove a movement toward "old time" fundamentalist Christianity. The fundamentalists struggled with theological modernists throughout the decade in a battle for the soul of American Protestantism. While a deep strain of anti-Catholic sentiment pervaded the fundamentalist camp (and could be found among more moderate Protestants as well), the Klan directed most of their ire at the social vices and secularism fundamentalists associated with modernism. Chief among the secular threats stood evolutionary theory. For fundamentalists, evolution stuck at the very core of their beliefs: the exalted status of humanity and the Bible's infallibility. The strength of conservative Protestantism pushed several states to pass legislation banning the teaching of evolution in public schools. Tennessee's antievolution law, the Butler Act, spawned a legal challenge that became the Scopes Monkey Trial. The Scopes trial brought the fundamentalist–modernist struggle to a boil and became a national sensation. It perfectly encapsulated the social movements of the decade in which (perceived) traditional American ways clashed with the forces shaping a very different, modern nation.

TIMELINE

1920   The 19th Amendment is ratified.

National American Woman Suffrage Association converts into the League of Women Voters.

The Volstead Act is passed.

Al Capone arrives in Chicago.

1921   The Sheppard–Towner Act, which provided funds for rural prenatal and child care, is passed.

E. C. Yellowly becomes chief of special Prohibition agents.

KDKA begins regular broadcasting of religious programs.

First KKK chapter is established in Indiana in March.

1922   Hiram Evans succeeds William J. Simmons as Imperial Wizard of the KKK in November.

The Cable Act, which removed citizenship restrictions for women married to non-American citizens, is passed.

1923   D. C. Stephenson is appointed Grand Dragon of the KKK.

Aimee Semple McPherson's Angelus Temple opens in January.

1924   The National Origins Act is passed.

Nellie Tayloe Ross and Miriam Ferguson become first female governors in American history.

Simmons settles his lawsuit with Evans.

1925   Tennessee legislature passes the Butler Act.

Stephenson is convicted of murder.

Scopes "Monkey Trial" takes place in July.

William Jennings Bryan dies in July.

The Equal Rights Amendment fails in Congress.

Carrie Chapman Catt establishes the Committee on the Cause and Cure of War.

Bruce Barton's *The Man Nobody Knows* is published.

1926   "Sweet Daddy" Grace establishes the United House of Prayer for All People.

McPherson is "kidnapped" in May.

1927   Beginning in September, Stephenson helps destroy the KKK by publicizing organization's links to political corruption in Indiana.

Tennessee Supreme Court rules in favor of John Scopes on appeal in January.

1929   Saint Valentine's Day Massacre in Chicago.

Dry: Living with Prohibition

Political and Social Issues

During the early 19th century, alcohol consumption, viewed as an essential aspect of socialization and the workday by most Americans, came under fire as a disruptive influence on American society. Buoyed by the vast reform activism and renewed religious fervor of the period, the earliest exponents of temperance emerged. By the middle of the century, the moderate stance of the early temperance advocates had hardened into a position that advocated total abstinence ("teetotalism"). This stance developed from concerns over the rapidly growing population of American cities, which were increasingly viewed as dens of sinful behavior, and dramatic demographic shifts. For temperance reformers, the beer-loving German and whiskey-swilling Irish immigrants who flooded the county midcentury seemed to propel a decline of morality, religion, and social order. These concerns led to 13 states passing stringent temperance legislation during the 1850s. Most of these states repealed their prohibition laws during the next decade, and the federal government encouraged such moves to help generate "sin tax" revenue during the Civil War, but the successes of the early temperance advocates served as a shining example for later advocates.

After the Civil War, the temperance movement regrouped as both a political and social movement. A formal Prohibition Party ran presidential and local candidates with limited success, but the establishment of the Woman's Christian

New York City deputy police commissioner John A. Leach, right, watches agents pour liquor into the sewer following a raid during the height of Prohibition, ca. 1921. (Library of Congress)

Temperance Union (WCTU) in 1874 dramatically aided the movement. The WCTU engaged in grassroots organization that combined moral suasion, formal ties to evangelical Christianity, and lobbying of politicians. Although some WCTU members viewed the organization as part of a larger women's rights movement, the Union was fundamentally conservative in its outlook. Prohibition for them was a moral issue that required political regulation, not an effort to establish women in the political hierarchy.

The sweeping reform sentiment of the Progressive Era proved to be the catalyst for a stronger prohibition movement. Progressives attacked political corruption, corporate mistreatment of the working classes, and a variety of social ills. Alcohol restrictions emerged as part of this program because of the number of social problems associated with "demon rum." For temperance-minded progressives, the lure of alcohol and the male-dominated social world of saloons led to a squandering of personal income by factory workers, criminal activity, immorality and prostitution, and fissures in the family unit caused by drunkenness. Significantly, the male-dominated Anti-Saloon League (ASL), which attacked the social and criminal aspects of alcohol and downplayed religious aspects of temperance, supplanted both the WCTU and the Prohibition Party in significance by the early 20th century. This approach made prohibition and regulation of alcohol more palatable to liberal progressives troubled by the Christian trappings of earlier temperance organizations.

The intersection of progressive and ASL actions helped usher in a new era of successful prohibition legislation. Most spectacularly, ASL lobbying efforts resulted in nine southern states, an area hostile to temperance initiatives during the 19th century, passing prohibition laws in the first two decades of the 20th century. In early 1913, ASL campaigning helped win passage of the Webb–Kenyon Act, which helped keep alcohol from being transported into dry states. Later that year the ASL leadership decided to focus their energies on passage of a prohibition amendment to the Constitution. They believed that some states would never go dry; hence constitutional coercion represented the only avenue to national prohibition. To launch the drive, Prohibition advocates organized a massive rally in Washington. Local law enforcement declared the crowd that assembled on the Capitol steps to be the largest gathering ever held there, save for inauguration days (Foster 2002, 194).

The success of the amendment campaign resulted from a number of political developments in the last half of the 1910s. First, progressivism became the nation's dominant political force during that decade, which helped a variety of reforms including alcohol regulation. Prohibition advocates also grew in number thanks to concerns over the possible social problems related to the influx of eastern and southern European immigrants. Reformers feared these immigrants, if given unrestricted access to alcohol, would serve only to exacerbate the social problems of American cities. Finally, World War I altered America in ways that virtually ensured the success of a Prohibition amendment. The war discredited all things German, and with German brewers traditionally the most vocal opponents of prohibition, alcohol (especially beer) came to be viewed as "un-American," if not downright treasonous. Wartime food restrictions also aided the ASL. They successfully lobbied Congress to shut down all breweries and distilleries so that grain could be diverted for the war effort. With the nation already virtually dry, Congress approved a Prohibition amendment in December 1917. The 18th Amendment became part of the Constitution in January 1919. To close loopholes in the amendment's language banning only "intoxicating" beverages, which left the door open for legislative interpretation, the Congress passed the Volstead Act which defined "intoxicating" as anything more than 0.5 percent alcohol. A few states attempted to circumvent the Volstead Act by passing less stringent legislation of their own, but in the National Prohibition Cases of 1920, the Supreme Court established the Volstead Act as supreme.

Enforcing Prohibition

Enforcement of Prohibition laws proved extremely difficult. The language of the legislation reflected the ambivalent feelings of many congressional members who voted for the regulations. The Volstead Act, for example, proved to be a spectacularly unwieldy piece of legislation. Strict in regard to punishments of violators, the legislation also reflected congressional concerns over privacy, religious freedom, and expense that made total enforcement of the law simply impossible. And while the federal government assumed primary responsibility for regulation, the 18th Amendment itself made the states concurrently responsible for enforcement of Prohibition. By relying on the states for significant enforcement responsibilities, the 18th Amendment and Volstead Act created situations in which state governments in wet areas could undercut the legislation by underfunding enforcement agencies. By the early 1930s, as Prohibition staggered toward repeal, 28 states had eliminated all Prohibition enforcement funding from their budgets.

The 3,600 agents of the Treasury Department's Prohibition Bureau (who were appointed on the basis of political considerations and were exempt from civil service requirements) were expected to prevent the importation of alcohol across thousands of miles of unguarded national borders, to shut down illegal saloons and distilleries, and to regulate those businesses and individuals with legal permission to produce or distribute alcohol. Given the era's concerns over the cost of government, the Prohibition Bureau, not surprisingly, found itself chronically underfunded. By one estimate, thorough enforcement required an annual outlay of $50 million, but Congressional appropriations never exceeded $10 million (and many years hovered around $5 million) (Pegram 1998, 158). Lack of funding resulted in low pay for agents, which resulted in widespread corruption within the Bureau. During Prohibition's first six years, one out of every 12 agents lost their job over illegal activity.

A series of exemptions embedded in the Volstead Act also countered total enforcement and compliance. Permits were granted for the production and distribution of sacramental wine and for the medicinal use of alcohol (although a subsequent law prevented doctors from prescribing beer to their patients). Production of industrial alcohol, required for the nation's growing chemical industry, grew dramatically during Prohibition. While the denaturing process made industrial alcohol undrinkable, law enforcement officials found it impossible to prevent some of this alcohol from being diverted before it was denatured, which undoubtedly contributed to the spike in production. Similarly, brewers were allowed to market "near beer" with an alcohol content of 0.5 percent, which could only be produced by brewing real beer and then removing the alcohol. This also opened opportunities for diversion prior to alcohol removal. Finally, the Volstead Act contained provisions protecting the possession and use of alcohol in private homes. The home brewing of wines and hard ciders offered thirsty

Americans legal avenues around Prohibition. And Congress prevented the search of private dwellings unless authorities could prove illegal liquor made in them had been sold, which only encouraged home production.

Home Brewing

With the Volstead Act's allowance of personal production of 200 gallons of alcohol a year, a new home-brewing industry emerged. The ease with which citizens could produce their own homemade intoxicants had not been expected by either the ASL or the crafters of antialcohol legislation, hence the lenient provisions governing home production. Stores selling the equipment required for home brewing and distilling opened in almost every American city. Because they did not sell alcohol, the stores did not violate Prohibition. Malt tonic, which New York congressman Fiorello LaGuardia promoted as a flavor-adding additive to "near beer," corn sugar mash, and grape concentrate "bacchus bricks" became available in many neighborhood grocery stores (Burns 2004, 190–197). Home brewers, following readily available recipes, utilized kettles to distill pure grain alcohol, then mixed in various ingredients to approximate the flavor of traditional spirits. For example, mixing the pure grain alcohol with water, juniper oil, and glycerine produced "bathtub" gin. Not only was the process of making homemade alcohol simple, it was also inexpensive. The equipment required could be purchased for around $10.

Crime Wave

The passage of Prohibition legislation created a new avenue of criminal activity: bootlegging. Organized crime did not begin in the 1920s, but the drying of America gave it a significant boost. Previously, the activities of criminal gangs— prostitution, narcotics, and illegal gambling—fell beyond the pale of genteel society. With social drinking now a crime, respectable Americans now became potential customers for the criminal underworld. This led to a dramatic increase in the profits to be made from illegal, alcohol-related activities. Bootleggers bribed police and public officials, which caused public alarm, but it was their bloody turf wars (that occasionally caught innocent bystanders in the crossfire) that created fear of a Prohibition crime wave. Events such as the 1929 "Saint Valentine's Day Massacre," in which members of Al Capone's gang dressed as cops gunned down seven members of Bugsy Moran's rival gang, stirred a cauldron of anxiety that led some to question the benefits of Prohibition for American society.

While some criminal organizations distributed home-brewed alcohol to their clients, booze smuggled into the country offered a larger profit. Wealthier Americans willingly paid dramatically inflated prices for professionally produced spirits, and with the prosperity of the decade, more Americans possessed the means to do so than in previous generations. Bootlegging gangs utilized convoys of trucks to bring liquor into the country via back roads along the Canadian and Mexican borders. "Rum rows" of alcohol-laden ships lined parts of the coasts. Seagoing ships dropped anchor in international waters and then speed boats ferried the booze to the shore. Out-manned, out-gunned, and out-horsepowered, the U.S. Coast Guard could do little to stanch the flow. Rum-running did not constitute the most significant means of distributing illegal alcohol during Prohibition, but it represented "the most romantic" method (Parrish 1992, 100). When the Treasury Department admitted to seizing only about 5 percent of all the alcohol smuggled into the country, the staggering level of Prohibition-related crime—and the futility of law enforcement efforts—came into sharp relief for disquieted Americans.

Despite the cool-headed pronouncements of statisticians that the murder rate steadily climbed from the beginning of the 20th century, with the greatest increase occurring before the enacting of Prohibition, the bloody and well-publicized of actions of criminal gangs during the 1920s created a public impression of Prohibition-fueled lawlessness. Sensationalized newspaper accounts of the period often greatly exaggerated the actual level of bloodshed, making exact figures difficult to ascertain, but thousands certainly did die as a result of organized criminal behavior. Opponents of Prohibition also pointed out that undisciplined Prohibition Bureau agents often engaged in unnecessary gun battles that resulted in the loss of civilian life. The federal government acknowledged some 300 agents and civilians killed. In response, the Association Against the Prohibition Amendment (AAPA) issued the highly critical pamphlet *Reforming America with a Shotgun*. Although Prohibition advocates became deeply troubled by the murders and blamed organized crime for undercutting support for Prohibition, they also began to criticize the bootlegging gangs' customers—middle-class Americans for whom public drinking became a new form of entertainment.

Speakeasies

Despite the closure of America's saloons in January 1920, outlets for public drinking proved available in all American cities. The underfunding of federal agents, leniency by city governments, and outright political corruption helped an illegal drinking underground to flourish. While some of these establishments distilled their own alcohol, most purchased their booze from the criminal bootlegging gangs. Many were actually owned by organized crime figures. Middle- and upper-class patrons, therefore, contributed greatly to the success of criminal activity in the country, a point Capone made repeatedly (Burns 2004, 197). The profitability of providing illicit alcohol to the well-heeled led to the opening of more than 30,000 illegal dispensaries in New York City alone, with an estimated 219,000 across the country.

Dubbed speakeasies, these new public watering holes created a new form of amusement in stark contrast to the male-dominated saloons of old. The speakeasies often served quality meals and offered music and dancing that made them amenable to male and female customers. They benefitted not only from Prohibition, which shut down the saloons and drove up liquor prices, but also from new patterns of socialization and dating. During this period, motion pictures, radio, and automobiles dramatically changed dating patterns in the United States. Visiting a "speak" became part of this new method of courtship, particularly among the college-aged. Unlike pre-Prohibition saloons, where the only women present were likely to be prostitutes, both sexes came to view the public conviviality of the speakeasy as an environment both respectable and gender-neutral. According to Catherine Gilbert Murdock, women of the 1920s viewed entrance into speakeasies, as with voting, as part of a larger dissolution of the male sphere. The speakeasies of the 1920s, meeting places of the fun-loving and single of both sexes, became the models for post-repeal nightclubs.

Flapper hides a flask in her boot, Washington, D.C., 1922. The speakeasies of Prohibition brought women into the sphere of public consumption for the first time. (Library of Congress)

The "speaks" also permanently changed what respectable Americans drank in public. During the pre-Prohibition period, male-dominated saloons primarily served beer and straight liquor. Mixed drinks, in this macho milieu, appeared effete. With Prohibition, the cocktail, previously found only in up-scale establishments and cabarets, became ubiquitous. This alteration partly reflected the influx into speakeasies, of women who might prefer more flavorful drinks as part of their introduction into the world of public consumption. Mixed drinks also helped mask the foulness of cut-rate liquor. Perhaps more importantly, the drinking of cocktails made the speakeasy experience appear more cosmopolitan (a term that, not surprisingly, became the name of a popular cocktail); they linked the behavior of middle-class Americans to the carefree conspicuous consumption of the wealthy. As one historian noted, the cocktail "became a sign of economic distinction" (Burnham 1993, 63).

Repealing the "Noble Experiment"

By the end of the decade, only the most hardened dry advocates continued to believe in what Herbert Hoover dubbed the "noble experiment." Most Americans witnessed the corruption, crime, murder, decreased respect of authority and laws, and lax enforcement and concluded that Prohibition hurt the nation more than it improved it. The loss of middle-class support proved most decisive. This group helped propel the creation of several national anti-Prohibition groups, which were often supported by wealthy benefactors. Additionally, prominent business and professional organizations, including the American Bar Association, joined the crusade for repeal of the 18th Amendment. Led by the half-million member strong AAPA, the drive to alter the Constitution geared up in 1928. Despite Herbert Hoover's pledge that year to step up enforcement, the repeal advocates continued to gain momentum. A 1931 federal commission's report of Prohibition's failures served to speed up the process. The next year, Franklin Roosevelt made repeal part of his presidential platform. On December 5, 1933, Utah became the 36th state to ratify the 21st Amendment to the Constitution, which officially repealed national Prohibition.

Although popular mythology paints Prohibition as a widely violated failure, the reality is more complex. If viewed as a righteous crusade to completely eliminate alcohol as a social problem in the United States, a goal many proponents hoped to achieve, Prohibition did certainly fail. However, from the more circumspect and limited perspective of curbing alcohol-related excess, the Prohibition movement achieved some of its goals. Working-class drinking, because of increased prices and reduced opportunities, did decline during the 1920s. And the saloon culture viewed as the home of so many social ills never recovered from Prohibition. Even after repeal, regulation of public drinking establishments became tighter, which reduced prostitution, violence, and youth drinking in bars. Most significantly, Prohibition resulted in an overall decline in alcohol consumption, not just during the 18th Amendment period but also after. Not until the 1970s did the United States achieve per capita consumption rates equal to those pre-Prohibition.

THE SECOND KU KLUX KLAN IN THE 1920S

Causes

The 1915 premiere of D. W. Griffith's landmark film *The Birth of a Nation* (based on the novel *The Clansman* by Thomas Dixon) demonstrated that motion pictures could truly be considered a new art form. In addition, the film spurred former minister William J. Simmons to focus his fixation on the Old South on the Reconstruction-era white supremacy group the Ku Klux Klan. In the film, the

Klan represented Southern knights protecting white womanhood and traditional values. For Simmons, this notion struck a responsive chord. Troubled by a United States undergoing rapid demographic, cultural, and ethnographic changes, Simmons saw the re-creation of the Klan as a means of stanching the flow of forces he perceived as eroding the genteel tradition. Simmons perceived his Klan (often referred to as the "New" or "Second" Klan) as a protector of traditional American values under siege from groups far more threatening than just African Americans. Simmons, as with other nativists, believed the rural, Protestant majority that shaped American society in the 19th century appeared unable to protect their lifestyle from the corrosive elements found in America's increasingly significant urban areas. To thwart this threat, Simmons declared the rebirth of the Klan at a cross-burning rally atop Stone Mountain in Georgia in November 1915.

The 1860s Klan organized as a Southern response to Northern efforts aimed at establishing former slaves as integral players in the South's economic and political life. Unlike the original Klan, Simmons' Klan feared more than just African Americans. The "New" Klan found

Ku Klux Klan members attend an initiation ceremony in Baltimore, Maryland, in 1923. The Klan of the 1920s tried to restrict the influence of immigrants, Catholics, African Americans, and left-wing radicals— groups the organization viewed as "un-American." Klan members dressed in white robes and hoods to conceal their true identities. (The Illustrated London News Picture Library)

threats in the large numbers of Catholic immigrants who arrived in the early 20th century, Jews, the promiscuous popular culture, secularism, city-dwellers, trade unionists, and Communists. With its greatest strength in rural areas of the South, Midwest, and far West, the Klan reflected the concerns of small-town Americans unable to cope or keep up with the dizzying changes occurring in the cities. For the earliest Klansmen, their organization seemed the last line of defense against the destruction of their—in Robert Wiebe's famous phrase— autonomous "island communities." This destruction stemmed from the view that the new immigrants of the late 19th and early 20th centuries represented an unassimilable wave of swarthy, clannish, and Catholic Southern and Eastern Europeans. These immigrants landed in American cities and stayed in urban areas to provide inexpensive labor in dangerous industrial plants. Unlike prior immigrant

Table 6.1. Distribution of Ku Klux Klan Membership by Geographical Region (percent)

Region	1922	1924
North central (IN, OH, IL)	6.4	40.2
Southwest (TX, OK, AR, LA, NM, AZ)	61.0	25.6
South (includes KY, WV)	22.2	16.1
Midwest (MN, IA, NE, KS, MO, MI, ND)	5.0	8.3
West (OR, CA, ID, UT, WA, CO, WY)	5.1	6.1
North Atlantic (NY, DE, NJ, PA, MD, CT, MA, ME, VT, NH, RI)	0.3	3.7

Source: Adapted from Jackson 1967, 15.

groups, such as the Irish, who dispersed west or integrated themselves into traditional American society, the new immigrants established ethnic neighborhoods in American cities that, thanks to the discrimination toward and low wages of their residents, rapidly developed into urban slums. For nativist Americans, the growing significance of expansive urban areas, already seen as hothouses of immorality, caused alarm; for those cities to now swarm with non-English-speaking Catholics was cause for action.

Simmons's vision of a white, Anglo-Saxon Protestant America in need of defense benefited from the United States' involvement in World War I. The federal government promoted the war effort with a jingoistic patriotism that stressed "100 percent Americanism" and called into question anything that did not fit within this restrictive rubric. This campaign helped fuel anti-German sentiment during the war, an antiradicalism crusade in the war's immediate aftermath, and a xenophobic persuasion that achieved startling success during the 1920s. Chief among the beneficiaries of this propulsive nativist perspective stood the Ku Klux Klan.

Events

Klan Organization

Simmons's vision did not immediately translate into a national organization. By 1920, only approximately 5,000 members could be found in chapters located in Alabama and Georgia. Desperate to build a more significant movement, Simmons turned over business operations to Edward Clark and Elizabeth Tyler of the Southern Publicity Association. Clark and Tyler possessed a great deal of promotional experience, having previously worked as publicists for the YMCA and the Red Cross. They brought modern promotional techniques to the Klan that paid immediate dividends. Clark and Tyler developed a pyramid business structure that offered financial incentives to recruiters (known as Kleagles) of new members—a move that also directly benefited Clark and Tyler. The two promoters also propelled the organization's growth by enlarging its focus. They initially advanced the Klan as a Southern bulwark against the threat posed by the return of hundreds of thousands of African American veterans. When the feared race war failed to manifest, Clark and Tyler began to stress the Klan as a moral and conservative Christian organization. Under their guidance, the Klan began to more closely reflect the fraternal organization tradition that Simmons initially planned. The Klan became a vehicle for nativist Americans to gather and establish social communities based upon their image of America. Clark and Tyler oriented the Klan toward attacks on adulterers, prostitutes, Prohibition violators, and other immoral groups, with an undergirding hatred of immigrants and minorities. To help promote this vision, Klan auxiliaries were established for white Protestant women and children. The result of this campaign was a Klan that flourished throughout the South and Southwest.

The violent actions of Southern Klansmen spurred a series of exposés in Northern newspapers, most significantly a cluster of *New York World* articles in September 1921. These reports resulted in a House of Representatives investigation of the KKK. Thanks in large part to a dramatic and tearful testimony by Simmons, the House investigation fizzled in October 1921. Moreover, the publicity the Klan gained by this national attention allowed the organization to spread its tentacles into the North. During 1922, a massive Klan publicity campaign spurred phenomenal growth in Northern states (particularly the conservative Midwest). By 1924, 40 percent of the Klan's members could be found in Ohio, Illinois, and Indiana.

As an organization that stressed morality and conservative values, the Klan leadership needed to be above reproach. The inability to find quality leaders eventually helped destroy the organization, but in the early 1920s, internal upheavals within the Klan resulted in a reorganization that brought a true believer with grand ideas to power. In November 1922, Texas dentist Hiram Evans took control as the new Imperial Wizard of the Klan and expelled Clark, Tyler, and Simmons (all of whom had been involved in recent sex or alcohol scandals). Evans stressed the respectability of the Klan and promoted the notion of more active involvement in the political process to curb the pernicious effects of immigrants and the immoral. His vision brought the Klan to the pinnacle of its success during the 1920s.

Social Policy

Evans's campaign for respectability resulted in enormous growth in Klan numbers. By some estimates, Klan membership peaked at 5 million in the mid-1920s. Such remarkable numbers gave Evans a vehicle for his aspirations to affect the course of American politics. Education, law and order, and immigration reform loomed largest in Evans's political agenda. As the organization's official leader, Evans found himself able to shape the broad contours of the Klan's social/ political agenda (and he promoted these ideas through the Klan's national news-paper *Searchlight*), but the group's size, its diffusion across the country, and the relative autonomy of local chapters (Klaverns) hindered his ability to coordinate policy.

The result of this decentralization and localism was a disorganized program of local units promoting disparate elements of "100 percent American" reform measures. Fear of Catholicism in education, however, proved to be central to many of the Klan's reform campaigns. Across the country, Klan-backed school boards worked to oust Catholic schoolteachers from the public schools. In some states, Klan-influenced legislatures tried to fundamentally shape public educa-tion. In Ohio, the state legislature passed bills requiring daily Bible study in schools and made it illegal for Catholics to be employed by public school sys-tems. In Oregon, a referendum passed in 1922 that required all children between the ages of 8 and 16 to attend public schools. Such activity demonstrated the strength of the Klan but, conversely, also exposed the organization's weaknesses. In Ohio, the proposed legislation was vetoed by the governor because it vio-lated the separation of church and state. The Oregon law was ruled unconsti-tutional by the United States Supreme Court on the same grounds. The inability of Klan politicians to achieve promised goals eventually undercut national sup-port for the organization.

Despite the Klan's success at local and state levels, only a few Klansmen ever achieved national office. The U.S. Congress, therefore, never fell under Klan sway in the manner of the Indiana legis-lature. The small group of pro-Klan con-gressmen, however, did push the Klan's education and agenda at the federal level. A mid-decade attempt to create a cabinet-level Department of Education failed due to concerns over centrali-zation, but the Klan-led nativist move-ment succeeded in reducing the influx of Catholic immigrants. Beginning in 1921, the U.S. Congress maintained an emergency immigration law that curbed the number of Eastern and Southern Eu-ropean immigrants. Thanks to the "100 percent Americanism" campaign spear-headed by the Klan, Congress enacted the 1924 National Origins Act, which not only reduced the total number allowed to immigrate annually but also ensured

Ku Klux Klan members parade down Pennsylvania Avenue in Washington, D.C., in 1926. (Library of Congress)

The Klan in Indiana

The Klan found its greatest strength in the state of Indiana. Klan scholar Kenneth T. Jackson went so far as to dub the city of Indianapolis the "Center of Klandom" (Jackson 1967, 144). The Hoosier State achieved this level of significance largely due to the drive and desire of state Klan leader David Curtis Stephenson, who structured a remarkably large and well-ordered organization. An endorsement in the state organization's *Fiery Cross* newspaper could determine a politician's future. In 1924, Klan-backed candidates swept into office, winning control of the governorship and the state legislature.

The Klan's influence, however, did not translate to sweeping political change. The organization possessed the power to get candidates elected to office, but the blatant unconstitutionality of Klan social legislation doomed much of their program. Klan congressmen dutifully proposed legislation to require Bible studies in schools, to allow only public school graduates to work in public schools, to have public schools adopt Stephenson's manual *One Hundred Years of Health,* and to force parochial schools to use the same textbooks as their local public schools, but none of these measures became law. Their failure stemmed partly from the clearly unconstitutional nature of the legislation and partly from the divisiveness that befell the Indiana Klan.

D. C. Stephenson used his position as head of the state organization to become the most prominent Klansman in the country. His 1923 appointment to the position of Grand Dragon involved a rally in Kokomo's Melfalfa Park that brought 100,000 Klan members to the town. He parlayed the vast sums acquired from the organization to build a suburban mansion, a fleet of automobiles, and a yacht to entertain his girlfriends. His power proved to be a threat to the cohesion of the national Klan organization, and Stephenson and Evans became bitter rivals. The failure of Klan-inspired legislation directly resulted from this rivalry, as the elected supporters of the two leaders often voted against legislation proposed by the other faction.

Despite the Klan's public stance in favor of Prohibition, Stephenson also possessed a vast liquor cabinet, and only his political connections and power prevented his alcohol-fueled legal problems from becoming public. In 1925, however, Stephenson's flaunting of the law proved costly. On a train ride to Hammond, Indiana, he kidnapped and raped secretary Madge Oberholtzer, which led the distraught young woman to poison herself on the return trip to Indianapolis. Stephenson refused to take her to a physician until she was close to death. Before Oberholtzer died, she gave the police a full statement. The resulting trial shocked the public, left the Indiana Klan reeling, and resulted in a life sentence for Stephenson.

When Klansman governor Ed Jackson refused to pardon Stephenson, the Grand Dragon lashed back by informing authorities of the corruption within the state of Indiana. A number of state and local officials (including Jackson) found their careers ruined by the resultant publicity. But the primary victim of Stephenson's jailhouse confessions was the Indiana Klan. Already wracked by an internal power struggle between Stephenson and Evans, and then by various local leaders looking to replace Stephenson, by the end of the decade the once powerful organization dwindled to fewer than 5,000 members.

that British immigrants would predominate among those allowed into the country.

For the Klan, the restrictive immigration laws seemed to forebode a period in which the organization could wield enormous political power at the national level. To demonstrate their significance, the Klan staged a massive rally in Washington the next summer. The centerpiece of the rally was a parade of 40,000 hooded Klan members down Pennsylvania Avenue. Despite this chilling demonstration of strength, the Klan, buffeted by a number of factors, had already begun to decline in both numbers and influence.

Opposition to the Klan

Given their strident and restrictive notions of "100 percent Americanism," the rise of organized anti-Klan activity proved inevitable. A variety of individuals and groups, both secular and religious, from across the political spectrum responded to the Klan's rise by mobilizing opposition. Liberal defenders of civil liberties (and modernism) found the Klan to be a reactionary force that thwarted progress in this country. Civil rights organizations feared that the Klan, if left unchecked, would propel the establishment of Jim Crow laws across the country. Some opposition came from surprising sources. Thomas Dixon bitterly criticized the organization for claiming to be a successor of the original Klan, while American Legion posts assailed the Klan for denigrating the work of African American, Jewish, and Catholic soldiers during World War I.

American Catholics, however, proved to be the Klan's most problematic opponents. The American Church feared that Klan political strength, if left unchallenged, might threaten the very existence of the Catholicism in this country. Church leaders were particularly concerned about the Klan's threat to parochial schools. Several Catholic organizations sprang up to counter the Klan, but the most successful proved to be the American Unity League (AUL), headed by Irish-Americans. The AUL organized rallies that promoted the diversity of America and also published surreptitiously obtained Klan membership lists.

Catholic politicians and those with large Catholic constituencies found attacking the Klan a good way to maintain their political power. The mayors of Boston, New York, Chicago, and Cleveland all banned the Klan or barred the group from parading. Several state legislatures passed laws criminalizing the public wearing of hoods and masks, which prevented the Klan from recruiting those unwilling to be publicly associated with the organization. New York's legislature enacted the most stringent of these laws. The so-called Walker Bill not only banned the public wearing of hoods but also required all secret organizations to provide by-laws and membership lists to the secretary of state. The actions of state and municipal governments significantly hindered the Klan's growth in many of the country's urban areas. Also, because those cities with the largest

Catholic populations were often the ones the Klan could not enter, these actions made the Klan appear weak and unable to stand up to the organized power of American Catholicism and its allies.

Decline

Despite the Klan's enormous membership and political power, a rapid decline ensued. In part, outside forces mitigated the Klan's continued public role. Their militant nativist stance no longer appeared as necessary after restrictive immigration policies took effect, the power of Jim Crow in the South held, America's political radicals were driven underground, and the U.S. economy rebounded from its postwar slump. With an overall climate of political conservatism holding sway, the quasi-secret KKK no longer appeared necessary. For many nativist Americans, the defeat of Catholic presidential candidate Al Smith in 1928 signaled the victory of "100 percent Americanism" over the foreign menace.

These factors, however, did not automatically spell doom for the Klan. Internal issues, however, proved insurmountable. With recruiters paid by quantity, not quality, questionable individuals swelled the Klan's membership. The destructive public activities of these members hurt the Klan's reputation and troubled authorities concerned about the organization's lawlessness. Klan leadership posed an even more serious problem. Many of the group's leaders viewed the Klan as their own personal fiefdom, to be ruled and exploited at will. Enormous amounts of Klan funds eventually were embezzled and diverted, which led to increasing concern that the Klan itself was corrupt. Power struggles within state and local branches divided the Klan membership and weakened the organization.

This questionable leadership proved even more damaging by engaging in the sort of activities that the Klan publically decried. Dwight Stephenson's sensational trial certainly drew the most attention, but other Klan leaders undercut their state and local chapters through their involvement in sex scandals (Buffalo leader Rev. Charles Penfold, for example) or general patterns of lawlessness, a problem that plagued much of the Colorado branch. To many Americans sympathetic to the Klan's platform, the organization appeared to be engaging in the sort of "un-American" activities it originally combated.

Throughout the nation, state Klans faced similar decline as the 1920s drew to a close. Devoid of its former national prominence, the Klan retreated to the South, with small local organizations in the Midwest. The reduced Klan continued its traditional role as a defender of segregation and the racial status quo but found little success during the economic dislocation of the 1930s. With the development of the civil rights movement during the 1950s, the Klan once again gained membership and attention. Despite the well-publicized terrorist actions attributed to the group, the civil rights–era "Third" Klan never matched the size or significance of the Klan of the 1920s.

RELIGIONS NEW AND OLD

A Time of Tension

The 1920s marked a period of tension and anxiety for religious Americans of all types. Postwar prosperity created disposable incomes that propelled secular leisure activities often viewed as immoral. Scientific thought had broken with its traditional position as an explainer of God's cosmos and now openly challenged biblical teachings. Automobiles, telephones, feminism, and motion pictures threatened traditional standards of morality and gender roles. And America's cities—where, according to the 1920 census, most Americans now resided—appeared to be beacons of sin and crime that inexorably pulled young people toward temptation. In addition, religious Americans no longer found themselves able to offer a solid wall of defense against these challenges. Postwar efforts by liberal churchmen to unite American Protestants (an attempt exemplified by the abortive Interchurch World Movement) greatly angered conservatives. They viewed the relaxed standards and drift toward biblical interpretism required to achieve denominational unity as a veiled drive for modernism and apostasy. The faith of Americans fractured and turned in on itself as modernists battled with conservatives and old stock Protestants looked aghast at the waves of Catholics and Jews immigrating in the early 20th century.

The conservatives organized under the recently codified form of Protestantism known as fundamentalism. Despite their claims to represent "old time" religion, the fundamentalists adopted traditional ideas, but they transformed the shape of their faith by stressing particular beliefs. Central to the fundamentalist belief system were dispensationalism, premillennialism, and biblical inerrancy. They buttressed these ideas with criticism of modernism, evolution, and scientific theories that ran counter to biblical science. For the fundamentalists of this period, a conservative political, cultural, and gender stance also marked orthodoxy. The experience of World War I, which fundamentalists perceived as a battle between godly America and irreligious Germany, galvanized conservative Christians. In the war's aftermath, fundamentalists made a determined effort to unite against the forces of modernism arrayed against them.

The struggle by conservative Protestants to protect what they viewed as American values proved the most bitter fight. Despite the retreat of mainstream denominations from the Social Gospel and other reform activities, conservative Protestants believed the churches had not successfully purged themselves of the corrupting influences of modernism. Already troubled by developments in other parts of the country, falling farm prices made conservative rural Americans believe that their way of life stood under attack. A dogged defense of "old time" religion seemed the only path to survival. It was this sense that only strict adherence to traditional beliefs could protect cherished ways of life that made fundamentalists so determinedly opposed to the modernist Protestants who sought to reconcile religion with the new conditions of American society. While the Protestant conflict of the 1920s can be viewed as simply an extension of the centuries-old struggle between pietism and rationalism (or, in other words, faith versus reason), the societal alterations of the 1920s gave this clash new urgency. Fundamentalists perceived American society as spiraling out of their control. With modernism gaining the upper hand in the larger society, fundamentalists came to believe their activities represented the conservative tradition's last redoubt. This protracted and polarizing struggle between modernists and fundamentalists led Richard Hofstadter to dub the 1920s "the focal decade in the Kulturkampf of American Protestantism" (Hofstadter 1962, 123).

Fundamentalism on the March

Despite their gnawing fear of losing power, the fundamentalists managed to exert significant political strength during the decade. This stems partly from their ability to agree on dogma (such as biblical literalism and anti-Darwinism) and their success in coordinating actions. In 1919, some 6,500 fundamentalist leaders met in Philadelphia to establish the World Christian Fundamentals Association (WCFA). Led by William Bell Riley of Minneapolis, the WCFA issued a manifesto, *God Hath Spoken,* that outlined their beliefs and served notice to the modernists that the conservative tradition remained vibrant. Through the WCFA, fundamentalists promoted their beliefs, exchanged information, and plotted strategy. The organization helped conservative Christians engage in successful political battles over immigration, Prohibition, and evolution.

The battle for national Prohibition provided, if not fundamentalism's greatest success of the period, at least traditional Christianity's most successful effort at working with the modernists to obtain their goals. Prohibition's strange bedfellows, progressives and fundamentalists, developed out of differing notions of what temperance legislation might achieve. For the progressives, elimination of alcohol would help women, children, and families by reducing the destructive aspects of alcohol abuse among the working classes. For the fundamentalists, it meant removing the temptation of "demon rum" that led to social vices and immorality. The ratification of the 18th Amendment in 1919, therefore, represented a victory for both the "town" (progressives) and "country" (fundamentalists). Historian Sydney Ahlstrom called it "the last grand concert of the old moral order" (Ahlstrom 2004, 901).

The coalition that worked to enact Prohibition, however, could find little else to agree on. The fundamentalist impetus continued to succeed during the 1920s, however, because of the rightward turn of American society in general. Progressive reform withered in the face of prosperity and a conservative backlash that viewed the reformist tendencies of the previous decade as fostering an environment conducive to the social ills of the 1920s. Fundamentalists managed to exert their political will because of the overwhelming conservative climate of the times. For example, troubled conservative Protestants who lashed out against Catholics found audiences among American nativists who were worried about the ethnic slums of American cities. For the fundamentalist of the 1920s, the growing numbers of non-Protestant and non-Christian immigrant Americans explained the decline of the nation's urban areas. They perceived the cities to be overrun by "un-Americans" who either answered to the pope or denied Christ. To contain this threat, conservative Christians proposed limitations on immigration. Anti-immigrant pronouncements often decried the crime and vice that appeared in immigrant communities without commenting on religious factors, but the underlying notion always remained: these social ills sprang from the Catholic and Jewish nature of the immigrants. The anti-Catholicism of the fundamentalists coalesced with a larger xenophobia, born in part by the hyperpatriotism of World War I, to create a nativist sentiment capable of passing restrictive legislation. The National Origins Act of 1924, for example, significantly curtailed the immigration of both Southern and Eastern Europeans (primarily Jewish, Eastern Orthodox, or Catholic) and Asians.

The acceptance of scientific pronouncements by the modernists made it impossible for the fundamentalists to accept their brand of Christianity. While Prohibition and immigration restrictions allowed conservative Christians to work with politically oriented individuals not necessarily disposed toward the fundamentalist faith, the battle against science left them to struggle alone. It would be the fundamentalist attack on science more than any other effort of the period that created the impression fundamentalists were backward, reactionary, and primitive. While authors such as Albert Wiggam, whose 1923 book *The New Decalogue of Science* promoted salvation through science rather than scripture, raised the ire of fundamentalists, it was Charles Darwin (or, more accurately, his popularizers) who brought conservative Christians to a froth. Evolutionary theories threatened the very foundation of their faith. If humans represented simply one tiny part of a larger scheme governed by forces beyond anyone's control, the notion of humanity's creation in God's image crumbled. Moreover, the scientific notions undergirding evolution challenged God's omnipotence and omnipresence. For fundamentalist biblical literalists, this could not stand. They spearheaded campaigns throughout the country to pass legislation banning evolutionary theory from the public schools. Most famously, the legislature of Tennessee passed the anti-evolution Butler Act, which precipitated the 1925 Scopes Monkey Trial.

The momentum gained by fundamentalists with these successes, however, declined dramatically as the 1920s wound down. In 1927, even William Bell Riley noted that the WCFA no longer grabbed headlines in America's newspapers (Leinwand 2001, 207). The demographic changes that so troubled fundamentalists partly explained this decline. From the beginning of the decade until the year Riley lamented the WCFA's declining stature, almost 4 million rural residents migrated to America's cities. This movement sapped the overwhelmingly rural fundamentalist movement of many potential adherents. The exposure of the willful close-mindedness of many of fundamentalism's most rabid defenders during the Scopes trial also led many moderate Christians, who might have been sympathetic to some of the aims of the conservatives, to distance themselves from the movement. This shifting of stances within the churches dealt fundamentalism its most significant blow. Throughout the decade, intradenominational struggles over doctrine racked many of the nation's largest churches. By the end of the decade, however, the fundamentalists found themselves unable to gain control of the leadership of many denominations. While fundamentalism held sway in most Southern churches, the proponents of conservative beliefs lost the fight in "swing" churches such as the Northern Presbyterian and the Northern Baptist. These national defeats forced the fundamentalists to retrench in their Southern base and slowly work to build a national movement, a process that continues today.

Old Faith—New Forms

The science and technology that so troubled the fundamentalists also became a tool in their attempts to spread the gospel. Automobiles allowed circuit preachers to move from town to town more rapidly than ever before. Even the most isolated hamlet far from a railroad depot could now be a day trip for traveling evangelists. Newspaper wire services allowed fundamentalist pronouncements, such as T. T. Martin's during the Scopes trial, to be read across the country. Radio loomed largest of these developments. While radio could be decried as a tool for modernist propaganda, it could also be utilized as an instrument for spreading faith. Radio allowed distant audiences to connect with the nation's most prominent theologians and the infirmed to hear local sermons.

The power of radio transformed American evangelists. Some, such as the veteran Billy Sunday, continued to crisscross the nation in a seemingly endless series of "crusades," but other evangelists built up a local congregation, established a larger reputation through radio broadcasts, and then made lucrative appearances in areas in which their radio sermons were transmitted. Pittsburgh's KDKA began the first regularly scheduled religious programming in 1921. By 1925, religious organizations owned 10 percent of all American radio stations. Legendary radio preacher Charles Fuller started doing radio work in 1929 and began broadcasting sermons from his home church in 1930. During the 1930s, he went national with the "Old Fashioned Revival Hour," which made him the best-known Protestant minister in the country.

No minister of the 1920s better exploited modern techniques to promote traditional Christianity than Aimee Semple McPherson. Divorced twice by her early 30s, McPherson built the magnificent Angelus Temple in Southern California to

Media-savvy evangelist Aimee Semple McPherson was a shining star in the religious revival of the early 20th century. (Library of Congress)

serve as the center of her ministry. McPherson wore fashionable clothing, dyed her hair blond, and made a fortune promoting faith healing, speaking in tongues, and preaching the fundamentalist creed of Pentacostalism. Her success lay in part in her adoption of the vaudevillian trappings that made Sunday's sermons so successful. She utilized bands, light shows, animals, and stage tricks to convert the church experience into show business. McPherson spread her celebrity not only by being the first woman to preach on the radio but also by being the first American to establish a religious radio station. Her popularity waned somewhat after a 1926 escapade in which McPherson claimed to have been kidnapped for five weeks (she had actually run off with a married man), but "Sister Aimee" continued to be a religious force until the 1940s, and her Church of the Foursquare Gospel spawned an independent Pentecostal sect.

Defending Catholicism

The nativist fear of Catholic immigrants stemmed from a demographic fact: no single Protestant denomination could muster as many supporters as the Roman Catholic Church had. Even with the restrictive immigration acts of the early

1920s, some 23 million Americans claimed to be Catholic. These larger numbers engendered the hatred and concern of nativists and provided an opportunity to defend their faith from Protestant attacks. However, this proved to be a herculean task. Unlike the Irish Catholics of the 19th century who helped undercut an earlier wave of anti-Catholicism through patriotic sacrifice during the Civil War, Catholics of the 1920s found themselves in a period of peace, prosperity, and xenophobia that offered few overt opportunities to prove their contribution to the country. Much of the virility of 1920s anti-Catholicism, in fact, stemmed from wartime experiences that hardened attitudes and undercut Catholic claims to patriotism. Pope Benedict XV's call for all belligerents to lay down their arms as the Central Powers collapsed, the Irish church's role in preventing conscription in Ireland when the British army desperately needed men, and the American Church's adoration of Sinn Fein leader Eamon de Valera (who toured the United States in 1919–1920) all propelled a nativist sentiment that viewed Catholicism as treasonous.

The American Catholic Church immediately tried to counter this notion by positioning the Church as a vehicle of aid and social welfare. In 1919, both the "Bishops Program" of social reform and the National Catholic Welfare Council were established. The need to adopt a defensive stance in the face of organized bigotry, however, sapped these endeavors of much of their energy. A larger attempt to demonstrate that Catholicism felt at home in America involved the holding of the Twenty-eighth Eucharistic Congress in Chicago, the first such congress to occur in this country. By some estimates half a million Catholics crowded into the city for the 1926 religious pageant. A mass in Soldier Field drew an astonishing 150,000 people. Although the congress intended to show Catholicism as part of the fabric of American life, the virtual siege of Chicago by Catholics merely reinforced nativist fears of "papist" power.

If the Eucharistic Congress represented only a partial victory for American Catholics, the nomination of Al Smith for the presidency proved the depth of anti-Catholic sentiment, even as it showed the Church could marshal significant strength. As the Catholic governor of New York, Smith had already proven he could carry out the functions of his office without being beholden to the Vatican. But his status as an anti-Prohibition Catholic made his victory in the 1928 election impossible. Smith managed to gain the nomination of the factionalized Democratic Party, but nativist sentiment doomed his campaign to failure in the general election. Smith's potential victory was decried by "100 percent Americans" as the vanguard of a Catholic takeover of the United States in which the pope would make foreign policy, the Jesuits would act as secret police, and wine would flow freely. While no Democrat stood a chance against Herbert Hoover in 1928, the anti-Catholic smear campaign against Smith hurt his chances and confirmed the continued virulence of nativism. Still, Smith's respectable showing gave hope to some American Catholics, who continued to proclaim their contribution to America. In the end, his campaign helped begin the realignment of the Democratic Party that reached fruition under Franklin Roosevelt, a realignment that included American Catholics as part of the New Deal Coalition.

The Man Nobody Knows

The most successful religious book of the decade, *The Man Nobody Knows,* perfectly mirrored a staunchly probusiness era in which executives achieved the level of public heroes and successful ministers openly flaunted their vast wealth. The book attempted to reconcile Christ with President Coolidge's declaration that the "chief business of the American people is business." Written by advertising executive Bruce Barton (the son of a Congregationalist minister), the book promoted Christ as the foremost businessman in world history. Barton posited that Christ should be emulated and praised not only for his morality and teachings but also for his promotional and organizational abilities. He claimed that Christ succeeded, even though he faced competition from other faiths, because of his ability to sell followers on the need to become Christians. Undergirding *The Man Nobody Knows* was the notion that modern Americans needed an updated version of Christ that satisfied their desire for religion without forcing difficult questions about the nature of American capitalism. Barton's book represented the pinnacle of religious modernism in an era of modernism. He had not simply reconciled Protestant faith with science, as many liberal theologians of the decade attempted; he had also converted Christ into a 20th-century American. Not surprisingly, *The Man Nobody Knows,* along with Sinclair Lewis's anticlerical screed *Elmer Gantry,* was frequently excoriated by fundamentalists. Despite the controversy surrounding it, the runaway success of Barton's book led him to follow it up in quick succession with sequels *The Book Nobody Knows* (1926) and *What Can a Man Believe?* (1927).

The Varieties of African American Religious Experience

If fundamentalists and modernists could not reconcile their differing belief systems, they did, in general, unite over issues of race. The nativist "100 percent American" attitudes that spawned the Red Scare, National Origins Act, and Ku Klux Klan might have shifted some bigoted Americans' attention toward Catholics, immigrants, and radicals, but it did not eliminate racial animosity toward African Americans. Not only did African Americans continue to face hostility but they also became increasingly disabused of the notion that the North represented freedom and equality. During the first decades of the 20th century, a massive migration of African Americans from the rural South to industrial jobs in the urban North brought to light the racism that also prevailed north of the Mason-Dixon Line. For African Americans of the 1920s, as had been the case since emancipation, the church remained a haven of community, assistance, and compassion in a hostile environment.

Mainstream African American churches flourished during the 1920s. The African Methodist Episcopal Church, African Methodist Episcopal Church–Zion, and the Colored Methodist Episcopal all claimed hundreds of thousands of members during the decade. The various congregational Baptist churches, although difficult to quantify, undoubtedly possessed a six-figure membership total as well. Chicago's Olivet Baptist sported a congregation of more than 8,000, which made it the largest Protestant church in the United States. These churches offered a variety of social services, ranging from job training and housing assistance to child care facilities for working parents, all of which made the transition to urban living more palatable.

Elements of the new urbanized African American minority responded to the challenges of the time by joining a welter of newly established sects that revolved around the personal appeal of a charismatic leader. These new sects varied widely in terms of goals and doctrine, but many emerged from the Pentecostal movement and stressed personal piety, strict (although subjective) morality, and personal fealty toward the group leader. Among the most significant of these groups were Father Divine's interracial Peace Mission Movement, Charles "Sweet Daddy" Grace's United House of Prayer of All People, Ida Robinson's Mount Sinai Holy Church, and Charles Harrison Mason's Church of God in Christ. Given the pervasive climate of racism during the 1920s, some of the new sects not surprisingly went beyond the promotion of racial equality and expounded racial separatism or African racial superiority. Although primarily a social movement, Marcus Garvey's Universal Negro Improvement Association developed significant religious trappings as part of its separatist message. And the radical separatist Nation of Islam emerged from the teachings of Fard Muhammad, who began preaching in Detroit in 1930.

Spiritualism

While most religious Americans found themselves involved in the Protestant versus Catholic or modernist versus fundamentalist debates, a vibrant community of American spiritualists also operated during the 1920s. Although American spiritualism dated back to the early 19th century, it underwent decades of decline thanks to public ridicule, scandals, and fraudulent claims. Nonetheless, the spiritualist impulse—the desires to make contact with the deceased and scientifically prove metaphysical theories—underwent something of a rebirth in the early 20th century. A certain measure of respectability was granted by the interest in spiritualism exhibited by prominent figures such as Victor Hugo, Alfred Russel Wallace, and William James. The 1907 reorganization of the American Society for Psychical Research (ASPR) gave the movement a significant boost.

During the 1920s, American spiritualism gained renewed attention thanks to tours by prominent spiritualists. Sherlock Holmes creator Sir Arthur Conan Doyle made a series of highly successful lecture tours during the decade. And Sir Oliver Lodge, recognized as the world's most famous spiritualist writer, also traveled to the United States. The ASPR itself gained attention by offering prizes to individuals who could provide scientific proof of life after death (a move that motivated Thomas Edison to attempt to build a machine to communicate with the deceased). Their campaign paid off handsomely in the well-publicized activities of Margery Crandon, who spewed "ectoplasm" while in a trance. By the end of the decade, ASPR efforts led to the establishment of a psychical research center headed by J. B. Rhine at Duke University.

THE SCOPES TRIAL

Causes

The battle between the those who embraced modernism and those who saw it as a destruction of American society took many forms. The Ku Klux Klan's drive to organize conservative, native-born Protestants may have been the most spectacular and frightening aspect of this conflict, but the Klan avowed only to be defending a diffuse set of values that constituted "100 percent Americanism." A court case in a sleepy Tennessee town proved to be the decade's most famous example of conservative Christianity directly challenging the forces advocating secularism and science. The 1925 Scopes "Monkey Trial" clearly demonstrated that the genteel tradition and its defenders continued to hold sway over swaths of the United States. That the trial ended so inconclusively only served to illuminate that the chasm that existed between Americans arrayed in "urban" and "rural" camps would not be soon bridged. As Michael Parrish noted, John Scopes's trial represented one of the prime examples of how the United States had become "one nation, divisible" (Parrish 1992, 114–134).

The Scopes trial emerged as a challenge to Tennessee's Butler Act. Written by John W. Butler, a rural legislator concerned about his children's education, the Act made it illegal to "teach any theory that denies the story of the Divine Creation of man as taught in the Bible, and to teach instead that man has descended from a lower order of animals" in any school that received public funds. Butler's bill had overwhelmingly passed both houses of the Tennessee legislature in early 1925. Very little public protest emerged during the bill's debate. Only after its passage did any Tennessee newspapers question the impression of the state that the legislation might create outside of the Volunteer State. Nor did professional educators mount any significant attempt to block passage. Both the University of Tennessee and the state Department of Education had important (primarily budgetary) legislation pending, and neither wished to cross the legislature. Given his later significance to the Scopes trial, surprisingly, one of the few public critics of Butler's bill had been William Jennings Bryan. Despite his status as the apostle of rural America, Bryan feared the proposed penalties for violation of the law would doom it (as had been the case with a similar bill in Kentucky). Bryan suggested Tennessee follow Florida's lead in passing an act that made teaching evolution a crime that included no penalty for violation. For Bryan, this symbolic legislation would demonstrate the sentiments of Christian Americans without raising the ire of civil libertarians or free-speech advocates. The Tennessee legislature, however, decided to make violations of the Butler Act punishable by fines of no less than $100 and no more than $500.

Despite the inclusion of monetary penalties for violation of the Butler Act, many in the Tennessee government, including Governor Austin Peay, viewed the legislation as a symbolic act. This view of the Butler Act can be discerned in the lack of immediate enforcement. The Act's passage did not affect the state's educational system in any meaningful way. Teachers in the state continued to teach science as they had before and continued to use the same textbooks. The Act's passage did stir some public criticism, however. The *Chattanooga Times,* for example, while silent during the bill's debate, issued editorials against the Butler Act. And a variety of Tennessee citizens pondered legal challenges to the Act's constitutionality.

Events

The passage of the antievolution act prompted the American Civil Liberties Union (ACLU) to issue a call for a legal challenge. ACLU advertisements that appeared in Tennessee newspapers asked for a willing plaintiff to launch a test case against the "monkey law," as the Tennessee legislation had been dubbed. Led by civil engineer George W. Rappleyea, a group of upright citizens who frequently met for sodas in Dayton, Tennessee's F. E. Robinson drugstore made the fateful decision to organize the test case. They hoped that the resultant publicity would help bring positive attention to their hometown, whose economy had stagnated in the 20th century. In one of the great twists of the trial, their efforts brought more attention to bear on Dayton than anyone imagined, but the publicity proved to be relentlessly negative. The Rhea County hamlet became synonymous with Bible-thumping anti-intellectualism.

The Dayton "boosters" persuaded the town's young science teacher John Thomas Scopes to confess to violation of the Butler Act. Despite his eventual status as the center of the debate over evolution, Scopes initially contributed nothing to the plan but his name. He expressed his concerns over the anti-evolution statute but had no inclination to challenge the law until pushed by the Rappleyea group to do so. For the Dayton boosters, Scopes was the perfect choice for a defendant. The young teacher was popular, not viewed as a radical, had no local family who might suffer because of the trial, and—perhaps most importantly—was willing to accept the role of Butler Act violator to help the community.

On May 7, 1925, the local constable arrested Scopes for violating the state's antievolution law, despite that fact that Scopes used Tennessee public schools' officially adopted biology text, George W. Hunter's *A Civic Biology: Presented in Problems*. Residents then contacted the ACLU and out-of-town newspapers with the news that the Butler Act would be challenged in Dayton; events quickly spiraled beyond the control of Dayton's boosters. The ACLU sent a defense team to Dayton led by Clarence Darrow, an avowed atheist who loved to publicly attack fundamentalism. Darrow offered his services free because he wanted the chance to go head-to-head with William Jennings Bryan, the most prominent member of the eight-person prosecution team and the nation's leading antievolutionist. From the trial's beginning, Darrow's focus was on attacking fundamentalism, not defending John Scopes. Fundamentalism (and Bryan) angered Darrow so much that he agreed, for the only time in his career, to work pro bono. Along with the august jurists, some 200 reporters and thousands of tourists descended on Dayton. The crowd that gathered included those truly interested in the case as well as many who simply wanted to provide entertainment. Dayton became clogged with street performers, itinerant preachers, vendors, and people with pet monkeys. Those who wished to stay abreast of the trial but could not make the trip to Dayton could listen to the proceedings through the new medium of radio. Scopes became the first American trial to be broadcast.

The trial itself began on the blisteringly hot morning of July 10 and spanned a scant 12 days. The strategies of the two legal teams became clear on the first day of the proceedings. Bryan and the prosecution planned to focus on the narrow legal argument that Scopes had admitted to violating the Butler Act. They had not only his confession but also the testimony of several students stating that Scopes had taught from Hunter's textbook. School superintendent Walter White testified that Scopes could not teach the biology textbook without teaching evolution. It seemed, from the prosecution table, an open-and-shut case. For the defense, the Dayton trial presented an opportunity to demonstrate the unconstitutionality of the anti-evolution legislation, but Scopes's legal team also recognized that a victory in this trial could be disastrous. They needed Scopes to be found guilty so they could appeal to a higher court; only at the state or federal level could the Butler Act be ruled unconstitutional. Absolved from having to make a strong defense for his client, Darrow used the trial as a pulpit for attacking fundamentalism, and he perceived the proceedings as an opportunity to engage Bryan in a religious debate.

For Darrow, the need to lose the case but make a strong showing created an unusual situation. During the trial's first few days, the defense team used a variety of tactics to demonstrate the unconstitutionality of the anti-evolution leg-

American lawyer and politician William Jennings Bryan (1860–1925) argues for the prosecution during the Scopes "Monkey Trial," Dayton, Tennessee, 1925. (Hulton Archive/Getty Images)

islation. Darrow and the defense variously claimed that the Butler Act violated the separation of church and state embedded in both the United States and Tennessee constitutions, that it broke the Tennessee constitution's protection to worship according to the dictates of conscience, and that the law violated protected free speech. Judge John Raulston, however, ruled that the legislature possessed the power to make uniform rules for the state's public schools and ruled against the defense. The defense expected (and needed) this defeat and had engaged in this line primarily to lay the foundation of an appeal, so they shifted focus on day five and began both to assail the thinking behind the Butler Act and to posit that Christianity and science could be compatible. On this latter point, Darrow argued for the necessity of bringing in expert witnesses, scientists and liberal theologians alike, to explain the complicated issues at play to the jury. The prosecution mounted a furious attack against this move. Judge Raulston's banning of expert witnesses on Friday July 17 seemed to bring the trial to a close. Many of the reporters congregated in Dayton felt this was so and departed over the weekend. Those who stayed witnessed the trial's most dramatic turn.

On Monday Raulston moved the proceedings outside to escape the court-room's stifling heat, inadvertently creating an audience for the culminating showdown between Darrow and Bryan. Darrow called Bryan to the stand as an expert on the Bible. Despite Bryan's right, as an attorney for the opposition, to refuse, he agreed to take the stand. This most famous incident of the trial need never have occurred. Not only could Bryan have refused to take the stand but Raulston could have also prevented the debate. In the end, he allowed the theatrics to go on but ruled Bryan's testimony would not be part of the trial record. The judge even excused the jury before Bryan began to testify. Legally pointless, the Darrow–Bryan sparring match ensured the trial a notorious place in American history.

On the courthouse lawn, some 3,000 spectators watched Darrow mercilessly grill Bryan. Although he ranged across several topics, Darrow's primary focus was to expose what he viewed as the inconsistencies of biblical science. The "Great Commoner" found himself forced to defend the creation of the earth in six days but also to admit there were "days" before the sun's creation on the fourth day. Darrow's attack on the lack of biblical accounts of those people living outside of the Holy Land culminated in the defense attorney suggesting that Bryan had never lived "near anybody of learning" (Caudill and Lawson 2000, 17). Darrow's relentless attack included forcing Bryan to admit Jonah had been swallowed by a whale and to defend the biblical account of a great flood in 4004 B.C.E. Bryan, exhausted and defeated, finally conceded that not all of the Bible's accounts (such as Joshua making the sun stand still) could be interpreted literally. Although Bryan had not been a biblical literalist, Darrow's line of questioning put Bryan in the awkward positions of appearing to be one and of defending this basic tenet of fundamentalism. Bryan's concession meant nothing in the context of the trial, but for Darrow it represented a personal victory over "the fool ideas that no intelligent Christian on earth believes."

Despite Darrow's masterful performance, the verdict was never in doubt. Scopes had admitted to teaching evolution, which the defense team did not dispute. For Darrow, the entire circus in Dayton served only as a prologue for the real fight. The next day the jury took just nine minutes to find Scopes guilty. In fact, it took them longer to weave their way through the crowd to reach the room in which they deliberated than it did to reach the verdict. Raulston immediately fined the science teacher $100. Scopes had achieved the status of martyr for the cause of science; Bryan gained the same position among fundamentalists by dying in Dayton five days after the trial's end. Within days of his death, supporters began collecting funds to establish the fundamentalist Bryan College in Dayton.

Darrow and the defense achieved the result they desired in Dayton, but the Tennessee Supreme Court squashed their chance to repeal the Butler Act. In January 1927, that court overturned Scopes's conviction on appeal, but only because Raulston violated Tennessee law by not consulting the jury before hand-

Historians' Debate:
Who Won and Who Lost in the Scopes Trial?

The inconclusive end to the Scopes trial created an environment in which this most famous battle between modernism and fundamentalism offers a multiplicity of interpretations. Scopes lost his case, but public opinion generally ridiculed the backwardness of southern fundamentalists. Scopes won his appeal, but the Butler Act remained on the books. And the fundamentalist sentiment continued to hold sway in elements of American society but fell back in the face of modernism and science. Under such circumstances, historians continue to grapple with the question of who actually won the Scopes "Monkey Trial."

The dominant view of midcentury historians was that Scopes and Darrow lost the battle in Dayton but eventually triumphed thanks to the thorough discrediting of the antievolutionist worldview, which appeared ignorant and narrow-minded. Building upon the Depression-era work of journalist Frederick Lewis Allen, these historians planted fundamentalism as a last gasp effort to halt the force of modernism, which swept the anti-evolutionists aside as a new American society emerged. Richard Hofstadter firmly established this view in several of his influential works. William Leuchtenburg followed suit in his popular *The Perils of Prosperity, 1914–1932.* In his seminal 1958 monograph on the trial, Ray Ginger offered a full-length explication of this interpretation.

More recent scholarship has offered a more cautious assessment of modernism's triumph. Edward J. Larson, perhaps the current leading authority on the trial, noted that the humiliation of Bryan and fundamentalism little affected areas already under the influence of conservative Christianity. Newspaper accounts that ridiculed southerners as backward reactionaries meant nothing in the South itself. And the Tennessee Supreme Court's skillful blocking of constitutional challenges to the Butler Act allowed other states to enact similar legislation. From this perspective, one might argue that modernism eventually emerged victorious but that this development did not inevitably arise from the publicity surrounding the Scopes trial. To Paul Conkin, the eventual victory of science suffered a dramatic setback in Dayton and only overcame the forces arrayed against the teaching of evolution due to Cold War imperatives during the 1950s.

Religious scholar George Marsden has persuasively argued that the Scopes trial affected fundamentalism more than it did America. He posits that fundamentalists, recognizing the forces allied against them in the North and cities, retreated to their Southern bastion and gathered strength to create an independent subculture devoid of the pernicious "-isms" of mainstream society. This tactical retreat guaranteed their survival in a hostile America. Along similar lines, Ferenc Szasz sees the Scopes trial as a watershed event for conservative Christians who utilized the event to propel their anti-evolutionist movement. Scopes becomes, as Larson has noted, part of a long struggle that continues to this day with the battle over "intelligent design." Advocates of intelligent design can now point to Scopes, as do Marvin Olasky and John Perry in their recent book on the trial, as a reference point for the evolving nature of creationist legal tactics. In an ironic twist, the Scopes trial, therefore, becomes an example of close-mindedness for both sides. Olasky

Continued on next page

Historians' Debate:
Who Won and Who Lost in the Scopes Trial?, Continued

and Perry posit that the move from uncritical biblical literalism to a stance that embraces the scientific method represents the modernization of creationism. For them, the Scopes trial becomes both a legal victory and a tactical learning tool. Like Thomas Paine and populism, the Scopes trial appears to be infinitely malleable, embraceable as a victory for both sides, and destined to continually stir debate.

---

ing down his fine; the court upheld the constitutionality of the Butler Act. Therefore, Darrow could not pursue that case further. Despite occasional protests, the Butler Act remained in effect until 1967.

THESE MODERN WOMEN: THE EMERGENCE OF FEMINISM

Background

In 1848, Lucretia Mott, Elizabeth Cady Stanton, and a small group of political activists gathered in Seneca Falls, New York, to discuss a host of reform issues. Chief among their concerns, however, was the political and economic marginalization of American women. During the Seneca Falls convention, Stanton drafted the "Declaration of Sentiments," a document that outlined the goals, including the franchise, of the women's rights movement. These events of 1848 launched the movement in the United States. Historians have divided the American feminist movement into periods ("waves") based upon chronology and aims. The activities of the 19th century are known simply as women's rights; those of the early 20th century are "first wave" feminism.

The early 20th century brought sweeping political changes to both America and the women's movement. Feminists (a phrase that entered the American lexicon during this period) began to augment their traditional natural-rights appeals with discourse on the social benefits of female suffrage. They began to promote women's roles in reinforcing morality as an instrument of social reform. By this logic, if women obtained the right to vote, they would help clean up political corruption and work to pass legislation addressing social ills such as prostitution, alcohol abuse, and child labor. This embrace of progressive reform sentiment derived from a new generation of leaders who came to the fore during the early 20th century. These women imbued the National American Woman Suffrage Association (NAWSA) with a sense of being part of a larger reform movement. Thanks to their efforts, six more states granted women the right to vote during the early 1910s. Buoyed by these successes, in 1916 Carrie Chapman Catt unveiled an elaborate "winning plan" that called for concerted pressure on public officials and total cooperation among local NAWSA branches. The plan served as the organization's guiding principle until national suffrage was achieved.

Not all feminists agreed with the NAWSA's peaceful, piecemeal approach to suffrage. In 1913 Alice Paul, who witnessed the militant British feminist movement first-hand earlier in the century, broke with the NAWSA and established the Constitutional Union. Paul believed the direct-action approach used in England should serve as the template for activities in this country. Moreover, she believed the staid NAWSA's focus on individual states created an unnecessary delay in the achievement of equality. Paul argued that the discarded 19th-century tactic of obtaining a constitutional amendment to guarantee a national franchise should be readopted by feminists. Her National Woman's Party (NWP) launched a public campaign of propaganda and demonstrations to persuade Congress pass a suffrage amendment.

The grass-roots efforts of the NAWSA, public protests by the NWP, and momentum that developed during the 1910s finally bore fruit in 1918. In January of that year, President Woodrow Wilson announced his support for a constitutional amendment, and the House of Representatives passed the 19th Amendment. In June 1919, the Senate finally did the same. After a desperate national campaign for passage, and Wilson's pleas to state Democratic parties, Tennessee became the 36th state to ratify the 19th Amendment, thereby making it part of the Constitution. In the end, only 10 states voted against the amendment.

Feminist Social Policy in the 1920s

After obtaining the franchise, American feminist leaders attempted to organize American women into a powerful voting block to exert pressure on the political system. However, this endeavor yielded no successes as stirring as the 19th Amendment. American feminists quickly discovered that the unifying effect of fighting for the cause of suffrage crumbled with the granting of the franchise. Rather than invigorating American women to stand and vote together for further reform, participation in the electoral process divided American women. The majority of women simply aligned themselves with the two major political parties; these affiliations made the unity of female voters impossible. For many feminist leaders, the 1920s forced them to accept the bitter fact that many who stood alongside them in the fight for suffrage did so because they simply wanted to be part of the political process, not because they sought to fundamentally reform American society. Those who remained in the movement also faced another divisive fight over tactics (and goals), which sapped much of their remaining momentum. Additionally, the decade ushered in a period of prosperity, peace, popular culture, and consumerism that encouraged an ethic of domesticity that made feminists appear to be out of step with mainstream American society. The 1920s would prove to be a very difficult decade for the women's movement.

In the aftermath of ratification, Maud Wood Park and Carrie Chapman Catt reorganized the NAWSA as the League of Women Voters (LWV). Lack of an overriding "women's" issue led many American women to decline invitations to join the new group. The LWV's initial membership constituted a scant one-tenth of the NAWSA's at the time of the 19th Amendment's ratification. Still, LWV leaders hoped the organization would serve as a vehicle for training women for political activism and to educate them about issues that directly related to their lives. The LWV stressed its nonpartisanship and focused on particular issues (and those politicians who supported them). Because the issues the LWV promoted fell within the broad purview of "reformism," however, they rarely supported conservative politicians. Nor, despite their determined efforts, could the LWV members motivate women to vote. A frequently cited "lack of interest in politics" resulted in a lower percentage of women than men participating in elections. In many states, less than half the eligible female voters cast ballots (Chafe 1972, 29–37).

Part of the LWV's program involved electing more female officials. Their inability to organize women to vote as a block significantly hampered this program. In 1922, 27 women ran for Congress, but only one was elected. Although two women became the first female state governors in American history in 1924, their successes had little to do with the organizing activities of the LWV. In Texas, Miriam Ferguson ran as a substitute for her husband Jim after he was banned from running for reelection. And in Montana Nellie Taylor Ross ran only because her husband William had died in office. This pattern occurred at the federal level as well. Of the women elected to Congress during the decade, two-thirds succeeded their husbands.

The LWV did manage to achieve some success by directly lobbying Congress to pass legislation dealing with social issues. The 1921 Sheppard–Towner Act provided funds for educational programs geared toward lowering infant mortality rates. Even more striking in an era of xenophobia, 1922's Cable Act removed the citizenship penalties leveled against women who married aliens. However, the recognition that the League could not mobilize enough women to swing elections eventually undercut their ability to propel legislation. The Child Labor Amendment to the Constitution, which many feminists promoted, failed to be ratified. According to one historian, this setback led to the "ebb tide of social feminism" (Lemons 1973, 228–247). And Sheppard–Towner's reduced support in Congress led to the act's repeal at the end of the decade.

The general political conservatism of the decade certainly affected feminists' ability to shape legislation, but internal divisions also factored significantly. Alice Paul and the NWP created a rift in the movement over the fight for total equality. Paul proposed what she called the Lucretia Mott Amendment, a proposed constitutional amendment that simply stated "men and women shall have

National Woman's Party motor convoy in Rapid City, South Dakota, in 1927. The delegation, consisting principally of western women, met President Coolidge and asked for his support of the Equal Rights Amendment then pending in Congress. (Library of Congress)

equal rights throughout the United States and every place subject to its jurisdiction." The Equal Rights Amendment (ERA) created a firestorm of controversy with the women's rights movement. LWV members and leaders from specialized women's organizations, such as the Women's Trade Union League (WTUL), believed the ERA would undermine the work of early-20th-century women's rights activists, who had succeeded in getting woman-specific protective legislation passed. Critics of the ERA feared the amendment would force women to give up the separate but equal status that granted them alimony, widows' pensions, workplace protections, and immunity from military conscription. For Paul, however, the ERA represented the culmination of the fight for equality.

The debate over the ERA became a battle over "sameness versus difference" that wreaked havoc on the feminist movement. Paul argued that sex-based labor legislation represented a pernicious form of sex discrimination that threatened to keep American women in the position of second-class citizens by promoting a mind-set that viewed women as inferior to male workers. For Paul, legislation such as maximum daily working hours for women curtailed women's ability to

advance in their occupations and to earn a living. The LWV and WTUL, however, viewed protective legislation as essential to maintaining proper living conditions for American women. They noted that the weakness of organized labor
and probusiness stance of the federal government meant that the removal of
protective legislation for women would inevitably result in tragedy for working-
class women. The divided nature of the women's movement over the issue of
ERA doomed the amendment when it was debated in Congress.

The Workplace

Protective legislation came to be so contentious within the women's movement
partly because so many working women faced the vicissitudes of low-paying,
low-level work. Some 10 million American women worked for wages during
the 1920s, many in demeaning factory, sales, or domestic work. Although governmental studies found women employed in most of the occupational categories listed in the census, almost 90 percent worked in female-designated
occupations. They made less money than male workers because they were
viewed as inferior or unskilled workers. In 1927, the average weekly wage for
an American man was $29.35; for women it was $17.34. For activists such as
Alice Paul, this disparity underscored the need for the ERA; for other feminists
the realization that employers denigrated the contributions of women made protective legislation an essential tool in offsetting gender imbalances.

Despite the hoopla surrounding "New Woman" professional workers, the
decade of the 1920s did not usher in a period of significant occupational advancements. The percentage of women in the workforce only grew by 1 percent during the decade. And while the percentage of women in the workforce
classified as "professionals" continued to climb slowly, the vast majority of these
women found themselves in circumscribed "female" jobs in education, nursing,
and social work. Graduate and professional schools often utilized quotas that
kept the number of female lawyers and doctors very low. In fact, the percentage of doctors who were women declined during the decade. And with the
growing medical specialization of obstetrics, the traditionally female occupation
of midwife virtually disappeared.

Many new professions did open up for American women in the 1920s, but
here again, female workers faced what later came to be known as the "glass
ceiling." For example, during the decade, the number of women in the banking
industry increased, but they never achieved the highest positions in the industry. Often women were hired solely to work with female clients. These women
never rose above the position of assistant cashier. Business executives justified
the lack of promotions for women by claiming that most women quit working
when they become wives and mothers, which made them a bad investment in
terms of training and responsibilities. Such attitudes prevailed in all occupations,

which made the struggles of feminists doubly difficult. With few women achieving the highest levels of their given professions, those arrayed against women's rights could offer "proof" that women were inferior. And the limits on women's career achievements reduced both the number of role models for the younger generation of feminists and the funds available to continue the fight for equality.

Liberated and Apolitical

Alice Paul's fractious campaign for the ERA helped divide the women's rights movement into "social" feminists and "hardcore" feminists, but forces outside the movement undercut its broad-based support. To the consternation of the activists, the postwar generation of young women, whom they had hoped would be the next generation of movement leaders, engaged in rampant dissipation and activities that simply reinforced gender stereotypes. Women's movement leaders discovered that many young women viewed equality as a license to engage in social pleasures traditionally within the domain of men, and that many older women equated it with technological developments in housekeeping. While the rift between the NWP and the LWV caused the women's movement to founder, it sank in a sea of cosmetics, cigarettes, and washing machines.

College-aged women of the 1920s often used the mantle of liberation and equality as a justification for social activities denied their mothers. The stereotype of the "flapper," with her bobbed hair, sheath skirt, and rouged face, never represented the majority of young women during the decade, but the lure of drinking and sexual liberation that it embodied siphoned off much of the educated middle class that feminists hoped to attract. Buttressed by the vulgarized Freudianism that became popular during the 1920s, college women promoted frank and open sexuality, not political activism, as their primary vehicle for attacking traditional gender roles. As Paula Fass noted about college-age youth of the decade, they were "little interested in political or economic issues, they neither pressed for change nor partook actively in political discussions" (Fass 1977, 328). What angered feminists the most about the flapper image was that it reinforced traditional gender roles concerning beauty and sexuality. Liberated young women defined themselves not only by their appearance but also by their ability to attract male suitors. College women may have subverted the traditional notion that dating was an immediate prelude to marriage, but their social ideas still revolved around their physical attributes being interpreted by men. Equally troubling was the tendency of college women to judge each other on the basis of physical beauty, rather than to attempt to unite for political and social reform. Despite the fundamentally apolitical attitude of flapper types, their scandalous activities—overt sexuality, smoking, drinking, and publically exposed flesh—became associated with the women's movement by more conservative elements of American society. More traditionally minded American women, who might have entertained the notion of involvement with the movement, avoided participation in women's rights activities because of such hedonism.

American advertisers and purveyors of popular culture also promoted the cults of beauty and domesticity to great effect during the 1920s, actions which both angered and hampered the women's movement. The cosmetics and beauty industries exploded during the decade. They took the notion of liberation, moving it from the political to the personal, by launching advertising campaigns that reinforced the notion that "modern" woman was young and beautiful. The motion picture industry also served to reinforce the cult of beauty. Female stars of the period fit into only a few circumscribed roles. From the vamps (Theda Bara) to the sexually promiscuous (Clara Bow) to the flapper (Louise Brooks), screen actresses built their careers around appearance and gender-prescribed image. The acceptance by American women of such superficial representations brought damning criticisms from veteran feminists. These jeremiads, however, served only to illuminate the differences between the generation of women who organized the suffrage campaign and the younger women enjoying the carefree liberation of the 1920s. Charlotte Perkins Gilman criticized sexualized young women for their "selfish and fruitless indulgence," but those she hoped to influence paid her no heed. One female writer of the decade dubbed the younger generation "Feminist-New Style." As Frank Stricker noted, these women "desired a measure of economic independence and satisfying work, but she would not sacrifice marriage and family for work" (quoted in Cott and Pleck 1979, 478).

For middle-aged or less adventurous young women, advertisers and the media equated liberty and freedom of choice with activities associated with homemaking. Reputedly time-saving cooking and cleaning devices, prepackaged foods, and mass-produced clothing of the period did not eliminate the traditional responsibilities of American housewives, but they did erode older notions of home production. These women, with the plethora of items for sale, became a significant part of a consumer society that required the advice of professional home economists to ensure that homes were safe, clean, and modern. Scientific child rearing stressed the active participation of mothers. To keep up with developing technologies and medical practices required significant attention and time, which left less of both for activity outside of the home. With cultural forces stressing a woman's duty to provide the best home possible for her husband and children, political activism became both selfish and a less important luxury. And with the collapse of the economy in 1929, protection of the home became even more difficult and time-consuming.

The cult of youthful beauty also induced middle-aged women to pay more attention to their appearance. Advertisers promoted countless products that promised to restore beauty and vigor. American women were encouraged to adopt the styles of their daughters in order to remain "young and modern." The advertisers of the decade made staying thin and attractive central activities for married women as well as for the single. These promotional techniques proved highly successful. One 1927 study found that 90 percent of the women polled wore face powder. That the generation of American women old enough to have previously been denied the vote embraced such rhetoric angered feminists even more than their desertion by the young. They viewed the married and middle-aged as the generation most available for continuing the fight for equality. To many feminists, the inability to mobilize these women demonstrated most clearly how marginalized the movement had become and how difficult the fight for women's rights would be.

BIOGRAPHIES

Al "Scarface" Capone, 1899–1947

Criminal Gang Leader

Born in 1899 in Brooklyn, Al Capone dropped out of school at 14 and became a bouncer, bartender, and small-time hoodlum. A 1917 bar fight left him with a knife wound across his face (hence the nickname "Scarface"). In 1920, Capone moved to Chicago to work for organized crime boss John Torrio. Capone quickly became the head of Torrio's bootlegging operations and helped organize a territorial agreement with other bootleggers to reduce intergang violence.

In 1924, Capone found himself pushed out of Chicago by a reformist mayor; he moved to nearby Cicero. He gained national attention when the press began reporting on his control of the local government of Cicero. After Torrio's 1925 conviction for liquor violations, Capone reorganized the gang, with himself as the senior partner. That same year the Chicago bootleggers' truce broke down and Capone established his gang as the preeminent provider of illegal alcohol in the city. His control of the Windy City's liquor trade made Capone a millionaire.

Al Capone, the son of Neapolitan emigrants, is America's most legendary gangster. (Library of Congress)

Capone's willingness to talk to the press, charisma, and penchant for explosive violence made him a notorious figure and something of a folk hero. This attention also made him a target for law enforcement officials. During the winter of 1927, Chicago reformers succeeded in pressuring Capone to leave that city; he moved to Miami. Although he returned to Illinois on occasion, this exile allowed his influence to wane. After a 1929 summit of the nation's leading bootleggers, Capone was arrested for carrying a concealed weapon and received a one-year prison sentence. Then in early 1931, federal investigators charged Capone with income tax fraud; Capone was sentenced to 11 years in prison. He was released in 1939 because of good behavior and his deteriorating health caused by advanced syphilitic dementia. Capone died in Miami in 1947.

Carrie Chapman Catt, 1859–1947

Women's Rights Leader

Born Carrie Lane in 1859, Catt attended college in Iowa before becoming a high school teacher and administrator. In 1885, she married Leo Chapman and assisted him in editing a newspaper. After her husband's 1886 death, she was active as a freelance writer and lecturer. In 1890, Catt participated in the creation of the National Woman Suffrage Association (NWSA). That same year she married engineer George Catt. She steadily moved up the hierarchy of the NWSA, serving as president during the early 20th century. She also established the International Woman Suffrage Alliance in 1902.

During the 1910s, Catt again became head of the NWSA and spearheaded the organization's grassroots campaign to gain women's suffrage. Catt and the NWSA promoted a state-by-state method of gaining the franchise, with lobbying of the Congress as a secondary tactic. After ratification of the 19th Amendment in 1920, Catt helped convert the NWSA into the League of Women Voters (LWV). She attempted to use the LWV as a means to increase women's involvement in the political process, a campaign that met with only qualified success during her lifetime.

In 1925, Catt organized the Committee on the Cause and Cure of War. The Committee lobbied international bodies as well as the United States government to adopt diplomatic solutions to conflict, a campaign that culminated in the Kellogg–Briand Pact. She remained a dedicated peace activist for the remainder of her life. During the 1930s, she became deeply involved in lobbying support for the World Court and League of Nations. Catt died in New York in 1947.

Clarence Darrow, 1857–1938

Attorney, Civil Liberties Activist

Born in 1857 in rural Ohio, Clarence Seward Darrow started his law career in Andover, Ohio, before moving to Chicago. Initially a corporate attorney in the railroad industry, Darrow's conscience propelled him to become a labor lawyer. Among his most prominent early clients were American Railway Union president Eugene V. Debs, labor leader "Big" Bill Haywood, and the United Mine Workers. Darrow's successful defenses of both Debs and Haywood and his outspoken stance as a civil libertarian made the attorney a national figure. He did not always win his cases, but even in defeat, Darrow served his clients well. Darrow became a controversial figure in part because his personal disgust with the death penalty led him to defend obviously guilty clients. He managed to avoid the death penalty for the McNamara Brothers, whose terrorist act left 20 dead. Most famously, he kept teenage "thrill killers" Nathan Leopold and Richard Loeb from being executed thanks to an insanity defense.

Darrow agreed to represent John Scopes pro bono in 1925 because of the jurist's deep rooted hatred of fundamentalist Christianity. His masterful dissecting of William Jennings Bryan during the 1925 Scopes "Monkey Trial" made Darrow one of the nation's most prominent defenders of evolution. After the Scopes trial, Darrow largely retired from active practice. His last significant case was the successful defense of Henry and Ossian Sweet, two Detroit African Americans accused of killing a member of a white mob that had surrounded their family home. Darrow served as chairman of the National Recovery Review Board during the mid-1930s. He died in Chicago in 1938.

Father Divine, ca. 1870–1966

Religious Leader

Father Divine was born George Baker in Georgia during the late 1870s (the exact date is unknown). Baker's youth is obscure, but he is known to have moved north around the dawn of the 20th century and settled in Baltimore. He became a traveling minister in the early 1910s, before establishing himself in New York in 1915. Because of his claims to embody divine spirit, Baker eventually changed his name to Father Divine. In 1919, he moved his small band of communally living followers to Sayville, Long Island.

Divine's group became one of the many small, pietistic sects organized around a charismatic leader during the 1920s. His claim to be God on Earth proved to be controversial, as did the interracial nature of his following. Divine promoted a program of chastity, peace, and racial equality. His ultimate goal was total human harmony and the elimination of all racial distinctions.

By the 1930s, Divine's Peace Mission Movement, based in Harlem, gained significant strength, thanks in part to the copious amounts of free food they handed out during the depths of the Depression. In the early 1940s, Divine moved his base to Philadelphia and, more controversially, married a white woman 50 years his junior. Although his public stature never regained its previous height, Divine continued to fight for peace and racial harmony until his death in 1967.

Aimee Semple McPherson, 1890–1944

Evangelist

Born into a deeply religious family in 1890, Aimee Kennedy broke with her family's Methodism as a teenager and became a Pentecostal. She married minister Robert Semple in 1908, and the two became missionaries in China. After Semple's death, Aimee returned to the United States and married Harold McPherson. The two divorced after a few years of marriage. Aimee worked tirelessly as a traveling evangelist and faith healer during World War I and slowly built up a national reputation.

McPherson's success on the circuit allowed her to build the Angelus Temple in 1923. The southern California auditorium became the home of her Church of the Foursquare Gospel. The highly controversial McPherson brought the theatricality of preaching to new heights. With her peroxide blond hair and trademark blue cape, McPherson led services replete with exotic animals, bands, dramatic portrayals of biblical events, and light shows. At her mid-1920s peak, McPherson preached 21 sermons per week. She became the first woman to preach on the radio. Her success led to the establishment of the nation's first religious radio station, a Bible college, and a telephone-counseling ministry.

In 1926, McPherson disappeared for five weeks, eventually emerging from a Mexican desert with a tale of being kidnapped. Authorities believed she had spent the time in Mexico with a married man and brought obstruction of justice charges against the evangelist. Although the charges were later dropped, McPherson's reputation was dealt significant damage. Her church (and private life) suffered badly during the 1930s. Financial problems and competition from other media-savvy evangelists eroded her status. McPherson transferred control of her church to her son, Rolf, shortly before her death in 1944. Her Foursquare Church later blossomed into an independent Pentecostal sect.

Alice Paul, 1885–1970

Women's Rights Leader

Born in Moorestown, New Jersey, in 1885, Alice Paul grew up in a comfortable Quaker home. She attended Swarthmore College, the University of Pennsylvania, Washington College of Law, and American University, earning two Ph.D.s and a law degree. She went to Europe in 1907 to engage in a career in social work but quickly became immersed in the English women's suffrage movement. Paul experienced first-hand the direct action tactics of the movement and came to believe similar methods should be adopted in the United States.

When Paul returned to this country, she became a leader of the National American Woman Suffrage Association's (NAWSA) Congressional Committee. A disagreement over tactics led Paul to establish her own independent Congressional Union in 1913. She later renamed the Union the National Woman's Party

(NWP), which served as Paul's primary organizational affiliation for the rest of her career. During the 1910s, she used confrontational techniques to publicize her campaign for women's suffrage, a move that angered and alienated more moderate women's rights activists. After ratification of the 19th Amendment, Paul focused her energies on the passage of an Equal Rights Amendment (ERA), which she had personally crafted. Her fight for the abortive ERA further distanced Paul from other leading feminists.

During her later career, Paul attempted to get international organizations to approve equal rights statements and fought for the inclusion of sex discrimination language appended to civil rights legislation. Paul succeeded in having sex discrimination added to the employment provisions of the Civil Rights Act of 1964, which helped rekindle the women's movement in the 1960s. Paul also achieved some level of vindication when all major women's organizations eventually adopted pro-ERA stances. She died in 1977.

As a feminist and suffragist favoring the use of militant tactics, Alice Paul devoted her life to fighting for women's rights. She also wrote the Equal Rights Amendment and worked hard, though unsuccessfully, to secure its passage. (Library of Congress)

John T. Scopes, 1900–1970

Educator

Born in 1900 in Paducah, Kentucky, John Thomas Scopes grew up in Salem, Illinois (William Jennings Bryan's hometown). After attending the University of Kentucky, Scopes became an educator, eventually settling in Dayton, Tennessee, to teach science and math and to coach football. His decision to serve as the defendant in a Butler Act test case made him a household name. The Scopes "Monkey Trial" of 1925 helped harden the differences between traditional, conservative rural Americans and the proponents of modernism and secularism associated with the cities. Scopes won his appeal in 1927, by which point he was no longer employed by the Rhea County school system. After the trial concluded, Scopes informed one reporter that he had not even violated the anti-evolution law. Local "boosters" had convinced him to admit his guilt even though he had not actually taught a lecture on evolution.

The publicity associated with the trial—and his newfound status as America's most prominent teacher of evolution—made it difficult for Scopes to remain in Dayton. He subsequently pursued a master's degree in geology at the University of Chicago. Scopes worked as a surveyor in the oil industry until retirement in 1964. His role in the "Monkey Trial," however, remained a central aspect of his life. Scopes helped promote the 1960 motion picture *Inherit the Wind,* which provided a fictionalized account of the trial, and his 1967 autobiography, *Center of the Storm,* revolved primarily around the case. He died in 1970.

William J. Simmons, 1880–1946

Ku Klux Klan Organizer

Born on a farm in Harpersfield, Alabama, in 1880, William Joseph Simmons became a circuit-riding minister for the Methodist Episcopal Church in the early-20th century. A dispute with church leaders led Simmons to leave the clergy and drift through periods as an insurance salesman for the Woodmen of the World (a fraternal organization that bestowed the honorary title "colonel" on Simmons) and as a professor of Southern history at Atlanta's Lanier University. Deeply imbued with the myths of the Old South, Simmons found inspiration in *The Birth of a Nation* to reestablish the Klan in 1915 as a purveyor of conformity to traditional white supremacist social and moral values. Influenced by his experience with the Woodmen, Simmons modeled the "new" Klan along the lines of the widely popular fraternal organizations of the period.

Simmons's vision of the Klan, however, proved beyond his personal abilities. He found himself forced to bring in outsiders to help organize and promote his organization, which sapped much of his authority. Despite being acknowledged as the founder of the reestablished Klan, Simmons found his position challenged by aggressive state leaders. An internal power struggle resulted in Simmons losing his position as Imperial Wizard in 1922. He immediately began a series of lawsuits to regain control of the Klan. In 1924, Simmons agreed to drop his suits in return for a lump sum payment of almost $150,000. Simmons then retired to suburban Atlanta. He died in 1946.

Dwight Curtis Stephenson, 1891–1966

Ku Klux Klan Leader

Born in Texas in 1891, Stephenson drifted through a variety of jobs, states, and political positions before settling in Evansville, Indiana, in 1920. A masterful self-promoter and salesman, Stephenson found the Klan to be the perfect vehicle for his personal and political ambitions. Thanks to his support of Hiram Evans, Stephenson became Grand Dragon of 23 Northern states. His 1923 coronation as

Grand Dragon drew 100,000 Klan supporters to Kokomo, Indiana. His grandiose acceptance speech made it clear that Stephenson believed he was now one of the most powerful men in the country. The Indiana Klan leader's personal political ambitions included plans for a Senate run, then possibly a bid for the White House.

From his Indianapolis base, Stephenson built the Indiana Klan into the most powerful state organization in the country. By some estimates, one-third of the native-born white male residents of the state belonged to the Klan in the mid-1920s. Stephenson utilized the Klan as a personal shadow government and military. The Indiana Klan leader mobilized his organization to elect a governor and a senator, and he could marshal the support of the state legislature. He leveraged politicians by threatening to withhold Klan support, and he kept the organization under close watch through personal allegiances and informants.

Stephenson's empire crumbled in 1925 with his conviction for the kidnapping, rape, and murder of Madge Oberholtzer. Angered by the Indiana governor's refusal to pardon him, Stephenson publicized the state's widespread, Klan-influenced corruption in 1927. Stephenson was paroled in 1950 but violated his parole and returned to prison the next year. Released in 1956, the former Klan leader dropped into obscurity. He died in Tennessee in 1966.

Billy Sunday, 1862–1935

Evangelist

Born in 1862 in Story County, Iowa, William Ashley Sunday Jr. grew up in rural poverty in Iowa before spending much of his adolescence in orphanages. In 1877, he became a semipro baseball player and volunteer fireman. Sunday joined the Chicago White Stockings in 1883 and played professional baseball until 1890. A renowned base stealer, he retired in his prime to become a Bible teacher and traveling evangelist.

In 1893, he became an associate of traveling evangelist J. Wilbur Chapman. When Chapman left the circuit in 1896, Sunday launched his own career. Sunday's relentless touring and boundless energy made him the nation's most famous traveling preacher. Despite never attending seminary, Sunday was ordained by the Presbyterian Church in 1903. He led hundreds of crusades, preached to an estimated 100 million people, and converted close to 1 million during his services. His theatrical preaching style and quick wit earned him a vast personal income and inspired future generations of evangelists. Sunday strongly believed in marshaling Christians to shape public morals, and he used his fame to promote a variety of social causes, particularly Prohibition. In 1920, he attempted to become the Republican presidential candidate to advance his conservative social agenda. Despite this political failure, Sunday remained wildly popular as a circuit preacher. He continued to lead crusades until his death in 1935.

Billy Sunday, evangelist (1862–1935). (Library of Congress)

E. C. Yellowly, 1873–1962

Federal Law Enforcement Official

Born in Mississippi in 1873, Edward Clements Yellowly grew up in North Carolina. After a brief period operating the family farm, Yellowly began working as a Bureau of Internal Revenue alcohol revenue collector in 1899. His success in apprehending moonshiners and rumrunners led to a series of transfers and promotions. By 1919, Yellowly worked as a regional supervisor in San Francisco and had created a field audit system for the bureau.

In 1921, Yellowly became the chief of a cadre of special Prohibition agents assigned to areas in which local law enforcement struggled. While working in New York, Yellowly became famous for his inventive use of disguises for his agents. He and his agents worked in almost every state before Yellowly was assigned to focus on lawless Chicago. The difficulty of battling Al Capone in that city led Yellowly to organize a group of agents immune to bribery (popularly known as the "Untouchables"). He left active Prohibition enforcement in 1930 but continued to work for alcohol-related units of Internal Revenue until his retirement in 1946. Yellowly died in Chicago in 1962.

REFERENCES AND FURTHER READINGS

Ahlstrom, Sydney E. 2004. *A Religious History of the American People.* 2nd edition. New Haven, CT: Yale University Press.

Alexander, Charles C. 1966. *The Ku Klux Klan in the Southwest.* Lexington: University of Kentucky Press.

Bergreen, Laurence. 1994. *Capone: The Man and the Era.* New York: Simon and Schuster.

Blee, Kathleen M. 1991. *Women of the Klan: Racism and Gender in the 1920s.* Berkeley: University of California Press.

Burnham, John C. 1993. *Bad Habits: Drinking, Smoking, Taking Drugs, Gambling, Sexual Misbehavior, and Swearing in American History.* New York: New York University Press.

Burns, Eric. 2004. *The Spirits of America: A Social History of Alcohol.* Philadelphia: Temple University Press.

Caudill, Edward, and Edward Lawson. 2000. *The Scopes Trial: A Photographic History.* Knoxville: University of Tennessee Press.

Chafe, William H. 1972. *The American Woman: Her Changing Social, Economic, and Political Roles, 1920–1970.* New York: Oxford University Press.

Chalmers, David A. 1981. *Hooded Americanism: The History of the Ku Klux Klan.* 3rd edition. New York: Franklin Watts.

Clark, Norman H. 1976. *Deliver Us from Evil: An Interpretation of American Prohibition.* New York: W. W. Norton.

Coben, Stanley. 1991. *Rebellion against Victorianism: The Impetus for Cultural Change in 1920s America.* New York: Oxford University Press.

Collins, Gail. 2004. *America's Women: 400 Years of Dolls, Drudges, Helpmates, and Heroines.* New York: Perennial.

Conkin, Paul K. 1998. *When All the Gods Trembled: Darwinism, Scopes, and American Intellectuals.* Lanham, MD: Rowman & Littlefield.

Cott, Nancy F. 1987. *The Grounding of American Feminism.* New Haven: Yale University Press.

Cott, Nancy F., and Elizabeth H. Pleck. 1979. *A Heritage of Her Own: Toward a New Social History of American Women.* New York: Touchstone.

Dye, Nancy Schrom. 1980. *As Equals and as Sisters: Feminism, the Labor Movement, and the Women's Trade Union League of New York.* Columbia: University of Missouri Press.

Epstein, Daniel Mark. 1993. *Sister Aimee: The Life of Aimee Semple McPherson.* New York: Harcourt Brace Jovanovich, 1993.

Evans, Sarah M. 1989. *Born for Liberty: A History of Women in America.* New York: Free Press.

Fass, Paula. 1977. *The Damned and the Beautiful: American Youth in the 1920's.* New York: Oxford University Press.

Flexner, Eleanor, and Ellen Fitzpatrick. 1996. *Century of Struggle: The Women's Rights Movement in the United States.* Enlarged ed. Cambridge, MA: Belknap.

Foster, Gaines M. 2002. *Moral Reconstruction: Christian Lobbyists and the Federal Legislation of Morality, 1865–1920.* Chapel Hill: University of North Carolina Press.

Ginger, Ray. 1958. *Six Days or Forever? Tennessee v. John Thomas Scopes.* London: Oxford University Press.

Goldberg, David J. 1999. *Discontented America: The United States in the 1920s.* Baltimore: Johns Hopkins University Press.

Goldberg, Ronald Allen. 2003. *America in the Twenties.* Syracuse, NY: Syracuse University Press.

Grebstein, Sheldon Norman. 1960. *Monkey Trial: The State of Tennessee vs. John Thomas Scopes.* Boston: Houghton Mifflin.

Greenberg, Martin Alan. 1999. *Prohibition Enforcement: Charting a New Mission.* Springfield, IL: Charles C. Thomas.

Higham, John. 1955. *Strangers in the Land: Patterns of American Nativism, 1860–1925.* New Brunswick, NJ: Rutgers University Press.

Hilfer, Anthony Channell. 1969. *The Revolt from the Village, 1915–1930.* Chapel Hill: University of North Carolina Press.

Hoffman, Dennis E. 1993. *Scarface Al and the Crime Crusaders: Chicago's Private War against Capone.* Carbondale: Southern Illinois University Press.

Hofstadter, Richard. 1957. *The Age of Reform: From Bryan to F.D.R.* Englewood Cliffs, NJ: Prentice-Hall.

Hofstadter, Richard. 1962. *Anti-intellectualism in American Life.* New York: Alfred Knopf.

Israel, Charles A. 2004. *Before Scopes: Evangelicalism, Education, and Evolution in Tennessee, 1870–1925.* Athens: University of Georgia Press.

Jackson, Kenneth T. 1967. *The Ku Klux Klan in the City, 1915–1930.* New York: Oxford University Press.

Kerr, K. Austin. 1985. *Organized for Prohibition: A New History of the Anti-saloon League.* New Haven, CT: Yale University Press.

Kirschner, Don S. 1970. *City and Country: Rural Responses to Urbanization in the 1920's*. Westport, CT: Greenwood.

Kraditor, Aileen S. 1981. *The Ideas of the Woman Suffrage Movement, 1890–1920*, Rev. ed. New York: W. W. Norton.

Larson, Edward J. 1997. *Summer for the Gods: The Scopes Trial and America's Continuing Debate over Science and Religion*. New York: Basic Books.

Lears, T. J. Jackson. 1981. *No Place of Grace: Anti-modernism and the Transformation of American Culture, 1880–1920*. New York: Pantheon.

Leinwand, Gerald. 2001. *1927: High Tide of the 1920s*. New York: Four Walls Eight Windows.

Lemons, J. Stanley. 1973. *The Woman Citizen: Social Feminism in the 1920s*. Urbana: University of Illinois Press.

Leuchtenburg, William E. 1958. *The Perils of Prosperity, 1914–1932*. Chicago: University of Chicago Press.

Lippy, Charles H. 1989. *Twentieth-Century Shapers of American Popular Religion*. New York: Greenwood Press.

Marsden, George M. 1980. *Fundamentalism and American Culture: The Shaping of Twentieth-Century Evangelicalism, 1870–1925*. New York: Oxford University Press.

Marty, Martin E. 1986. *Modern American Religion*. Vol. 2, *The Noise of Conflict, 1919–1941*. Chicago: University of Chicago Press.

Moore, Leonard J. 1991. *Citizen Klansmen: The Ku Klux Klan in Indiana, 1921–1928*. Chapel Hill: University of North Carolina Press.

Moore, R. Laurence. 1977. *In Search of White Crows: Spiritualism, Parapsychology, and American Culture*. New York: Oxford University Press.

Moran, Jeffrey P. 2002. *The Scopes Trial: A Brief History with Documents*. Boston: Bedford/St. Martins.

Morone, James A. 2003. *Hellfire Nation: The Politics of Sin in American History*. New Haven, CT: Yale University Press.

Murdock, Catherine Gilbert. 1998. *Domesticating Drink: Women, Men, and Alcohol in America, 1870–1940*. Baltimore: Johns Hopkins University Press.

Olasky, Marvin, and John Perry. 2005. *Monkey Business: The True Story of the Scopes Trial*. Nashville: Broadman & Holman.

Parrish, Michael E. 1992. *Anxious Decades: America in Prosperity and Depression, 1920–1941*. New York: W. W. Norton.

Pegram, Thomas R. 1998. *Battling Demon Rum: The Struggle for a Dry America, 1800–1933*. Chicago: Ivan R. Dee.

Sinclair, Andrew. 1962. *Prohibition: The Era of Excess*. Boston: Little, Brown and Company.

Szasz, Ferenc Morton. 1982. *The Divided Mind of Protestant America, 1880–1930*. Tuscaloosa: University of Alabama Press.

Tucker, Richard K. 1991. *The Dragon and the Cross: The Rise and Fall of the Ku Klux Klan in Middle America*. Hamden, CT: Archon.

Wade, Wyn Craig. 1987. *The Fiery Cross: The Ku Klux Klan in America*. New York: Simon and Schuster.

Wiebe, Robert H. 1967. *The Search for Order, 1877–1920*. New York: Hill and Wang.

The End of the 1920s

OVERVIEW

The popular perception of the 1920s presents the decade as a period of unbridled prosperity. Growing rates of automobile and radio ownership, the development of tourist destinations, tales of fantastic "get rich quick" schemes, and the fabulous growth in industrial production all seemingly support this belief. Nor can one find counterviews in the public pronouncements of the nation's business leaders or presidents. Boosterism proved to be one of the hallmarks of the age. As with many stereotypes, tales of 1920s prosperity contain a kernel of truth. Nor were the captains of industry lying with their pronouncements of success. Business did flourish during the Republican Decade. Technological developments resulted in new consumer products and more efficient means of producing older goods, our federal government was friendly, and we emerged from World War I with our industrial base unscathed; all of these things helped propel remarkable gains for American corporations. Underneath the glowing success of business, however, the issue of prosperity becomes far more complicated. Thanks to higher wages, the middle class enjoyed the fruits of prosperity by purchasing a wealth of consumer and luxury items that had been previously out of their financial reach. Yet despite the increased income of the middle class, their actual purchasing power did not match their acquisitiveness. America's middle class managed to soak up so much of the nation's industrial output only by purchasing many of their consumer goods on credit. The previously much-decried action of going into debt (or, as it was more ominously referred to, living beyond one's means) became an accepted by-product of enjoying modern conveniences. For working-class Americans, most of the consumer goods they helped manufacture stood well beyond their financial ability to consume. Limited wage increases, some measure of employer largesse in improving working conditions, and the benefits of increased municipal social services represented their circumscribed portion of prosperity. The notion of the 1920s as a period of astonishing wealth, then, only tells part of the story of how Americans lived during the decade.

In their renowned 1929 account of life in Muncie, Indiana, sociologists Robert and Helen Lynd found a city thoroughly stratified not just in the expected differences of age, social values, or ethnicity but, most importantly, in quality of life. The Lynds uncovered what most Americans instinctively knew but chose to ignore: some citizens struggled simply to survive while others enjoyed immense wealth. They noted that a tiny fraction of Muncie ("Middletown" in the book) controlled the economic wealth of the city. And while a "business-class" portion of the citizenry enjoyed a middle-class lifestyle by providing services for the wealthy, some 70 percent of the city's residents found themselves facing periodic unemployment and frequent economic hardship as part of the "working class." The Lynds also noted a pervasive reluctance to address social problems and economic inequalities. They commented that "as Middletown has become reluctantly conscious from time to time of discrepancies in its institutional system, it has frequently tended to avoid 'doing something about' these 'social problems' of 'bad times,' 'the younger generation,' 'corrupt politics,' 'housing,' 'street traffic,' and so on, by blaming the difficulty on the 'nature of things' or upon the willfulness of individuals" (Lynd and Lynd 1929, 501).

Had economists undertaken similar studies of America's cities, they would have discovered that the economic inequalities uncovered by the Lynds in Muncie actually became more pronounced during the 1920s. Not only did the prosperity of the decade only benefit a small portion of the nation's citizenry but also the wealthiest Americans actually increased their economic control of the nation. Fabulous business profits translated into growing riches for the elite that dwarfed the slight improvements in quality of life for the working class. In other words, the rich grew richer faster than the poor grew less poor. During the 1920s, an already unbalanced distribution of wealth grew increasingly skewed toward the top. That such conditions did not result in social upheaval resulted from a number of factors. America's political leaders, overwhelmingly drawn from the social elite, often personally gained from the success of business while they continued to maintain a traditional view of the government's responsibilities. They believed the federal government had a responsibility to provide basic protections for consumers and workers (a legacy of the Progressive era) but did not view government as an instrument of regulation or social welfare. Those who sought to redress the maldistribution of wealth through governmental action were faced with an intractably probusiness, antiunion Washington wedded to the economic status quo. Equally important, the successes of business, to an extent, trickled down into improved conditions for the middle and working classes. Business prosperity required consumption, and the expansive increase in personal credit benefitted industry and gave the middle class a sense of partaking in the prosperity. The working class also enjoyed a rise in their living conditions (which seemed princely compared to the living conditions of workers in Europe); this muted their discontent. The degraded status of workers, vast personal debt on the part of the middle class, and massive industrial overproduction eventually coalesced into a dangerous condition that contributed to both the onset and continuation of the Great Depression, but this reckoning occurred only at the end of the decade.

By the tail end of the decade, some measure of union activism blossomed. In many industries, conditions for workers grew even more dehumanizing as industrialists attempted to extract maximum profits by reducing wages and increasing workloads. Disgruntled employees in several industries, particularly textiles, staged a series of protests and strikes in an effort to improve their conditions. For many of these workers, the decision to engage in unionization and work stoppages only emerged as a last-ditch effort to counter the impossible demands of employers. Faced with poverty-level wages and body-destroying work-rate expectations, these workers struck out of a sense of desperation. In most cases, these attempts to stem industrialist excesses failed through a combination of union weaknesses, internecine fighting, and governmental support of employers. However, these failures helped to lay the foundation for the labor movement's growth during the 1930s.

A number of the strikes of the decade were led by American Communists. In the wake of the Bolshevik Revolution, left-wing Americans deserted the Socialist Party to establish a revolutionary Communist movement. The persecutions of the postwar Red Scare dealt the movement a devastating blow, but the remaining American Communists managed to keep the movement alive by going underground during the early 1920s. In 1925, an aboveground party, the Workers Party of America (WPA), began the slow process of establishing a legitimate communist organization in this country. While the party's views of existing labor organizations changed over time, from its inception the WPA attempted to become active in unionization efforts, which prompted communist involvement in the strikes of the late 1920s. Internal struggles over doctrine and power wracked the WPA, but some measure of unity was achieved by the end of the decade. Reflective of the new consensus, American Communists changed the name of their party to the Communist Party, USA (CPUSA) in 1929. As with the labor movement in general, the limited successes of the 1920s helped lay the groundwork for CPUSA successes in the next decade.

The feverish desire for prosperity exhibited by the wealthy and its emulation by the middle class also fueled a series of speculative ventures. Economist John Kenneth Galbraith posited that Americans of the 1920s inhabited a "world of speculative make-believe" (Galbraith 1988, 3). One of the overriding concerns of the decade was to "get rich quick." Such sentiment led to a growth in the total number of businesses and a record growth in patents but also to less savory endeavors as well. The decade's most famous "quick buck" scheme involved an ex-convict and former Boston clerk named Charles Ponzi. He perfected the pyramid scheme whereby a person contributes a certain amount of money to a fake business enterprise (in Ponzi's case, he claimed to be dealing in foreign currencies) with a "guaranteed" return. In reality, Ponzi simply paid those who participated in the scheme earlier with the money contributed by those who joined later. By doing so he managed to pay the promised profits, but only as long as more contributed. Those who got in on the scheme at the end, with no one behind them in the pipeline, lost their money. Ponzi managed to take in an estimated $15 million before being exposed. His 1921 conviction for mail fraud should have served as a cautionary tale for those looking to make a quick fortune, but many Americans failed to learn the lesson that spending today against future profits was a fundamentally unsound business practice.

The amount of funds involved in the Ponzi scheme paled in comparison to those involved in the Florida land boom. With its wonderful climate and reputation as a playground for the wealthy, Florida's popularity as a tourist destination and retirement area grew steadily from the mid-1910s on. Those who purchased property in Palm Beach or Miami prior to World War I realized an enormous profit on their initial investments thanks to the burgeoning population of Florida. This inescapable fact, combined with a massive advertising campaign fueled by a combination of civic boosterism and outright chicanery, propelled one of the great land bubbles in American history. Middle-class Americans swooped in to purchase any land they could find, underwater or not, in the belief that the property would continue to escalate in value. Blinded by tales of property increasing in value by 400 percent or more, American investors propelled an explosion in new developments across southern Florida. Those with little disposable income found participation in the boom facilitated by the widespread practice of purchasing land for 10 percent down. Typically, these small investors expected to sell the land for a profit before having to pay off the other 90 percent. The boom peaked in 1925, but a combination of natural disasters, crooked deals, ridiculously inflated prices, and—most importantly—a lessening confidence in the long-term potential for land values led to a rapid end to the boom. Like those involved with Ponzi, individuals who entered the boom at the end found themselves facing economic difficulties.

Responsible Americans might view the activities in Florida with disdain, believing those who suffered only had themselves to blame for involvement in such a questionable venture, but the stock market, with its links to America's most successful companies and businessmen, seemed to offer a means of enjoying prosperity for even the most skeptical. Vast business profits propelled the stock market continually upward from the middle of the 1920s. The market's growth escalated dramatically in 1927 and seemed destined to continue climbing. Such confidence in the market fueled increased speculation, which only helped to increase belief in continued growth by inflating prices. Concomitantly, a host of questionable business practices, from easy credit to speculation to overproduction, made the economy appear falsely strong. In October 1929, this economic house of cards collapsed. While only an estimated one million Americans suffered reversals due to their direct involvement in the market, the collapse created a downward spiral that sucked in businesses and banks. The interlinked nature of the economy, therefore, brought the collapse home to all Americans. By the dawn of the 1930s, no one could ignore the nation's economic woes as the onset of the Great Depression shattered the optimism of the previous decade.

The sheer magnitude of the Great Depression forced a fundamental adjustment to the federal government. Past administrations allowed economic downturns to run their course, believing they were part of a natural cycle, with little interference in either the economy or social welfare programs. Traditionally, aid to the indigent and dispossessed fell within the provenance of private charities, with local governments helping only when needed. President Hoover initially followed this pattern in dealing with the Depression. Hoover attempted to convince business and labor to voluntarily work together to minimize the effects on the economy while he made rosy statements to boost the morale of the American people. The failure of Hoover's plan to rebuild the economy, coupled with the unprecedented suffering that accompanied 25 percent unemployment, forced the creation of new policies. Much to his consternation, Hoover, however haltingly, enlarged the responsibilities of the federal government to include direct involvement in employment and public aid. Although he often appeared aloof and uncaring, Hoover actually began the creation of the modern welfare state through his legislative activities in 1932. His program did provide some measure of relief, but, more importantly, he laid the groundwork for Franklin Roosevelt's New Deal.

TIMELINE

1920	The postwar depression begins.
	The United Communist Party is established.
1921	Carl Fisher begins using an elephant to promote Miami Beach.
	The Workers Party of America is established.

1922   George Merrick begins development of Coral Gables, Florida.

The coal strike begins in April.

The railroad strike begins in July.

Nation begins recovery from postwar economic slump.

1923   *Adkins v. Children's Hospital* strikes down D.C. minimum wage law.

1924   State of Florida abolishes all state income and inheritance taxes.

1925   Florida land boom peaks.

Addison Mizer begins Boca Raton, Florida, development in April.

Florida railway embargo begins in October.

The Workers Party of America becomes the Workers (Communist) Party of America.

The International Labor Defense is founded.

1926   Passaic, New Jersey, strike begins in January.

Hurricane hits Miami, September.

The University of Miami is established.

Fisher attempts to make Mantauk, Long Island, the "Miami Beach of the north."

1927   Last striking Passaic workers return to jobs in February.

McNary–Haugen bill is first introduced.

Robert and Helen Lynd study Muncie, Indiana.

1928   Hurricane hits Okeechobee, Florida.

Textile strike hits New Bedford, Connecticut, in April.

"Dixie Highway" is completed.

"Third Period" of communist movement begins.

1929   Elizabethtown strike begins in March.

Gastonia strike begins in April.

Communist League of America (Opposition) is established in May.

Gastonia 7 convicted in October.

Wall Street stock market crash in October.

Agricultural Adjustment Act is passed in November.

Workers (Communist) Party of America becomes Communist Party, USA.

1920s ECONOMICS: THE DISTRIBUTION OF WEALTH

An Age of Prosperity

The 1920s began with a serious economic downturn thanks to the difficulties that accompanied the transition back to a peacetime economy. During the war, unemployment—thanks to the large number of men in uniform—had been virtually nonexistent, and government contracts had bolstered the industrial and agricultural sectors. With the end of the war, most of these contracts ended, and a wave of veterans returned and began the process of obtaining their previous jobs. By 1922, after a confusing period marked by a series of rapid boom-and-bust cycles, the American economy had not only recovered, it also began a period of robust growth and prosperity. Bolstered by new technologies, little labor unrest, the support of the general public, and a pliant federal government, American business interests wallowed in one of the greatest waves of corporate success in the nation's history. The gaudy profits of American business gave rise to a widespread belief that the United States had achieved a miraculously high level of prosperity.

During the 1920s, production, income, and business profits soared. The national income rose from $64 million at the beginning of the decade to $87 million in 1929 (Faulkner 1954, 606–607). Accompanied by a lack of inflation, this meant an exceptional increase in purchasing power. There were plenty of goods for affluent Americans to spend their income on and industrial production nearly doubled. Unfortunately, this expansion in the number of consumer goods available outpaced demand. Increases in income and population were not sufficient to offset overproduction as the 1920s wound down. This imbalance would prove to be one of the factors leading to the catastrophic depression at the end of the decade.

Not surprisingly, in an effort to link themselves to the notion of a successful America, the series of Republican presidents during the decade loudly trumpeted the prosperity of the period. Much of the economic optimism of the time (and later perceptions of the 1920s) derived from the rosy pronouncements of the federal government. In 1927, the Internal Revenue Service (IRS) reported that Americans enjoyed the highest standard of living in world history (Leinwand 2001, 34–36). President Calvin Coolidge declared that the nation as a whole benefited from the prosperity. His successor, Herbert Hoover, in a remark that followed him for the rest of his life, declared that poverty in the United States faced an imminent demise. The onset of the Great Depression in 1929 proved the hollowness of Hoover's claim. A close examination of the distribution of wealth during the 1920s betrays a similar emptiness in the assertions of Coolidge and the IRS.

Most Americans felt some measure of gain from the decade's business prosperity. However, the determinedly probusiness federal government put few checks on the growth of corporate interests and steadfastly refused to ensure that the prosperity was diffused throughout the American population. The Republican-controlled executive and legislative branches avoided regulation of the economy, as did the conservative Supreme Court. For example, in *Adkins v. Children's Hospital,* the court struck down the District of Columbia's minimum wage for women law. The result of this laissez-faire approach was a society increasingly economically stratified. A horribly skewed distribution of wealth enabled the few at the top of the economic pyramid to achieve new heights in their standard of living while a large economic underclass struggled simply to survive.

This maldistribution of wealth continued to escalate as the decade progressed. By 1929, less than 3 percent of the populace qualified as wealthy, yet the 60,000 richest families in the country possessed a personal wealth greater than the 25 million poorest families. The top 1 percent represented 14.5 percent of the total national income. Reflecting the fact that the disparity in wealth distribution increased during the decade, the top 1 percent's share of the national wealth had grown by 19 percent since 1920 (Goldberg 2003, 128–129). Also by 1929, only about 20 percent of American families could be considered middle class. Some three-fourths of the nation's families lived below middle-class status. Although the generally accepted minimum working-class budget for a family of four was $2,000 per year, the average industrial wage only reached the $1,300 per year mark shortly before the economic downturn of 1929. While the Great Depression created economic dislocation of unprecedented levels, many Americans faced dire circumstances long before it began.

The Wealthy

The succession of probusiness presidents during the Republican Decade stressed free enterprise; they believed it was unfair to tax heavily those who prospered from free enterprise. This hands-off approach toward the wealthy was directed by Andrew Mellon. As treasury secretary under all three Republican presidents during the 1920s, Mellon wielded enormous political influence. He also stood to benefit from low personal income tax policies; Mellon made a fortune controlling Gulf Oil and Alcoa. When Harding appointed him to serve in the cabinet,

Secretary of the Treasury Andrew Mellon lays the cornerstone of the Internal Revenue Building, May 20, 1929. (Library of Congress)

Mellon stood as the third richest man in the United States. Mellon helped to craft legislation that dramatically reduced taxes on all income levels, with especially significant cuts for those at the highest income levels. Loopholes in the laws allowed many of the nation's wealthiest citizens to avoid paying any taxes at all. Those at the top of the economic pyramid who could not find a means of avoiding income taxes altogether still found themselves enjoying the benefits of the revised tax schedule. Over the course of the decade, the tax on incomes over $1 million dropped by 31 percent. As part of this program, Mellon also succeeded in eliminating inheritance and gift taxes. Elizabeth Stevenson later laconically noted, "to see the twenties whole, it is necessary to acknowledge the quite conscious manipulation of the economy for the benefit of one element" (Stevenson 1998, 131).

While the number of people in the highest income brackets increased over the course of the decade, which gave an impression of the diffusion of prosperity, their control of the nation's total wealth also increased. The number of millionaires in the United States increased from 65 in 1919 to 513 in 1929 (Williamson and Lindert 1980, 75–80). However, the share of the nation's total income possessed by the wealthy increased from 22.9 percent to 26.1 percent during the decade (Bernstein 1960, 63–64). The combined incomes of the top 0.1 percent of the nation's families were greater than the combined incomes of the bottom 42 percent of families. While the distribution of wealth had been increasingly skewed toward the wealthy since the Civil War, this increase represented a dramatic jump.

This enormous purchasing power spurred speculation and investment as well as the sale of luxury goods. Wealthy Americans contributed to the flurry of stock market activity and engaged in furious land speculation in Florida, southern California, and Muscle Shoals, Alabama. Although land speculation could be exceptionally dangerous (as when the Florida land boom imploded), for those wealthy enough to participate, the potential gains could be enormous. At its peak in this decade, real estate income (primarily rent and interest) exceeded the income of agriculture or any group of manufacturing industries. Sales of luxury items such as motorboats also soared. Privately owned watercraft increased by 90 percent during the 1920s. The number of golf courses, the traditional orbit of the well-to-do, grew by 200 percent.

The Middle Class

Although middle-class Americans did not benefit from Mellon's tax policies to the same extent as the rich, the "Coolidge Prosperity" of the middle decade did increase their consumer purchasing power. The coupling of increased disposable income and shorter work weeks led middle-class Americans to devote more attention to both leisure and consumption. To facilitate consumerism, businesses began to offer a wealth of expensive products to Americans through the wonder of "installment buying." No longer forcibly constrained to be thrifty, Americans gobbled up automobiles ("Ride Now, Pay Later," trumpeted the manufacturers), refrigerators, washing machines, and radios with 10 percent down and pledges to make monthly payments. During the decade, more than 85 percent of all furniture sold in the United States would be bought on credit. The ability to obtain goods through a payment schedule allowed the middle class to achieve a significantly higher standard of living, but at a dear cost. By 1927, Americans purchased 15 percent of all goods sold on credit. Consumers had racked up $3 billion in personal debt. This bloated figure led the National Association of Credit Men, an organization that represented manufacturers and retailers, to issue a call for curbing the "explosiveness of credit . . . for undoubtedly in a credit pinch this condition would prove a very disturbing factor" (Mowry 1963, 32–33). The end of prosperity two years later would demonstrate just how costly living beyond one's means could become.

For middle-class Americans the lure of buying against future earnings proved irresistible. The 1920s ushered in the era of "hard-sell" advertising and planned obsolescence (Lears 1994, 218–234). To move their overproduced goods, American manufacturers unleashed an unprecedented storm of advertising on American consumers. Advertisers connected social status with consumption and posited that modern life required a battalion of new "necessities." In his 1922 novel, *Babbitt,* which thoroughly denounced modern business and advertising, Sinclair Lewis lampooned the middle-class Americans who swallowed whole cloth the pronouncements of advertisers. Lewis carefully cataloged all the new "necessities" required in a modern, prosperous home as a means of assailing those whose "god was Modern Appliances" (Lewis 2002, 5–16). What Lewis failed to recognize was the way advertisers connected installment buying and modern household accessories with middle-class aspirations to affluence. Advertisers linked the endless cycle of work-purchase-consume to the very survival of American civilization. In *Middletown,* their examination of life in Muncie, Indiana, sociologists Robert and Helen Lynd found that the obsession to purchase more goods became a matter of patriotism. They related a newspaper editorial that declared "the American citizen's first importance to his country is no longer that of citizen but that of consumer" (Lynd and Lynd 1929, 88). To consume, even at the risk of financial peril, denoted one's success in achieving the American dream, a dream of leisure, comfort, and wealth. Through keeping up with modern products and technology, middle-class Americans both established their superiority over the drudgery of working-class existence and connected themselves with the wealthy. By consuming on the installment plan, middle-class Americans tasted some of the delights of wealth, and by consuming beyond their means they placed themselves in a position that required they continue to work diligently for their employers. Middle-class Americans, therefore, derived both pleasure and pain from the unequal distribution of wealth.

The shift toward middle-class status being defined by one's consumption also helped those in the economic middle more readily accept how the nation's wealth was distributed. The 1920s witnessed a dramatic alteration in the perception of the wealthy. The Republican presidents of the 1920s scaled back antitrust suits, which both reduced the impression that all captains of industry exploited the country and, coupled with their relentlessly probusiness policies, allowed for corporate mergers on an unprecedented scale. This consolidation meant prosperity and a raft of consumer goods for the middle class; they became connected and supportive of the wealthy. Social commentator Gilbert Seldes noted that at the turn of the century average Americans believed millionaires "had because they lacked; . . . [and] enjoyed because they suffered." However, by the 1920s, the perception had shifted to "[they] had because they had; [they were] rich only because they were prosperous; [they] luxuriated because they lived, a little beyond their means, in comfort, on the installment plan" (Seldes 1993, 18–19). That some Americans became fabulously wealthy during the decade only reflected the prosperity enjoyed by all. In other words, for there to be prosperity, there had to be some who became ultrarich. For the middle manager, then, that the growth in the income of a duPont or Rockefeller outpaced the growth of his income created little concern.

Farmers

The war proved a bonanza for American agriculture. While much of Europe was impossible to cultivate and millions of men in uniform required sustenance, American farmers reaped unimagined profits. To meet the increased demand, many went into debt purchasing new (often marginal) land and mechanizing their operations. This proved lucrative in the short term, but had disastrous long-term consequences. The postwar return to normal agricultural production in Europe significantly reduced the need to import American commodities, which led to a glut in the domestic market. By early 1921, prices had dropped to only one-third of their 1920 levels. Rural banks failed and land values collapsed. Farm wages dipped by 40 percent from 1920 to 1924. Nearly one million farmers lost their homes to foreclosure that year alone. Those who managed to maintain the title to their land also suffered. The value of farmland tumbled as commodity prices fell. Total farmland values in this country decreased by a staggering $20 billion during the decade.

Between 1919 and 1924, 13 million acres of land were taken out of production. For the first time in American history, the acreage of land being cultivated for crops decreased. While in the past this reduction in acreage would have translated into decreased production and increased commodity prices, non-cultivation during the 1920s did not help improve the lot of American farmers. Agricultural production actually increased 5 percent during the first half of the decade. Thanks to tractors and combines, yield per acre had increased. However, the enormous costs of mechanization pushed small farmers out of the market. The large corporate farm, with its battery of low-paid agricultural workers, increasingly became the norm.

America's family farmers attempted to address their dire financial circumstances by promoting parity and farm cooperatives. Embedded in the concept of parity was the notion that the government should establish minimum prices for commodities to ensure both fair market value and economic security for farmers. To do so, the federal government would purchase commodities at a price profitable for producers and then resell the commodities to consumers. Any surplus would then be dumped on international markets, which, in theory, would keep prices high in the United States. Beginning in 1927, Congress repeatedly passed the McNary–Haugen bills to establish this practice, but President Coolidge's concern over price fixing led him to veto the bills repeatedly. The farm cooperatives were attempts by farmers to stabilize production and prices through voluntary associations. In the face of uncontrollable international markets and the enormous number of uncooperative individual producers, these

Tenant farmer and his family sit in front of the dilapidated shack they rent, Sissonville, West Virginia, October 1921. Lewis Hine photo. (Library of Congress)

organizations failed to stem the suffering of farmers. Agriculture's share of the national income fell by 50 percent during the 1920s.

The failure of farmers to achieve relief from the federal government and the consolidation of agricultural wealth into large, corporate farms caused a downward spiral in the standard of living for those involved in agricultural work. The increasingly marginal status of American farmers can be seen in the rise in farm tenancy during the 1920s. Although farm tenancy rates had steadily risen since the 1880s, the rate spiked dramatically during the Republican Decade. By the end of the 1920s, 40 percent of all farmers rented the land they worked. The nature of tenancy also changed as the percentage of renters rose. In the past, farm tenancy (for white agricultural workers) often served as a rung on the ladder toward independent ownership of land for young farmers (Grant 2002, 36–56). By the 1920s, tenancy had become part of a descent toward landless farm laborer. Tenant farmers faced dramatic reductions in both social status and living conditions. Nationally, houses on rented farms had lower values than those owned by their residents. Landlords routinely allowed rented farm houses to go unpainted, unrepaired, and unelectrified in order to maximize profits. Tenants also faced the inescapable problem that two people—the tenant and the landlord— made their living off one piece of property.

The Working Class

For American workers, one reason more of the vast business profits did not trickle down involved the weakness of the labor movement. The immediate postwar period saw American workers attempt to build upon gains made through National War Labor Board rulings. In 1919, some 4 million workers participated in strikes. The optimism that generated such support for unionization efforts, however, proved short-lived. A rightward drift by the federal government and corporate efforts to link trade unionism with Bolshevik radicalism helped undermine private and public support for the strikes. Most of the postwar strikes, therefore, ended in victory for business interests. Crushing defeats for the unions in major industries such as steel and textiles left workers virtually defenseless against the machinations of corporate leaders. And the inability of unions to offer protection for workers led many industrial workers to foreswear the labor movement for the rest of the decade, which served only to further undercut their socioeconomic status.

The surge in labor unrest as World War I ended did result in gains for workers in a few industries. Far more workers, however, benefited from the fear among corporate leaders that the pattern of frequent strikes might continue to disrupt business operations. To placate workers, large employers adopted measures typically known collectively as welfare capitalism. A 1926 survey of the nation's 1,500 largest companies found that 80 percent engaged in some form of welfare capitalism. In some cases, this involved tangible economic benefits for loyal service to employers through such programs as stock options, pensions, profit sharing, and group insurance. Other aspects of welfare capitalism addressed the morale of workers. Companies built cafeterias, established sports teams, and refurbished work areas in attempts to keep employees content. The carrot of welfare capitalism was accompanied by the stick of the open shop. At its heart, the improved living conditions for workers embedded in welfare capitalism were intended to prevent unionization. Employers stressed that they could help workers because they did not have meddling labor unions interfering in their relationship. Maintaining the open shop (which became euphemistically known as the "American Plan" during the 1920s) became integrally linked to continuing the worker benefits of welfare capitalism. Furthermore, the actions of corporate leaders in determining the exact nature of welfare capitalism's parameters demonstrated that the policy was undergirded with "the paternalistic assumption that the employer knew what was best for his help" (Brandes 1976, 28).

Mellon's argument that a reduction in taxes for corporations and the wealthy would result in trickle-down gains for American workers proved partially accurate. General prosperity and the desire to keep workers on the job resulted in both welfare capitalism and a rise in working class wages. How much of the decade's prosperity actually reached the working class remains contentious. Real wages for blue-collar workers rose by 14 percent during the decade. However, from 1923 to 1929—the peak period for the nation's economy—real wages increased by less than 5 percent (Soule 1989, 122–123). Much of this more modest gain only affected the upper tier of the working class. Auto and railroad workers, construction workers, and printers, in particular, saw their wages rise while less skilled workers obtained far more modest gains, if any. To put the increasing economic gap of the decade in perspective, while industrial wages increased by 14 percent, corporate dividends increased by more than 100 percent.

Working-Class Predicament

While industrial workers were responsible for the construction of the plethora of new consumer items available during the 1920s, their lack of purchasing power constrained their ability to purchase the fruits of their labors. For a working-class family, there simply was not enough extra income after paying for necessities. Economist Emma Winslow calculated that 95 percent of a working-class family's monthly income went to food, clothing, housing, and utilities. This left a scant 5 percent for education, health, recreation, and luxury items. She also noted that such a lifestyle left no money for savings, which made significant improvements in the quality of life for working class families very difficult, if not impossible (Berridge, Winslow, and Flinn 1925, 168–170). Installment buying made some items available, but large purchases such as automobiles often remained too expensive. Blue-collar Americans had to make do with less costly "major" purchases such as radios and irons. While they could enjoy a taste of the decade's consumer culture, workers found themselves bombarded with advertising images for a range of products promoted as requirements for remaining modern and up-to-date but which they simply could not afford.

For workers angry over their inability to consume or the dehumanizing regimentation of the assembly line there was little redress. Employers had successfully deflected the threat of widespread unionization while they benefitted from their ability to draw from a large pool of potential employees. Corporate America managed to maximize profits through two primary means. First, they plowed wartime profits into modernizing and mechanizing American industry. Second, most corporations adopted some measure of Frederick W. Taylor's "scientific management" system, which sought to organize assembly lines in ways that achieved maximum production, efficiency, and speed. The result of these two developments was a decreased need for unskilled industrial workers (often referred to as "technological unemployment"). The federal government did not maintain unemployment figures during the decade, but the consensus among historians is that unskilled or semiskilled workers faced double-digit unemployment throughout the 1920s. In their study of Muncie, Indiana, Robert and Helen Lynd found high unemployment rates and a pervasive pattern of under-

Table 7.1. Production and Employment in American Manufacturing Plants

Year	Production	Employment
1914	100	100
1915	110	107
1916	120	111
1917	129	117
1918	138	122
1919	148	129
1920	130	112
1921	114	99
1922	139	112
1923	164	125
1924	158	116
1925	170	117
1926	172	118
1927	170	115

Note: 1914 = base index number 100.

Source: Adapted from Sautter 1991, 222.

employment. Most of the working-class residents they interviewed detailed abrupt, unannounced short-term layoffs during slack business periods. They noted, "to the working man . . . unemployment as a 'problem' varies from a cloud the size of a man's head when 'times are good' to a black pall in a time of 'easy labor market' that may overspread all the rest of their lives" (Lynd and Lynd 1929, 56–64). Easily replaced and without organized support, the disgruntled worker who spoke out against the unequal distribution of wealth quickly found himself out of a job.

That more working-class Americans did not protest their status after 1922 reflects a number of factors. The ability of employers to bring in replacement workers, thanks to "technological unemployment," looms large, but it does not fully explain the pacific nature of working-class Americans. Because wages did increase, however slightly, over the course of the decade, laboring Americans perceived themselves as benefiting from the general prosperity. The growth in municipal social services in areas such as education, libraries, and health facilities also contributed to the notion of improved living conditions. And finally, despite their exploitation and limited share of business profits, American workers enjoyed one of the highest standards of living in the world. The vast number of immigrants and second-generation Americans in the industrial workforce possessed vivid memories of European poverty, which colored their perceptions of conditions in this country. To these workers, the meager scraps thrown to them by employers did represent prosperity.

African Americans

Issues of work and distribution of wealth took on a new character for African Americans in the 1920s. Previously concentrated in agricultural work in the American South, the opportunity to obtain better paying industrial jobs north of the Mason-Dixon Line during World War I propelled a massive internal migration. Recently relocated African Americans frequently found employment in the automobile, metalworking, and food packing industries. The end of the war, however, severely crippled the upward mobility of these people. As Irving Bernstein noted, African Americans "were the last to be hired and the first to be fired, were seldom allowed to do skilled work and almost never given supervisory jobs, were assigned the older, dirtier, and less pleasant work places, were paid less for the same work, and were often denied membership in unions" (Bernstein 1960, 58).

The widespread discrimination faced by African Americans in the workplace blunted their ability to benefit from the prosperity of the 1920s, but their demographic shift toward the industrial regions of the country did serve to increase their share of the nation's wealth. Industrial jobs, despite discriminatory practices, paid better than Southern sharecropping and farm tenancy, and the northern migration created large new African American neighborhoods conducive to the creation of minority-owned businesses. Some of these businesses blossomed into large commercial concerns. According to one government-funded study, immediately prior to the onset of the Great Depression some 70,000 businesses across the country were owned and operated by African Americans, including 33 banks (Woofter 1933, 199). The result of these endeavors was the blossoming of a (primarily Northern) African American middle class; however, this measured prosperity withered after the crash of 1929.

BOOSTERISM AND BUSTS:
THE FLORIDA LAND BOOM

The Dream Begins

In 1821, the United States completed the process of obtaining from Spain the area that became the state of Florida. Although Florida became the 27th state in the Union in 1845, the state was viewed as a fringe area of the county until late in the 19th century. Florida's wonderful climate and the drainage of swamps beginning in the 1880s helped propel a nascent tourism industry, but the state's lack of infrastructure made it difficult for holiday-makers to visit. The development of a modern and efficient transportation network at the turn of the 20th century helped usher in increasing numbers of vacationers and set the stage for the Florida land boom of the 1920s. With property values steadily climbing throughout the first two decades of the century, Florida land came to be viewed as a solid investment. And with a small army of boosters and hucksters promoting this land, Americans across the country found that investing in property they had never seen was far too easy.

The transportation system initially served as a vehicle for bringing America's wealthiest families to Florida to enjoy the area's mild winters. Standard Oil Company executive Henry Flagler deserves the credit for creating the notion of Florida as a winter playground for the rich. Flagler began developing his Florida East Coast Railway in the 1880s with an eye toward facilitating the travel of his socioeconomic equals to the sunny clime. As his railway continued to snake farther south, Flagler built magnificent hotels along the way. In 1894, Flagler reached Palm Beach and decided to make the community an earthly paradise for the rich. Flagler built a grand hotel, the Royal Poinciana, and also began to develop Palm Beach as a planned community. To translate his vision into reality, Flagler hired architect Addison Mizner. The homes that Mizner designed for Palm Beach created an atmosphere of classical opulence mingled with gaudiness calculated to demonstrate extravagant wealth. Palm Beach became the living embodiment of Thorstein Veblen's concept of "conspicuous consumption." Supporters branded the architectural style "Mediterranean Revival," but Mizner's biographer offered the more descriptive phrase "Bastard-Spanish-Moorish-Romanesque-Gothic-Renaissance-Bull-Market-Damn-the-Expenses Style" (Johnston 1953, 213). The architect explained his quixotic vision as resulting from "sometimes start[ing] a house with a Romanesque corner, pretending that it has fallen into disrepair and been added to in the Gothic spirit, when suddenly the great wealth of the New World has poured in and the owner has added a very rich Renaissance addition" (Boulton 1990, 89). Despite criticisms, Mizner's unique architectural style became thoroughly linked in public imagination with the state of Florida. "Mediterranean Revival" eventually served as the de facto design for the vast number of buildings that went up during the land boom.

A series of killing frosts in the mid-1890s propelled Flagler to extend his railway further south. He decided to try again to build paradise some 60 miles south of Palm Beach in the Biscayne Bay area. Flagler's new home, incorporated as the city of Miami in 1896, eventually became the hub of the Florida land boom. He dredged canals, built water and electricity systems, and established a newspaper in Miami. Within a few years, Miami achieved Flagler's vision of an American Riviera. Modern, glamorous, and sun-splashed, Southern Florida became fixed in the minds of Americans as the holiday fantasyland of John D. Rockefeller, J. C. Penney, various DuPonts, and other captains of industry. This image of Florida added an allure to the state that helped drive the subsequent land boom as Americans sought to capture some of this glamour by moving to South Florida.

Selling the Dream

The land boom rested in part on the establishment of South Florida as the stomping grounds of America's elite, but the confluence of a number of other factors precipitated the manic land rush. The industrialization of the nation, growth in public transportation, and widespread economic prosperity created an environment in which large numbers of Americans possessed the ability to establish second homes or engage in land speculation. The work of early Florida boosters such as Flagler and Mizner helped ensure that this excess capital made its way to the Sunshine State. A second generation of promoters and developers recognized the economic potential of recruiting a more diverse body of investors. The nation possessed a limited number of ultra-wealthy families, but a burgeoning upper-middle class offered a seemingly limitless supply of new migrants. The Florida of the boom would become, in George Tindall's phrase, a "subdivision civilization" (Tindall 1965, 79). To attract this economic "second-tier," Florida's boosters launched a massive publicity campaign in the mid-1910s. Their sales brochures emphasized Florida's invigorating climate (Ponce de Leon and the Fountain of Youth often figured heavily in promotional material), leisure opportunities, and prognostications of the state's great future and continuing prosperity. They also gained free publicity from those associated with the construction of the Panama Canal (which involved significant amounts of construction materials that first passed through the port at Key West) and those stationed in new military facilities constructed in Florida during World War I. This transient population often returned to homes across the country singing the praises of Florida.

Florida historians William Frazer and John J. Guthrie convincingly delineate the Florida land boom as beginning in 1915, growing steadily to a mid-1920s crest, and then collapsing in 1925. While their book *The Florida Land Boom* is primarily an economic assessment of the boom, they do insightfully point out the significant psychological aspect of the event (Frazer and Guthrie 1995, xv). The emotional appeal of leisure and association with America's elite is part of this, but so is a particular economic perception of Florida. The boom, they argue, could not have occurred had not Americans believed that purchasing land in distant Florida represented a good investment. In other words, those who clambered to purchase Florida real estate bought into the image created by the state's boosters partly because they felt it involved no personal risk. One piece of Palm Beach land sold for $84,000 in 1915, $240,000 in 1922, $800,000 in 1923, and $1,500,000 in 1924. Shortly before the boom ended in 1925 the parcel was estimated to be worth $5,000,000 (Tindall 1965, 109). Land buyers believed that values and prices, given the joys of the region, stood only to continue rising. This notion made the purchase of land in Florida more than simply a status symbol; it also offered a means of turning a profit. If one tired of frolicking in the

Bathers enjoy the winter sun at Miami Beach Casino, March 1923. (Library of Congress)

sun, so the logic goes, there would always be someone else eager to purchase the property. And when people came to believe that Florida property did not have the potential to increase in value the boom abruptly ended.

The second-generation booster chiefly responsible for instigating the boom was Carl G. Fisher. After making a fortune in the automobile industry, Fisher moved to Miami. Exemplifying the energy and vision of those who inaugurated the boom, Fisher literally made his own land to sell. After completing a bridge from the mainland to Miami Beach in 1913, Fisher dredged up Biscayne Bay, then used the dirt and sand to fill in the swamps and expand the size of that island. Miami Beach went from submerged mangrove swamp to highly valued real estate almost overnight. His remarkable exploits proved captivating to Americans. Folk humorist Will Rogers commented that Fisher made "the dredge the national emblem of Florida" (Burnett 1986, 204). Fisher and his partners then began a massive promotional campaign to attract buyers to his lot auctions. He used elephants, carnivals, bathing beauties, and bands to get people to the auctions.

Transporting the Masses

Fisher also attracted potential buyers in part because of an ever-increasing transportation network. Flagler's Florida East Coast Railway soon faced competition from the Atlantic Coast Line and Seaboard Air Line Railway. Indicative of the increasingly more middle-class clientele of the promoters, a number of new highways afforded means of traveling to South Florida for those who could not afford the private Pullman cars of Flagler's customers. The "Dixie Highway" section of U.S. Highway 1 reached Miami by the mid-1920s. A number of privately financed toll roads also served those desirous of becoming part of the land boom. The Tamiami Trail cut across South Florida (with disastrous ecological effects) and linked the Gulf and Atlantic coasts. Similarly, speculator William "Fingy" Connors constructed his own toll road to allow prospective buyers access to his land. Like the Tamiami, the Connors Highway severely damaged the environment (in this case the Everglades region). The Florida legislature ensured such roads would receive ample usage by not requiring the state's motorists to possess drivers' licenses. Reflecting both the fact that everything moved fast in Florida and the desire to keep the "tin can" tourists in their Fords coming south, the legislature also established the nation's highest speed limit—45 miles an hour (Crossen 2005).

The highly developed transportation network spurred an explosion in new developments. While many were simply hastily plotted lots on freshly cleared land intended as nothing more than a vehicle for turning a quick profit, other developments involved significant planning. Coral Gables, situated southwest of Miami, epitomizes the latter type. The city represented the singular vision of flamboyant Florida promoter George Merrick. He developed Coral Gables as a completely planned community. Merrick proclaimed Coral Gables to be "America's most beautiful suburb"—a Palm Beach for middle managers. Merrick proved to be a masterful promoter of the Florida way of life. He operated some 35 real estate offices across the country to sell his land to those who did not want to make the trip south. Merrick even enlisted veteran politician and religious figure William Jennings Bryan, merely one of the developer's some 3,000 salesmen, to shill for Coral Gables. Bryan gave public speeches that mixed Bible study with boosterism to the crowds that gathered in Coral Gables. Merrick is also credited with being the first promoter to stress palm trees in his advertising materials, an item that subsequently became ubiquitous in sales brochures (Allen 1964, 228). His efforts paid off in Coral Gables land sales of close to $100 million in 1925 alone. Although driven by the desire to profit from his venture, Merrick also possessed a deep strain of civic responsibility. He viewed Coral Gables as a model community and strove to make it a pleasant living environment. Among his lasting gifts to Florida is the University of Miami, which he opened in 1926.

The work of Flagler, Fisher, Merrick, and others made South Florida the center of the state's land boom. Although Jacksonville, as a rail hub and political center, prospered during the boom, South Florida became the state's economic and population center. Northern Florida remained poor and rural while the Southern part of the state became prosperous. Prior to the boom, most of the state's population resided in the north, but the boom dramatically altered this.

Despite the transient nature of tourism, a significant number of people made South Florida their permanent home because of the land boom. Among the long-term effects of the boom was the increased political and economic power wielded by the Southern half of the state.

Miami and the Florida "Lifestyle"

Within the South Florida boom zone, Miami emerged as the area's most important community. The population of Dade County grew by almost 500 percent between 1910 and 1930. It became, in the hyperbolic press of the time, "The Wonder City," "The Fair White Goddess of Cities," "The World's Playground," and "The City Invincible." As the home of the boom real estate industry, business district property in Miami skyrocketed in value. A typical downtown structure that sold for $1,000 at the beginning of the 20th century cost several hundred thousand dollars by 1925. Hundreds of real estate offices were located in the city. In 1922, the *Miami Herald* became the heaviest newspaper in the world, thanks to its bloated real estate section. The frenzied real estate business led the city government to ban the sale of land or unfolding of maps in public places because of the traffic congestion created by sidewalk sales. The massive influx of buyers and speculators put an enormous strain on the city's infrastructure and utilities and created a severe housing shortage. Homelessness and vagrancy became a severe problem while prescient Miamians rented out their front porches to those who could not find legitimate lodging.

For those with money, however, South Florida offered an enormous variety of leisure pleasures, both legal and illicit. To attract buyers, developers often built entertainment facilities as integral parts of their new communities. These efforts ranged from the mundane and ubiquitous tennis and golf courts to the more exotic attempts to replicate Venice, Italy, with canals and gondolas. The "Florida lifestyle" of leisure also included, thanks to the actions of the Florida legislature, horse racing and dog racing. Going to the track to gamble became a central aspect of life in South Florida. Winning a wager on the greyhounds and thoroughbreds in Florida was especially sweet because the state legislature abolished all state income and inheritance taxes in 1924. For those who wished to engage in other forms of gambling, Miami boasted a variety of illegal casinos. The state was a favorite haunt of organized crime figures such as Al Capone, who often wintered in Miami. Capone and his ilk set up casinos in Florida and used the state's long, ragged coastline to bring illegal liquor in from Cuba and the Bahamas. Prohibition enforcement was notoriously lax in South Florida because local officials did not want to drive away the tourists by curtailing their amusements. As a result, Miami's nightlife became a notorious draw for pleasure seekers during the 1920s.

The End of the Dream

Like all speculative bubbles, the Florida land boom had to end. In this case, the end proved swift and costly. To a significant degree, the same psychological factors that created the boom led to its demise. By 1926, many Americans came to believe that the ridiculously inflated prices simply could not hold. With public sentiment drifting toward a belief that Florida real estate no longer represented a good investment, the pool of potential buyers began to diminish. The end of the allure spelled the end of the boom. Many Americans, still buoyed by the prosperity of the Republican Decade, began to look elsewhere for investments. Perhaps the greatest irony of the Florida land boom is that many Americans, at the end of the boom, decided to place their surplus money in what they viewed as a safer and more reputable investment—the stock market.

Far more mundane factors than mass psychology, however, played a role in ending the boom. Many of those who wanted to be part of the Florida real estate market found it increasingly difficult to do so. The prices for lots reached such dizzying heights by the end of 1925 that substantial capital was required before one could purchase land. This effectively squeezed middle-class buyers out of the market. Many people became part of the boom not to reside in Florida but to buy a parcel and then sell it for profit as prices escalated. The dramatic rise in prices, however, made this small-scale speculating impossible.

Others who had gotten involved in the market found themselves burned by unscrupulous developers and agents and, with their initial funds gone, could not continue to participate in the land boom. The frenzy of the market, not surprisingly, pulled swindlers into the Florida real estate business. False advertising of properties and subdivisions (including the notorious sales of undrained swamplands) and falsely inflated prices duped many in the north who wanted to be part of the boom without actually going to Florida. Such activities led some states to pass "blue sky" laws that stopped dishonest real estate firms from selling land in their states.

Those who found themselves unable to participate in the Florida real estate market, however, counted their blessings as a series of events in 1925 and 1926 made the supposed joys of the state appear very false. In January the *Prinz Valdemar,* a 240-foot schooner, sank in the mouth of Miami's harbor. The difficulty in removing the old Danish warship, slated to become a floating hotel, brought shipping to the city to a standstill and raised concerns that the rapidly developing communities of South Florida did not have the infrastructure to deal with expanding populations. With concerns over the welfare of South Florida's population growing, the state's rail lines declared a moratorium on all imperishable goods. Beginning in the summer of 1925 the railways would only ship foodstuffs into South Florida. Intended both to allow repairs on the state's overtaxed railway system and to stave off a looming famine among the swollen population

Boats swept from their docks by the Miami Hurricane, September 18, 1926. (Library of Congress)

of South Florida unable to cope with the area's staggering inflation, the move effectively stopped the flow of both potential buyers and building materials.

The events of the first half of 1925 demonstrated that the Florida real estate market was a house of cards. Bereft of new buyers, contractors and developers began calling in their debts, which speculators could not cover. The widespread practice of buying "binders" (putting 10 percent down on a property with the hope of selling it for a profit before the other 90 percent of the price had to be paid) proved disastrous. Real estate agencies, developers, construction companies, and contractors went bankrupt in droves. Florida's cities that had borrowed heavily for infrastructure and public service programs in the belief that the flush times would not end now found themselves teetering toward the economic brink. By the end of 1925, all of the nation's cities with the highest debt load per citizen were located in Florida.

Things grew even worse in 1926. With Florida's cities and speculators scrambling to revive the real estate market, a natural disaster ended all hope for rebuilding the shattered economy. In September, the Miami Hurricane swept across the Southern part of Florida. The jerry-built houses of the boom washed away. Some 400 Floridians perished. The image of South Florida as a paradise went with them. In addition, investigative reporters surveying the damage filed numerous stories that claimed local officials had deliberately minimized both the death toll and the extent of the damage in an effort to help the real estate market. The local governments of Florida came to be viewed with the same disdain as con man real estate agents. Florida's land boom had officially ended.

The Nightmare of Boca Raton

The end of the land boom caught many real estate agents and speculators unable to pay their debts and stuck with unsellable properties purchased at ridiculously high prices. Many went bankrupt and countless developments went unfinished. The most dramatic of these failures was a planned community 27 miles north of Miami named Boca Raton (dubbed "Boucoup Rotten" by rival developers). The brainchild of Addison Mizner, the grand plan for Boca Raton included a world-class hotel, a smaller inn, and the world's widest highway (which featured 20 lanes with a canal in the middle) (Tindall 1965, 109). The development covered an enormous 16,000-acre tract of land. To fulfill his vision, Mizner had enlisted T. Coleman duPont and other wealthy backers to create the Mizner Development Corporation. Had Boca Raton been completed it would have been the most ambitious development in Florida. Mizner's brother Wilson only half-jokingly claimed that he expected Palm Beach to become the servants' quarters for Boca Raton.

However, Boca Raton was never finished. Mizner announced the development in April 1925, just as the boom peaked, and initial interest in the project was very high. By that fall, though, the market had undergone a dramatic transformation. With concerns about Florida real estate growing, duPont pulled out of the project. Mizner could not continue construction without his financial backers. His only hope was to use the money garnered from the sale of lots to continue the project, but buyers proved scarce as the year wound down. Without buyers or backers, Mizner could not pay his contractors. Unpaid, the contractors refused to continue construction. By the summer of 1926, Mizner's company fell apart. The architect was forced to sell all of his remaining assets, including the Boca Raton buildings that had been completed. Financially ruined, Mizner died in 1933.

The Cold Light of Morning

The end of the boom caused dramatic problems in the state of Florida. Overextended city governments faced long-term problems in paying off their debts, and many announced as early as 1926 that they could not honor their bonds. The web of personal debt and false wealth created by the boom ruined individuals and businesses alike. As with any boom, those who got in early and then sold made a profit, but those still holding Florida property in 1926, such as Addison Mizner, found themselves in a difficult position. Having purchased land as an investment and with the intention of quickly turning the property around (colloquially known as "passing the baby"), they could not pay off what they owed. This meant that those who continued to own Florida property suffered, and those who had sold the land to them paid the price as well because they could not collect what was owed to them. In some cases, property reverted to those who had owned the land before the boom occurred, as the cord of overlapping unpaid binders unraveled.

For Florida, the end of the land boom sent shockwaves through the state that effectively meant the onset of the Great Depression half a decade before it convulsed the rest of the country. As early as 1926, the state's banking industry collapsed because of the massive number of loan defaults. This resulted in the closure of many Florida banks, which significantly reduced public confidence in the banks. Concerned private citizens then began pulling their money out of the banks, which led to more closures. The infamous "runs" on banks associated with the early years of the Great Depression had begun. In 1928, the Okeechobee Hurricane ripped through Southern Florida with a wave of destruction almost the equal of the 1926 Miami Hurricane. Shortly afterward, the Mediterranean fruit fly arrived in Florida and wreaked havoc on the state's citrus industry. Things had turned so bad so quickly in Florida that it was viewed as one of the states damaged the least by the onset of the Great Depression. But for the rest of the nation to sink to their level was cold comfort for Floridians.

FIGHTING BACK: ORGANIZED LABOR AT THE END OF THE 1920s

Early 1920s Woes

For organized labor, the decade of the 1920s posed a host of problems. The wave of 1919 strikes materially helped some workers but not all benefited. Even more troubling, concerted efforts to equate the actions of workers with radicalism and "un-American" activity fueled a widespread antipathy to the efforts of labor unions. A succession of Republican governments and their probusiness agendas only added to these difficulties. With the crumbs of welfare capitalism thrown to workers by American business interests, labor unions found many industrial workers unwilling to risk their jobs for other material gains. Unionization efforts were also hindered by the attitudes of American unions themselves. Fearful of the taint of radicalism, many unions shied away from confrontations with business leaders. The notoriously conservative American Federation of Labor (AFL) also failed to overcome its traditional aversion to organizing unskilled or minority workers during the decade.

American workers, typically unorganized and without employment protections, faced a series of setbacks following the recession early in the decade. Employers attempted to extract maximum profits by reducing wages, extending working hours, increasing production expectations, and jobbing out piecework as often as possible. Confronted with an increasingly dire situation, American workers lashed out. In April 1922, 500,000 coal miners walked off the job. Over the summer, 400,000 railroad workers did the same. During 1922, more than 1,500,000 workers went on strike. Unlike the optimistic struggles of 1916 and 1919, the 1922 work stoppages represented a defensive action as workers attempted to simply maintain a subsistence living. The internal weaknesses of the labor movement, the Harding administration's willingness to use federal troops, and labor injunctions coalesced into an imposing counter to these work stoppages.

The New England textile strike illustrates the failure of labor during the early decade. Beginning in February, some 60,000 textile workers walked off the job. After accepting a 22.5 percent pay cut in 1921, the workers balked at another 20 percent cut coupled with an extension of the workweek from 48 to 54 hours. The workers managed to maintain the strike for several months but finally agreed to the longer workweek in return for the mill owners abandoning the 20 percent pay cut. Still, the extension of the work hours represented a reduction in hourly wage. Defeated on all fronts, disgruntled workers meekly

In an effort to garner attention for his cause, a striking Pennsylvania coal miner traveled to New York City to picket in front of the Berwind White Coal Mine Company. The 1922 work stoppage was an attempt to improve working conditions for miners and to obtain recognition of the union. (Underwood & Underwood/Corbis)

returned to work. For the already struggling unions, the strikes of 1922 proved disastrous. In particular, the railroad, mining, and textile unions saw dramatic decreases in membership. Setbacks of this magnitude served as cautionary tales for workers contemplating work stoppages. During the tumultuous year 1919, 1 American worker out of every 5 left his or her job as part of an industrial dispute; in 1925, the percentage had dropped to 1 worker out of every 50 (Zieger 1969, 249).

Passaic

Passaic, New Jersey, developed into a significant textile center in the decades bookending the turn of the 20th century. Staffed primarily by European immigrants, the city's mills became highly regarded for the quality of their woolen and worsted products. However, the successes of the area's mill owners (organized as the Wool Council) did not result in immediate benefits for the city's industrial workers. To remedy this situation, labor unrest became a hallmark of the Passaic mills. Beginning in 1912, workers staged work stoppages with regularity. Most of the minimal gains achieved by these strikes were lost during the cost-cutting activities that accompanied the textile depression of 1924–1925. Wool Council members rolled wages back by 10 percent and reduced overtime payments.

The worsening conditions for Passaic mill workers corresponded with a concerted drive by representatives of the Workers Party to unionize textile workers. This small communist party sent the energetic Albert Weisbord to New Jersey in 1925 to organize mill workers. Weisbord succeeded in coordinating a January 1926 walkout to protest the pay cut. At the peak of the strike, more than 20,000 workers left their jobs. In a show of remarkable solidarity, Passaic workers at mills that had not yet cut wages also left their jobs. As the first communist-led mass strike in American history, Passaic seemed to augur great progress for the country's left wing. The strike gained national attention and supporters of various political stripes helped fund relief efforts to sustain the workers.

Weisbord's tactics, however, raised troubling issues for American Communists. As part of his struggle to keep the workers united, Weisbord played upon their ethnic prejudices. For example, he generated support for the strike among Slavic workers by referring to mill owners with a variety of slurs that played upon their Germanic heritage (Blatt and Norkunas 1996, 220). Such actions ran counter to the nondiscriminatory stance of the communist movement. Even more problematic, the Comintern had directed national parties to work within existing labor organizations rather than establishing rival dual unions. The AFL's United Textile Workers (UTW) union had failed to gain a foothold during the 1919 unrest in Passaic, so Weisbord simply ignored the UTW in his drive to organize New Jersey mill workers. Under strict party orders, Weisbord and his communist associates turned over leadership of the strike to the UTW in September. The removal of the able Weisbord proved costly. Relief funds slowed to a trickle and the conservative UTW began negotiations with the Wool Council that did little to improve the lot of the striking workers. Over the winter of 1926–1927, the UTW signed a series of agreements with individual plants that eliminated the wage cut but did nothing to guarantee union recognition. Hence, the last of Passaic's workers returned to their jobs in February 1927 under conditions exactly as they had been in December 1925 but after losing a year's pay. Nor did the AFL continue to work on behalf of Passaic's workers. In fact, when communists led New Bedford, Massachusetts, textile workers in a 1928 strike, the tiny Passaic branch of the UTW, in recognition of Weisbord's 1926 efforts, publicly supported the New England strike, which prompted the AFL to expel the local.

New Bedford

The decline in textile prices proved to be a harsh blow to the previously flourishing textile industry of New England. The overproduction and high wages paid to company officials drove mill owners to slash prices in an effort to increase profits. In April 1928, New Bedford mill owners announced a 10 percent reduction in the already depressed wages of workers, which ignited a wave of protests. Thanks to a change in Communist policy that advocated the establishment of dual unions, two distinct labor organizations participated in the New Bedford strike, unlike in Passaic. The moderate Textile Council (TC) represented skilled, native-born Caucasian workers while the communist-led Textile Mill Committee (TMC) organized unskilled, primarily immigrant workers. The rift between the two groups and their varied responses to management demands starkly illustrated the chasm of interests and attitudes that prevented the creation of a united labor movement. In this case, the TC struck to protest the proposed wage reduction and made no effort to cooperate with the TMC while the TMC viewed the New Bedford strike as a vehicle for extracting sweeping demands for industrialists. The Committee declared that its members would not return to work until there was a 20 percent increase in wages, a 40-hour workweek, and the elimination of child labor and racial discrimination.

Mill owners attempted to reopen their plants in July, but 20,000 picketers prevented strikebreakers from entering the mills. This would be the last significant cooperation between the TC and the TMC. That fall, owners and TC representatives began negotiations to end the strike, with both sides agreeing to exclude the TMC from the proceedings. Over TMC protests, the TC agreed to a 5 percent pay cut compromise in October. Fred Beal and the TMC leadership, however, refused to agree to the compromise and pledged to keep the mills closed. Their efforts to maintain the strike met with violence from local authorities, who took a much dimmer view of the radical TMC than the TC. TMC meetings were disrupted and the leadership arrested, which destroyed the Committee. Members found their efforts to thwart the compromise carried significant consequences. Those who were allowed to return to work faced pay cuts of 15 percent instead of 5 percent. The refusal of TC members to stand up for the unskilled workers of the TMC served to harden communist attitudes toward existing "reactionary" labor organizations. In the wake of the bitter New Bedford fight, American Communists established the National Textile Workers Union in an effort to avoid collusion with the AFL-affiliated United Textile Workers in future textile industry disputes.

Piedmont Revolt

Over the course of the 1920s, American textile production became increasingly dominated by southern manufacturers. A number of factors contributed to this drift. First, even the paltry unionization efforts of the North outdistanced worker effort in the Southern states, which made work stoppages less likely among southern workers. The overwhelmingly conservative state governments south of the Mason-Dixon Line also helped squelch worker protests. And a large potential replacement workforce for Southern mills, whose only other employment option involved the even lower paying agricultural sector, helped keep workers compliant. The confluence of these factors led to demeaning and degrading working conditions for Southern mill hands. They received the lowest industrial wages in the nation, worked the longest hours (60–72 hours per week), had to accept that their wives and children would have to staff the night shifts in Southern mills, and found themselves completely under the control of mill owners due to requirements that they live in company-owned "mill villages." The mid-decade textile depression made conditions even worse for the 300,000 Southern mill workers. Mill owners not only slashed wages but also increased the use of nighttime female and child workers (who were both paid less than adult males) and implemented the "stretch-out," a forced speed-up of production without a concomitant raise in pay.

The pitiful working conditions in the Southern mills eventually propelled a wave of labor protests that gripped the South in 1929. Workers in the area often found these efforts hamstrung by the lack of union organizations. The UTW fielded no Southern locals until nonunion workers forced their hand by staging spontaneous walkouts that year. In March 1929, nonunion workers began the year's first large strike in Elizabethtown, Tennessee. Angry at low wages, they stopped working and hastily organized a UTW local. The conservative UTW, however, offered little to counter the mass arrests and bombings faced by striking workers or the hundreds of state police who swarmed into the city to enforce a labor injunction. Battered by the forces arrayed against them, the UTW settled in May with no tangible benefits for workers. After the strike ended, Elizabethtown plant owners blacklisted almost 1,000 workers and succeeded in preventing the unionization of those still at their jobs.

Gastonia

The AFL's inattention to Southern textile mill workers prior to Elizabethtown led to these workers becoming a focus of communist efforts to organize industrial workers. By 1929, the American communist movement had adopted a stance, partly in recognition of the anticommunist position adopted by the AFL, to attempt to create left-wing dual unions. For Southern mill hands this shift meant attention from the new National Textile Workers Union (NTWU). Because it was the largest mill in the South, the Loray mill in Gastonia, North Carolina, became the initial site of these organizational efforts. New Bedford strike veteran Fred Beal helped lead the Loray walkout against a 20 percent pay cut on April 1. The strike helped demonstrate the deep clefts that communism created in the labor movement. Although the UTW had made no effort to organize the Loray workers prior to the strike, AFL president William Green publicly denounced the work stoppage (primarily due to the communist influence in Gastonia). The actions of Beal and other communist labor organizers (including William Z. Foster) in Gastonia also illustrated the disconnect with the workers of the region. The NTWU's demands included calls for racial equality (which the majority white strikers did not agree with) and a plea to the National Guardsmen called in to protect mill property to mutiny and join the strike (which only confused the locals and led to an undercutting of support in North Carolina for the "revolutionaries").

Much like the Harlan County coal strikes in the next decade, the Gastonia work stoppage became a rallying point for the American left. However, their support proved futile in overcoming the typical combination of big business, local politicians, and state government they faced. By mid-April, National Guard troops succeeded in protecting strikebreakers who reopened the mill. From this point until the tragic proceedings culminated in September, the Loray strike proved to be a series of deadly humiliations for the mill workers. Most agreed to return to work with no improvement to their conditions after the strikebreakers reopened the mill. The remainder found themselves evicted from their company-owned homes. Local law enforcement officers attempted to roust these homeless workers from a tent colony in June. A bloody scuffle ensued that left one policeman dead. Beal and 16 others were charged with conspiracy to commit murder. A mistrial resulted in widespread mob violence against the NTWU and communist organizers in Gastonia. Ella May Wiggins, the communist balladeer of the strike, was murdered during the unrest. In September a second trial resulted in convictions against seven defendants. Released on bail while appealing their convictions, all seven promptly fled to the Soviet Union. The NTWU's efforts to organize Gastonia's workers went with them.

An Unaffiliated Future

After the disastrous unionization efforts in Elizabethtown, Gastonia, and a crushing blow in Marion, North Carolina, Southern mill workers continued to lobby for improvements in their working conditions, but they did so without any official affiliations. Over the summer of 1929, a series of spontaneous work stoppages protesting the stretch-out occurred in South Carolina. In many cases these were successful but only because the striking workers limited their demands simply to the elimination of that loathsome practice. Recognizing that calls for unionization accompanying strikes often brought the wrath of the authorities, the South Carolina mill workers made clear they were unaffiliated and steadfastly refused to allow either of the national unions to participate in the strikes.

The bloody Southern encounters also affected the AFL. At their October 1929 national convention, the federation adopted a historic shift in policy and declared the beginning of a campaign to unionize Southern workers. In keeping with their traditional cautious approach, however, the AFL tried to convince mill owners to willingly cooperate with the UTW, rather than pursue a course of confrontations and strikes. These efforts met with little success. The intractable mill owners maintained their antipathy to unionization, and then the onset of the Great Depression gutted the industry itself. Even after New Deal–era legislation guaranteed collective bargaining rights, the South would prove to be the most difficult region of the nation to unionize.

Red Rising: The Rebirth of American Communism

Origins of the American Movement

The Bolshevik Revolution sparked the birth of an avowed communist movement in the United States. Initial strength emerged from factions within the well-established Socialist Party. Unable to agree upon a united approach to communism, these factions organized the competing Communist Party of America and Communist Labor Party. Combined, the two parties contained somewhere between 25,000 and 40,000 members. The catastrophic setbacks of the postwar Red Scare, however, immediately reduced the nascent American Communist movement to a shell of its initial size. Although the governmental excesses of the Red Scare were not repeated, the decade of the 1920s proved to be a very difficult period for American Communists. Constant government scrutiny and seemingly endless rounds of internecine warfare buffeted the movement. Only at the very end of the decade did a relatively united Communist party emerge.

After the persecutions of the Red Scare, the remaining elements (about 25 percent of the initial membership) of the American Communist movement went underground. Rather than attempting to establish an active, public political party, American Communists engaged in a series of propaganda campaigns against each other, as a variety of small organizations sought official recognition as the American branch of the Comintern (the Moscow-based organization of national Communist parties). The CPA itself broke into two separate parties, with both confusingly claiming the same name, in April 1920. The smaller of the two CPAs, led by Walter Ruthenberg and Jay Lovestone, attracted most of the English-speaking American Communists. The larger CPA maintained the allegiance of most of the foreign-language federations. Some measure of order was restored later that year when the Ruthenberg–Lovestone CPA merged with the CLP to become the United Communist Party (UCP). The UCP's primary doctrinal difference with the rump CPA involved a more moderate approach to armed insurrections and an advocacy of participation in peaceful labor strikes.

Friends of Soviet Russia

During the underground period, American Communists attempted to improve U.S.–U.S.S.R. relations by establishing the Friends of Soviet Russia (FSR) over

An estimated 30,000 Communists and supporters of the Union of Soviet Socialist Republics celebrated the anniversary of that country's founding during an August 1929 mass rally in New York. Similar events were held throughout the world. (Bettmann/Corbis)

the summer of 1921. Despite being controlled by Communists, the group was ostensibly open to anyone with an interest in the new Soviet Union. As an effort to attract non-Communists, the FSR strongly promoted its work in alleviating the suffering caused by the Russian famine of 1921. While this humanitarian aspect initially took center stage, a political agenda lay at the heart of the FSR.

By the next year, the political aspects of the FSR became clear. They continued to lobby for humanitarian aid but also stressed the need for the United States to develop closer ties with the U.S.S.R. Among the FSR's demands were full diplomatic recognition of the Soviet government by the United States, financial credit available to Moscow, a more balanced reporting of Soviet activities, and a pledge by the United States to no longer interfere with the political affairs of the Soviet Union. Despite the issuance of a steady stream of well-produced publications to promote their efforts, the FSR failed to achieve its goals. The organization officially disbanded in 1930.

Road to Reunion

Seeking to gain recognition from the Moscow-based Comintern (Third, or Communist, International) as the "official" American Communist party, both groups sent delegates to the Soviet Union over the summer of 1920. The Comintern demanded that the bickering groups resolve their differences and establish a united party. In May 1921, the bickering factions finally reached a compromise that led to a single American Communist party, which retained the CPA moniker. This conference also adopted a new, Comintern-ordered stance for the still-underground party. They were to step back from calls for destroying "reactionary" current labor unions and enter these mainstream unions. The notion of creating dual unions fell away. Another turn in the Comintern line led the CPA to establish an aboveground party for mass mobilization. In December 1921, the aboveground Workers Party of America (WPA), initially headed by James Cannon, emerged with the CPA continuing to operate as the underground controller of the new WPA.

Those within the party wedded to the principles of maintaining a secret, vanguard party found the creation of an aboveground organization intolerable. This disgruntled group (known within the party as the "goose" faction) then decided to follow the letter of the Comintern law by establishing the United Toilers of America, but the group continued to stress the importance of underground activities. This newest split only ended with an unusually successful series of conventions of American Communists in 1922. A compromise program emerged whereby the aboveground United Toilers organization would be abandoned with the underground CPA remaining in place but slowly being phased out. By early 1923, the CPA had been abandoned in favor of the aboveground party, which, in 1925, changed its name to the Workers (Communist) Party of America (WCPA).

The post-1922 aboveground organization adopted a far more cautious approach toward the eventual overthrow of capitalism. The Workers Party stressed involvement with existing labor unions to gain a voice within them (the "boring from within" tactic). This approach would, in theory, allow the Communists to help workers achieve immediate gains, thereby endearing the Communists to them. Immediate demands by workers could then be used as stepping stones toward the eventual demise of capitalism. Nor would American Communists openly disclose to the workers they helped organize their ultimate goal of seizing power. A duplicitous rhetoric developed whereby the Workers Party members stressed immediate demands to the workers without explaining that these moves simply built momentum for an armed revolution in the future.

Reaching Out

The directive to work with existing liberal organizations propelled the Workers Party into alliances with a variety of trade organizations. American Communists, however, faced difficulties in establishing themselves in existing unions. The postwar animosity toward radicals did not immediately dissipate. Union leaders sought to keep the struggling labor movement from losing its already minimal gains by not allowing communist affiliation to discredit labor groups. Further, this concern over public reaction to communist involvement in the labor union was coupled by a mistrust of communist intentions. Many labor leaders felt the Communists, despite their public calls for simple redress of current worker issues, possessed an agenda that could eventually destabilize the labor movement, if not the nation itself.

William Z. Foster's Trade Union Educational League (TUEL) represented the opening salvo in Communists' attempts to bridge the gap between themselves and established labor organizations. The TUEL operated within the American Federation of Labor (AFL), a group long hostile to radical politics, as a propaganda unit to push the organization toward the political left. Foster proved highly adept at the "boring from within" strategy, and the TUEL achieved success in developing close ties with the AFL's central union councils in several Midwestern cities. TUEL's advances, however, proved short-lived. In 1923, progressive elements from the AFL attempted to hatch a new political party that would bring together all working-class Americans and farmers. By creating paper unions, the Workers Party was able to flood the founding convention with delegates. These delegates then used the numerical majority to give the Communists control of the new Federal Farmer-Labor Party. Angry AFL leaders not only scuttled the new party but also worked to eject TUEL representatives from local union organizations. The collapse of the WPA's connections to the Farmer-Labor movement led the party to promote its own slate of candidates in 1924. Foster's efforts were rewarded in his nomination as the WPA presidential candidate; he earned a scant 33,000 votes. The Comintern, however, insisted that Ruthenberg become the actual head of the WPA.

The WPA also attempted to connect with workers outside the channels of existing labor organizations. In consultation with the Comintern, James Cannon established the International Labor Defense (ILD) in 1925. To show their concern and support for all labor activists, the ILD pledged to provide legal and financial support to all labor activists—regardless of their political affiliations—who were facing legal proceedings that stemmed from their labor efforts. The ILD proved to be one of the movement's more successful 1920s creations. Over the course of the decade, it evolved into an organization that provided legal services to all members of the working class. During the 1930s, the ILD gained notoriety for its assistance to African Americans, particularly the Scottsboro 9.

Other WCPA efforts to reach out to organized labor suffered a mixed fate. Communists managed to gain control of elements of the Fur Workers Union and, after they successfully led a 1926 strike, later obtained leadership of the entire union. Workers Party members attempted to repeat this success by leading a 1926 strike among locals of the International Ladies Garment Workers Union. When the strike failed, however, the Communists found themselves pushed out of the union. The Passaic textile strike probably best illustrated the uneven achievements of the "united front" period. Al Weisbord's efforts to organize the workers seemed to portend an important development in the growth of communist strength among unskilled laborers, but Comintern orders to defer to the weak AFL textile union in order to avoid creating a dual union not only destroyed his efforts but also led to a disappointing conclusion for workers.

New Schisms and Approaches

In March 1927, WCPA leader Walter Ruthenberg's death sparked another round of internecine struggles over control of the party. Several of Ruthenberg's lieutenants, a Foster-Cannon faction, and Jay Lovestone grappled for leadership. Once again, Comintern intervention alleviated the deadlock. They instructed the party to place Lovestone in charge as the WCPA general secretary. Foster retained a significant place in the party, but his authority was primarily restricted to union work (which was his perceived area of expertise). Lovestone promoted a form of "American exceptionalism" that significantly shaped the WCPA's policies. At its heart, exceptionalism posited that the communist revolution in America would be temporarily forestalled by the abundance and material wealth of the nation. Unlike the decaying imperialism of European states, the United States was still ascending as an imperial nation, which gave capitalism in this country an increased staying power. Exceptionalism's adherents, therefore, argued against immediate confrontational actions, which would later prove futile. Rather, American Communists needed to settle in and prepare for the unavoidable capitalist crisis of the future. A far cry from the expectation of immediate, global revolution that fueled the communist movement at the dawn of the decade, American exceptionalism reflected the sobering realities of the 1920s.

The convoluted political machinations within the Soviet Union resulted in an abrupt Comintern about-face in 1928. Joseph Stalin, as part of his consolidation of power, declared an assault on the "Right Danger" within the communist movement at the Sixth Comintern Congress. The Comintern's drift leftward represented, according to Stalinists, the beginning of the global communist movement's "Third Period." Communist tactics now included severing ties with nonrevolutionary organizations, the establishment of the previously decried dual unions, and a significant escalation in fiery rhetoric to announce the impending revolution. This tactical change destroyed almost a decade's worth of efforts by American Communists to obtain voices within the labor movement. Tiny dual unions appeared during the fall of 1928; their Communist leaders were now faced with the daunting task of building a labor movement from scratch. Tainted by its connections to the AFL, the TUEL became the Trade Union Unity League, which served as the umbrella organization for all the new communist unions.

Concern over the "Right Danger" also meant another upheaval at the top of the WCPA. Lovestone and his staunchest supporters, with their conservative exceptionalist stance, found themselves supplanted by the party's left wing. The general secretary grudgingly accepted the Third Period strategy, but his earlier views cost him control of the party. While some converts to the left, such as Foster, managed to survive, Lovestone represented too much of a threat to remain within the WCPA. In June 1929, the party expelled Lovestone and his closest allies. Another 200 members deserted the WPA in protest and followed Lovestone into his newly created Communist Party (Majority Group). Even more members, finally cognizant of the American party's lack of autonomy from the whimsical dictates of the Comintern, simply abandoned official affiliation with any Communist party. The convolutions within the party resulted in the rise of Earl Browder. The new general secretary proved to be the ideal of the national party leaders Stalin hoped to establish. Browder offered little in the way of original communist theory, so he did not present a challenge to Stalinist orthodoxy, and he willingly submitted to the dictates of the Comintern, which assured some measure of stability and support in the American movement if Comintern policies shifted. The final year of the decade also witnessed a final change in party name. The WCPA became the Communist Party, USA (CPUSA). As the CPUSA, the major Communist party in the nation would soon achieve the height of its success thanks to the economic dislocation of the Great Depression.

Trotskyists

During the tumultuous year of 1928, the "Right Danger" of the Lovestone faction was not the only wing of the American communist movement to face censure. Before his own ejection from the party, Lovestone himself oversaw the hearing that removed several veteran members from the WCPA. Their offense had been to support the exiled Leon Trotsky in his condemnations of the increasing bureaucratization of the Comintern and to support Stalin's questionable machinations in consolidating his power. Those within the American party who raised the issue found out firsthand the validity of Trotsky's complaints; their dissent from Stalin's line resulted in expulsion from the party in October 1928. Led by James Cannon, the Trotskyists initially hoped to reform the party itself rather than create a rival organization. Quickly recognizing the futility of this attempt, Cannon and his followers established the Communist League of America (Opposition). The League served as the American wing of Trotsky's proposed Fourth International. The organization remained a small, albeit vocal, endeavor. With a membership that never topped 200, Cannon eventually realized the difficulty of maintaining the organization as an independent body. Therefore, in 1934, the League merged with the American Workers Party.

Playing the Market: The Effects of the Great Crash

The Stock Market

The stock market stood as one of the primary factors contributing to the notions of prosperity during the 1920s. Thanks to the enormous profits being made by America's corporations, the stock market began a remarkable climb during the middle of the decade. With stock values continually rising, the market became flooded with small-scale speculators looking to get rich quick as well as ill-informed middle-class investors hoping to pay for their retirement with dividends. To facilitate the entry into the market of those with little ready capital, stock brokers began the dangerous practice of issuing seemingly unlimited credit. Just as there were binders for Florida land and installment plans for washing machines, those who wished to enter the market could buy stock on the "margin" by paying 10 percent down and the rest with future profits. As long as prices continued to climb, the system held out; but when confidence broke and the great sell-off of 1929 began, those involved in this risky practice found themselves devastated.

Early in the decade, stock prices continued to be relatively low. When the country emerged from the postwar slump, this resulted in highly lucrative yields. During the last half of 1924, stock prices began a slow but steady climb. For example, the *New York Times* average of the prices of 25 leading industrial stocks rose by 20 points over that period. Stock prices continued to increase, with occasional minor losses, over the course of the next two years. Beginning in 1927, however, a continual, large increase in prices began. By early 1928, the market had become a "mass escape into make-believe" (Galbraith 1988, 11). Small, middle-class investors began to seep into the market. False hopes of becoming an overnight millionaire through involvement in the market developed in a pattern first elaborated in the Florida land boom. The examples of the fortunate few were cited by market boosters as representative cases. After a slight correction in December 1928, the market rebounded with record highs, which served only to further the delusion that a major adjustment would not occur.

During the summer of 1929, the market reached new heights. The average price of the 50 leading stocks had risen to $176 by March 1928; in September 1929, they soared to $307. Swollen values pulled even more small speculators into the market. The early September prices began to fall by the middle of the month. Their continual decline spooked many investors, and confidence in the market sagged. This resulted in a vicious circle of sales, which lowered prices, which forced brokers to call in debts from margin sales, which forced more sales. Prices skittered downward until the market finally bottomed out on "Black Tuesday"—October 29. On that date, nearly 16.5 million shares of stock changed

Distressed investors and speculators mobbed the New York Stock Exchange in 1929 in the wake of the great stock market crash. (Library of Congress)

hands in a flurry of activity that saw industrial stocks drop by an average of 43 points. Market value dropped by $2 million per hour until the gong that announced the end of trading mercifully rang at 3:00 p.m. For those left holding stock, the era of prosperity was over; for the rest of the country, the end lay just around the bend. The 1920s began with a postwar economic slump, and they ended with the worst depression in American history.

After the Crash

The crash did not immediately result in a complete national economic dislocation —that would come later—but it did change the national mood. The giddy optimism exemplified by the federal government's pronouncements evaporated. An estimated 10,000 people crowded around the New York Stock Exchange on "Black Tuesday" to watch their dreams of wealth melt away. From this central point, a stunned disillusionment radiated and would soon reach across the nation. Folk humorist Will Rogers declared New York to be the new home of the "Wailing Wall." The city's mayor, Jimmy Walker, urged the motion-picture exhibitors visiting New York for their annual convention to show only positive films to help keep up the nation's morale.

Those involved in the market—estimated to be between one and three million Americans—found themselves immediately confronted with a changed world. Previous economic status meant nothing. In an effort to protect themselves, brokers called in all debts, regardless of who the debtor might be. Entertainers Irving Berlin and Eddie Cantor found themselves ruined. Cantor eventually recouped a fraction of the $2 million he lost by writing *Caught Short!*, a humorous account of his travail. Comedian Harpo Marx joked that all he had left was his harp and a croquet set. Herbert Bayard Swope possessed a fortune, on paper, valued in September at $14 million. By the end of October, he found himself $2 million in debt (Klingaman 1989, 286–288).

Some of the nation's largest business concerns collapsed in the wake of the crash. Americans who had invested in these firms learned to their horror that many firms gave out false financial information to lure investors and then plowed their money into the market (in some cases investing in other firms as unsound as their own). W. B. Foshay's Minneapolis-based company proved to be one of the larger immediate casualties, but its story was not unique. Foshay cobbled together public utilities companies in 13 states to create a paper empire. He paid false dividends out of the new capital that poured in from speculators. In the fall of 1929, the 32-story Foshay Tower, which resembled the Washington Monument, arose in downtown Minneapolis as a demonstration of the company's wealth. When the market collapsed, however, the overextended Foshay could not pay his debts. On November 1, the Foshay Company went into receivership with liabilities of $20 million. Foshay eventually went to prison for securities violations, but the empty Foshay Tower stood as a reminder to his ruined stockholders of how the stock market collapse changed their lives.

An immediate ripple effect from the crash was felt by businesses involved in finance or the luxury items so popular during the boom. Far too much of the total funds in the nation's banks were tied up in speculation for them not to suffer. Jewelers saw Christmas orders cancelled. Theaters, steamship lines, and tourist destinations all witnessed a drop in customers. Pawnshops, however, found themselves flooded with business. Trying to sell, rather than consuming, had become a new national pastime. Perhaps most reflective of the change in mood, the speakeasies that surrounded Wall Street shuttered over the course of the winter.

By December, the sinking economy reached the middle class. Sales of low-priced consumer goods fell faster than luxury items that month. Even budget retailer Woolworth's reported a sharp drop in sales when compared to December 1928. Unemployment crept toward 20 percent as the new year rolled around. Local entrepreneurs found their tailor shops, theaters, and restaurants sliding toward bankruptcy for want of customers. Those able to keep their families fed did so in new ways. Even those with essential skills had to adjust. For example, Rochester physician Lynn Rumbold continued to practice medicine over the winter, but his payments now consisted of vegetables, offers to clean his house, and a pedigreed dog. His patients could no longer pay him in currency (Schactman 1979, 307); their cash had gone to pay for, in F. Scott Fitzgerald's memorable phrase, "the most expensive orgy in history."

BIOGRAPHIES

James Cannon, 1890–1974

Leader of American Trotskyists

James Patrick Cannon was born near Kansas City, Kansas. From a left-wing family, Cannon became a member of the Socialist Party in 1908. During the next decade, he became an organizer for the Industrial Workers of the World. He helped the Socialist Party's left wing break away to establish the nascent American Communist movement. Cannon became a leader of John Reed's Communist Labor Party (CLP).

In 1925, Cannon founded the International Labor Defense (ILD) as a vehicle for providing legal services to jailed union agitators. He headed the ILD until his expulsion from the Workers Party in 1928. Cannon's removal from the party stemmed from his advocacy of Leon Trotsky's criticisms of Joseph Stalin and the Comintern. Trotsky argued that Stalin had led the Comintern (and the Soviet Union) away from Leninism and toward totalitarianism. Cannon and his followers attempted to sway American Communists to this stance but found themselves outmaneuvered. After his ejection from the American party, Cannon established the Communist League of America (CLA) as an American Trotskyist party. After a variety of alliances, Cannon helped found the Socialist Workers Party (SWP) in 1938. Cannon spent part of World War II in prison on conspiracy charges but resumed his leadership of the SWP upon release in 1945. He continued to serve as an important part of the SWP organization until his death in Los Angeles in 1974.

Carl Fisher, 1874–1939

Florida Developer

Carl Graham Fisher was born in Greensburg, Indiana, in 1874. He dropped out of school at age 12 and, after working a variety of jobs, became involved in selling and racing bicycles and automobiles. In the early 20th century, Fisher became very wealthy through his involvement in the auto parts industry. In

1909, he led the group of investors that built the Indianapolis Motor Speedway. Fisher's work in the auto industry led him to become active in the plans for transcontinental highways. As part of these activities, he became interested in the state of Florida, which was to be the terminus of a proposed north–south highway.

In the early 1910s, Fisher began to purchase Florida real estate in the Miami area. His greatest triumph was the dredging of Biscayne Bay to build the resort community of Miami Beach (previously a swampy, half-submerged speck of land). To sell his properties, Fisher engaged in increasingly outlandish stunts and promotions. His efforts proved instrumental in creating the public interest in Florida that spurred the land boom. These efforts also significantly increased Fisher's personal fortune.

The end of the Florida land boom proved especially damaging to Fisher. He plowed much of his wealth into a proposed summer resort at Montauk, Long Island. Florida debts ended that project. The 1926 Miami Hurricane destroyed much of his Florida property, and the 1929 stock market crash wiped out his fortune. Fisher spent the final years of his life living in a small cottage in Miami Beach. He died in 1939.

W. B. Foshey, 1882–1957

Developer
Wilbur Burton Foshey was born in 1882 in Ossining, New York. His family's financial difficulties forced Foshey to work a series of low-level jobs in the railroad and utilities industries during his youth. His work in utilities, however, convinced Foshey of the potential profits to be made in that industry.

In 1916, Foshey moved to Minneapolis. After obtaining a small loan, he began the process of buying small public utilities operations. By streamlining these operations Foshey made them more efficient and profitable, which allowed him to purchase more utilities. By the mid-1920s, his vast multistate utilities empire made Foshey a multimillionaire. In 1929, as a monument to his own success, Foshey commissioned the Foshey Tower in downtown Minneapolis. Modeled on the Washington Monument, the 32-story skyscraper became the city's tallest building. The elaborate grand opening included a host of dignitaries and a John Philip Sousa theme song specially commissioned by Foshey. The utility magnate's reckless speculating in the stock market, however, brought down his empire within weeks of the tower's opening. Destroyed by the 1929 crash, the W. B. Foshey Company went into receivership with an estimated $20 million in liabilities. Foshey served three years in prison before being released in the mid-1930s. He spent the rest of his career working as a Chamber of Commerce booster for Salida, Colorado. Foshey died in Minneapolis in 1957.

William Green, 1870–1952

Labor Leader

William Green was born in Coshocton, Ohio. After receiving an eighth-grade education, Green followed his father's lead and became a coal miner. The Greens stressed trade unionism and Baptist piety in equal measures. In 1886, William joined the Progressive Miners' Union. He became an official of his United Mine Workers of America local in 1891 and slowly rose in the union's hierarchy over the next decade. In 1912, Green became an Ohio state senator, running as a progressive Democrat. The next year, while still serving as a state legislator, Green was elected secretary-treasurer of the UMWA and also became the vice president of the American Federation of Labor (AFL).

When AFL president Samuel Gompers died in December 1924, Green became his compromise replacement. During the difficult decade of the 1920s, Green focused on keeping the organization as united as possible, sought to distance the AFL from communism and the taint of radicalism, and headed a massive public relations campaign. This campaign aimed at convincing business leaders of the benefits of dealing with organized labor. Despite the great attention he gave to this attempt to sell unionism, his efforts proved generally unsuccessful. The number of unionized workers actually decreased over the course of the decade.

The 1930s would prove an even greater challenge to Green. The depredations of the Great Depression severely crippled the already weak labor movement. While the AFL president welcomed the spate of New Deal legislation geared toward workers, he also steadfastly tried to stave off the radicalism that often followed in the wake of these new laws. His fundamentally conservative view on the role of the unions led Green to oppose militant strikes, and he worked to remove the Congress of Industrial Organizations (CIO)–affiliated unions from the AFL. His reserved approach eventually contributed to a waning of his authority as more activist leaders came to the fore. Green finally gave up the presidency in 1952. He died in Coshocton in 1970.

William Green entered the coal mines at 16 and rose to be president of the United Mine Workers and then of the American Federation of Labor. (National Archives)

Jay Lovestone, 1897–1990

Dissident American Communist Leader

Lovestone immigrated to the United States from Lithuania in 1907. He became an avowed socialist while attending the City College of New York. Lovestone broke with the socialists in 1919 and helped found the Communist Party of America (CPA).

During the 1920s, Lovestone's primary function in the communist movement was as a writer and newspaper editor. He was closely linked to party head Charles Ruthenberg. When Ruthenberg died in 1927, Lovestone emerged as the party's new leader. He became closely connected to the theory of "American Exceptionalism," which holds that the peculiar nature of capitalism in America meant that the communist revolution in this country would be temporarily delayed. This rightist stance eventually cost Lovestone his position. When the Comintern shifted to the left in 1928, the "Right Danger" element was expelled. He attempted to leverage his broad-based support within the American movement into a drive to maintain his position, but the American party chose to side with the Comintern.

He subsequently formed his own communist group, which operated under a variety of names. By the 1940s, Lovestone had moved into the American Federation of Labor, where he served in several organizations. Lovestone's bitterness over his treatment by the Comintern and the American party led to his disavowal of communism and the adoption of a rabidly anticommunist stance. During this period, he also became a government informant, with most of the information he forwarded regarding the work of communists in the labor movement. Lovestone continued to work in the union movement, primarily as a foreign affairs specialist, until 1974. He died in 1990.

George Merrick, 1886–1942

Florida Land Developer

George Edgar Merrick was born in Pennsylvania in 1886. Merrick and his family moved to the Miami, Florida, area when he was an adolescent. As a young man, he became involved in local politics, eventually serving as a Dade County commissioner. While working for the county, Merrick became a firm proponent of building roads throughout the state to encourage tourism.

After his father's death in the early 1920s, Merrick began to develop his vision of an aesthetically pleasing planned community. Using land inherited from his father as a base, Merrick began to build the city of Coral Gables, southwest of Miami. His stated desire was to make the city "America's most beautiful suburb." During the Florida land boom of the early 1920s, Merrick opened real estate offices across the country to sell his land to those eager to participate in the leisurely Florida lifestyle. In 1926, Merrick established the University of Miami in Coral Gables as part of his civic vision.

The end of the boom, the hurricane of 1926, and the onset of the Great Depression destroyed Merrick's empire. After rebuilding his life, Merrick attempted a similar venture in the Florida Keys during the 1930s but again his plans were dashed by a hurricane. Merrick spent his last few years serving as the Miami postmaster. He died in 1942.

Addison Mizner, 1872–1933

Architect and Florida Developer

Addison Cairns Mizner was born in California in 1872. Because his father was a diplomat, Mizner traveled a great deal as a child. He continued this nomadic existence as a young man before settling in New York to work as an architect in 1904. Mizner specialized in designing unique and eclectic country homes for wealthy patrons.

In 1918, he moved to Florida and began designing homes in Palm Beach. His signature style blended elements from a variety of sources onto a Mediterranean base. This "Mediterranean Revival" style became the standard for design in Florida during the early-20th century. Despite the clashing styles embedded in his work, Mizner actually obsessed over even the smallest details in his designs. He claimed that his projects represented the melding of all of the best aspects of the different styles, and he strove to give the homes character and a feeling of history. Mizer became notorious for developing means of making furniture, woodwork, and floors appear to be antique. The success of his work made Mizner both highly sought after and wealthy.

In 1925, he attempted to capitalize on the Florida land boom by creating the Boca Raton development on 16,000 acres north of Miami. The elaborate plan worked out by Mizner and his partners would have made Boca Raton the most impressive of all the land boom developments. His efforts, however, came just as the boom ended. After construction of a few buildings and homes, the development had to be abandoned. Financially broken, Mizner maintained a much-reduced lifestyle with sporadic architectural projects before dying in Palm Beach in 1933.

Charles Ponzi, 1882–1949

Confidence Man

Born Carlo Pietro Giovanni Guglielmo Tebaldo Ponzi in Lugo, Italy, on March 3, 1882, Ponzi came to the United States in 1903 and worked a series of menial jobs for the next few years. He spent 20 months in prison for forgery and another

Ex-convict and con artist Charles Ponzi. (Bettmann/Corbis)

two years in jail for illegally smuggling Italian immigrants into the country. During World War I, he established himself in Boston as a clerk for an import-export firm.

In 1919, Ponzi established the Securities Exchange Company allegedly to make investments in foreign currencies. He built his company by advertising a 50 percent rate of return on all investments within 90 days. By paying investors off with the money of other investors, Ponzi built a personal fortune and kept his fraudulent company flush with funds. In August 1920, however, he was arrested for mail fraud. Through a combination of federal and state convictions, he remained in prison for most of the next 14 years. Upon release, he was deported to Italy. Ponzi then moved to Brazil. He died penniless in Rio de Janeiro in 1949.

Charles Ruthenberg, 1884–1927

American Communist Leader

Ruthenberg grew up in New York City as a child of Russian Jewish immigrants. While attending Columbia University in the early 20th century he became involved with the Socialist Party of America (SPA). During the 1910s he worked as a traveling lecturer and organizer for the SPA, gaining most acclaim for his widely distributed 1917 pamphlet, *Are We Growing Toward Socialism?* He also ran in several elections as a Socialist candidate. Ruthenberg's 1918 arrest for organizing antidraft activities led Eugene V. Debs to make the antiwar speech that led to the Socialist leader's conviction for violating the Espionage Act.

Ruthenberg left the SPA in 1919 to become one of the leaders of the new Communist Party of America (CPA). He spent parts of the early 1920s in Moscow. During his time in the United States, Ruthenberg frequently found himself under arrest for violating criminal syndicalism laws in several states. Although he avoided jail time in most cases, his 1923 conviction in Michigan led to a lengthy appeals process that challenged such laws on grounds that they violated First Amendment rights. In 1925, Ruthenberg became head of the newly created Workers Party of America. His appeal reached the U.S. Supreme

Court in 1927, but the decision was moot because of Ruthenberg's death that year.

Ella May Wiggins, 1900–1929

Labor Activist, Songwriter

Wiggins was born September 17, 1900, in Sevierville, Tennessee. Her poverty-stricken family moved a great deal during her early life. By the time Ella May was 20, both her parents were dead and she was married to John Wiggins. Her husband worked in the textile mills of South Carolina. After a 1926 move to Gaston County, North Carolina, John deserted her and their five children.

Wiggins worked in the mills herself and became active in the union movement during her time in North Carolina. She worked to unionize mill employees and attempted to help involve African American workers in the labor movement. When the Gastonia strike began in April 1929, Wiggins was instrumental in convincing the National Textile Workers Union local to integrate. Her song "A Mill Mother's Lament" became the anthem of the strike. On September 14, 1929, the truck she was riding in with other striking workers was ambushed outside Gastonia. Wiggins was fatally wounded. Her accused killers were acquitted in 1930.

REFERENCES AND FURTHER READINGS

Akin, Edward N. 1991. *Flagler: Rockefeller Partner and Florida Baron*. Gainesville: University Press of Florida.

Allen, Frederick Lewis. 1964. *Only Yesterday: An Informal History of the 1920's*. New York: Harper & Row.

Ballinger, J. Kenneth. 1936. *Miami Millions: The Dance of the Dollar in the Great Florida Land Boom*. Miami, FL: Franklin Press.

Beiberman, Harold, Jr. 1991. *The Great Myths of 1929 and the Lessons to Be Learned*. Westport, CT: Greenwood Press.

Bernstein, Irving. 1960. *The Lean Years: A History of the American Worker, 1920–1933*. Boston: Houghton Mifflin.

Berridge, William A., Emma A. Winslow, and Richard A. Flinn. 1925. *Purchasing Power of the Consumer: A Statistical Index*. Chicago: A. W. Shaw.

Blatt, Martin Henry, and Martha K. Norkunas, eds. 1996. *Work, Recreation, and Culture: Essays in American Labor History*. New York: Garland.

Boulton, Alexander O. 1990. "The Tropical Twenties." *American Heritage* 41 (May/June 1990): 88–94.

Brandes, Stuart D. 1976. *American Welfare Capitalism, 1880–1940*. Chicago: University of Chicago Press.

Bremer, William W. 1984. *Depression Winters: New York Social Workers and the New Deal*. Philadelphia: Temple University Press.

Burnett, Gene M. 1986–1991. *Florida's Past: People and Events that Shaped the State*, 3 vols. Sarasota, FL: Pineapple Press.

Carter, Paul, A. 1977. *Another Part of the Twenties*. New York: Columbia University Press.

Crossen, Cynthia. 2005. "Land in 1920s Florida Was So Hot, People Sold Underwater Lots." *Wall Steet Journal*, August 3, B1.

Curl, Donald W. 1984. *Mizner's Florida: American Resort Architecture*. Cambridge, MA: MIT Press.

Daniel, Clete. 2001. *Culture of Misfortune: An Interpretive History of Textile Unionism in the United States*. Ithaca, NY: Cornell University Press.

Dubofsky, Melvyn. 1994. *The State and Labor in Modern America*. Chapel Hill: University of North Carolina Press.

Faulkner, Harold Underwood. 1954. *American Economic History*. 7th ed. New York: Harper & Brothers.

Frazer, William, and John J. Guthrie Jr. 1995. *The Florida Land Boom: Speculation, Money, and the Banks*. Westport, CT: Quorum Books.

Galbraith, John Kenneth. 1988. *The Great Crash of 1929*. Boston: Houghton Mifflin.

Goldberg, David J. 1999. *Discontented America: The United States in the 1920s*. Baltimore: Johns Hopkins University Press.

Goldberg, Ronald Allen. 2003. *America in the Twenties*. Syracuse, NY: Syracuse University Press.

Grant, Michael Johnston. 2002. *Down and Out on the Family Farm: Rural Rehabilitation in the Great Plains, 1929–1945*. Lincoln: University of Nebraska Press.

Gray, Ralph, and John M. Peterson. 1974. *Economic Development of the United States*. Rev. ed. Homewood, IL: Richard D. Irwin.

Hosen, Frederick E. 1992. *The Great Depression and the New Deal: Legislative Acts in Their Entirety (1932–1933) and Statistical Economic Data (1926–1946)*. Jefferson, NC: McFarland.

Houck, Davis W. 2001. *Rhetoric as Currency: Hoover, Roosevelt, and the Great Depression*. College Station: Texas A&M University Press.

Johnston, Alva. 1953. *The Legendary Mizners*. New York: Farrar, Strauss, & Young.

Kazan, Abraham E. 1937. "Cooperative Housing in the United States." *Annals of the American Academy of Political and Social Science* 191 (May): 137–143.

Klingaman, William K. 1989. *1929: The Year of the Great Crash*. New York: Harper & Row.

Kuznets, Simon. 1941. *National Income and Its Composition, 1919–1938*. New York: National Bureau of Economic Research.

Ladenburg, Thomas J., and Samuel Hugh Brockunier. 1971. *The Prosperity and Depression Decades*. New York: Hayden.

Lears, Jackson. 1994. *Fables of Abundance: A Cultural History of Advertising in America*. New York: BasicBooks.

Leinwand, Gerald. 2001. *1927: High Tide of the Twenties*. New York: Four Walls Eight Windows.

Lewis, Sinclair. 2002. *Babbitt*. New York: Modern Library.

Lynd, Robert S., and Helen Merrell Lynd. 1929. *Middletown: A Study in Contemporary American Culture*. New York: Harcourt, Brace.

Montgomery, David. 1987. *The Fall of the House of Labor: The Workplace, the State, and American Labor Activism, 1865–1925*. Cambridge: Cambridge University Press.

Morgan, Ted. 1999. *A Covert Life: Jay Lovestone, Communist, Anti-Communist & Spymaster*. New York: Random House.

Mormino, Gary R. 2005. *Land of Sunshine, State of Dreams: A Social History of Modern Florida*. Gainesville: University Press of Florida.

Mowry, George E., ed. 1963. *The Twenties: Fords, Flappers, & Fanatics*. Englewood Cliffs, NJ: Prentice-Hall.

Murphy, Paul L., David Klassen, and Kermit Hall. 1974. *The Passaic Textile Strike of 1926*. Belmont, CA: Wadsworth.

Odum, Howard, William Fielding Ogburn, and the President's Research Committee on Social Trends. 1933. *Recent Social Trends in the United States*. New York: McGraw-Hill.

Perrett, Geoffrey. 1982. *America in the Twenties: A History*. New York: Simon and Schuster.

Plesur, Milton, ed. 1969. *The 1920's: Problems and Paradoxes*. Boston: Allyn and Bacon.

Ricci, James M. 1984. "Boasters, Boosters, and Boom: Popular Images of Florida in the 1920s." *Tampa Bay History* 6 (Fall/Winter): 31–57.

Romasco, Albert U. 1965. *The Poverty of Abundance: Hoover, the Nation, the Depression*. New York: Oxford University Press.

Salmond, John A. 1995. *Gastonia, 1929: The Story of the Loray Mill Strike*. Chapel Hill: University of North Carolina Press.

Sautter, Udo. 1991. *Three Cheers for the Unemployed: Government and Unemployment before the New Deal*. New York: Cambridge University Press.

Schactman, Tom. 1979. *The Day America Crashed*. New York: G. P. Putnam's.

Seldes, Gilbert. 1933. *The Years of the Locust (America, 1929–1932)*. Boston: Little, Brown.

Sklar, Martin J. 1992. *The United States as a Developing Country: Studies in U.S. History in the Progressive Era and the 1920s*. New York: Cambridge University Press.

Soule, George. 1989. *The Prosperity Decade: From War to Depression*. Armonk, NY: M. E. Sharpe.

Standiford, Les. 2003. *Last Train to Paradise: Henry Flagler and the Spectacular Rise and Fall of the Railroad that Crossed an Ocean*. New York: Three Rivers Press.

Stevenson, Elizabeth. 1998. *Babbitts and Bohemians: From the Great War to the Great Depression*. Rev. ed. New Brunswick, NJ: Transaction.

Thomas, Gordon, and Max Morgan-Witts. 1980. *The Day the Bubble Burst: A Social History of the Wall Street Crash of 1929*. New York: Penguin.

Tindall, George B. 1965. "The Bubble in the Sun." *American Heritage* 16 (August): 76–83, 109–111.

Vickers, Raymond B. 1994. *Panic in Paradise: Florida's Banking Crash of 1926*. Tuscaloosa: University of Alabama Press.

Watkins, T. H. 1999. *The Hungry Years: A Narrative History of the Great Depression in America*. New York: Owl Books.

Williamson, Jeffrey G., and Peter H. Lindert. 1980. *American Inequality: A Macroeconomic History*. New York: Academic Press.

Wilson, Joan Hoff. 1975. *Herbert Hoover: Forgotten Progressive*. Boston: Little, Brown.

Woofter, T. J., Jr. 1933. *Races and Ethnic Groups in American Life*. New York: McGraw-Hill.

Zieger, Robert H. 1969. *Republicans and Labor, 1919–1929*. Lexington: University of Kentucky Press.

People and Events in the 20th Century

THE 1900s

THE 1910s

THE 1920s

THE 1930s

THE 1940s

THE 1950s

THE 1960S

THE 1970s

THE 1980s

THE 1990s

1920s Index

About the Authors

Linda S. Watts, professor of American Studies in the Interdisciplinary Arts and Sciences Program at the University of Washington, Bothell, is author of *Rapture Untold: Gender, Mysticism, and the "Moment of Recognition" in Writings by Gertrude Stein* (1996), *Gertrude Stein: A Study of the Short Fiction* (1999), and *Encyclopedia of American Folklore* (2006).

Alice L. George earned her Ph.D. in history from Temple University in 2001 after 20 years as an editor at newspapers including the *Detroit Free Press* and the *Philadelphia Daily News*. She is the author of *Awaiting Armageddon: How Americans Faced the Cuban Missile Crisis* (2003), *Old City Philadelphia: Cradle of American Democracy* (2003), and *Philadelphia: A Pictorial Celebration* (2006). She works as an independent historian in Philadelphia.

Scott Beekman is an assistant professor of history at the University of Rio Grande. He lives in Athens, Ohio, with his wife, historian Kimberly K. Little, and son, Miller. Beekman is currently under contract for a book examining the role of NASCAR in modern Southern identity.